Large-Scale Data Analytics with Python and Spark

A Hands-On Guide to Implementing Machine Learning Solutions

Based on the authors' extensive teaching experience, this hands-on graduate-level text-book describes how to carry out large-scale data analytics and design machine learning solutions for big data. With a focus on fundamentals, this extensively class-tested text-book walks students through key principles and paradigms for working with large-scale data, frameworks for large-scale data analytics (Hadoop, Spark), and explains how to implement machine learning to exploit big data. It is unique in covering the principles that aspiring data scientists need to know, without detail that can overwhelm. Real-world examples, hands-on coding exercises and labs combine with exceptionally clear explanations to maximize student engagement. Well-defined learning objectives, exercises with online solutions for instructors, lecture slides, and an accompanying suite of lab exercises of increasing difficulty in Jupyter Notebooks offer a coherent and convenient teaching package. An ideal teaching resource for courses on large-scale data analytics with machine learning in computer/data science departments.

Isaac Triguero is Distinguished Senior Researcher at the Department of Computer Science and Artificial Intelligence, University of Granada, and Associate Professor of Data Science at the School of Computer Science, University of Nottingham. He won the 2019 (Level 2) School of Computer Science – University of Nottingham Award for Teaching.

Mikel Galar is Associate Professor of Computer Science and Artificial Intelligence at the Department of Statistics, Computer Science and Mathematics, Public University of Navarre. He is a co-founder of Neuraptic AI and won the 2020 Excellence in Teaching Award of the Public University of Navarre.

T0293133

Large-Scale Data Analytics with Python and Spark

A Hands-On Guide to Implementing Machine Learning Solutions

ISAAC TRIGUERO
University of Granada and University of Nottingham

MIKEL GALAR
Public University of Navarre

Shaftesbury Road, Cambridge CB2 8EA, United Kingdom

One Liberty Plaza, 20th Floor, New York, NY 10006, USA

477 Williamstown Road, Port Melbourne, VIC 3207, Australia

314–321, 3rd Floor, Plot 3, Splendor Forum, Jasola District Centre, New Delhi – 110025, India

103 Penang Road, #05–06/07, Visioncrest Commercial, Singapore 238467

Cambridge University Press is part of Cambridge University Press & Assessment, a department of the University of Cambridge.

We share the University's mission to contribute to society through the pursuit of education, learning and research at the highest international levels of excellence.

www.cambridge.org
Information on this title: www.cambridge.org/highereducation/isbn/9781009318259

DOI: 10.1017/9781009318242

First published 2024

Printed in the United Kingdom by CPI Group Ltd, Croydon CR0 4YY

A catalogue record for this publication is available from the British Library.

A Cataloging-in-Publication data record for this book is available from the Library of Congress.

ISBN 978-1-009-31825-9 Paperback

Additional resources for this publication at www.cambridge.org/TrigueroGalar

To the memory of my late father and brother, and to my ever-present mother, whose love, strength, and guidance have shaped my journey.

Isaac Triguero

To my beloved wife, for her support, understanding and patience.
To my lovely daughter, who fills every day with joy.
And to my family, for making this journey possible.

Mikel Galar

Contents

Preface

Motivation

It is nearly twenty years since the term "big data" started to become popular, but many still struggle to understand what it really means. There are several reasons for that, including a lack of consensus on what big data is and the many "faces" and aspects that the term big data refers to; for example, data acquisition, security, storage/computational infrastructure, or analytics/mining. This book focuses on the analytics side of things, i.e., on large-scale data analytics, in which the aim is to use machine learning and data science techniques at a large scale. Throughout this book we will use indistinctively the terms big data and large-scale data analytics.

Data science and machine learning techniques have proved to be instrumental in gaining insights and actionable knowledge from data. Whilst most data scientists work on the basis that "the more data the better" – which may not necessarily be true – they soon encounter problems in tackling big datasets because of their size, the need to process them quickly, or their diversity in format and shape, among others. Fortunately, many platforms such as Hadoop, Spark, Flink, or Dask have arisen to enable us to deploy data science techniques in the context of big data by distributing their processing across multiple computers.

While there are plenty of books and online resources about these platforms, one of the main challenges that anyone wanting to get up to speed with big data and machine learning faces is to find a single resource that not only tells you how to use a particular platform but also provides the underlying foundations and principles for designing machine learning solutions in large scale problems. To design machine learning solutions for big data, there is a need to understand some of the most important elements of the underlying technology. However, technology evolves very quickly and there are some details that a data scientist will need to know, but they might not need to know the nitty-gritty detail of the underlying platform. Currently, there is a gap between how to design machine learning in big data, which is mostly in the form of scientific publications, and technology, for which we find many technical books and online documentation. The purpose of this book is to bridge that gap, providing a single concise source of information to help data scientists exploit big data with machine learning from scratch following a hands-on approach.

Approach

This book aims to teach the key concepts for implementing machine learning with big data in a concise and hands-on manner. Rather than attempting to cover all the technical aspects of the current big data frameworks, which may rapidly change and may not be directly relevant for data scientists (e.g., the implementation details of a distributed file system), this book is unique amongst all existing resources in that it introduces key principles and new concepts for designing big data solutions for machine learning. Having said that, we do teach the high-level features of these platforms, learning to identify why they may be of use in designing big data solutions for machine learning and what their expected performance is.

As this is a textbook, we approach the learning experience with a diverse range of teaching strategies to realize different learning outcomes: knowledge and understanding (KU), intellectual skills (IS), and professional/practical skills (PPS), which are summarized at the beginning of each chapter. To combine theory and practice, the concepts are presented following a hands-on approach in which we combine explanations, code, and real examples. Throughout the chapters, various challenges/questions are left to the reader to foster reflective thinking. Solutions to those challenges are later provided to ensure the concepts are clear. In addition, numerous exercises and lab assignments are provided to assess knowledge, comprehension, and ability to apply the concepts. Solutions to those exercises and assignments are provided to instructors. At the end of each chapter, we provide a take-home message with the key information and an additional section for those readers who want to learn more, including numerous links and references.

Audience

This textbook is primarily aimed at undergraduate and masters students taking courses on machine learning for big data with a prior background in programming and machine learning / data science. The content is based on the big data and machine learning courses that the authors teach at their respective universities. We also expect this book to be useful for researchers and engineers who apply data science to various problems and encounter the need to deal with large-scale data analytics.

The skills readers will acquire by studying this book will make them capable of designing innovative solutions for real-world big data problems – skills that are in high demand in research and industry.

Structure

The book is divided into three main parts. Part I covers the basic concepts for understanding big data and the key principles and programming paradigms for dealing with it. Part II dives into the technology of big data, introducing the most established big data frameworks, namely Hadoop and Spark. This involves key technical details and how to efficiently program with distributed data structures. Finally, Part III focuses on how to use machine learning and data science in the presence of large volumes of data, learning how to use existing libraries and how to design efficient and effective solutions to adapt data science techniques (including preprocessing, learning, and model deployment) to this scenario.

The book contains many examples, and each chapter includes various challenges for the reader and a series of exercises. The supplementary material includes lab assignments that comprise larger coding projects at various levels. It also provides a practical tutorial for getting started with Python and Spark.

How To Read This Book

Part I sets the scene with some basic concepts that are extremely important for the remainder of the book. Readers are strongly recommended to work through the materials and, in particular, the exercises on Map Reduce – pen and paper in hand – to cover the material of this part. Having said that, these concepts will be reinforced in Parts II and III.

In Part II, after a chapter on Hadoop, we delve into the hands-on section on Spark. It is vital for readers to write code as they go along. The challenges, exercises, and lab assignments are key to learning how to work with distributed datasets. For many readers, the Spark SQL style may be a bit odd, and it will require time and effort to absorb some of the material in this part.

Part III builds upon the previous parts, but at the same time it will allow readers to keep practising with the Spark application programming interface (API) to find the appropriate operations for designing big data solutions for machine learning. To successfully complete this last part of the book, we advise readers to run their own experiments, test what they learn in various datasets, and play with the exercises and challenges without looking at the solutions.

Here are a few practical things to remember when reading this book:

- Code is presented in boxes of the following type:

```
# This is a block of code - the output follows
2+2
```

- Output is presented in boxes of the following type:

```
4
```

- Errors and print statements are shown in a different output box. The following block of code,

```
print("This will be printed in a different type of box")
```

prints the sentence in a box of the following type:

```
This will be printed in a different type of box
```

- We purposely show errors when running some code. These are usually shortened to three or four lines, so readers can replicate them when practising.
- Sometimes we may have shortened the output within the code itself (e.g., slicing the output [:5]). Do not forget to remove that bit if you want to see the full output.
- There are various notes around the book that look like this:

> These notes present additional information that is not key to understanding the chapter but clarifies some aspects or delves a little deeper.

- We recommend doing the challenges when you find them. Do not leave them for later, as the following sections might spoil them.
- At the beginning of each chapter you will find the key learning outcomes, categorized as KU, IS, and PPS. We suggest readers go back to these at the end of the chapter and ensure they feel they have learned those points.

Teaching with This Book

The book has been designed to teach a comprehensive course on machine learning for big data, and we recommend instructors follow the same presentation order if the goal of your course is similar. However, depending on your audience and the timeline for your course, Parts I and II could still be used to teach an introductory course on big data technologies, and how to do distributed computing, without going into the machine learning side of things. If your students are familiar with Spark, you could use Part II as a refresher and jump into Part III.

The supplementary material provides lab assignments which instructors could use to assess the knowledge of their students. These have been designed with various levels, so that the instructor can go as far as they can depending on their available time. In addition, the online resources for instructors include the Jupyter Notebooks used to write this book, PowerPoint slides, a large collection of exercises, exams, and solutions based on the material in the book. We teach the content of this book as a mixture of slide-based presentations and (interactive) live coding. During the live coding sessions, we use Google Colab, so that our students can get (read-only) real-time access to the code that we are writing. This has proven to help with interaction and questions.

Why Python and Apache Spark?

In this book we have adopted Python as the programming language and Apache Spark as the big data framework. However, the concepts introduced here remain agnostic of the programming language and the underlying big data platforms and their future developments.

There are various reasons why we opted for Python. It is currently the most popular programming language among data scientists due to its vast community and prominent libraries for machine learning such as scikit-learn, TensorFlow, or PyTorch. Python is also a clean and expressive programming language with a simple syntax, which usually means a relatively shallow learning curve. In addition to this, Python is multi-platform (i.e., the same code works on Windows, MacOS and Linux) and allows for multiple programming paradigms (e.g., functional or object-oriented programming). Last, but not least, Python is an interpreted language and offers different tools, like Jupyter Notebooks, that allow us to explore the language and the concepts presented here in an interactive way, which is great for teaching and learning purposes. In fact, the entire book has been written in Jupyter Notebooks.

From the existing big data platforms, we have chosen Spark over other rising, and promising, platforms such as Apache Flink or Dask. Our main motivation for this is that Spark is well established, with a very active community, and it is additionally supported by the company Databricks. Thanks to that, Spark can easily be deployed in cloud platforms like Azure or Amazon Web Services, and it is probably the most widely adopted platform in industry. It is worth noting that Spark offers APIs for various programming languages like Scala, Java, R, or Python. Additionally, there are many resources online from which we learned how to do large-scale analytics.

This does not mean that these are perfect choices, and there may be various counterarguments. For example, Spark is natively implemented in Scala, and although the Python API is improving quickly and provides almost the same features and functionality, it may not always be the best choice. However, as mentioned before, the choices of programming language and big data framework do not change the principles we aim to convey in this book.

> We have used Python >= 3.8 and Spark 3.3.0 in writing this book. You will find various links to different operations from Spark throughout the book, referencing that specific version to avoid issues with future editions of Spark.

What This Book Is *Not* About

The keywords involved in this book are widely used and the reader might have some expectations about what it is about. For this reason, here is a non-exhaustive list – in no particular order – of what this book is *not* about:

- Although we use Python as the main programming language and readers might learn a few tricks in this book, we are not explicitly teaching any Python features.
- We explore the Python API of Spark and discuss the efficiency of many of its operations, but this book should not serve as a reference manual for it.
- We aim to distribute the computation of machine learning and data science algorithms, and this will involve quite a few details of some selected algorithms, but we are not explaining machine learning per se.
- This book does not directly cover the parallelization of the training of deep learning models with big data, which is usually accelerated using graphics processing units (GPUs). While it is certainly possible to combine big data and GPU parallelization (e.g., using Spark and TensorFlow), we do not cover how to train deep learning

models with big data. However, we do showcase how to deploy a deep learning model to classify millions of examples in Spark (see Chapter 8).

- As mentioned before, we focus only on the analytics side of big data, but even within that, we mostly focus on the volume of the data. Other aspects, such as its variety (structured and non-structured data) and data fusion approaches to exploit it are not discussed here as they are usually more problem dependent (see Chapter 1 for more detail).

Acknowledgments

The content of this book has been put together based on the research and teaching activities that both authors have been conducting since 2013. This includes various tutorials at conferences (e.g., the World Conference on Computational Intelligence), numerous research papers, and the courses we teach at our respective Universities.

Thus, the list of acknowledgments is obviously *big*. The final structure and specific content you can find in this book is the result of several years of reviews and feedback from our students and teaching assistants who have been using this material, and we are extremely thankful for this. The enthusiasm of our students and the progress they were making motivated us to write this book. Likewise, through the tutorials we have run in international conferences and numerous research projects, we have received feedback from various peers. Special thanks are due to our research collaborators, Salva Garcia, Francisco Herrera, Alberto Fernandez, and Mikel Elkano, and more generally to the computational intelligence and machine learning communities.

While writing the book, we have received help from the R&D Tracasa team, and more specifically, from Christian Ayala and Ruben Sesma with the case study we deploy in Chapter 9 about image segmentation in remote sensing. Last, but not least, the book has been reviewed by several colleagues who are using it for their teaching. We want to thank Professor Chris Teplovs (University of Michigan), Professor Grazziela Figueredo (University of Nottingham), and Professor Daniel Peralta (Ghent University) for their invaluable feedback.

Part I

Understanding and Dealing with Big Data

1 Introduction

Learning Outcomes

  [KU]   Learning the principles of big data and its importance
  [KU]   Understanding that scale-out is the way to address big data problems
  [KU]   Understanding that big data processing requires data locality and a
         new big data computing paradigm

1.1   What Is Big Data?

Even if we might not be fully aware of it, we are all generating lots of data. As an example, when we use applications on our phones or computers, our interactions with those applications may be logged and later processed to, perhaps, improve user experience. Big data is a term that has widely been used by many for several years now, not only in the context of computer science but also in many other fields such as finance, biology, physics, or medicine.

The term "big data" is frequently used to refer to the idea of exploiting lots of data to obtain some benefit. We are under the impression that this data may be advantageous in some way, which is why we collect loads of information in the hope of utilizing it somehow to gain insights and, more importantly, value out of it. But when it comes to answering the question of what big data is, people start talking about gigabytes of data, or terabytes of data, focusing only on the volume; the thing is, there is no standard definition of what big data actually is. For that reason, some people tend to call big data anything that might be no more than standard machine learning and data science problems.

It is actually impossible to define big data based only on a specific amount of data. Although there is no standard definition, we very much like this one:

> *Big data involves data whose volume, diversity, and complexity requires new*
> *techniques, algorithms, and analyses to extract valuable (hidden) knowledge.*

So, if you ask us whether we are talking about 20 megabytes, 8 gigabytes, 100 terabytes, our answer will be: "Well, it depends." It depends on what you want to do with that data, the kind of analyses you need to perform on the data to obtain the knowledge you are seeking. In layman's terms, if you can do that analysis on your laptop, that is not big data. You have to use distributed solutions to handle such data.

It is common to refer to big data in different ways. For example, some may call it *data-intensive* applications, and others may refer to it as *large-scale data processing*, in which data is the core of the problem and the solution. For the sake of simplicity, we generally use the term big data. It is also important to remember that what we call big data today might be almost nothing tomorrow, as the computer power available to us is growing every day as well.

1.2   Success (and Failure) of Big Data

There have been many examples of successful big data applications. For example, the large retail company Target improved their return on investment using guests' data to predict pregnancy.[1] Using big data in this way has not been without controversy,[2] whether or not this was a true example.[3] This example is not far from how Amazon use their recommender systems to increase their sales.[4] Netflix has also been recognized for their recommender system.[5] There are also good examples in finance,[6] physics,[7] and medicine (Agrawal and Prabakaran, 2020).

However, one must be cautious when analyzing tons of data, since erroneous conclusions may produce unpredictable consequences affecting large populations. Google Flu Trends is a well-known example that was very successful at first but ended up suffering from inadequate interpretation of the data. Let's consider this case in a little more depth. A while ago, there was a fear of a pandemic due to a new strand of swine flu (H1N1). At the time, the Centers for Disease Control and Prevention (CDC) took some time to process incoming data about this disease, so they were only able to get a global view of the situation with one to two weeks' delay. Google soon realized this and came up with a very innovative solution.

They used search query data, that is, searches made on Google, and found a strong correlation between the real historical data about the disease and some specific terms that people were using in their searches. Thus, they developed Google Flu Trends, which allowed them to monitor the spread of swine flu in real time (avoiding the

---

[1] "How Target gets the most out of its guest data to improve marketing ROI": www.predictiveanalyticsworld.com/machinelearningtimes/how-target-gets-the-most-out-of-its-guest-data-to-improve-marketing-roi/6815/.

[2] Kashmir Hill article at Forbes: www.forbes.com/sites/kashmirhill/2012/02/16/how-target-figured-out-a-teen-girl-was-pregnant-before-her-father-did/?sh=68744a66686d.

[3] Gregory Piatestsky research: www.kdnuggets.com/2014/05/target-predict-teen-pregnancy-inside-story.html.

[4] The history of Amazon's recommendation algorithm: www.amazon.science/the-history-of-amazons-recommendation-algorithm.

[5] "How Netflix's recommendations system works": https://help.netflix.com/en/node/100639.

[6] Fraud detection using VISA: https://usa.visa.com/visa-everywhere/security/outsmarting-fraudsters-with-advanced-analytics.html.

[7] "The big data challenge at the Large Hadron Collider": www.innovationnewsnetwork.com/big-data-challenge-large-hadron-collider/11359/.

CDC delay). More information about how Google Flu Trends worked can be found in Ginsberg et al. (2009).

But, the key question for us is, *why is this big data?* They certainly needed to parallelize their data analytics tools to handle more than 3000 million searches every day, comparing the most common 50 million search terms against a database of flu propagation from 2003 to 2008. Having said that, it is not only about the volume, but the need to parallelize their analyses and handle lots of incoming data rapidly to get a global view in real time. In particular, they used a solution based on Hadoop MapReduce.

You might be thinking, wow, so Google made a real-time solution for pandemics . . . why didn't it work with COVID-19, though? They actually stopped Google Flu Trends in 2014 after they overestimated the flu levels in 2013. There were various reasons for this, including how people changed their behavior around their searches, the influence of the media when talking about this, and the modeling itself may have overlooked considerable information which could also have been captured with standard statistical methods. This exemplifies how machine learning and data science models need to be fed with quality data and may required updating with new data so that they are constantly adapted to the current data distribution; this is usually called data stream mining. If you want to know more about the traps behind Google Flu Trends, see Lazer et al. (2014).

This example is interesting because it is not just a representative case of success in big data, but also of how misinterpretations can lead to wrong conclusions. Although this book is focused on how to do machine learning and data science at scale with massive amounts of data, one must keep in mind the difficulties of working in big data analytics, a relatively young field in computer science that is changing extremely quickly.

1.3 Big Data Evolution and Definition

Our world revolves around data. Science, business, medicine, industry, energy, anything you can imagine: they all generate and store data. Looking at some figures from well-known examples, you will have an idea of the amount of data we are talking about. The Large Hadron Collider from The European Organization for Nuclear Research (CERN) is the largest particle collider in the world and its experiments generate about 90 petabytes of data per year.[8] Twiter, YouTube or Spotify need to be able to gather, process and distribute huge amounts of data to maintain their services and improve user experience (6,000 tweets every second[9], 500 hours of video uploaded to YouTube every minute[10] and 60,000 tracks uploaded to Spotify everyday[11] More than 300 billion emails are sent each day.[12] These are just figures, but they can give

---

[8] CERN storage: https://home.cern/science/computing/storage.
[9] Six thousand tweets every second: www.dsayce.com/social-media/tweets-day/.
[10] Five hundred hours of video uploaded to YouTube every minute:
    www.tubefilter.com/2019/05/07/number-hours-video-uploaded-to-youtube-per-minute/.
[11] Sixty thousand tracks uploaded to Spotify every day: www.musicbusinessworldwide.com/over-60000
    -tracks-are-now-uploaded-to-spotify-daily-thats-nearly-one-per-second/.
[12] www.templafy.com/blog/how-many-emails-are-sent-every-day-top-email-statistics-your-business-nee
    ds-to-know/

us a hint of the difficulty in managing them. The previous examples were from private companies/institutions who own the data, but there are also instances of freely available big data that we could be exploiting right now. The Sentinel-2 satellite, put into orbit by the European Space Agency, scans the whole world every five days, generating one terabyte of data every day.[13] Even though this data is freely available, you would need a large computing capacity just to download and store the data required to perform multi-temporal analysis over several years.

There are also statistics about how big the digital universe is. At the beginning of 2020, it was estimated at 64.2 zettabytes of data and is expected to grow to more than 180 zettabytes by 2025.[14] Take a look at the paper by Martin Hilbert and Priscila López[15] that compares the amount of analogue and digital data over time, and also analyzes how computational capacity has evolved. To put it into perspective, back in 1986, 41% of the world's computing capacity was available in calculators. This is just an anecdote showing how fast the world is evolving and the new possibilities offered by the digital age.

The truth is that we don't really know how accurate those figures are, but we certainly do generate way too much data, and going from analogue to digital storage has increased our ability to store it immensely. At some point we started storing data, valuable or not, and the need for processing that data to gain knowledge has now arrived. Somehow we are under the impression that data is the *new gold*. With the advent of the Internet of Things, we must take advantage of it to turn it into profitable products. Having said all of this, is it all about volume? Shall we just collect and store data for the sake of it?

Although we have said there is no formal/standard definition of what big data is, in 2001 Gartner defined/characterized big data using the three Vs: volume, velocity, and variety (Laney, 2001); see Figure 1.1.

- **Volume** is the obvious one. We have seen an increase in the amount of data that is being generated every second. In data science, datasets have seen enormous growth in the number of examples and features. We are expanding from gigabytes to petabytes of information and, unfortunately, you cannot currently have a petabyte drive on your laptop/desktop computer to store and process it.
- **Velocity** means the speed at which the data arrives, and also the speed at which we have to process the data if we want to take advantage of it. We are moving from traditional batch applications to real-time ones, in which late decisions may imply missed opportunities.
- **Variety** or the different formats and structure that the data may have is changing. From traditional structured data/tables such as tables and relational databases for which we know the schema to semi-structured data such as XML or JSON files, for which we can still infer the schema, or completely unstructured data such as text,

---

[13] www.thalesgroup.com/en/critical-information-systems-and-cybersecurity/news/sentinel-2-so-much-data-so-little-time
[14] https://www.statista.com/statistics/871513/worldwide-data-created/
[15] www.martinhilbert.net/worldinfocapacity-html/

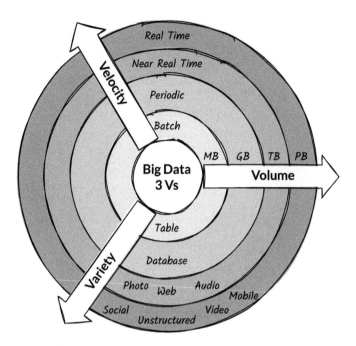

Figure 1.1 The three Vs of big data: volume, velocity, and variety.

images, audio, and video for which we do not know the schema and on which might want to impose some structure prior to doing any analyses.

Big Data is expanding on these three fronts at an increasing rate. Others have expanded the definition to five Vs by including veracity and value.

- **Veracity** refers to the problem of trusting your data. We have so much data coming from different sources that there is uncertainty about its quality. Data may be missing, ambiguous, or, simply put, wrong.
- **Value** is central; all the other Vs that characterize big data are useless without it. With bigger datasets, we (supposedly) have an opportunity to find better patterns and better insights into a problem. Although, as we state later, more data does not necessarily imply better results. Some would argue that the value is not in itself a property of the data, in comparison to the previous Vs, but the objective to achieve from using the data. For us, it is not really important to define the value as a property or an objective, but there is an expectation of obtaining some benefit/value from analyzing it.

Many researchers have become very creative, and you will find additional Vs online (we lost count at 10). But we think that these five really give you a flavor of what we are talking about here.

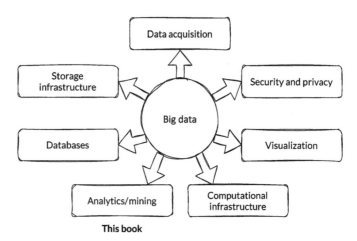

Figure 1.2 The "faces" of big data.

1.3.1   The Faces of Big Data

The concept of big data has often been confused because of the multiple aspects that it may involve. We could say that the world of big data has many different faces or areas of interest that are affected by the different Vs we described. The areas that we consider the most relevant are represented in Figure 1.2.

First of all, the data needs to be *acquired*, which may not be trivial. This could include, for example, deploying specialized sensors or equipment depending on the application (e.g., air quality sensors) or gathering information from existing devices (e.g., our smartphones) that are interconnected and can feed some information back to us. That data needs to be *stored* somewhere, and although we said before that there have been incredible advances in storage capabilities with huge hard drives, when talking about big data we need a sophisticated *storage infrastructure* that allows us to read/write data efficiently and safely. The data we are storing should be appropriately *protected and secured*, and if personal information is being used we should be able to guarantee the preservation of *privacy*, so complex computer security protocols and ethical procedures need to be put in place when talking about big data applications. The design of *databases* that can allow for efficient data queries may also be influenced by the different Vs of big data (e.g., NoSQL databases). Likewise, *data visualization* and *data analytics/mining* are two key areas in data science that contribute directly to obtaining value from the data, and they need to be reconsidered in this scenario. Last, but not least, we will need to process that data, so will need a suitable *computational infrastructure*, capable of handling the processing reliably in conjunction with the storage infrastructure.

The key focus of this book is on the data analytics side of things and how to efficiently apply methods to extract (hidden) knowledge in big datasets. More specifically, we will focus on how to design, develop, and apply machine learning models in big data. To do this, we will have to briefly cover some basic concepts of the computational and storage infrastructures needed to carry out such analyses.

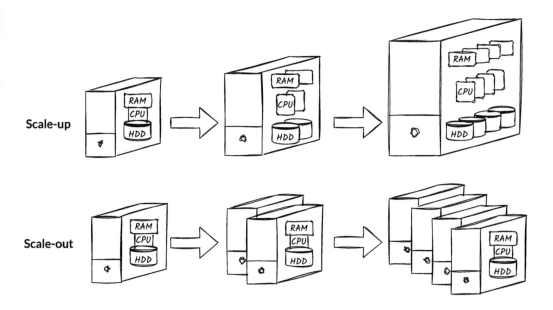

Figure 1.3 Scale-up versus scale-out.

1.4   How to Deal with Big Data?

Let's assume we embark on exploring 100 terabytes of data. To begin with, a single machine wouldn't be able to store that data, and of course it would lack the processing capabilities to process so much data in a reasonable amount of time. As a trivial example, you could think of the time required just for reading that data. A standard mechanical hard disk drive with an optimal reading speed of 160 MB/s would take about two hours just to read one terabyte, assuming no overhead in the process. This would amount to more than eight days to read the whole dataset sequentially.

So, what do we do? What is the solution? Well, probably not a surprise to most computer scientists: a *divide-and-conquer* approach. Rather than trying to make a single machine more powerful by adding more memory, getting a bigger hard drive, and so on (which, by the way, could actually be very expensive and the improvements would be limited), why not try spreading the processing across more than one computer?

Adding more resources to a single computer is what we call *vertical scalability* or *scale-up*, as opposed to *horizontal scalability* or *scale-out*, which involves using more than one computer. Figure 1.3 illustrates these concepts.

The good thing about using multiple machines to address this problem is that they may not need specific hardware (i.e., high-end specs) to tackle big data, so they can be cheaper, and if we need more computing power we just add more computers. However, this horizontal scalability is not free of issues. Table 1.1 summarizes the advantages and disadvantages of each approach.

Table 1.1 Scale-up versus scale-out: advantages and disadvantages.

Scale-up	Scale-out
Key idea	*Key idea*
Add more memory, processors	Add more (cheaper) nodes
Advantages	*Advantages*
✓ Less energy consumption	✓ Cheaper
✓ Less expense on cooling systems	✓ Fault tolerance possible
✓ Easier to implement solutions	✓ Easy to grow
Disadvantages	*Disadvantages*
× Price	× More physical space
× No fault tolerance	× Energy costs (electricity and cooling)
× Limited hardware upgrades	× Network equipment required

We could be tempted to always follow a scale-up approach as it is much simpler to implement at the expense of much higher (sometimes unaffordable) costs. Unfortunately, acquiring very specific hardware with lots of RAM, big hard disk drives, and many CPUs would quickly become very expensive, and the upgrades we may be able to get may be limited. Nowadays, we can easily equip a server with 128 GB of RAM, but it would be difficult, or even impossible, to get a total capacity of the order of terabytes. Conversely, in scale-out, we can use multiple computers to cope with the storage and computation needs of big data. Scalability itself may be straightforward in this case, since new computers can be directly added to a network to grow almost on demand. And, more importantly, the growth becomes almost unlimited.

For big data in particular, the idea of scale-out can be implemented with lots of commodity hardware servers together to improve the computing and storage capacity. The term "commodity hardware" is usually used to refer to computers without cutting-edge hardware, and that is the kind of hardware usually expected for Big Data processing. This will obviously be much cheaper than buying very specific components, as required for scale-up, but will also provide other advantages.

Another important factor that makes horizontal scalability very appealing is the possibility of making our applications *fault tolerant*. If you have a single very powerful machine that, for whatever reason, crashes, this will be a problem in processing big data, especially if it fails suddenly after several days of computation. However, even using commodity hardware which could perhaps fail more frequently, having multiple machines may allow us to be fault tolerant, so that other machines may pick up on the work the failed machine was doing.

However, not everything is good. In horizontal scalability the computers are connected through a network, which not only means that we need network equipment but also adds complexity to the design of any software as there will be a need to coordinate actions across computing nodes. When considering scale-out, there are many other issues we should bear in mind: we will need more physical space, maintenance, energy costs (electricity and cooling systems), and so on. Thus, opting for a scale-out approach needs to be well justified. To solve a problem that simply requires (a bit) more RAM

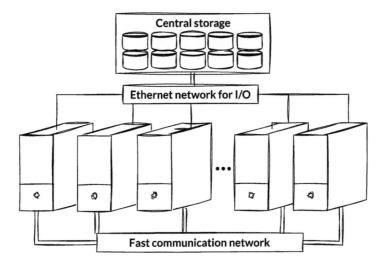

Figure 1.4 Simplified representation of an HPC architecture.

or a new CPU, we would advise not considering horizontal scalability since this may just not be a big data problem.

Despite these limitations, horizontal scalability is the way to go for big data. The advantages clearly outweigh the disadvantages of this type of scalability, especially because there is no limit to growing at an affordable cost, and it can be done in a flexible manner and with the possibility of implementing fault tolerance. We hope this helps you understand why big data technologies are based on horizontal scalability to be able to handle the different Vs that characterize big data.

1.4.1   High Performance Computing versus Big Data Computing

When we started talking about horizontal scalability, the term high performance computing (HPC) may have come to your mind. If you know what HPC is, you are probably now thinking that if we are going to be dealing with big data, we will have to use that kind of facility and not just a single laptop/desktop computer.

If you don't know what HPC involves, it would be a cluster of independent computers (nodes) that are connected using a communication network (e.g., Infiniband [if you're lucky]) and they usually have access to a central storage device (typically via an Ethernet network). Each of these nodes has one or more multi-core CPUs, and their own RAM and hard (or solid-state) disk. In an HPC setting, these nodes typically use the Linux operating system. It is perhaps obvious, but it is important to note that any application that runs on a node can only access that node's RAM, and not another node's. This is called a *distributed memory* architecture. A simplified example of an HPC architecture is depicted in Figure 1.4.

If we are going to have a lot of computers connected through a network, how do we implement a distributed/parallel program? To answer that question, we need to keep in mind that in an HPC cluster, one of the nodes will usually act as the *master node*, and this will be in charge of orchestrating all the communication and synchronization across the nodes of the cluster. The remaining nodes, *the workers*, will perform the actual calculations.

One of the classical ways of dealing with distributed computing is with MPI (Message Passing Interface). Without going into too much detail, MPI is a communication protocol used in parallel programs that is based on two main functions: `scatter` and `gather`. In essence, the former function sends a message to the computing/worker nodes with information about the operation that needs doing; the workers perform it and return a response to the master node. The latter function receives/collects the results from the worker nodes.

One issue with MPI is that you need to explicitly determine what each node is going to do. This means we need to keep the distributed architecture in mind when programming and must decide how to divide the work between the master and the workers, putting a major part of the responsibility for the distribution of the computing on the programmer. The technologies we look at in this book are based on the opposite principle since they hide the details of the network communication as much as possible. Although it may perhaps be a little counterintuitive, the idea of hiding the networking details is usually referred to as being *transparent* to the programmer. That is, we work at a higher level of abstraction and do not need to worry about how the communication occurs on a distributed system. Nevertheless, we still need to know what is going on to distribute the work efficiently. Another significant disadvantage of traditional MPI is that it is not *fault tolerant* by definition, and hence not very appropriate for big data.

Besides these two issues, which could possibly be addressed, there is a key reason as to why an HPC architecture may not be appropriate for big data problems. Traditionally, HPCs have been used to tackle problems that require lots of computation but relatively little data. In this scenario, all nodes can quickly access the data, and the key focus of distributed solutions is in spreading the (time-consuming) computation across the nodes. Usually, the different subtasks tackled by each node are not independent, so there is a need to communicate intermediate results (i.e., calculations). However, these "messages" are usually not "very big." As a remark, the different nodes usually have their own local storage, but it is not intensively used during job execution. Figure 1.5 illustrates this idea.

Do you see a problem here if you aim to work with massive datasets? If we were to have a large single central storage capable of storing all our data, then the network would be the main bottleneck, since all the computers would be trying to read data continuously, making it impossible to scale. The more computers, the greater the limitations in terms of input/output (I/O). Figure 1.6 illustrates the problems when dealing with large datasets in HPC.

For big data, applications will devote most of their time processing and manipulating the data, which results in lots of time spent in I/O, which is moving data across the network in an HPC setting, and this will be a very slow process. Hence, applying standard HPC solutions to big data problems does not scale, simply because the central

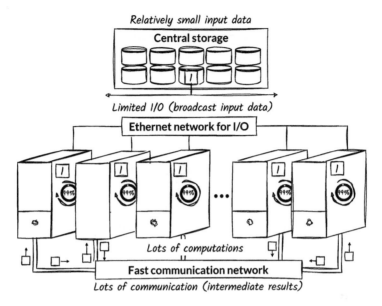

Figure 1.5 The traditional HPC way of doing things (inspired by a keynote talk from Professor Jan Fostier). We expect a small amount of input data and high CPU utilization. The figure shows 99% to highlight the high CPU utilization, but that is certainly too idealistic.

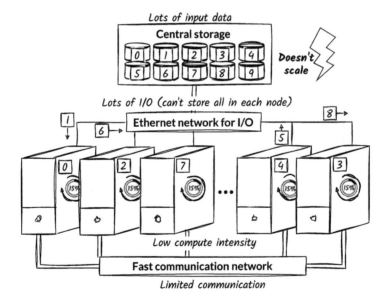

Figure 1.6 Problems for HPC in dealing with data-intensive applications. We expect a large amount of input data and lower CPU utilization compared to standard HPC due to the data access bottleneck. The figure shows 15% CPU utilization to show how the I/O affects the ability to perform much computation on the data.

storage and/or I/O network cannot deliver the data to the worker nodes at a sufficient rate to keep the worker nodes busy. In summary, big data is not HPC, they are different

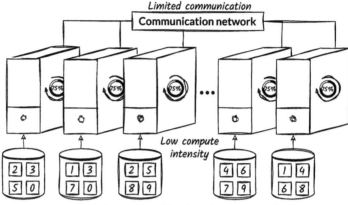

Figure 1.7 The principle of data locality to tackle data-intensive jobs. Using the local drives to implement data locality, we can reduce the traffic across the network and increase CPU utilization. The figure illustrates this with 75% CPU utilization to indicate that in big data we may not be CPU-bound, but having the data close by will allow us to perform the necessary operations with it much more quickly.

computation models and we need a different hardware architecture to run on, although both share the idea of distributed computing.

What Do We Have To Do Differently To Tackle Data-Intensive Jobs?

The limiting factor for big data processing in an HPC setting is the amount of data that must be read/written through the communication network, since storing data in a central place and moving all data to the computing nodes when executing a job yields poor performance. Therefore, it becomes crucially important to minimize data movement across the network. Cluster architectures for big data solutions should ensure that data and computing power are colocated, avoiding data transfer through the network as much as possible. In other words, the data should reside very close to where actual computations will take place.

As mentioned before, in HPC, local drives are not really being used, so why don't we use them to keep a fraction of the data in every single node? This is referred to as the principle of *data locality*. Data locality is what distinguishes big data clusters from HPC clusters. The idea is to use the local drives of the computing nodes as distributed storage, so that, during the execution of a big data solution, we should ensure that each computing node uses (as far as possible) the data stored in it. In this way, data transfer through the communication network only occurs when it is absolutely necessary for the processing.

Additionally, to provide fault tolerance, there is a need for some data replication in the distributed storage, so that if one node fails there is another one capable of handling that part of the data. Figure 1.7 shows what a big data cluster might look like, and illustrates data replication with factor two (each chunk of data is present in two nodes).

You can see that, for example, chunk 2 is stored in both the first and the third nodes, and the rest of the chunks are replicated in the same way. This is what protects us from

Table 1.2 Big data vs. HPC: key differences.

Big data	HPC
Focus on data-intensive jobs	Focus on computation-intensive jobs
Hardware failure common	Surprised by hardware failure
Code: data science, graphs	Code: simulation, optimization
Usually mix CPU/GPU and data	Mix CPU/GPU
Job moved to where the data is located	Data moved to where it will be processed
SIMD model:[a] data parallelism	SIMD/MIMD[b] model (more general parallelism)
Commodity hardware acceptable	Needs specialized hardware

[a] Single Instruction Multiple Data
[b] Multiple Instruction Multiple Data

failures either when a node gets stuck or dies. However, when processing this data the system must ensure that chunk 2 is processed in just one of the nodes (e.g., the first or the third node to exploit data locality), but it will also be continuously checking for the node in charge of the processing, so that if there is any problem or it takes too long, that chunk can be processed in the other node. Again, one key point in big data is that the complexity behind decisions like where to store the data, replication, where to run the processing, or handling node failure, is transparent to the programmer. Big data frameworks provide the implementation to deal with such duties, so that the programmer can focus on the algorithmic side of things.

In summary, in comparison to traditional HPC clusters, a big data cluster focuses on data-intensive jobs rather than compute-intensive jobs. For this reason, HPC clusters are usually equipped with high-end computers that will keep the CPUs (or GPUs) very busy. However, for big data we may spend some time manipulating data and we will be more limited by the I/O performance and the amount of main memory we need to use, and less likely to be CPU-bound. This is why in big data clusters we use the term commodity hardware to refer to the kind of servers required.

The fact that standard hardware is used makes failures more probable over time (more probable if you have a computing cluster with thousands of nodes). Therefore, mechanisms to deal with faults are implemented to avoid stopping running jobs each time a node fails. From a software point of view, we could say that a big data cluster is suited to dealing with applications in data mining/science, while HPCs are perfect for other applications such as simulation or optimization (e.g., physics or engineering simulations, or the traveling salesman problem) that do not require as much data but lots of computation. Table 1.2 summarizes the key differences between big data and HPC.

1.4.2   Distributed Systems for Data-Intensive Jobs

When describing the main properties of a big data cluster, we have been discussing why we need a different computation infrastructure to process big data. We would like now to summarize the key principles and assumptions that are needed to design distributed systems for data-intensive applications. We could say that big data processing is the problem of applying an operation or task to all the data we have, assuming that one machine cannot process or store all of it. For example, you could think of computing statistics or training a machine learning model.

Obviously, we will use a big data cluster to do the job, but we are not really interested in knowing which specific machine stores what fraction of the data, as long as we get the result we are looking for in a timely manner. Likewise, if there is any failure in one particular machine (or even worse, straggler nodes), we still want the original task to be completed, even if that means that part of the processing needs to be repeated in a different node. If you allow us to put one more thing on the wish list, we do not need to know much detail about which node is executing what. Thus, we are looking for an abstraction of the complexity of distributed systems. When programming data-intensive applications, it is important to know and understand that there is a distributed system underneath, but we must be aware that big data frameworks will provide us with a suitable level of abstraction, allowing us to almost forget about the distributed system.

Of course, these frameworks must be especially cautious to preserve the data locality principle and avoid data transfer between machines as far as possible. In fact, the new programming model we introduce in the next chapter, MapReduce, is based on the following idea:

> *Moving computation is cheaper than moving computation and data at the same time.*

In summary, data will be distributed among nodes using a distributed file system. We will program the functions/operations to process data, and those pieces of code will be distributed to all the computing nodes; each computing node will work with the data stored locally. Only the necessary data should be moved across the network, as there will be occasions in which data movement is indeed required. In the next chapter we introduce this new programming model.

1.5   Take-Home Message

This chapter has introduced what we mean by big data, its importance, and the key principles for handling it efficiently. The take-away messages of this chapter are:

- Big data is not all about *volume* of data, and there are many other aspects that need to be considered such as velocity and variety.
- The world of big data has multiple faces and challenges such as databases, infrastructure, and security and privacy, but we are interested here in the idea of analyzing and extracting knowledge from big data with machine learning techniques.
- *Scale-up* is not the way to go for big data. That is, if you could analyze your data on a single computer, that is probably not big data. We will require to use multiple computers to process big data, that is, *scale-out*.
- The characteristics and requirements of a big data cluster are different from those usually used in high performance computing. The focus is on data-intensive jobs

rather than pure computation, where hardware does not have to be high-end and failures may happen.
- The principle of *data locality* tells us that to deal effectively with big data we should reduce data movement across the network, aiming to keep the data on the nodes that are going to process it (whenever possible).

This calls for a new big data computing paradigm, which is introduced in the next chapter.

1.6 To Learn More

As we mentioned before, there is no real consensus about what big data / large-scale analytics really is, but there has been quite a lot of literature discussing the potential benefits of dealing with large datasets. Here is a short selection of useful references.

Mayer-Schönberger and Cukier (2013) was one of the most influential books back in 2013 about the ways in which processing big data would transform our society.

Marx (2013) is an interesting article that discusses various applications of big data in biology and physics.

Pietsch (2021) is a philosophical book about big data, studying the epistemology of the tools and techniques applied.

While introducing the concepts of big data, we have come across the concepts of HPC and MPI. The following references will help if you want to familiarize yourself more with these topics.

Severance and Dowd (2010) is an open book on HPC, discussing different architectures, programming models, and parallel systems.

Gropp et al. (2014) is a great book about MPI and how to write parallel programs.

Apart from those references, if you want to learn more about scalability and data-intensive computing, please keep reading!

1.7 Exercises

1.1 What are the main three Vs that were initially used to define big data?
   (a) velocity, value, volume
   (b) variety, velocity, veracity
   (c) variety, volume, velocity
   (d) volume, velocity, value

1.2 Indicate whether the following statements about big data are true or false:
   (a) Big data always involves terabytes of data.
   (b) The definition of big data is independent of the kind of analyses we need to perform on the data.

(c) There is no standard definition of what big data is.

(d) In big data, we expect data to be in many formats, from structured to completely unstructured data.

1.3 Why do we say that big data has many faces? Briefly explain your answer, providing an example of one of those faces of big data.

1.4 In big data, we tend to prefer horizontal scalability over vertical scalability. Using your own words, explain why this is the case.

1.5 List two advantages of scale-out over scale-up when dealing with big data.

1.6 Indicate whether the following statements about scale-up and scale-out are true or false:

(a) It is always best to follow a scale-out approach independently of the size of the data.

(b) It is cheaper to achieve horizontal scalability than vertical scalability.

(c) Fault tolerance is not possible in scale-up.

(d) Implementations become more complex in scale-out.

1.7 To analyse a dataset, you are given two options:

(a) Option 1: 1 computer, 8 GB of RAM, 4 cores, 1 TB drive

(b) Option 2: 2 computers, 4 GB of RAM each, 2 cores each, 1 TB drive each

Which option would you choose? Explain the advantages and disadvantages of one option over the other.

1.8 Why is making our applications fault tolerant so important in big data? Explain your answer.

1.9 What are the key differences between a traditional HPC cluster and a big data cluster? Explain your answer.

1.10 What are the main disadvantages of traditional communication protocols like MPI when dealing with big data?

1.11 Why is the principle of data locality so important in big data? Explain your answer.

1.12 In big data, we do not necessarily require computers with high-end specifications. Using your own words, briefly explain why this might be the case.

1.13 Could we run a simulation or an optimization algorithm on a big data cluster? Would you expect it to be as fast as in an HPC? Explain your answer.

1.14 In the context of big data and networks, what does being transparent to the programmer mean? Explain your answer.

1.15 What is a big data framework? Briefly explain your answer.

2   MapReduce

Learning Outcomes

[KU]   Learn a functional programming paradigm for distributed computing with big data

[KU]   Understand why transparency and fault tolerance are desirable in big data

[IS]   How to use MapReduce in practice for problem solving

[IS]   How to exploit MapReduce to preserve data locality principles, minimising data movement

To deal with data-intensive jobs we need a change of programming model in distributed computing. We need something that allows us to move only computation and avoids moving data across the network as much as possible, which is, as discussed in the previous chapter, simply a very slow process when tackling big data.

In this new programming model, we will assume that all the data is distributed in a cluster of computers and we will implement the functions/operations that will have to be applied to the different chunks of the data. Each node will only work with the data that is stored in it, and we will only move data across the network when strictly necessary. This new model is known as MapReduce.

2.1   What Is MapReduce?

MapReduce is a parallel programming model that follows a simple divide-and-conquer strategy to tackle big datasets in distributed computing. The name "MapReduce" comes from the two main functions it uses to perform the computations: map and reduce. Relatively similar to MPI and its scatter and gather functions, MapReduce divides a big dataset into smaller (more manageable) chunks and performs an operation on them (the *map* phase), and then it combines, merges, or aggregates the results from the previous step (the *reduce* or *conquer* phase).

The key distinguishing features of MapReduce are its simplicity and transparency to programmers, as well as its assumption of data locality. It was first introduced by Google (Dean and Ghemawat, 2004), but it became popular thanks to the open-source project Hadoop[1] in 2006. We will cover more about the implementation details of Hadoop, but it is important to understand that Hadoop simply provides an implementation of the MapReduce programming model.

MapReduce is based on functional programming, and before going into the distributed computing side of things, we would like to discuss what these two functions map and reduce do.

2.2   Map and Reduce Functions in Python

If you already have some experience with Python and functional programming, you probably know that Python provides the map and reduce functions. In functional programming, we say that these are higher-order functions because they receive other functions as parameters. These functions work on iterable collections, for example, lists. Let us show you an example using the following list:

```
lst = [1, 2, 3, 4]
```

We'll start with the map function. This function takes two parameters: (1) a function and (2) a collection to whose elements the function is applied one by one.

For example, if we want to compute the square of all the integers in the list, we can either do a for loop over the elements of the list computing the square of each element, or we can apply a map function that takes two parameters: (1) a function to compute the square of an integer and (2) the collection in which we want to apply that function:

```
map(lambda x: x*x, lst)
```

```
<map at 0x17a531460a0>
```

Perhaps that's not the output we were expecting. This is because map does not return a list directly, but an iterator. We need to coerce it to a list if we want to see its content:

```
list(map(lambda x: x*x, lst))
```

```
[1, 4, 9, 16]
```

What happened? What map is doing here is applying the function lambda x: x*x to every single element of the list, giving, as a result, a new iterator with the resulting values. If you wonder what an iterator is, you can think of it as a way to traverse a collection sequentially. That's why we had to coerce that iterator into a list to see the actual content of the list.

By the way, we have used an in-line lambda (anonymous) function, which is a shortcut to avoid defining short functions. This would be the equivalent code without using a lambda function:

```
def square(x):
    return x*x
```

---

[1] https://hadoop.apache.org/

```
list(map(square, lst))
```

```
[1, 4, 9, 16]
```

As you can see, `map` can be a great way to avoid `for` loops, among other attractive properties from functional programming such as lazy evaluation (Hutton, 2016). Also, `lambda` functions come in handy in many situations where we just need to define a simple function. We will be using them throughout the book.

The `reduce` function is also available in Python, but, since Python 3, we need to import it from the `functools` library:

```
from functools import reduce
```

The idea behind the `reduce` function is to provide a simple way to combine the elements of a collection to make a single value. To do so, it takes two parameters like the `map` function: (1) a function with two parameters and (2) a collection to be reduced by applying the function *pairwise*.

In this case, the function given as a parameter takes two elements of the collection and returns a single one. Let's see an example that replicates the built-in Python function sum(⟨*collection*⟩) using `reduce`. sum(⟨*collection*⟩) gives us the sum of the values of an iterable collection (e.g., a list):

```
sum(lst)
```

```
10
```

We can do the same using the `reduce` function:

```
reduce(lambda x, y: x + y, lst)
```

```
10
```

The key point here is that `reduce` transforms the list into a single value by recursively applying the given function in pairs. Let's try to understand it better without using an anonymous function:

```
def add_reduce(x, y):
    out = x + y
    print(f"{x}+{y}-->{out}")
    return out
```

We want to know how the function we passed to the `reduce` function has been used, so we are "debugging" our code by printing out the values of x, y, and out.

```
reduce(add_reduce,lst)
```

```
1+2-->3
3+3-->6
6+4-->10
```

```
10
```

As you can see from this output, it took the first two elements of the list and added them; then, the result of that was added to the next value (i.e., 3); finally, the result of that was added to the last element, which means that we have added up all the elements of the list. In Python, the reduce function is implemented as a left reduction (fold left) because the function is applied left to right.

The operation we have used (addition) does not care about the order in which the reduction happens because it is *commutative* and *associative*, meaning that the result of add_reduce(x,y) is the same as add_reduce(y,x), and add_reduce (add_reduce (x,y),z) would be the same as add_reduce (x,add_reduce(y,z)).

In distributed computing, it is important to make sure the reduce function does not depend on the order of the elements to perform an operation. This is because we may need to apply it in different computing nodes to reduce overhead through the network. Generally, we cannot expect the elements of a collection to come in any particular order.

Obviously, we can do many more things than just adding up values using reduce and we will have to design specific functions for different problems. For example, if you wanted to compute the average of that list [1, 2, 3, 4], we should get 2.5. Could we just calculate the average of each pair? That is:

```
reduce(lambda x,y: (x+y)/2,lst)
```

```
3.125
```

What is happening? To compute that mean we use division, which is not an associative operation; for example, (1/2)/2 = 0.25, which is not the same as 1/(1/2), that is, 2. Thus, you should generally ensure that your reduce function is commutative and associative.

In the MapReduce programming model we will combine these two functions, one after the other. The first aims to make some transformations to the input data, and the latter reduces it and yields a final result. We can combine both in Python in the same line of code, so we could first obtain the square of each element of a list and then add them up:

```
reduce(add_reduce, map(lambda x: x*x, lst))
```

```
1+4-->5
5+9-->14
14+16-->30
```

```
30
```

In summary, the map and reduce functions in Python are great for reducing code complexity by avoiding unnecessary for loops. In the MapReduce programming model, they become the key components. Here is a hint about why this is the case: map can be easily applied in parallel, whereas reduce can be used for aggregating information coming from several sources and can be done in phases (given that the function used is commutative and associative).

2.3   "Hello World" in Big Data: Word Count

We now understand how the map and reduce functions work sequentially, but how do
we split the work among computers when we have big data? To answer this question,
we are going to use the big data equivalent of "Hello World," which is known as "Word
Count".[2]

The task consists of counting the frequency of words in a document or collection of
documents. To understand what we want to achieve, let us create a simple string with
some content that could represent a document:

```
text = "Welcome to the Big World of Big Big Data Welcome World \
        bye World Hello MapReduce GoodBye MapReduce\
        This Book on Big Data is fun"
```

If we want to count the words in that string with Python, you might think you could
split this by the blank spaces and then use a dictionary to keep every single word as a
key; the value could be the number of times it appears in the text. Something like this:

```
dic = {}
for word in text.split(" "):
    if word not in dic.keys():
        dic[word] = 1
    else:
        dic[word] += 1
```

And, voilà:

```
dic
```

```
{'Welcome': 2,
 'to': 1,
 'the': 1,
 'Big': 4,
 'World': 3,
 'of': 1,
 'Data': 2,
 'bye': 1,
 '': 14,
 'Hello': 1,
 'MapReduce': 2,
 'GoodBye': 1,
 'This': 1,
 'Book': 1,
 'on': 1,
 'is': 1,
 'fun': 1}
```

But, what if this was a very big document file? So big that it wouldn't fit in the
memory of your computer? One would probably think of applying a divide-and-
conquer strategy. Let's see if this could solve the problem.

If the document is very big, then we must assume that it is distributed among several
computing nodes that we can use for parallelizing the job. For example, let's assume

2 Content inspired by BerkeleyX CS105x
   https://courses.edx.org/courses/course-v1:BerkeleyX+CS105x+1T2016/

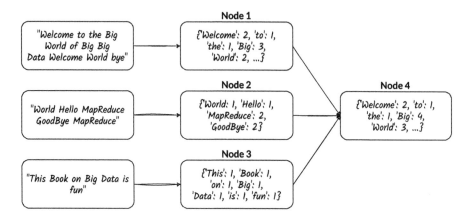

Figure 2.1 Attempt to parallelize Word Count using four computing nodes.

we have three nodes and each one has (locally) a chunk/partition of the document following the data locality principle. Now it would be straightforward to apply the previous code (i.e., the for loop) in each chunk of data, so that we can obtain partial word counts. When all the nodes have done their job, an additional node could receive all the partial (intermediate) results from each node and merge/aggregate them into a single dictionary. Figure 2.1 plots this potential solution.

Do you see any problems with this plan? Well, for starters, we are assuming that all the intermediate results (i.e., dictionaries) will fit in the main memory of a single computer to perform the aggregation, which might not be the case (in general). Also, in the most extreme case, the size of the output from each node could be even bigger than the chunk of the text itself if there were no repetitions. Of course, this will not be true in most cases, as the number of words in a language is limited (e.g., around 470 000 in English!), and there will definitely be repetitions. Nevertheless, we must abstract ourselves and think "big." So, assuming that a single node may deal with all the results is not scalable, and not desirable in big data.

Maybe you could think of a way to alleviate this by using some nodes in the middle (between the first three machines and the final one) that could aggregate partial results. But that wouldn't work either for all cases, because the final result still needs to fit in one single machine, which in big data might not be true.

Then, how do we solve this? Rather than sending all the intermediate results to a single node, wouldn't it be better to send just a subset of the words (that would fit in the memory of one computer) to a particular node that will only take care of aggregating that subset and keep the final word count for them? Figure 2.2 shows this alternative.

In this example, different nodes take care of different keys, for example node 4 deals with the subset "welcome," "to," "the," and "World." Actually, there is no need for three new nodes in this example – the original three nodes could take care of the second stage.

You might now be wondering whether it's necessary to program which words go to which node. Not really, that's part of the "magic" of MapReduce. Apart from the map and reduce phases, there is an intermediate phase that we have not yet named, known

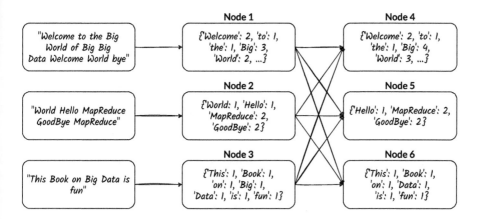

Figure 2.2 Parallelizing Word Count using six computing nodes (only three different ones would actually be needed). The output remains distributed across nodes 4, 5, and 6.

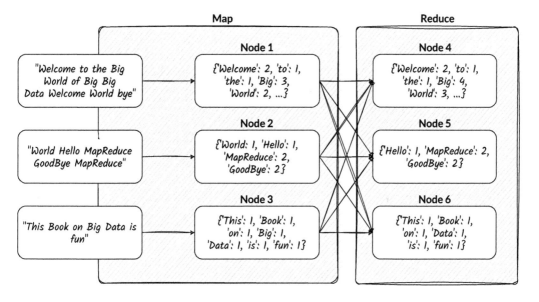

Figure 2.3 High-level representation of the two main stages of MapReduce.

as the *shuffle* phase. This is precisely the phase where certain keys and their values are sent to particular nodes, and this happens automatically in MapReduce. At the end of the process, we will have the final result distributed in multiple machines. We will come back to this in a couple of sections.

This is the main idea of MapReduce, where the map phase performs some initial operation in different chunks of the data and reduce will merge all intermediate results with the same key into a single one, keeping the output distributed. You can visualize these two phases in Figure 2.3.

> ## Challenge #2.1
>
> How would you create a ranking of the words to determine which word is the most frequently used?
> Considering the previous example, the final results should be distributed across nodes as follows:
>
> - *Node 1* would keep "World," "Hello," and "MapReduce" because they are the most popular ones (three, two, and two repetitions, respectively);
> - *Nodes 2* and *3* would keep the other ones ... or maybe we don't even need a third node in this case.
>
> Can you do this in a single MapReduce step? If you need more than one MapReduce step, remember that conceptually you do need to perform entire MapReduce phases.

So far we have solved the algorithmic part of how to do the word count by making use of the data locality principle in a distributed fashion both in terms of computation and the final result. However, in the previous chapter we mentioned that horizontal scalability allows for fault tolerance; at the moment, the process could end even if one node failed. Imagine that a computer only encounters a hardware problem once in three years – if we have 10 000 nodes, even if each one only fails every three years, we may have ten failures per day!

Then, how does MapReduce get to be fault tolerant? The idea behind it is rather simple. If a node fails, then the process being executed by that node is launched in

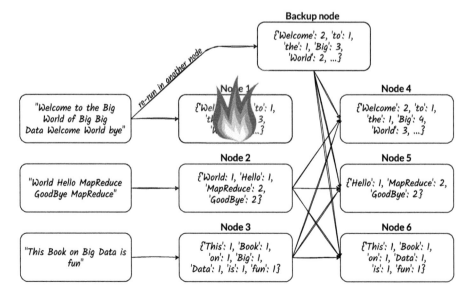

Figure 2.4 Fault tolerance in MapReduce. Node 1 fails or is not responding, so another node takes over that computation.

another one, looking for a node that holds a copy of the required data (or the majority of it). Likewise, when a node is taking longer than expected to provide an answer, or hasn't been responsive, speculative execution of the same process is launched in another node. If the node were to recover from a temporary glitch, the first process that finishes will provide the result, the other being discarded. Figure 2.4 illustrates this idea.

In conclusion, the MapReduce programming model helps us deal with some of the challenges of deploying distributed solutions for big data, including a new level of abstraction and fault tolerance mechanisms. For correctness, we must admit that MapReduce does not itself provide fault tolerance, but the framework implementing the MapReduce programming model is what gives us that level of abstraction and transparency. We will come back to this in the next chapter.

2.4   Working with Key–Value Pairs

We now introduce MapReduce a bit more formally. As we already mentioned, MapReduce is based on functional programming and it operates on (*key, value*) pairs, which are simply tuples (like in Python). For example:

- For a text file, the *key* could be the line number, and the *value* would be the actual text in that line. Following the previous example, we could have something like:

```
(1, "Welcome to the Big")
(2, "World of Big Big")
(3, "Data Welcome World bye")
...
```

- If we think of a classification dataset in machine learning, the *key* could be the instance number and the *value* the actual instance with its corresponding features and class label:

```
(1, ((0.4, 0.2), 1))
(2, ((0.5, 0.4), 0))
(3, ((0.6, 0.9), 0))
(4, ((0.3, 0.3), 1))
(5, ((0.7, 0.8), 0))
...
```

We must assume that we are working with very large files, so that, they need to be divided into chunks and stored across different nodes. Again, we don't need to take care of this, since a distributed file system will be doing this job for us (as discussed in the next chapter).

In MapReduce, the user must only implement two functions, one for each phase: map and reduce. Note that we sometimes talk about the map and reduce functions or phases indistinctly, although we do not really implement map and reduce, but the functions that are run within those phases. Both phases will work with (*key, value*) pairs, but they have different purposes. Additionally, as we mentioned earlier, there is

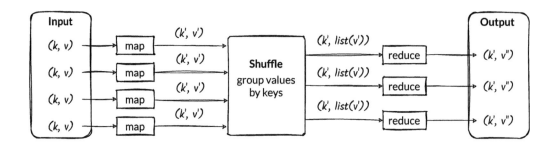

Figure 2.5 Formal definition of MapReduce.

an intermediate phase that occurs between map and reduce, known as shuffle, which happens automatically, and it is part of the *magic* behind MapReduce.

Figure 2.5 summarizes the whole MapReduce process. In a nutshell, map takes a key–value pair as input and returns another key–value pair (or a list of key–value pairs). Shuffle groups all pairs with the same key and creates a list with their values. Finally, reduce takes a list of values for each key and combines it into a single value.

We wouldn't be surprised if you are finding it difficult to understand such a definition, as we did when we first read about MapReduce. To help with this, let's break each phase down.

2.4.1   Map

For the map phase, a programmer must design what we call the map function, which transforms a certain input key–value (k, v) pair into zero or more intermediate $\langle k', v' \rangle$ pairs (i.e., a list of key–value pairs), where both k' and v' can be arbitrary, user-defined objects (a string, an integer, a data structure, etc.). It is common not to use the input key k of the map function, since it may not provide useful information (it is usually metadata like the filename, line number, and so on). The value is usually where we must focus to output the new $\langle k', v' \rangle$ pairs.

For example, we can design a map function map(k,v) that returns (abs(v),1) as a key–value pair. Therefore, the absolute value of a given input value (v) becomes the output key k', and the output value v' will always be 1. Note that in this map function the input key (k) is not relevant at all.

If we apply such a function to the list of key–value pairs...
```
[(1, 2), (2, -1), (3, 1), (4, 3), (5, 6)]
```
it would output (see Figure 2.6)
```
[(2, 1), (1, 1), (1, 1), (3, 1), (6, 1)]
```
In this example, the map function only returns one intermediate $\langle k', v' \rangle$ pair for each input $\langle k, v \rangle$ pair. You will soon realize that you must design your map function depending on what you need in your reduce function.

Remember that we are programming in a distributed environment, so we must assume that each $\langle k, v \rangle$ pair may be in a different node. For the map function, this means that you will not have access to other $\langle k, v \rangle$ pairs in the input to generate the new

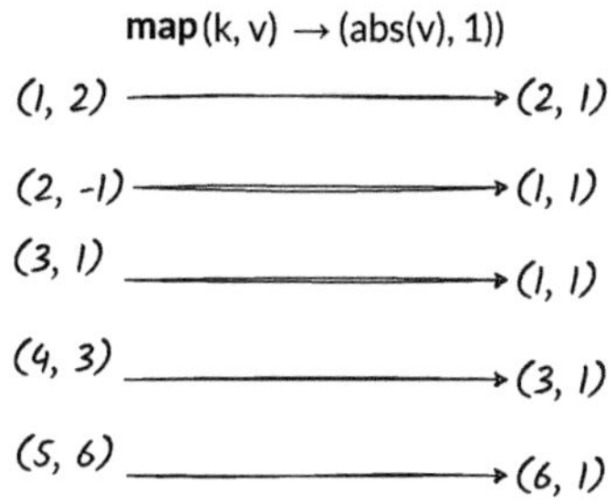

map (k, v) → (abs(v), 1))

(1, 2) ────────────────→ *(2, 1)*

(2, -1) ════════════════→ *(1, 1)*

(3, 1) _____→ *(1, 1)*

(4, 3) _____→ *(3, 1)*

(5, 6) _____→ *(6, 1)*

Figure 2.6 Map example. For each input tuple, the map function returns (abs(v),1).

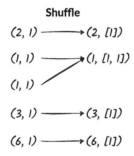

Shuffle

(2, 1) ──────→ *(2, [1])*

(1, 1) ──────↗ *(1, [1, 1])*

(1, 1) ↗

(3, 1) ──────→ *(3, [1])*

(6, 1) ──────→ *(6, [1])*

Figure 2.7 Shuffle example. For each output from the map, the shuffle operation will group together those values with the same key.

output $\langle k', v' \rangle$. This is why the map function can be run in parallel, and in fact we could parallelize as many processes as there are input $\langle k, v \rangle$ pairs. However, in practice we will see that they are grouped in data partitions and that the degree of parallelization will be limited by the number of partitions.

2.4.2 Shuffle

After performing the map function on all input $\langle k, v \rangle$ pairs, the resulting $\langle k', v' \rangle$ pairs are automatically grouped by k', and for each k' a list(v') is generated with all the values associated to k', obtaining new pairs formed of a key and a list of values: $\langle k', \text{list}(v') \rangle$.

In a distributed environment, this phase will require data movement across the network, so that, all the values v' associated with the same k' are sent to the same place (node), regardless of where they were generated. Therefore, we must be cautious when designing the map phase to avoid unnecessary data transfer during the shuffle phase, since it may become a bottleneck.

Continuing with the previous example, the input to the shuffle would be...
```
[(2, 1), (1, 1), (1, 1), (3, 1), (6, 1)]
```
and the output of the shuffle phase would be (see Figure 2.7)
```
[(2, [1]), (1, [1, 1]), (3, [1]), (6, [1])]
```
It is important to mention here that we cannot expect list(v') to be in any particular order. In this example they are just 1s, but if they were something else, you cannot

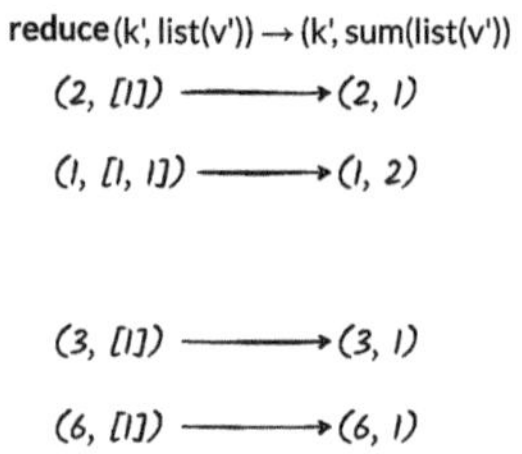

reduce (k', list(v')) → (k', sum(list(v'))

(2, [1]) ———————→ (2, 1)

(1, [1, 1]) —————→ (1, 2)

(3, [1]) ———————→ (3, 1)

(6, [1]) ———————→ (6, 1)

Figure 2.8 Reduce example. For each input tuple, the reduce function returns sum(list(v')).

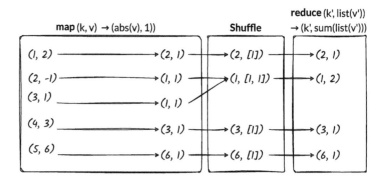

Figure 2.9 Complete MapReduce example.

expect them to be sorted in any particular way. This may have some implications for the way we design the next step. Additionally, we should not assume that we will have access to the whole list(v') in the next phase. In fact, we could find ways to concatenate all the values; however, we should avoid as far as possible working with the whole list because it might not fit in the main memory of a single node.

2.4.3   Reduce

After the shuffle phase, in the reduce phase we must define a function that receives a ⟨k',list(v')⟩ pair and aggregates (reduces) the list of values list(v') to a single value v'', returning a final ⟨k',list(v'')⟩ pair.

Following the same example, the input would be the result of the shuffle:

[(2, [1]), (1, [1, 1]), (3, [1]), (6, [1])]

If our reduce function was to compute the sum of all the elements in the list, sum(list(v'), the output would be (see Figure 2.8)...

[(2, 1), (1, 2), (3, 1), (6, 1)]

Figure 2.9 puts all the phases together to visualize the whole process. You can see that with these map and reduce functions we have been able to count the number of times each absolute value v was present in the initial list. Although this exercise may seem too simple, it is very common in MapReduce to do similar calculations, since many tasks may require counting.

Before discussing how to implement the Word Count example with MapReduce, we would like to highlight a few considerations on designing a MapReduce solution.

> **The reduce function must be commutative and associative**: The reduce phase works by pairs on the list provided by the shuffle phase, and you cannot expect the reduce to happen in any particular order. But, why is that? Because, otherwise, you would be assuming that the whole list of values of a given key would fit into the memory of a single node, and as mentioned before that may not be true in big data (or at least, not a good idea). Additionally, working by pairs allows us to limit the information sent across the network in the shuffle phase (see Section 2.5).

> **Design a complete MapReduce cycle**: Conceptually, MapReduce would always carry out the above steps, namely, map, shuffle, and reduce. So, if you need to perform successive MapReduce operations, you would need to define how both map and reduce would work.

2.4.4   Implementing Word Count with MapReduce

We have already seen the key challenges to implementing Word Count in big data, and presented the map/shuffle/reduce phases in detail. So, we are now ready to put this together and show how to conceptually implement the map and reduce functions for Word Count. For simplicity, let's say that the input is a simplified version of the one we used previously, where each key–value pair is composed of the line number and the content of that line.

```
(1, "Welcome to the Big")
(2, "World of Big Big")
(3, "Data Welcome World bye")
```

Rather than performing the word count directly in the map phase, we could simply use the map phase to split that input string into words and return each word as the key. So, for each word, we are going to return a pair ⟨*word, value*⟩. But, what should the *value* be? As we are merely counting words, it could be a 1, meaning that the word has appeared once (and that will allow us to do the counting later).

Therefore, the map function would be something like this: map(k,v) => list((word(v), 1)). We represent this as a "list" of (word(v), 1) to note that different key–value pairs are output for the same input key–value pair (i.e., we will get as many key–value pairs as words in the string). Focusing on our input sample, for the first line (k == 1), the output will be composed of (Welcome, 1), (to, 1), (the, 1), and (World, 1). Figure 2.10 completes this idea with the other inputs.

After the map, the shuffle phase will automatically bring together all the values with the same key from the map phase, creating a list of values for each key. In this case, all the values for the same word will be grouped. Ensuring that all the values corresponding to the same word go to the same place, we enable the counting of the number of occurrences. Figure 2.11 shows the result of the shuffle phase. Note that each arrow from map to shuffle means that this information will be sent over the network (if

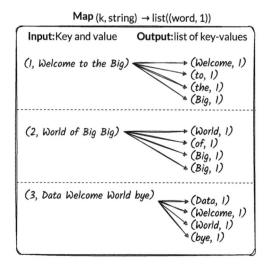

Figure 2.10 Word Count map phase.

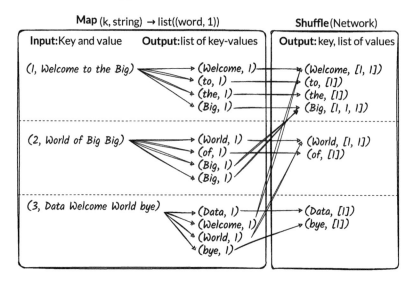

Figure 2.11 Word Count shuffle phase.

required). If we imagine that the dotted lines distinguish between three different nodes (each takes one line of text), there will be some data movement involved.

After the shuffle phase, the reduce function will receive a list of 1s for each key (i.e., each word), and its duty is to reduce that list into a number that is the final count of repetitions of that word. The implementation of this will be very similar to what we saw in the previous example (and before with Python): lambda x, y: x + y. Since this operation is commutative and associative, we will have no problems with the random order of the values that should be expected. Remember that we should

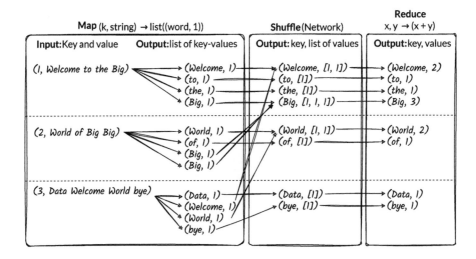

Figure 2.12 Complete Word Count MapReduce diagram.

not expect to access the list of values as a whole, but should reduce it by pairs. The complete MapReduce process is displayed in Figure 2.12.

Challenge #2.2

We have been provided with a large file that contains temperature data at different times in the following format:

```
2015-07-13; 24
2012-07-11; 24
2011-08-13; 43
2015-09-11; 17
```

How would you determine the maximum temperature each year using MapReduce?

2.5   Combiners

In the Word Count example you may have noticed that we could have optimized some of the data transfer among nodes. Whenever a word is repeated more than once in the same node, we could pre-aggregate the 1s to send a single key–value pair containing the word and the number of times it appears in the node instead of sending multiple key–value pairs. This could significantly reduce the network overhead when there is significant repetition in the intermediate keys produced by each map task.

To do so, in MapReduce we can implement something called a *combiner*, which can be understood as a local aggregator within the map phase. Combiners work very similarly to the reduce phase, but they are applied before the shuffle. In fact, usually, the same code is used. The idea is to reduce the values corresponding to the same key that reside in the same node, before sending them across the network.

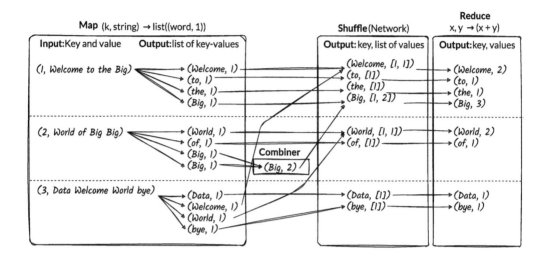

Figure 2.13 Combiners help reduce data movement across the network by applying the reduce function locally.

The way in which MapReduce works enables the implementation of combiners. However, different implementations of MapReduce (e.g., Hadoop or Spark) may decide to use a combiner or not depending on what is faster. Although combiners are very interesting for reducing network data transfer, we focus on how to design the map and reduce functions (especially for the suggested lab assignment) as combiners typically share the same code as the reduce function, and this can be seen as an implementation "trick" to boost the efficiency.

Figure 2.13 shows the effect of a combiner on our Word Count example. For the case of "Big" in node 2, we can combine the values before the shuffle, getting the tuple (Big, 2), by simply using the very same code of the reduce function on those local values that share the same key. You may see here why commutativity and associativity are essential for the reduce function to be applied, since otherwise, the result may vary if combiners are applied.

2.6   Internal Working

To fully understand how MapReduce works, we need a few more details about the processes that are involved when the execution of MapReduce takes place. As described in the next chapter, MapReduce is a programming model that needs to be implemented. The first well-known implementation is Hadoop, which we cover in the next chapter. But we will now give you a hint on how a MapReduce job is executed in Hadoop.

When running a MapReduce process, data is assumed to be already distributed across nodes in several chunks/partitions (on a distributed file system). These blocks are usually quite big, typically 64 or 128 MB.

In Hadoop, there are two main processes in charge of the execution of a MapReduce job, known as mappers and reducers, each one focused on the map and reduce phases, respectively.

- A *mapper* is a process that executes the map function we have programmed for each key–value in a partition of the data. A mapper can manage multiple blocks, and there can be more than one mapper in a single node.
- A *reducer* is a process that runs our reduce function for each key k'. The same reducer can deal with multiple keys k', and there can also be more than one reducer in a single node.

The mapper will take a partition of the data and produce new $\langle k', v' \rangle$ pairs using the map function. Then, the new pairs are partitioned (i.e., it is decided to which reducer each key will go) and sorted according to their target reducer, where they are further processed. After the shuffle phase, the reducer takes the $\langle k', \text{list}(v') \rangle$ pairs, also in the form of partitions, and produce the final outputs $\langle k', v'' \rangle$ by applying the reduce function.

There is one main issue in this process that we will discuss more thoroughly when we talk about Hadoop, but we want to give you a bit of a hint now. In Hadoop, these mapper processes write their outputs to a buffer in memory which is then written to disk. This slows things down because the shuffle process must read its input from the drive and send it to reduce, which will store data on the disk if it does not fit into memory. Finally, the reducers read the data again from the drive (if they are not in the buffer), and then write the result to the drive again (in this case, in the distributed file system). The key message here is that lots of I/O operations still happen with the disk drives, which are very slow compared to main memory.

2.7   Take-Home Message

We have seen that, conceptually speaking, MapReduce is relatively similar to other parallelization strategies like MPI, but the key distinguishing features are:

- It provides a whole new level of abstraction to the programmer. We don't really need to worry about how things are being run, but we do need to know that things will be happening in parallel.
- It is fault tolerant, which is very much needed when processing big datasets.
- It assumes data locality and redundancy through distributed file systems (we will see the Hadoop distributed file system in the next chapter).

Key points about how it works:

- MapReduce is composed of three main stages, map, shuffle, and reduce, where the shuffle phase happens automatically and we only have to program the functions that are executed in the map and reduce stages.
- The shuffle phase is where the data movement across the network happens, and it is influenced by the key–value pairs generated in the preceding map phase. We need to be careful how we design our map and reduce functions to avoid unnecessary traffic on the network. Combiners help in this case.

- The reduce function must be commutative and associative, otherwise it will not work as expected.
- Internally, the data is split into a number of partitions (which determine the degree of parallelism), and the MapReduce implementation coordinates different processes (e.g., mappers and reducers) to run the map and reduce functions on each key–value pair in a given partition.

2.8   To Learn More

Do you want to know more about MapReduce? We suggest you look at the following resources:

Dean and Ghemawat (2004) was the first paper on MapReduce, if you want to know all the details about MapReduce and how it was conceptualized. In particular, we suggest further reading on combiners (Dean and Ghemawat, 2004, Section 4.3).

Dean and Ghemawat (2010) is a good resource for further reading on MapReduce from its creators.

If you are not very familiar with functional programming, you may be interested in looking at the following books:

Hutton (2016) is a great resource for learning everything related to functional programming. The programming language is Haskell, which is quite different from what we use here, but the concepts and ideas about functional programming may be of interest.

Chiusano and Bjarnason (2014) is another great book about functional programming. In this case, the programming language is Scala, which may also be useful for doing big data stuff.

2.9   Solutions to Challenges

Challenge #2.1

How would you create a ranking of the words to determine which word is the most frequently used?
Considering the previous example, the final results should be distributed across nodes as follows:

- *Node 1* would keep "World," "Hello," and "MapReduce" because they are the most popular ones (three, two, and two repetitions, respectively);
- *Nodes 2* and *3* would keep the other ones ... or maybe we don't even need a third node in this case.

Can you do this in a single MapReduce step? If you need more than one MapReduce step, remember that conceptually you do need to perform entire MapReduce phases.

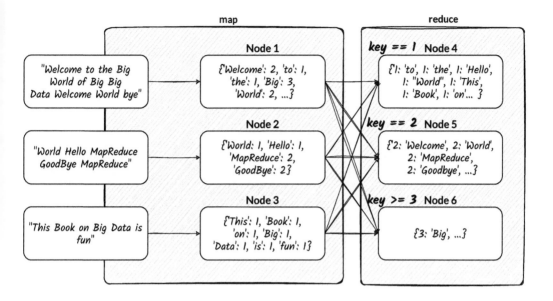

Figure 2.14 Wrong attempt to compute the most repeated words with a MapReduce philosophy; you can see how we may find words like "World" that are counted wrongly.

We discussed how to split the work across computers to count word frequencies in a big document using two stages:

1. Apply our original sequential solution to count the words in a chunk of data; this returns a dictionary with keys (the words) and values (the counts).
2. Combine/aggregate the solutions from the previous stage. We said that a way to do this would be to send a subset of words to a specific node that would take care of counting the frequencies of those words; a different node would take care of another subset, and so on. So, we get the final word count distributed across different computers.

We were asking you to find alternatives to directly computing which are the most repeated words. This is almost the same as being able to directly rank the words by frequency of appearance.

What we would be expecting you to try/do is to swap the key and the value, and initially perform the same "map" operation, and then, instead of sending a subset of words, send out the word count to the nodes according to the count frequency. Figure 2.14 presents this attempt.

But, as you can already see in the figure, is that actually correct? Or is this a joke rather than a challenge? Well, that certainly wouldn't do the trick. You wouldn't get the word count correctly and you would have the same word in different nodes (with different frequencies).

We set this challenge for you to see that MapReduce might not be able to do everything in one single stage. To solve this challenge, the idea was good, but you

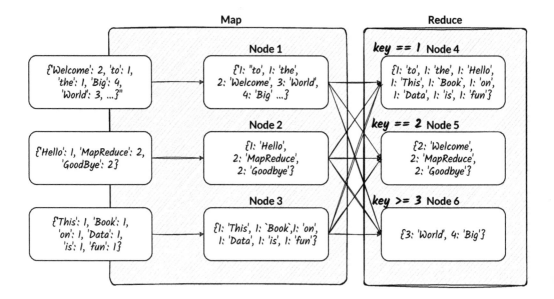

Figure 2.15 Computing the most repeated words with a MapReduce philosophy, using the output of Word Count as input.

should start off from the output of the word count; so, yes, we can concatenate two MapReduce processes (Figure 2.15).

The input to the map function would be something like this:

```
(1, "2015-07-13; 24")
(2, "2012-07-11; 24")
(3, "2011-08-13; 43")
(4, "2015-09-11; 17")
```

Here, the key is the line number and the value is the actual content. The desired final output would be a set of key–value pairs in which the key is the year, and the value is the maximum temperature observed in that year. For the above input, we should get:

```
(2015,24)
(2012,24)
(2011,43)
```

Therefore, we want to make sure that after processing each line of this file, we keep the year and the temperature, but the day and month could be disregarded as they are not important for what we've been asked to do.

As we would like to find the maximum temperature for each year, the map phase could process that input value, and send out the year as the output key and the temperature as the output value. Why? Because we want to make sure that the shuffle phase will group together all the temperatures associated with a year (e.g., (2015, [24,17])), so that the reduce phase will be able to compute the maximum of that list of values.

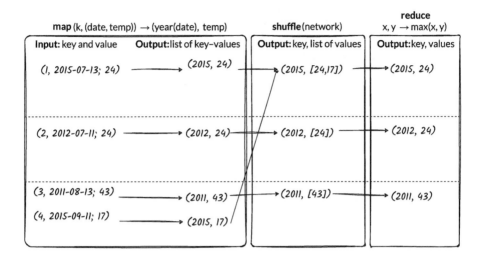

Figure 2.16 MapReduce approach to computing the maximum temperature per year.

Thus, the map function could look like this:

```
map(key, value):
    // key: line number; value: text in line
    year, temperature = value.split(";")
    return (year, temperature)
```

The reduce function will have to compute the maximum of each pair of values in the list. Using Python style for the reduce function, this would look like `lambda x, y: max(x,y)`. Is this associative and commutative? Try to check yourself.

Visually, a MapReduce solution for this is shown in Figure 2.16.

2.10   Exercises

2.1 In a MapReduce program, what is the correct sequence of stages?
  (a) map, reduce, shuffle
  (b) shuffle, map, shuffle, reduce
  (c) map, reduce, shuffle
  (d) map, shuffle, reduce

2.2 Indicate whether the following statements about MapReduce are true or false:
  (a) MapReduce guarantees that no data movement across the network will happen.
  (b) It is based on object-oriented programming.
  (c) In contradistinction to MPI, MapReduce requires explicit programming of the communication between nodes.
  (d) Hadoop implements the MapReduce programming model.

2.3 MapReduce is said to work on key–value pairs. Briefly explain whether the following statements are true or false:

(a) The input keys to the map phase are extremely important in minimizing data movement.

(b) The keys in all stages (map, shuffle, and reduce) need to be numeric.

(c) The output values of the map phase could be a tuple containing any data type, for example another tuple ('Big', 3), so that it outputs a tuple like (k', ('Big',3)).

(d) The reduce phase does not work on key–value pairs, which are only useful for the map and shuffle phases.

2.4 Indicate whether the following statements about the map phase are true or false:

(a) You can access any other key–value pair residing in any other partitions.

(b) It may output one or more key–value pairs from a single input (k', v').

(c) The output values of this phase are usually irrelevant and disregarded.

(d) In Hadoop, a process called the mapper runs this function in a partition of the data.

2.5 Indicate whether the following statements about the shuffle phase are true or false:

(a) Programmers have to specify the behavior of this phase as a function.

(b) It may involve data movement across the network.

(c) It groups all pairs with the same values and creates a list with their keys.

(d) Its performance may be influenced by how we define the map function.

2.6 Conceptually speaking, can we concatenate more than one MapReduce process? Briefly explain your answer.

2.7 Why do we say that MapReduce is transparent to the programmer and fault tolerant, but MPI is not? Explain your answer.

2.8 In your own words, briefly explain the role of combiners in the MapReduce paradigm and why they usually use the same code as the reduce function.

2.9 In the MapReduce paradigm, why does the reduce function have to be commutative and associative? Explain your answer, and provide an example where a non-commutative/associative reducer function could cause issues.

2.10 We have designed a map function map(k, v) that returns (v * k, k) and we apply it to this list of key–value pairs: [(0, 15), (15, 0), (2, 0)]. What is the output of applying this function?

2.11 Using the output from the previous exercise, what would be the output of the shuffle phase?

2.12 For the output of the previous shuffle, we define a reduce function as lambda x, y: x * y. What is the output of this phase?

2.13 Instead of the product, we now try subtraction: lambda x, y: x - y. What is the output? Do you anticipate any issues with it? Briefly explain your answer.

2.14　We have defined the following `reduce` function:

```
def special(x, y):
    if x > y:
        return x
    else
        return y
```

Would this be an associative and commutative operation? Briefly explain your answer.

2.15　Using the same input data as we used for Word Count,

```
(1, "Welcome to the Big")
(2, "World of Big Big")
(3, "Data Welcome World bye")
```

we have defined the map phase to return, for each word of the input value, a key–value pair like: `(1, length(word))`, where `length` is a function that gives you the length of the string. The reduction function is implemented as `lambda x, y: x + y`.

What will be the output of executing such a MapReduce process? Briefly describe what task is being performed by this MapReduce process.

Part II

Big Data Frameworks

3 Hadoop

Learning Outcomes

[KU]	How a big data application is distributed in Hadoop
[KU]	How a distributed file system enables data locality for big data processing
[KU]	How transparency and fault tolerance are implemented in Hadoop
[KU, IS]	Limitations of Hadoop for different data processing approaches

In the previous chapter we started talking about MapReduce as a programming model for big data. We said that the key features that make this model interesting are its transparency, its data locality assumption, and the fault tolerance capabilities. However, this is, let's say, a concept. Who is in charge of implementing that transparency, that is, the communication across computers? Or, who's ensuring data locality and the fault tolerance mechanisms?

We need an actual implementation/framework to use that concept. There are different implementations of MapReduce, but let's start off with Hadoop as the precursor and first open-source implementation of MapReduce.

3.1 What Is Hadoop?

Hadoop[1] is an open-source framework, written in Java, for big data processing and storage that is based on the MapReduce programming model presented by Dean and Ghemawat (2004) and the Google File System proposed by Ghemawat et al. (2003). Doug Cutting created this framework back in 2006, initially as part of the Apache Nutch project.[2] Are you wondering where the name and the logo (the elephant) came from? Well, he simply named it after his son's toy elephant.

Originally, it was composed of two main modules: one that implemented the MapReduce programming model and another (HDFS) that provided a distributed file system to implement the principle of data locality. As a bit of a spoiler, using the Hadoop implementation of the MapReduce programming model may perhaps not be the best

---

[1] https://hadoop.apache.org/
[2] https://nutch.apache.org/

choice now, but we will show you later how it works. In addition, there are two more important modules: YARN, available from the second version of Hadoop, is the resource manager in charge of coordinating any MapReduce process running in a Hadoop cluster; and Common, which is a utility library to support the other modules. Several modules have been added and deleted from Hadoop since its conception, and many of them have become independent projects built on top of Hadoop. We are actually talking about more than 150 projects! That's why it's known as the *Hadoop Ecosystem*.

Before providing more details about the different elements of Hadoop and how to execute Hadoop MapReduce, we would like to show you what a MapReduce program looks like.

3.2   Word Count Using Hadoop MapReduce

As you will see later, implementing Word Count on Hadoop can be a bit pointless now because it is a bit awkward to program and not very elegant, but it allows us to introduce how complex this used to be with Hadoop. So, don't panic if you are not a Java expert or a professional programmer, you will see later that with Spark and Python it will be much easier to get started.

We have borrowed the implementation of Word Count from the Hadoop MapReduce tutorial.[3] Let's start off with the implementation of the map function. To do this, we needed to define a class that extends the class Mapper, and define a function map:

```
public static class TokenizerMapper
      extends Mapper<Object, Text, Text, IntWritable>{

    private final static IntWritable one = new IntWritable(1);
    private Text word = new Text();

    public void map(Object key, Text value, Context context
                ) throws IOException, InterruptedException {
      StringTokenizer itr = new StringTokenizer(value.toString());
      while (itr.hasMoreTokens()) {
        word.set(itr.nextToken());
        context.write(word, one);
      }
    }
}
```

The output from the map function (given through context.write()) needs to be of specific data types implemented in Hadoop. Hadoop uses its own types, for example, Text instead of String, or IntWritable instead of Integer. Why do you think that is? Well, String and Integer are simply too "fat" for big data processing. So, Text and IntWritable provide a much lighter abstraction on top of byte arrays to represent the same type of information.

As we mentioned before, there is quite a lot of I/O happening locally for each drive at different stages: from map to shuffle, and from shuffle to reduce. But, what are we

---

[3] https://hadoop.apache.org/docs/stable/hadoop-mapreduce-client/hadoop-mapreduce-client-core/MapReduceTutorial.html

exactly writing/reading between stages? The key and values defined as the output of each stage need to be written and later read. This is done via a process known as *serialization*, which consists of converting the state of an object into a byte stream that can be written to disk, so that the state of the object can be reverted (i.e., deserialized) back into a copy of the object when reading. As this process has some costs, and the "thinner" the data type the better, the Hadoop framework came up with its own I/O classes to replace Java primitive data types.

You can also see in that code that when extending from the `Mapper` superclass, we indicated the data types of the input and output key–value pairs (`<Object, Text, Text, IntWritable>`). The implementation of the `map` function is quite self-explanatory. The input value is converted to `StringTokenizer` and read word by word, and the `map` function outputs each word as the key, and a one as the value, using Hadoop data types.

For reduce, we have to do something very similar and create a new class that extends from `Reducer`, indicating the input/output data types (`<Text, IntWritable, Text, IntWritable>`).

```
public static class IntSumReducer
     extends Reducer<Text,IntWritable,Text,IntWritable> {
  private IntWritable result = new IntWritable();

  public void reduce(Text key, Iterable<IntWritable> values,
                     Context context
                  ) throws IOException, InterruptedException {
    int sum = 0;
    for (IntWritable val : values) {
      sum += val.get();
    }
    result.set(sum);
    context.write(key, result);
  }
}
```

Note that the `IntSumReducer` class extends the `Reducer` class with an `IntWritable` input value type, but the actual `reduce` function is defined as an iterator, with the class `Iterable`, and this allows us to traverse the list of values that come with the same key from the previous phase. The reduce implementation is a "left-to-right" reduction, but again you can't assume that the list of values arrives in any given order. The code of `reduce` is quite simple: the integer values in the iterable list are summed and taken as the resulting new value.

Finally, we need a `main` function that sets up the entire job, specifying the classes we have implemented and the data types of the output key and values. As a side note, you can see below how we use the class `IntSumReducer` for both the combiner and the reducer.

```
public static void main(String[] args) throws Exception {
  Configuration conf = new Configuration();
  String[] otherArgs = new GenericOptionsParser(conf, \
                                  args).getRemainingArgs();
  if (otherArgs.length < 2) {
    System.err.println("Usage: wordcount <in> [<in>...] <out>");
```

```
    System.exit(2);
  }
  Job job = Job.getInstance(conf, "word count");
  job.setJarByClass(WordCount.class);
  job.setMapperClass(TokenizerMapper.class);
  job.setCombinerClass(IntSumReducer.class);
  job.setReducerClass(IntSumReducer.class);
  job.setOutputKeyClass(Text.class);
  job.setOutputValueClass(IntWritable.class);
  for (int i = 0; i < otherArgs.length - 1; ++i) {
    FileInputFormat.addInputPath(job, new Path(otherArgs[i]));
  }
  FileOutputFormat.setOutputPath(job,
    new Path(otherArgs[otherArgs.length - 1]));
  System.exit(job.waitForCompletion(true) ? 0 : 1);
}
```

You may have noticed how verbose and tedious it is to write a simple program with Hadoop MapReduce, requiring us to know these specific data types and define those classes, and it certainly doesn't feel like functional programming. Luckily for us, newer frameworks such as Spark, Dask, or Flink provide easier ways to implement MapReduce programs. Apart from the implementation of MapReduce, Hadoop provides much more than that, and this is what we are going to cover in the remainder of the chapter.

> **Challenge #3.1**
>
> If you have installed Hadoop on your own computer, run the Word Count example.

3.3   Resource Negotiator: Internal Working

As you probably guessed already, to run a MapReduce program there will be quite a few processes handling its execution, as we need to coordinate the execution of the map and reduce functions in multiple computers (transparently) and ensure tolerance to failure. We mentioned in the previous chapter that there are mapper and reducer processes running our MapReduce application, but how is that actually implemented?

Hadoop follows a classical master/worker architecture (Figure 3.1), in which a "master" node coordinates everything and a number of nodes (known as "workers") do the actual job. Remember that when we talk about a cluster of computers we mean a number of computers connected by a (high-speed) local network, as explained in Chapter 1.

3.3.1   Components

Hadoop has evolved quite a bit from its first version. Originally, the MapReduce module coordinated everything related to the execution. This meant that any additional module

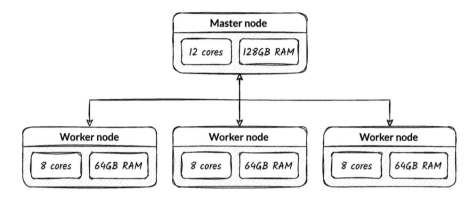

Figure 3.1 Master/worker architecture. The physical RAM and number of cores are indicated in the internal boxes.

that wanted to make use of Hadoop had to be based on MapReduce, which was not very flexible. That is why, from the second version of Hadoop, resource administration was taken away from the MapReduce module, creating a resource manager named YARN (Yet Another Resource Negotiator). This has a significant advantage for other projects that are built on top of Hadoop, as they can use the resource manager and the HDFS without using the Hadoop MapReduce implementation.

There are four important components and concepts you need in order to understand how things work in Hadoop (from Hadoop V2).

- *Resource Manager*. The process that manages the resources available in the cluster (for all applications); it has global vision of the cluster, knowing how much RAM is there in total, how many cores, and so on. It runs on the main/master node and communicates with the client applications. It orchestrates all the work and assigns tasks to Node Managers. In essence, it is a scheduler that optimizes the use of the available resources, negotiating their usage and managing the priorities of the different processes.
- *Node Manager*. A Node Manager process is tasked to launch and track processes assigned to worker nodes. There is a Node Manager process running at each worker node, and it is also in charge of feeding back information to the Resource Manager about the "health" of the node. Whereas the Resource Manager has a global view of the cluster resources, the Node Managers will have a local view of each node. Figure 3.2 can help understand this architecture.
- *Container*. A container is a subset of the resources of the cluster, defined by a number of cores and the amount of RAM (basically, a simplified virtual machine) that is held on the YARN cluster for the execution of an application. If you are not very familiar with virtualization techniques, we can understand a container as a subset of a node's capabilities that can be allocated to perform a given task (e.g., a mapper process) by negotiating with the Resource Manager. Why do you think we do this? Apart from tracking how many resources are currently being used in the cluster, containers help to provide isolation. Containers running applications submitted by different users

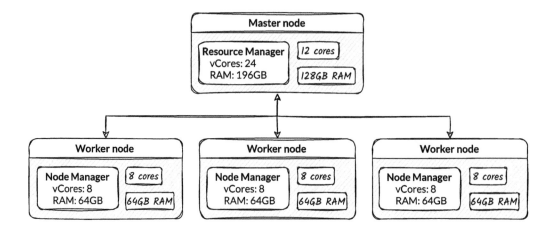

Figure 3.2 Resource and Node Manager processes. The Resource Manager knows all the available (virtual) cores in the cluster (24) and the total amount of RAM (196 GB); the Node Manager only knows about the resources available in a worker node.

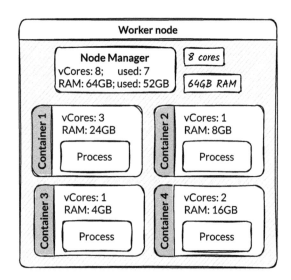

Figure 3.3 A worker node with four independent containers of different sizes, using a total 52 GB of RAM and seven cores of the node's resources.

should be isolated and unable to access each other's memory, files, and directories. Figure 3.3 gives an idea of how containers make use of the resources in a worker node. You can see how multiple containers may live within a single worker node, and they may be of different "sizes."

- *Application Master*. This process manages a particular application (e.g., your MapReduce program), and runs on a container. It is responsible for negotiating with the Resource Manager access to the containers required to run the application;

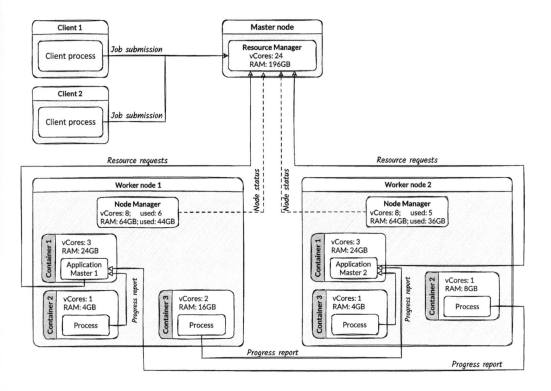

Figure 3.4 Resource negotiation process (see the Hadoop documentation). Two client processes are running on the cluster, each of which has its own Application Master residing in independent containers. Each Application Master controls different containers that are executing the job. Note that containers may live in different nodes, and those running the tasks will report progress to the Application Master.

it works with them once allocated, and with the Node Managers to monitor and execute the tasks. It is also responsible for fault tolerance.

Figure 3.4[4] can help visualize where each process sits and how different containers communicate. We will go into this in more detail in the next section.

3.3.2 Executing a MapReduce Process on YARN

Once we have written our MapReduce program using Hadoop, we are ready to run it (assuming you have installed Hadoop). However, note that the program does not necessarily have to be a Hadoop Java application, and other applications can also run on YARN. When running an application we usually indicate the number of mappers (or containers) we will consider, and we can also specify the required memory for each one. It is also common to refer to the application as a *job* to be run on a cluster.

[4] Hadoop's documentation:
https://hadoop.apache.org/docs/stable/hadoop-yarn/hadoop-yarn-site/YARN.html.

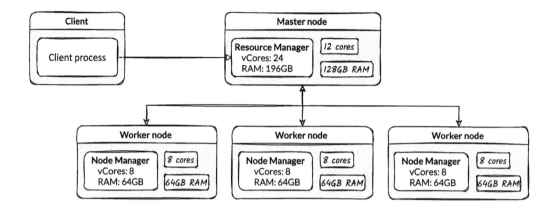

Figure 3.5 Step 1: A client application is submitted, communicating with the Resource Manager.

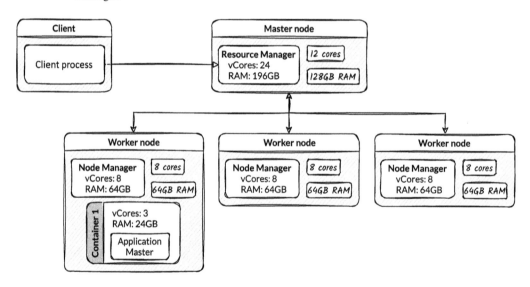

Figure 3.6 Step 2: The Resource Manager provides a single container (in a worker node) where the Application Master starts running and begins negotiations with the Resource Manager to request containers for the job it is coordinating.

To run the application, there will be a client process (usually, in a client node) that will submit a job (our application) to the Resource Manager in the master node (Figure 3.5). The Resource Manager is the communication/entry point for any client process. Every job is made up of one or more tasks that have to be run. When receiving a job, the Resource Manager will need to check whether it is currently possible to run the application (subject to resource availability) or if it must be queued. Thus, it is certainly possible to run more than one job simultaneously in a cluster, given enough resources.

After checking the status of the cluster, the Resource Manager will try to allocate a *single container* where the Application Master will be executed (Figure 3.6). It has to

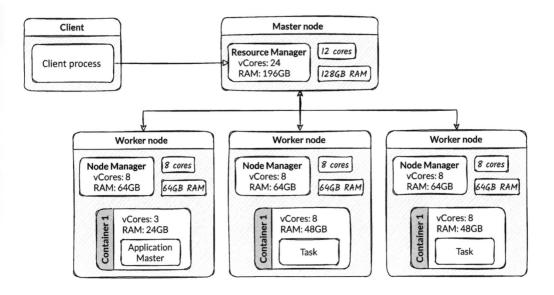

Figure 3.7 Step 3: The Application Master has obtained different containers where the different tasks associated with the job are executed.

negotiate with the corresponding Node Manager to determine if the requested container is available. Once a container has been granted on a worker node, the Application Master will start running on it. This will be the process in charge of executing the submitted job. If the Application Master controls the execution of the job, why do you think the Application Master lives in a worker node rather than in the master node? Well, as briefly mentioned above, we may have more than one job running on the cluster, and keeping all the Application Master processes in the master node may not be feasible or even safe.

The first step for the Application Master is to request subsequent containers from the Resource Manager to execute all the required tasks (Figure 3.7). Those tasks will do most of the status communication with the Application Master itself. Several containers can be run on the same node, but it is common to distribute the computing load among workers, exploiting data locality.

All the tasks are executed in the containers, which are released once their tasks are finished (Figure 3.8). A container may run multiple tasks corresponding to several data partitions in the same node.

Once all the tasks of the job have been executed, the Application Master exits, and the last container is deallocated from the cluster (Figure 3.9). Finally, the client application exits too.

In summary, there will be multiple tasks, each running in a container on a worker node somewhere in the cluster. At the same time, on the YARN side, the Resource Manager will work together with the Node Managers and the Application Master(s)

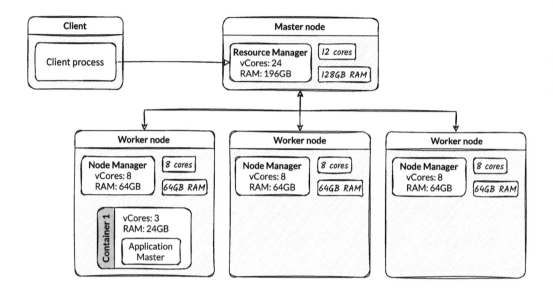

Figure 3.8 Step 4: Once the tasks of a job are completed, containers are deallocated.

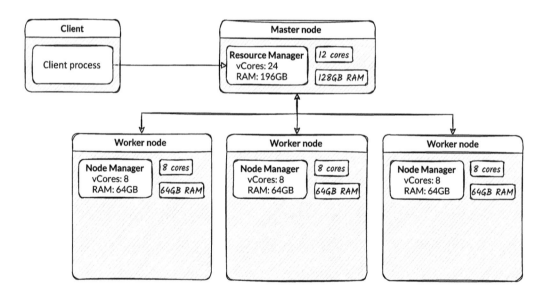

Figure 3.9 Step 5: The Application Master finishes and its container is released.

to manage the cluster's resources and ensure that all the tasks of an application are completed successfully.

By the way, you don't really need a cluster to play with Hadoop. Hadoop allows three different ways to run applications.

Local/standalone mode. In this mode, your application is run on a single Java virtual machine (JVM) on a single computer. This may become very useful for debugging your Hadoop MapReduce application when implementing it.

Pseudo-distributed (cluster simulator) mode. This will create multiple processes in one single computer to simulate how a cluster would work, and will provide some level of parallelization. However, it is important to highlight that in this mode we will not be taking into consideration potential network costs (e.g., due to some unavoidable data movement). So, don't be surprised if your solution runs very fast in this mode and doesn't seem to scale up well on a real cluster.

Fully distributed (cluster) mode. This is the fully distributed mode of Hadoop described in this chapter, in which multiple computers connected through a network communicate with each other to coordinate the execution of a big data program.

3.4   Hadoop Distributed File System

Before we talk about the Hadoop Distributed File System (HDFS), the first question we would like to ask is: What actually is a file system? It is a system that controls how data is stored and retrieved from a storage device (e.g., a hard drive or a solid state drive). In big data, we are more likely to be using hard drives as they are cheaper and allow for bigger storage capacity. In addition to this, the most important point in big data is that we will have lots of hard drives distributed in several nodes, and we look for transparency, that is, we would like to see them like a single drive where we can put our data and process it without having to think about how all the complexity behind it is managed.

If you have studied operating systems before, you might remember that the layout of the file system and the allocation of files to sectors heavily influences the number of seek movements on hard drives, and therefore the efficiency of reading and writing data. If you don't have previous experience with operating systems, you need to understand that, at a high level, a disk is composed of a number of blocks. A file is simply an abstraction that an operating system provides for the user to understand data, and is composed of one or more blocks. Many different implementations of how disk blocks are allocated to files exist (e.g., linked list, FAT32, inodes, NTFS), which usually aim at providing efficiency and resiliency when reading and writing information from a single drive.

3.4.1   What is the HDFS?

So, what are the differences between traditional file systems and the HDFS?

The HDFS is a scalable and flexible distributed file system written in Java for Hadoop. In the HDFS, the files, rather than being stored in a single hard drive in your computer, might be stored in multiple computers in a cluster of thousands of nodes that are connected to one single distributed file system through a network. In this case, the blocks associated with a file will be distributed among the different nodes of the cluster, which allows us to exploit data locality.

Since distributed file systems are network based, all the complications of network programming kick in, which poses different challenges than regular disk file systems. For example, preventing data loss is a key aspect of the design of these distributed file systems; this can be achieved via data replication, or with more efficient methods like erasure coding, which can reduce disk usage.

The HDFS was designed to deal with big data analytics, so there are some key principles that drove its design:

- Files are assumed to be *very large*, typically several gigabytes, containing many objects.
- A particular data access pattern known as *streaming data access* (write once, read many times) is considered. In this pattern, most operations are either read (usually the entire file or a large proportion of it) or appended, but random updates to the content of the files are rare (random access is not required). Likewise, the HDFS is designed to read files from start to end, giving more importance to reading throughput than latency. In other words, a dataset is typically stored, and then various analyses are performed on that dataset over time. In this case, the ability to read lots of data at once is more important than the latency in obtaining it.
- *High-specification computers are not expected.* The entire Apache Hadoop project is designed to work on relatively inexpensive hardware, where node failure is the norm. Hence, the HDFS is fault tolerant, allowing disks to fail without losing data thanks to data redundancy.

These design principles allow Hadoop to provide an appropriate file system for many big data applications; however, it is not adequate for *every* application. For example:

- *Accessing data with a low latency*, for example in the tens of milliseconds range. This will not work well with HDFS as it is optimized for delivering high data throughput at the expense of latency (streaming data access). HBase would be a better option for low-latency access.
- *Accessing many small files.* Files come with metadata indicating their path, owner, permissions, size, and tracking information of where the data blocks are (in HDFS, distributed across multiple disks in different nodes). The master node, also known as the *Name Node*, is the one that holds all the metadata for all the files in the entire system, and keeps this information in RAM. Thus, there is a maximum number of files that can be managed, which is determined by the memory of the Name Node. HDFS federation may help with this by allowing multiple (independent) Name Nodes (available since Hadoop V2). Even so, access latency won't be optimized, making reading of many small files slow compared to traditional file systems.
- *Writing concurrently to a file.* While a file can be read by multiple jobs concurrently, files can only be written to by a single writer, and new content should always be

appended at the end of the file. There is no support yet for multiple writers, or for modifications at arbitrary offsets in the file, and if it were, it would likely be very slow due to the design of the HDFS. To clarify, here we refer to multiple applications/jobs writing to the same file. As we will see in the next section, a single job may certainly write the different blocks of a file in parallel.

In addition to this, there is another issue that may seem counterintuitive: the HDFS actually sits on top of other file systems. The HDFS is an abstraction layer to hide the complexity behind distributed storage, but actually, the I/O operations on the hard drive are managed by the operating system through its file system. In fact, when you install HDFS on your system, you don't need to format your hard drives, but you simply indicate a location on the local drive where you want the data to be stored (in a cluster you should repeat this for each node). This allows the HDFS to be compatible with multiple operating systems.

3.4.2 How HDFS Works

Data Block Abstraction

As previously stated, a disk drive is usually composed of a number of blocks. The block size is the minimum amount of data that can be read or written. Disk blocks are very small in size, usually 512 bytes, and this is transparent to the user who doesn't really need to know that.

In the HDFS we also use the concept/abstraction of a block. Files are indeed broken into block-sized chunks, which are stored as independent units, and hence can be stored in different nodes of the cluster. A key difference is that the block size in HDFS tends to be a much larger unit, using 128 MB as the default value. Nevertheless, whereas in a traditional filesystem storing a 1 byte file would take an entire block of 512 bytes, in HDFS, a file that is smaller than a single block will not occupy a full block of storage, thus saving storage.

But, why is the block size so large in HDFS? In traditional file systems, the drive is split into small blocks to allow files to grow more easily, and to allow random access and arbitrary modifications to the files. However, according to the HDFS principles, we are not anticipating having to write many times, and not arbitrarily; we are expecting to read the entire file on most occasions, and they are assumed to be really big files. For this reason, Hadoop aims to reduce the seek time, which is the time to find the block on a disk drive and tends to be the dominant time when loading a file. By making the block size larger, the transfer time will become proportionally much larger than the time to seek the start of the block, which is preferable to achieve the high reading speeds needed in HDFS.

Apart from accelerating the loading of a file, are there any other benefits of using the block abstraction in HDFS? For starters, it allows us to have files that are larger than a single disk in the network. There is nothing stopping us from storing the blocks of a file on different disks, which actually enables the data locality principle as well. It also simplifies the storage management, which is critical in a complex distributed

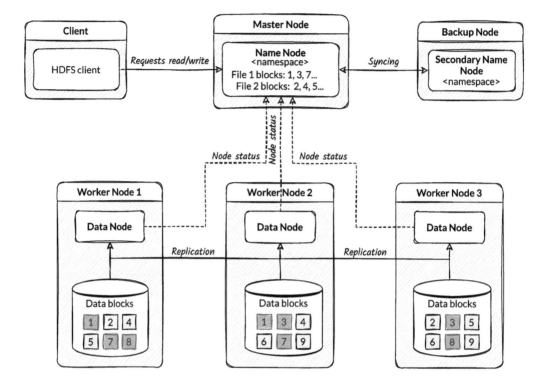

Figure 3.10 HDFS architecture (see the Hadoop documentation).

system in which the failure modes are so varied. For example, since blocks are of a fixed size, it is easy to compute how many can be stored on a given disk. It is also useful to separate metadata from actual data, which can be handled separately, which is very useful for distributed systems in which the Name Node will control where in the cluster the different blocks of a file are located. Last, but not least, it helps implement fault tolerance. To mitigate the effects of corrupted blocks and disk/machine failures, each block can be replicated to a small number of machines.

Architecture

The HDFS module also follows a master/worker architecture and is based on two main processes: the *Name Node* and the *Data Nodes*. The Name Node is usually at the master node, while Data Nodes normally run on the workers. Figure 3.10 presents a summary of how HDFS works and the different entities that are involved.

The Name Node manages the file system namespace, maintaining the file system tree and the metadata for all the files and directories in the tree. The Name Node also knows the whereabouts of the Data Nodes where the file blocks are located. This information is gathered from the Data Nodes when the system starts. As mentioned before, the Name Node stores all this information in RAM in order to rapidly respond to clients' requests. Although this limits the number of files that can be stored, this has been resolved with the HDFS federation feature, which allows for multiple Name Nodes, each one in charge of part of the namespace.

Without the Name Node, the HDFS cannot be used. Actually, if the Name Node crashes and the data in it is wiped, all the files in the HDFS would be lost since there would be no way to reconstruct the files from the Data Nodes' blocks. This is why Hadoop provides the ability to run a secondary Name Node that is in sync with the main Name Node to provide a backup. Since version 2, Hadoop allows for very fast recovery in the case of the failure of the primary Name Node through its high availability feature.

The Data Nodes, typically one per worker node in the cluster, store and provide access to the data blocks. Hence, they are responsible for managing clients' requests for I/O operations regarding data blocks. Additionally, they can also perform block operations, such as creation, deletion, or replication, as requested by the Name Node. Finally, they have to report back to the Name Node periodically with lists of the blocks that they store, and they also send "heartbeats" to confirm their availability.

Fault Tolerance: Data Redundancy

Currently, Hadoop provides two main ways to ensure fault tolerance.

- *Data replication.* This is the default mechanism for fault tolerance, which consists of replicating each data block multiple times in different Data Nodes. The default replication factor is 3, meaning that a data block is copied into three different Data Nodes so that, if one fails, the data will still be available in the other two. Thus, this incurs a 200% overhead in storage space and other resources (e.g., bandwidth when writing data).
- *Erasure coding.* This alternative was added with the third version of Hadoop to reduce the overhead caused by the replication strategy. Erasure coding uses far less storage than replication (approximately below 50% overhead), at the cost of higher CPU and network requirements. Part of the overhead to ensure fault tolerance is shifted to the reconstruction of lost data (in the case of a failure), which becomes more expensive with this strategy. Erasure coding is a branch of information theory which extends a message with redundant data for fault tolerance. Implementing this in Hadoop is not trivial and requires changes across many parts of the HDFS. If you already know about the parity check used in some RAID[5] configurations, erasure coding follows the same idea but implemented on top of HDFS and provided with greater tolerance to failures.

> From a developer / data scientist's point of view, whether HDFS is implemented with data replication or erasure coding is not particularly relevant unless the amount of storage available is limited.

---

[5] Redundant array of independent disks: https://en.wikipedia.org/wiki/Standard_RAID_levels.

Table 3.1 Basic command line operations with HDFS.

HDFS command	Explanation
`hadoop fs -ls <path>`	List files in a directory.
`hadoop fs -cp <src> <dst>`	Copy files from HDFS to HDFS.
`hadoop fs -mv <src> <dst>`	Move files from HDFS to HDFS.
`hadoop fs -rm <path>`	Remove files in HDFS.
`hadoop fs -rm -r <path>`	Remove files recursively in HDFS.
`hadoop fs -cat <path>`	Show the contents of a file in HDFS.
`hadoop fs -mkdir <path>`	Create a folder in HDFS.
`hadoop fs -put <localsrc> <dst>`	Copy files from local to HDFS.
`hadoop fs -get <src>`	Copy files from HDFS to local.

Accessibility

To access the HDFS, a client process can communicate with the Name Node on behalf of the user. It offers a POSIX-like interface to hide the implementation details. However, it is not a standard POSIX implementation, and it is not possible to browse the content of the HDFS directly as you would in other file systems. If you are a Linux command line user, the most annoying thing is that you won't be able to use tab completion. Table 3.1 presents some of the most frequent command line operations. You will notice that they are very much UNIX-like instructions, but it is necessary to indicate `hadoop fs -` prior to the command.

There are two main operations that can be carried out in HDFS:

- To *read* a file from HDFS, the client process sends a request to the Name Node for the locations of the data blocks. For each data block, the nearest Data Node with that data block is chosen and a read request is directly sent from the client to the Data Node, without further interaction with the Name Node. Note that when using MapReduce, a worker node may (ideally) be asking for data that is within the same node (exploiting data locality). If a block is corrupt or not accessible for any reason, a replica is chosen.
- To *create* a file, the client requests the Name Node to do so, and this checks that there is enough space and that the filename doesn't already exist. The file is created in the namespace without any blocks yet. Then, the client starts writing data to the first Data Node (indicated by the Name Node), which then replicates/propagates the block on the other Data Nodes where space was allocated for replicas (also by the Name Node). Hence, there is communication across Data Nodes for replication, and the Name Node awaits final confirmation.

3.5   Limitations: Technologies and Frameworks beyond Hadoop

We hope that by now you have understood the main advantages of Hadoop MapReduce, which allows us to handle big data in a simple and fault-tolerant way. It is definitely scalable and does not require specific hardware. However, it will not be the only solution we need for tackling big data. As discussed before, many projects have been created on top of Hadoop, and that happened because Hadoop has its own limitations; many "spin-out" projects appeared to tackle those and improve upon Hadoop.

Hadoop simplified big data processing, but data scientists quickly found multiple issues. On the one hand, implementing `map` and `reduce` functions in Java with the Hadoop API was a little bit cumbersome. On the other hand, as explained before, there is plenty of data serialization happening between the map and reduce phases, and that may become a bottleneck when performing data analytics. In particular, in problems that would require multiple MapReduce steps to complete their objective, this becomes a big issue. If you did the lab assignment in the previous chapter, you probably noticed that this may be common.

The key thing is that different algorithms may access data in different ways, that is, they may follow different data workflows. For example, there may be a need to iterate multiple times through a dataset to produce a machine learning model. You may also need to query a big database interactively to get, for example, some statistics, or subsets of the data. We said that big data may also bring data from different sources, and a successful way to handle such a variety of data is via graph-based models that don't follow a traditional way of storing and accessing data, but instead model data as nodes that are connected (e.g., web pages could be nodes, and they may link to each other). We also discussed the velocity aspect of big data and dealing with real-time (data streaming) processing that will need to continuously perform new computations based on incoming data. Whilst all of these examples may still be solved with the idea of MapReduce, the implementation provided by Hadoop would be very slow due to the serialization required between stages, the necessary replication, and all the disk I/O that these imply.

Thus, many new big data frameworks arose quickly to tackle these issues. At first, we found relatively quick solutions to the serialization problem. For example, systems such as Giraph[6] or GraphLab[7] to deal with graph-based models, or frameworks like Twister (Ekanayake et al., 2010) or Haloop[8] to allow for multiple iterations through the data. More recently, more comprehensive platforms such as Apache Flink,[9] Apache Spark,[10] and Dask[11] have emerged, and they are capable of handling various of those data workflows successfully.

You may now be wondering, does that mean that this is the end of Hadoop? Not at all! It is not the end, as Hadoop has become the basis for most other stuff, creating an entire ecosystem of platforms that build on top of it. For example:

[6] https://giraph.apache.org/
[7] https://github.com/graphlab-code/graphlab
[8] http://code.google.com/p/haloop/
[9] https://flink.apache.org/
[10] https://spark.apache.org/
[11] www.dask.org/

- Data services: tools to manipulate and process data easily. For example, Hive,[12] Pig,[13] HBase,[14] Flume,[15] and others.
- Operational services: helpful tools to manage the operations of a Hadoop cluster. For example, ZooKeeper,[16] Oozie,[17] and others.

The big data framework/tools landscape is big in itself. Here we have introduced Hadoop, and later we will discuss Apache Spark, but choosing the right technology very much depends on what you have to do with your data.

> ### Challenge #3.2
>
> If you are familiar with classical machine learning techniques, such as k-nearest neighbors, k-means, decision trees, or any other, would you be able to identify a method that may not work well with Hadoop MapReduce and briefly explain why?

3.6   Take-Home Message

This chapter has provided a gentle introduction to Apache Hadoop. We have seen that Hadoop is what we called a big data framework and that it is not *only* MapReduce, but it does provide an implementation of this programming model alongside two other main components: a resource negotiator (YARN) and a distributed file system (HDFS).

For the purposes of this book, describing all the details about Hadoop and its functioning may not be completely necessary, but it is important to be aware of some of the key concepts and its current progress:

- Implementing MapReduce programs with Hadoop may now be seen as a bit cumbersome, and will not probably be our final choice in many cases.
- Hadoop follows a master/worker architecture, in which a master node coordinates everything and delegates the actual computations to a number of worker nodes.
- The execution of a program on a Hadoop cluster is managed by multiple processes: Resource Manager, Node Managers, and the Application Master.
- The concept of a container is key to understanding how an application is deployed in a cluster, providing the necessary isolation to allow various applications to run at the same time safely.
- The distributed file system provided by Hadoop is managed by a Name Node process and various Data Node processes.

---

[12] https://hive.apache.org/
[13] https://pig.apache.org/
[14] https://hbase.apache.org/
[15] https://flume.apache.org/
[16] https://zookeeper.apache.org/
[17] https://oozie.apache.org/

- The HDFS was designed to comply with the following principles: accessing large files, high throughput, and no expectations of high-specification computers being available. Thus, it may not be good at providing low latency, access to many small files, or concurrent writes to a file from multiple applications.
- There are many technological advances happening in Hadoop (high availability, HDFS federation, erasure coding, etc.), and many more may appear in the near future. Learning the nitty-gritty detail of those may not be essential for a data scientist, but it is always good to keep an eye on the new developments.
- Hadoop has some limitations when it comes to applying various MapReduce processes in a row, and many new big data frameworks have emerged to deal with such cases. However, its distributed file system and resource negotiator are still very popular and are the foundation of many big data frameworks (the Hadoop Ecosystem).

As a final reflection; there are many big data frameworks out there, and choosing one may depend on what exactly you need to do. We like to say that choosing the right big data technology is similar to deciding which data structure is the most appropriate for a given problem. Many may do the trick, but doing it efficiently depends very much on your choice.

3.7   To Learn More

Do you want to know more about Apache Hadoop? The following may come in handy.

> White (2015) is the main book on Apache Hadoop. If you want to know all the details of the Hadoop architecture (especially YARN and HDFS), this book provides much more detail than we did here.

It is important to be up to date with the latest changes in Apache Hadoop.

> Keep an eye on the Apache Hadoop website[18] to find out about all the latest additions.

> We recommend Xia et al. (2015) to help understand the principles of the erasure coding fault tolerance mechanism.

We have talked about some concepts such as serialization or virtualization with which you may not be very familiar. If you want more information, we recommend the following resources:

> The concept of serialization[19] and how it works in Java[20] and Python with pickle.[21]

> Jain (2020) gives an overview of virtualization and how it is realized within Linux.

---

[18] https://hadoop.apache.org/
[19] https://en.wikipedia.org/wiki/Serialization
[20] https://docs.oracle.com/javase/tutorial/jndi/objects/serial.html
[21] https://docs.python.org/3/library/pickle.html

3.8   Solutions to Challenges

> **Challenge #3.1**
>
> If you have installed Hadoop on your own computer, run the Word Count example.

Here we summarize the key steps to run Word Count on your own computer. We assume you are using a UNIX operating system. Windows users may need to follow alternative tutorials.

Step 1. Create a Java file with the name of your class (e.g., WordCount, Common-Friends, etc.).

You can download the source code from the Hadoop MapReduce tutorial.[22]

```java
import java.io.IOException;
import java.util.StringTokenizer;

import org.apache.hadoop.conf.Configuration;
import org.apache.hadoop.fs.Path;
import org.apache.hadoop.io.IntWritable;
import org.apache.hadoop.io.Text;
import org.apache.hadoop.mapreduce.Job;
import org.apache.hadoop.mapreduce.Mapper;
import org.apache.hadoop.mapreduce.Reducer;
import org.apache.hadoop.mapreduce.lib.input.FileInputFormat;
import org.apache.hadoop.mapreduce.lib.output.FileOutputFormat;

public class WordCount {

  public static class TokenizerMapper
       extends Mapper<Object, Text, Text, IntWritable>{

    // member variable
    private final static IntWritable one = new IntWritable(1);
    private Text word = new Text();

    public void map(Object key, Text value, Context context
                    ) throws IOException, InterruptedException {
      StringTokenizer itr = new StringTokenizer(value.toString());

      while(itr.hasMoreTokens()){
          word.set(itr.nextToken());
          context.write(word, one);
      }
    }
  }

  public static class IntSumReducer
       extends Reducer<Text,IntWritable,Text,IntWritable> {
    private IntWritable result = new IntWritable();
```

---

[22] https://hadoop.apache.org/docs/stable/hadoop-mapreduce-client/hadoop-mapreduce-client-core/MapReduceTutorial.html

```
    public void reduce(Text key, Iterable<IntWritable> values,
                        Context context
                        ) throws IOException, InterruptedException {
        int sum = 0;
        for (IntWritable val : values){
            sum += val.get();
        }
        result.set(sum);
        context.write(key,result);
    }
}

  public static void main(String[] args) throws Exception {
    Configuration conf = new Configuration();
    Job job = Job.getInstance(conf, "word count");
    job.setJarByClass(WordCount.class);
    job.setMapperClass(TokenizerMapper.class);
    job.setCombinerClass(IntSumReducer.class);
    job.setReducerClass(IntSumReducer.class);
    job.setOutputKeyClass(Text.class);
    job.setOutputValueClass(IntWritable.class);
    FileInputFormat.addInputPath(job, new Path(args[0]));
    FileOutputFormat.setOutputPath(job, new Path(args[1]));
    System.exit(job.waitForCompletion(true) ? 0 : 1);
  }
}
```

> If you wish to practise further, you could implement the exercises from the lab assignment of Chapter 2. **Note**: For some of the exercises you might need to find the "tuple" data type of Hadoop (i.e., TupleWritable).

Step 2. Compile your code. We recommend you have a look at the tutorial we mentioned before if you struggle with this. You need an environment variable to be able to run your program:

```
export HADOOP_CLASSPATH=${JAVA_HOME}/lib/tools.jar
```

Then you can compile and create the jar file:

```
bin/hadoop com.sun.tools.javac.Main WordCount.java
jar cf wc.jar WordCount*.class
```

Step 3. Run your program.

```
hadoop jar wc.jar WordCount wordcount/input wordcount/output
```

Step 4. Check the output.

```
hadoop fs -cat wordcount/output/part-r-00000
Big 2
Bye 1
Data    1
Welcome 2
World   2
of  1
the 1
to  1
```

> **Challenge #3.2**
>
> If you are familiar with classical machine learning techniques, such as k-nearest neighbors, k-means, decision trees, or any other, would you be able to identify a method that may not work well with Hadoop MapReduce and briefly explain why?

Any iterative machine learning algorithm would have performance problems with Hadoop MapReduce as too many I/O operations would occur with HDFS. Well-known examples are k-means clustering, linear/logistic regression, or the page rank algorithm.

3.9   Exercises

3.1 List the main components/modules of Apache Hadoop.

3.2 Indicate whether the following statements about Hadoop are true or false:
   (a) Hadoop follows a scale-up strategy, so it can't add new computing nodes.
   (b) You need a cluster of computing nodes to be able to test Hadoop.
   (c) You cannot run more than one MapReduce job at the same time on a Hadoop cluster.
   (d) Hadoop uses the concept of containers to provide isolation of resources.

3.3 Why does the Hadoop MapReduce module provide its own data types (e.g., `IntWritable`) rather than using standard Java data types (e.g., `Integer`)? Briefly explain your answer.

3.4 Briefly explain why we need to serialize objects in a Hadoop MapReduce program.

3.5 Indicate whether the following statements about YARN are true or false:
   (a) You can only run Hadoop MapReduce jobs on YARN.
   (b) The Node Manager lives in the master node.
   (c) The containers of a given application must always be located in the same worker node.
   (d) The Application Master is the same for all jobs running on the cluster.

3.6 In YARN, the Resource Manager is in charge of allocating containers to run tasks for an application. Explain why we need those containers to execute an application.

3.7 In YARN, the Resource Manager process allocates a single container in a worker node where the Application Master is executed. Provide one reason why this Application Master process is not run in the master node.

3.8 Briefly describe the key steps to executing a MapReduce process on YARN.

3.9 Briefly mention the three execution modes available in Hadoop. Which of these modes would you use to debug your code?

3.10 Indicate whether the following statements about the HDFS are true or false:
   (a) The HDFS is good at reading big files, but not so good at making/writing random changes in the data.
   (b) The HDFS was designed to have a very low latency.
   (c) The concept of a block is important in HDFS to provide fault tolerance.
   (d) The Name Node knows about the whereabouts of all the files in a HDFS.

3.11 You are given a cluster of five computing nodes, in which each node has a local drive of 1 TB (fully) dedicated to the HDFS. Could we store a file that takes 5 TB? Briefly explain your answer.

3.12 You are given a cluster of four computing nodes, in which each node has a local drive of 1 TB (fully) dedicated to HDFS. We have two different files, one of 200 MB and the other 390 MB. Draw a diagram to show how these files are distributed in the HDFS. How many blocks do we need for each file? Assuming a replication factor of three, how much space is occupied in HDFS?

3.13 Why does the HDFS use a large block size of typically 128 MB? Briefly explain your answer.

3.14 Briefly explain how fault tolerance is currently achieved in Hadoop.

3.15 Provide two reasons why you may not want to use Hadoop MapReduce to implement a big data solution.

4 Spark

Learning Outcomes

[KU]	The importance of caching for efficient big data processing
[KU]	Extending MapReduce: the concept of resilient distributed datasets for big data
[KU, IS, PPS]	How to operate with resilient distributed datasets: lazy transformation versus actions
[KU]	How a Spark application is distributed to guarantee fault tolerance and transparency
[IS, PPS]	How to use Spark in practice for problem solving

In talking about MapReduce, we have already told you that there are some potential issues with the way we execute this programming model in the Hadoop framework. One of the problems we encountered is that in-between stages (i.e., from map to shuffle and from shuffle to reduce), we need to access the HDFS to read the input and write the output. While Hadoop MapReduce does help process big datasets as it allows us to reduce and control how much data is moved across the network to perform certain computations (using the principle of data locality), many I/O operations still happen locally for each drive, which is simply not very efficient.

This becomes even worse if we think of tasks/programs that may require multiple MapReduce stages. For example, to compute the histogram of word frequencies in a big document, we first ran a MapReduce program to obtain the word count, then we concatenated a second MapReduce program that counted how many words have a given frequency in the entire document.

You will easily find many different use cases in which Hadoop MapReduce is not suitable because of the serialization/deserialization to disk (see Figure 4.1). For example:

- We sometimes need to reuse the original dataset multiple times to be able to perform some calculations; we call these *iterative tasks*. Many machine learning methods require multiple passes through the data to learn a model or minimize some error, for example gradient descent for logistic regression or k-means for clustering.
- Or you may have a big database and you want to perform *interactive queries* on it. Every time you want to perform a single query, you would be reading data from the

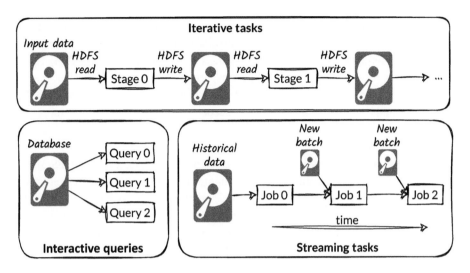

Figure 4.1 Tasks in which Hadoop MapReduce may not be efficient (see the Apache Spark documentation).

HDFS and loading the different chunks in the main memory of each worker node before carrying out the query.

- Big data promised to come fast (remember *velocity*), and sometimes it does so in the form of multiple batches of data that arrive continuously, known as *streaming data*. If you think of online learning/stream mining, we need to keep our models updated, which will require running multiple jobs in all of those incoming batches, and that needs to happen quickly!

In all of those cases, as shown in Figure 4.1, the key problem is the I/O from/to secondary storage, which is very slow compared to using main memory (and, of course, we won't normally have access to solid-state drives (SSDs) in a big data cluster). It is important to note that this is obviously not as slow as the network, which was the main problem we discussed Hadoop helping us address.

4.1   What Is Spark?

Spark, as defined by its developers, is a "fast and expressive cluster computing engine" that is compatible with Apache Hadoop. In other words, Spark is another big data framework, which promises to be 10 times faster than Hadoop on disk, and up to 100 times faster in memory. Although Spark is natively written in Scala, it provides rich APIs in different programming languages such as Java, Scala, Python, and R. Those APIs also improve the readability of the code in comparison with the cumbersome programming style of Hadoop. But, what is the key idea/novelty of Apache Spark? *They found a way to avoid serializing each MapReduce stage to drive.* But how?

In the past, the cost of RAM was quite high; nowadays it is not that expensive, meaning that we can have more memory in each worker node (as you probably guessed, for big data we not only need big hard drives, but also lots of RAM). And having more memory available is what Spark exploits to solve the problem. The developers decided to take advantage of RAM as if it was cache memory, reading/loading data only once, and reusing it as many times as needed by keeping it in main memory. Of course, you don't keep it in the memory of one single node, but each node will keep in memory a fraction of the entire dataset.

Simply put, for the first access we do read the data from HDFS, but then we keep things in main memory. This simple idea allows Spark to extend the MapReduce paradigm to interactive, iterative, and stream processing. For further details, have a look at the original paper where Spark was presented (Zaharia et al., 2010).

It is most important to highlight that this is a data-processing engine only. This means that Spark implements the MapReduce paradigm more efficiently than Hadoop, but it can still (and probably should) use HDFS (or other distributed storage systems); hence, it is claimed to be compatible with Hadoop. The core of Spark is actually designed to work on top of the Hadoop resource manager, YARN, or any other resource manager (like Mesos), but it also includes its own resource manager.

On top of the Spark core there are four libraries, depending on the type of processing you want to do: Spark SQL for structured data processing, Spark Streaming, MLlib for machine learning, and GraphX for graph processing (currently not available for the Python API).

4.1.1   The Goal of Apache Spark

The goal of Apache Spark is to provide distributed memory abstractions for a cluster of computers while retaining the attractive properties that MapReduce offers (e.g., fault tolerance, data locality, and scalability). To do so, Zaharia et al. (2012) came up with a way to provide distributed data structures, which they termed resilient distributed datasets (RDDs). They later extended Spark with DataFrames and Datasets; we will come to those in the next chapter.

What are they exactly? An RDD is a fault-tolerant collection of objects that can be operated on in parallel and, very importantly, can be cached for future reuse. In other words, imagine a list in Python, but rather than being only in the main memory of your laptop, it is distributed (transparently) across a cluster.

These distributed in-memory data structures allow for more operations than "just" the `map` and `reduce` functions. So, Spark not only implements the MapReduce paradigm more efficiently by reducing the serialization and deserialization to disk, but also extends it with additional functionality.

We are going to distinguish two types of operations with RDDs:

- A **transformation** is a lazy operation that builds an RDD from another RDD. Laziness is one of the main selling points of functional programming and allows us to perform operations such as map, filter, or groupByKey more efficiently by not evaluating them immediately.

* An **action**, on the other hand, does return a result or write something to disk.

This is a very important distinction to make because the laziness of transformations allows Spark to store a sequence of transformations as a recipe to be carried out (a logical execution plan), and it doesn't execute them until an *action* is triggered, allowing it to optimize the process and become more efficient.

As distributed data structures, RDDs are at risk of data loss if a computing node containing part of the information crashes. Spark has mechanisms designed to reconstruct them in case of failure.

4.2 Basic Concepts

Spark can be used with an interpreted language like Python in different ways:

* As an *interactive application* (probably the easiest way to learn Spark). You run either spark-shell for Scala or pyspark for Python and get an interactive interpreter. We will be using Spark from Jupyter Notebooks, which is also an interactive way of using Spark.
* As a *standalone application*. You write your code using your favorite integrated development environment (IDE) and then run it using spark-submit.

We could say that a Spark program is composed of two different programs, the *driver* program and the *workers* program, although we only see/implement one. The driver program runs anything that is sequential, and the workers program deals with anything that goes in parallel.

The first thing a Spark program must do is to create a SparkContext object, which is the main entry point to the Spark functionality. This tells Spark how to access a cluster (or your computer). If you are using the console (pyspark), the SparkContext is created automatically for you. If you are using Jupyter Notebooks as the driver for pyspark, you have also already initialized the SparkContext.

The SparkContext is created in the driver program to establish a connection with the Cluster Manager. Once connected, **executors** can be requested to run the different jobs. An executor is a process that performs the computation and stores the data in memory (similar to the mapper and reducer we discussed with Hadoop). To do this, the driver sends the code and tasks to the executors, and they inform the driver program when finished.

Figure 4.2 shows the key elements involved in the execution of a Spark program. It is important not to confuse these with the master/worker architecture that we mentioned before for Hadoop. Your Spark driver program may be running on a worker node if you use, for example, YARN to run it (note that you could also run the driver program on your own computer and connect to a cluster to run the tasks). Each program will have its own executors for isolation, that is, it prevents any data sharing between programs. A worker node may be running multiple executors.

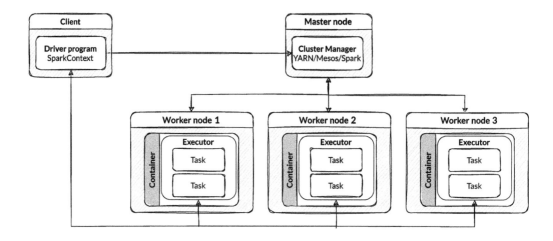

Figure 4.2 SparkContext and executors. The driver program will connect with the Cluster Manager, which requests the resources needed to run the different tasks.

To create a SparkContext you first need to build a SparkConf object that contains information about your application.

```
from pyspark import SparkConf, SparkContext
conf = SparkConf().setMaster("local[*]").setAppName("Chapter 4: pyspark")
sc = SparkContext(conf=conf)
```

After initializing Spark, you can track each task at http://localhost:4040. If that doesn't work, you can find the link by inspecting the content of the variable sc.

```
sc
```

```
<SparkContext master=local[*] appName=Chapter 4: pyspark>
```

In the above configuration, master is a Spark/Mesos or YARN cluster URL, or a special "local" string to run in local mode. We entered local[*] to tell Spark to use all the threads available as executors on the laptop on which we are running this. We also set the name of our application to "Chapter 4: pyspark". Although most of us forget about it because it is not a massive problem, it is good practice to stop the SparkContext before closing your Notebook by running sc.stop(). If you don't do this, you might end up creating multiple SparkContext instances, for example if you opened multiple Jupyter notebooks.

4.3   Resilient Distributed Datasets

As previously stated, an RDD is a distributed collection of objects. A few things to bear in mind:

- RDDs are immutable once created, meaning that you can't modify their content.
- An RDD can contain Python, Java, or Scala objects, including your own classes.
- A lineage of RDDs is kept to ensure fault tolerance.

We are going to show you now some examples of using RDDs. For a thorough list of operations with RDDs, see the official documentation.[1]

4.3.1   Creating RDDs

There are several ways to create an RDD:

- Parallelizing an existing data collection: `sc.parallelize(`⟨*Python collection*⟩`)`.
- Reading a dataset from your local drive or somewhere else (e.g., HDFS): `sc.textFile(`⟨*file*⟩`)`.
- Applying a transformation to an existing RDD.

Parallelizing an existing collection is the simplest way to create an RDD:

```
data = sc.parallelize([1, 2, 3, 4, 5])
```

`sc.parallelize()` is a lazy operation. This means that no computation happens just yet. At this point, Spark only records how to create the RDD.

What happens if you want to print `data`?

```
print(data)
```

```
ParallelCollectionRDD[0] at readRDDFromFile at PythonRDD.scala:274
```

Not much really: `print()` only tells you this is an object of type `ParallelCollectionRDD`. We will need to trigger a Spark action to get `sc.parallelize()` executed, for example `collect()` or `take()`.

Creating an RDD from an existing Python collection is obviously not very scalable, since we are parallelizing data that already fits into the driver memory. Hence, it is more common to load data from files (probably from a distributed or remote file system). You can load a file using `sc.textFile(`⟨*filename*⟩`)`:

```
bookRDD = sc.textFile("data/quixote.txt")
```

Note that `textFile()` is also a lazy operation; if you were to misspell the filename, you wouldn't get an error until you carried out an action on `bookRDD`.

> Throughout, we will be using the text of *Don Quixote*, the well-known Spanish novel by Miguel de Cervantes, to illustrate many of the operations we will be doing with Spark. The text is available from Project Gutenberg.[2]

From the way we specified the filename, the file `quixote.txt` is expected to be on your local filesystem, specifically, in the same folder as your Python program/notebook. However, you could have read this from an HDFS or from Amazon S3 by indicating

---

[1] https://spark.apache.org/docs/latest/api/python/reference/pyspark.html#rdd-apis
[2] www.gutenberg.org/ebooks/5921

the full path (IP address, port, and the actual path). If you have installed Hadoop on your computer and you put some files in your HDFS, you could do something like:

```
bookRDD_hdfs = sc.textFile("hdfs://localhost:9000/user/pszit/quixote.txt")
```

Let's check the type of bookRDD:

```
type(bookRDD)
```

```
pyspark.rdd.RDD
```

Spark partitions your file or collection automatically into a number of partitions depending on the resources available, but you can also indicate the level of parallelism when creating an RDD. Let's see how many partitions we have for bookRDD:

```
bookRDD.getNumPartitions()
```

```
2
```

By the way, is getNumPartitions() an action or a transformation? Well, neither, we would say. It simply fetches the metadata of this RDD. However, it will check that the book exists. If you wrote the wrong filename, at this stage Spark would return an error.

If you want to indicate the number of partitions when either reading a file or parallelizing a collection, you have to add this as a parameter:

```
bookRDD = sc.textFile("data/quixote.txt", 3)
```

```
bookRDD.getNumPartitions()
```

```
3
```

Note that each partition may be handled in different nodes (or threads). Figure 4.3 shows how the book may be split into three partitions (when an action actually triggers

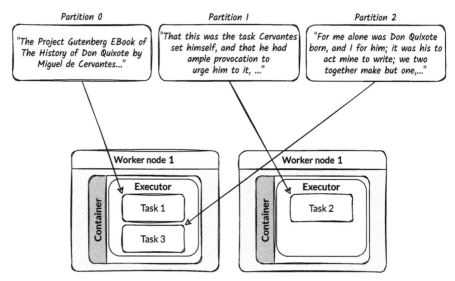

Figure 4.3 An RDD divided into three partitions. Partitions 0 and 2 are handled by worker 1 (one task for each partition), while partition 1 is managed by worker 2.

the reading of the file), each of which will contain a fraction of the book, and these partitions are processed by different tasks that are run by various executors.

4.3.2   Operations with RDDs

As mentioned before, when we work with RDDs we have two types of operations: transformations and actions. All operations on RDDs are executed in parallel according to the number of partitions defined, but the level of parallelization does depend on the number of nodes/cores available when executing your program. This means that if you partition your RDD into 24 chunks, but you only have 8 threads available, your program will process in parallel a maximum of 8 chunks at any one point in time. As the processing of one chunk is completed, the remaining ones will be processed.

Most Spark operations use high-order functions, which, as we saw in Chapter 2, are functions or methods that receive another function as a parameter. For example, to filter out the lines from an RDD we need to use a function, which can be an anonymous/lambda function:

```
quixote_lines = bookRDD.filter(lambda line: "Quixote" in line)
```

Remember that RDDs are immutable, so we are creating another RDD where we filter the lines with the word "Quixote." Let's see the content of the first line of that new RDD, `quixote_lines`:

```
quixote_lines.first()
```

```
'The Project Gutenberg EBook of The History of Don Quixote by Miguel de
Cervantes'
```

The funny thing is that the book was not read and filtered until we invoked this `first()` operation, which is an *action*! Also, as these operations are run in parallel, a `"Quixote"` `in line` instruction has been sent to all worker processes, which perform the filtering of that word in each partition of `bookRDD`.

4.3.3   Transformations

We have just seen an example of a transformation with `filter()` that allows us to transform an existing RDD (`bookRDD`) into a new one (`quixote_lines`). We now introduce other basic transformations that can be performed on RDDs.

Basic Transformations

Table 4.1 lists some basic transformations and their descriptions. Let's investigate these transformations, but first we are going to create a very simple RDD from our second-favorite list:

```
rdd = sc.parallelize([1, 2, 3, 4, 1, 2, 3, 4])
```

Table 4.1 Basic RDD transformations.

Transformation	Description
map<func>	Returns a new RDD built by applying the function `func` to each element of the original RDD.
filter<func>	Returns a new RDD composed of the elements of the original RDD that return `true` after applying `func`.
flatMap<func>	Similar to map, but each input element can be mapped to zero or more output elements (so `func` returns a sequence rather than a single item).

`map(func)`
Similar to what we did previously using the Python `map()` function on a list, we could use `map()` to, for example, multiply each element of the `rdd` by two. The behavior would be the same, but the main difference is that the `map()` function of Spark runs in parallel.

```
rdd.map(lambda x: x * 2)
```

```
PythonRDD[8] at RDD at PythonRDD.scala:53
```

Wait, we can't see anything. Have we changed the value of `rdd`? To see the content of this RDD we need to bring it to the driver. To do this, we can use `collect()`.

```
rdd.collect()
```

```
[1, 2, 3, 4, 1, 2, 3, 4]
```

Of course we didn't: RDDs are immutable. You need to allocate the result of the `map()` to a variable:

```
rdd_square = rdd.map(lambda x: x * 2)
```

If you now check the Spark WebUI, you won't see that `map()` function happening. This is a transformation, and therefore is "lazy". We have to use an action to trigger the transformation. Actually, you won't even see the `parallelize()` function until we trigger this `collect()`:

```
rdd_square.collect()
```

```
[2, 4, 6, 8, 2, 4, 6, 8]
```

If you now look at the Spark WebUI and investigate the last `collect()` operation, you can see the operations that were involved (Figure 4.4). There are a couple of things to highlight here. In that graph from Spark, we see that the `sc.parallelize([1, 2, 3, 4, 1, 2, 3, 4])` instruction was executed first, followed directly by the `collect()`. Wait, where is the `map(lambda x: x * 2)`? Well, that operation was concatenated with the `parallelize()` and doesn't show up on this tool.

Also, did you notice anything weird? We first read the data with `rdd = sc.parallelize([1, 2, 3, 4, 1, 2, 3, 4])` and did the `collect()` to see its

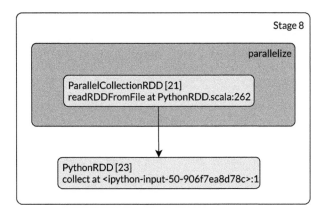

Figure 4.4 Spark WebUI view of the operations involved when running `collect()`.

content; as stated, the action triggers the data to be actually read. So, why is the data read again when we do `rdd_square.collect()`? If we want to reuse an RDD we need to cache it in memory, otherwise it will be read again. Note that caching is not done by default. We will come back to this in Section 4.3.9.

filter(func)
We already used this in a previous example. With `filter()` we can get rid of any elements of an RDD we are not interested in. For example, if we want to get rid of all the 1s:

```
rdd.filter(lambda x: x != 1).collect()
```

```
[2, 3, 4, 2, 3, 4]
```

Or if we want to keep only even numbers:

```
rdd.filter(lambda x: x % 2 == 0).collect()
```

```
[2, 4, 2, 4]
```

By the way, what is the data type of the data structure returned by `collect()`?

```
evens_rdd = rdd.filter(lambda x: x % 2 == 0).collect()
```

```
type(evens_rdd)
```

```
list
```

flatMap(func)
`flatMap()` is another very useful operation provided by Spark. But, what's the difference between `map()` and `flatMap()`? Let's test it:

```
rdd.map(lambda x: x * 2).collect()
```

```
[2, 4, 6, 8, 2, 4, 6, 8]
```

```
rdd.flatMap(lambda x: x * 2).collect()
```

```
-------------------------------------------------------------------------
Py4JJavaError Traceback (most recent call last)
C:\Users\MIKEL~1.GAL\AppData\Local\Temp/ipykernel_22464/3082495257.py in <mod-
ule> ----> 1 rdd.flatMap(lambda x: x * 2). collect()
...
```

Ouch, that didn't work. Why not? flatMap() is expecting that your input function func returns a *sequence* rather than a single item, and the sequences created will be then flattened/concatenated.

Okay, let us put the output of the function as a list:

```
rdd.flatMap(lambda x: [x * 2]).collect()
```

```
[2, 4, 6, 8, 2, 4, 6, 8]
```

Well, we don't see much difference. Let's see another example in which we have a few lines of text:

```
lines = sc.parallelize(["Welcome to the Big",
                        "World of Big Big",
                        "Data Welcome World bye",
                        "World Hello MapReduce",
                        "GoodBye MapReduce"
                        "This Book on Big Data is fun"])
```

```
lines.collect()
```

```
['Welcome to the Big',
 'World of Big Big',
 'Data Welcome World bye',
 'World Hello MapReduce',
 'GoodBye MapReduceThis Book on Big Data is fun']
```

We created an RDD in which the elements are strings, representing six lines of text. We are going to split those strings by blank space, aiming to get the words in that RDD.

```
words_map = lines.map(lambda line: line.split(" "))
```

What do you expect this to be?

```
words_map.collect()
```

```
[['Welcome', 'to', 'the', 'Big'],
 ['World', 'of', 'Big', 'Big'],
 ['Data', 'Welcome', 'World', 'bye'],
 ['World', 'Hello', 'MapReduce'],
 ['GoodBye', 'MapReduceThis', 'Book', 'on', 'Big', 'Data', 'is', 'fun']]
```

Each element of the original RDD has been split, but we still have six elements. If you look a little closer, you will see that the split function we used returns a list:

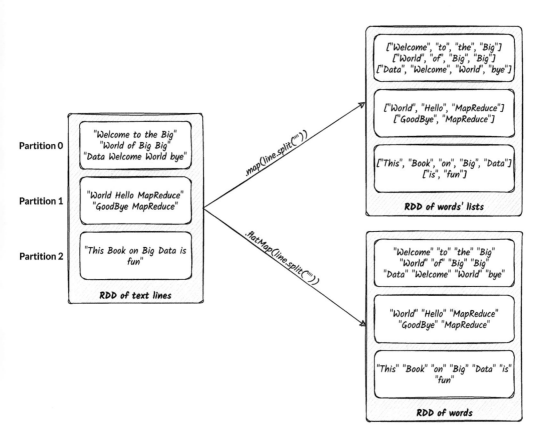

Figure 4.5 map versus flatMap on an RDD of text lines with three partitions.

```
"Welcome to the Big".split(" ")
```

```
['Welcome', 'to', 'the', 'Big']
```

If you wanted a single "flattened" list of words, that's when flatMap() comes in handy:

```
wordsFlatMap = lines.flatMap(lambda line: line.split(" "))
```

Let's collect it and show only the first five elements of the resulting list:

```
wordsFlatMap.collect()[:5]
```

```
['Welcome', 'to', 'the', 'Big', 'World']
```

That is, now we get an RDD of words (Strings) instead of lists because the lists have been flattened. Visually, we can see the differences between map and flatMap in Figure 4.5.

In Spark, it is quite common to concatenate multiple maps, filters, and flat maps to shape the data before applying any action. As we will see in Section 4.5, these operations are joined together and optimized.

Table 4.2 Transformations with pseudo-sets.

Transformation	Description
distinct()	Returns an RDD without repetitions. **Warning:** This requires a shuffle (sending data through the network)! May be slow!
union(rdd)	Returns the union of two RDDs (keeps duplicates).
intersection(rdd)	Returns the intersection of two RDDs (removes duplicates). **Warning:** This requires a shuffle!
subtract(rdd)	Returns the elements that are in the first RDD but not in the second (removes duplicates). **Warning:** This requires a shuffle!
cartesian(rdd)	Returns an RDD with all potential pairs of elements of both RDDs.

Transformations with Pseudo-Sets

RDDs are not really set structures as they allow duplicates. However, you can still use "set-like" operations on RDDs. The most important thing to remember in this case is that the RDDs involved must be of the same type. But we haven't told you yet the different types of RDDs we can have.

You can find full descriptions and examples for these functions on the Spark website.[3] Table 4.2 lists the functions and how they work. Let's create two RDDs of Strings to try these operations.

```
rdd1 = sc.parallelize(["water", "wine", "beer", "water", "water", "wine"])
rdd2 = sc.parallelize(["beer", "beer", "water", "water",\
                       "wine", "coca-cola", "lemonade"])
```

We can use distinct() to remove duplicates in an RDD:

```
rdd1.distinct().collect()
```

```
['water', 'beer', 'wine']
```

Interesting; were you expecting the list in a different order? In a distributed environment we can't expect any specific order, since it will depend on where the data is and how rapidly each executor responds.

With union(), we concatenate the elements of two RDDs. With intersection() we just get the elements that are present in both of them, whereas with subtract() we get those only present in the first RDD.

```
rdd1.union(rdd2).collect()
```

```
['water',
 'wine',
 'beer',
 'water',
```

---

[3] https://spark.apache.org/docs/3.3.0/api/python/reference/pyspark.html#rdd-apis

```
'water',
'wine',
'beer',
'beer',
'water',
'water',
'wine',
'coca-cola',
'lemonade']
```

```
rdd1.intersection(rdd2).collect()
```

```
['water', 'beer', 'wine']
```

```
rdd1.subtract(rdd2).collect()
```

```
[]
```

Note how both subtract() and intersection() remove duplicates, which provokes a shuffle (i.e., network traffic); they can therefore be slow operations depending on how big the RDDs are. The same is true for distinct().

Finally, cartesian() generates all pairs of elements combining those from both RDDs. Obviously, this can create huge RDDs even if the inputs are not so big, so you should try to avoid it as long as possible. Before applying this transformation to our RDDs, we are going to remove duplicates:

```
rdd1.distinct().cartesian(rdd2.distinct()).collect()
```

```
[('water', 'water'),
 ('water', 'beer'),
 ('water', 'lemonade'),
 ('water', 'coca-cola'),
 ('water', 'wine'),
 ('beer', 'water'),
 ('beer', 'beer'),
 ('beer', 'lemonade'),
 ('beer', 'coca-cola'),
 ('beer', 'wine'),
 ('wine', 'water'),
 ('wine', 'beer'),
 ('wine', 'lemonade'),
 ('wine', 'coca-cola'),
 ('wine', 'wine')]
```

4.3.4 Actions on RDDs

We have already used some actions to be able to understand transformations. These are described in Table 4.3 together with other basic actions. Let's check the actions that we haven't tried yet. We will first create an RDD to work with:

```
rdd = sc.parallelize([1, 2, 3, 4, 5, 6, 7, 8])
```

Table 4.3 Basic actions with RDDs.

Action	Description
reduce(func)	Aggregates the elements of an RDD using func, which takes two arguments and returns one. The function should be commutative and associative so that it can be computed correctly in parallel.
collect()	Returns all the elements of the dataset as an array to the driver program. This is usually useful after a filter or other operation that returns a sufficiently small subset of the data.
count()	Returns the number of elements in an RDD.
take(n)	Returns a list of the first n elements of an RDD.
first()	Returns the first element of an RDD.
takeOrdered(n, key=func)	Returns n elements in ascending order or in the order determined by the optional function func.
foreach(func)	Applies the function func to each element of the RDD. It doesn't return anything. It could be useful for inserting data into a database.

We can use count() to figure out the number of elements in our RDD, which can be useful for debugging.

```
rdd.count()
```

```
8
```

With take(n), we get the first n elements from an RDD. This must be the way to go in production, instead of using collect(), when we need to gather data from the workers. Why? Because we can't be sure that all the RDD will fit into the main memory of the driver, which could result in collect() producing an *OutOfMemory* error. With take() you can always control the amount of data you receive in the driver.

For example, we can take the first element from the RDD, which seems to be the same functionality as first():

```
rdd.take(1)
```

```
[1]
```

However, note that take() returns a list! But first() won't:

```
rdd.first()
```

```
1
```

You may find the reduce() action a bit confusing if you think of MapReduce as explained in the previous chapter. In MapReduce, we said that reduce() would keep things distributed, and wouldn't return anything back to the driver. However, in Spark, reduce() is an action, which behaves similarly to the reduce() function from Python, condensing all the elements of an RDD into a single one. The reduce function that will allow us to do standard MapReduce is called reduceByKey(), and it is a transformation that we will be looking at when working with key–value pairs (Section 4.3.5). Let's do a reduce() to sum the values in the RDD:

```
rdd.reduce(lambda a, b: a + b)
```

```
36
```

Let's now look at the takeOrdered() action, which is very much like take(), but allows us to get the elements in order, for which we can provide a function to alter the ordering. By default, it will take the elements in ascending order. For example, if we want to get only the first three elements of the list in ascending order:

```
rdd.takeOrdered(3)
```

```
[1, 2, 3]
```

Ok, that was simple, but how do we do it in descending order? We need to provide a function that returns a value for each element in the RDD, which will be used to get the elements in ascending order.

```
rdd.takeOrdered(3, lambda s: -1 * s)
```

```
[8, 7, 6]
```

In the above instruction, the function takeOrdered() took an anonymous function that basically inverts the sign of each element of rdd so that the highest number becomes the lowest.

4.3.5 Key–Value Transformations

So far we have seen "plain" RDDs, but you might be wondering, after all the fuss with MapReduce, have we entirely forgotten about key–value pairs?

Not really; Spark supports key–value pairs and they are another type of RDD. To create one of this kind, you simply need to define each element of an RDD as a tuple (⟨key⟩, ⟨value⟩). It is important to note that the key must be an immutable type of object; for example, lists cannot act as keys in Spark.

Basic Key–Value Transformations

Table 4.4 presents a list of basic key–value transformations together with brief descriptions.

Let's create our first RDD of key–value pairs:

```
rdd = sc.parallelize([(1, 2), (3, 4), (3, 6)])
```

We can apply any of the transformations we applied before, but we need to be aware that the elements of this RDD are tuples. For example, we could apply map() to take the value as key, and put a 1 as the output:

Table 4.4 Basic key–value transformations with RDDs.

Transformation	Description
groupByKey()	Returns a new RDD of tuples $(k, \text{iterable}(v))$. **Warning:** This requires a shuffle!
reduceByKey(func)	Returns a new RDD of tuples (k, v) where the values of each key k are aggregated using using the function func. This function should take two elements of type v and return the same type.
sortByKey()	Returns a new RDD of tuples (k, v) that has been sorted (in ascending order by default).

```
rdd.map(lambda k_v: (k_v[0], 1)).collect()
```

```
[(1, 1), (3, 1), (3, 1)]
```

In addition to those transformations, Spark has a few more designed for key–value RDDs. For example, we can now group rdd by key using groupByKey(). As a transformation, nothing will happen until we trigger an action. We are going to group by key and then directly collect it:

```
rdd.groupByKey().collect()
```

```
[(1, <pyspark.resultiterable.ResultIterable at 0x2e0d9d264f0>),
 (3, <pyspark.resultiterable.ResultIterable at 0x2e0d9d26e50>)]
```

Interestingly, it doesn't collect the list of values, but it returns an iterator for each key, which will allow us to go through all those elements and do something. To see the list of values, we would have to map every pair, and coerce the iterator to a list:

```
rdd.groupByKey().map(lambda x : (x[0], list(x[1]))).collect()
```

```
[(1, [2]), (3, [4, 6])]
```

Note that groupByKey() is quite inefficient because all the key–value pairs are shuffled around. If you plan to do some operation by key, it is probably best to use reduceByKey():

```
rdd.reduceByKey(lambda a, b: a + b).collect()
```

```
[(1, 2), (3, 10)]
```

All the elements with the same key will go the same node; they are also grouped together, and the function we defined reduces the list of values by adding them up. So, why is it better to use reduceByKey() than groupByKey() in some cases? Because reduceByKey() will apply some optimizations (using combiners) by performing local reductions before moving things across the network.

Something interesting you may have noticed: We explained that reduce() for RDDs is an action, and as such it returns a result to the driver. However, reduceByKey()

Table 4.5 Join-like transformations with RDDs.

Transformation	Description
join(rdd)	Inner join between RDDs; the key must be present in both RDDs.
leftOuterJoin(rdd)	Joins the elements of two RDDs; the key must be present in the second RDD.
rightOuterJoin(rdd)	Joins the elements of two RDDs; the key must be present in the first RDD.
fullOuterJoin(rdd)	Joins the elements of two RDDs; the key must be present in either of the RDDs.

is a transformation. The data remains distributed until we do the collect()! This makes a lot of sense since there could be lots of keys in our resulting RDD that won't necessarily fit into the main memory of the driver.

Challenge #4.1

Compute the word count of a list of strings using groupByKey() and reduce-ByKey(). Which one do you prefer?

Another interesting key–value transformation is sortByKey(), which allows us to sort (in ascending order by default) the pairs of a dataset (it doesn't modify them, but returns a new ordered RDD).

```
rdd2 = sc.parallelize([(3, 'a'), (2, 'c'), (1, 'b')])
```

```
rdd2.sortByKey().collect()
```

```
[(1, 'b'), (2, 'c'), (3, 'a')]
```

Join-Like SQL Transformations

When using key–value RDDs, you can apply different types of join operations, which are common when working with SQL databases. In summary, SQL joins mainly allow one to combine two tables based on a related column. In the case of RDDs, joins work by combining two RDDs using their keys. Hence, the idea is to concatenate the values of the elements of the RDDs having the same keys. The differences between the types of joins reside in how elements not having a key in the other RDD are treated. Table 4.5 introduces these transformations with brief explanations.

Here is a very quick example in case you find it useful. We will consider two tables (RDDs): one containing information about people and their age, and the other information about the hobbies people have.

```
people = sc.parallelize([("Lam", 35), ("Direnc", 35),\
                         ("Rebecca", 24), ("Edwina", 25)])
hobbies = sc.parallelize([("Lam", ["Triathlon", "Running", "Cycling"]),
                          ("Direnc", ["Lifting", "Running", "Reading"]),
                          ("Rebecca", ["Singing", "Dancing"]),
                          ("Grazziela", ["Running", "Music"])])
```

Notice that there may be people with unknown age or hobbies that would not be present in the people or hobbies RDDs, respectively.

join(rdd)

With join() we get the combination of the values associated with the common keys in the RDDs. For the example, we get the age and hobbies of the people present in both RDDs.

```
people.join(hobbies).collect()
```

```
[('Direnc', (35, ['Lifting', 'Running', 'Reading'])),
 ('Lam', (35, ['Triathlon', 'Running', 'Cycling'])),
 ('Rebecca', (24, ['Singing', 'Dancing']))]
```

You can check the result when there are repeated keys in any of the RDDs.

leftOuterJoin(rdd)

Similar to join(), with leftOuterJoin() we also get elements in the first RDD that are not matched with any element of the other RDD. The value for concatenation is set to None in these cases.

```
people.leftOuterJoin(hobbies).collect()
```

```
[('Direnc', (35, ['Lifting', 'Running', 'Reading'])),
 ('Edwina', (25, None)),
 ('Lam', (35, ['Triathlon', 'Running', 'Cycling'])),
 ('Rebecca', (24, ['Singing', 'Dancing']))]
```

rightOuterJoin(rdd)

This is the same as leftOuterJoin(), but the other way around. That is, we get the elements in the second RDD that are not matched with any element of the first RDD.

```
people.rightOuterJoin(hobbies).collect()
```

```
[('Direnc', (35, ['Lifting', 'Running', 'Reading'])),
 ('Lam', (35, ['Triathlon', 'Running', 'Cycling'])),
 ('Rebecca', (24, ['Singing', 'Dancing'])),
 ('Grazziela', (None, ['Running', 'Music']))]
```

fullOuterJoin(rdd)

fullOuterJoin() is like doing leftOuterJoin() and rightOuterJoin() simultaneously. That is, all elements from both RDDs are maintained. If they do not match with any from the other RDD, the corresponding values are set to None.

```
people.fullOuterJoin(hobbies).collect()
```

```
[('Direnc', (35, ['Lifting', 'Running', 'Reading'])),
 ('Edwina', (25, None)),
 ('Lam', (35, ['Triathlon', 'Running', 'Cycling'])),
 ('Rebecca', (24, ['Singing', 'Dancing'])),
 ('Grazziela', (None, ['Running', 'Music']))]
```

4.3.6   Key–Value Actions

Of course, we have actions for key–value RDDs. As before, you can still apply the actions we mentioned before for RDDs, but there are specific actions for key–value pairs (Table 4.6). Let's try them with our favorite key–value RDD:

```
rdd = sc.parallelize([(1, 2), (3, 4), (3, 6)])
```

Table 4.6 Key–value actions with RDDs.

Action	Description
countByKey()	Counts the number of elements for each key. Returns a dictionary.
collectAsMap()	Collects the RDD as a dictionary, but only provides one of the values.
lookup(key)	Returns the value associated with a given key.

You can still count the number of elements in total:

```
rdd.count()
```

```
3
```

But with key–value RDDs, we can also count by key:

```
rdd.countByKey()
```

```
defaultdict(int, {1: 1, 3: 2})
```

Note that if the number of keys were to be immensely large, countByKey() could cause memory issues in the driver. That's why we usually prefer to use a map() (to create a key–value pair like (key, 1)) followed by a reduceByKey() for counting (which simply adds the number of ones for each key).

You could transform your key–value RDD into a Python dictionary with collectAsMap():

```
rdd.collectAsMap()
```

```
{1: 2, 3: 6}
```

But note that we have lost the pair (3, 4)! it only provides one of the elements, since Python dictionaries do not allow for duplicate keys.

And finally, you can look up a specific key and get the values associated with it using lookup():

```
rdd.lookup(3)
```

```
[4, 6]
```

4.3.7   File I/O

Spark allows us to read and write files in different formats. This section introduces how to read/write with the RDD API.

Text Files

As we saw before, we can read text files from a file system, distributed or not, with `sc.textFile()`, but the most important thing is that all worker nodes can access the file.

We can actually read all the files in a directory by indicating the name of the directory:

```
lines = sc.textFile("data/")

lines.count()
```

```
43476
```

In this case, we put every single line of each file as an element of the `lines` RDD.

There is also the function `wholeTextFile()`, which provides a key–value RDD with the filenames as keys and their content as values.

```
files = sc.wholeTextFiles("data/")

files.count()
```

```
5
```

We can also save an RDD as a text file using `saveAsTextFile(filename)`. For example, we can first filter and then save:

```
bookRDD = sc.textFile("data/quixote.txt")

quixote_lines = bookRDD.filter(lambda line: "Quixote" in line)

quixote_lines.saveAsTextFile("data/quixote_lines")
```

But, `quixote_lines` will not be a single file, but a directory with multiple files (one file per partition). This is because each node will write it in different places.

Reading Other Formats

Can we read CSV or JSON files natively with Apache Spark? Unfortunately, not with the RDD API, but it is possible with Spark SQL (Chapter 5). For now, you will need to parse the files.

JSON Files

Here is one example for JSON files using the `json` library.

```
import json
json_rdd = sc.textFile("data/people.json").map(lambda x: json.loads(x))

print(f"Number of elements in the RDD from people.json: {json_rdd.count()}")
```

```
Number of elements in the RDD from data.json: 5
```

Let's see how the first element has been read:

```
json_rdd.first()
```

```
{'employee_id': 8761,
 'personal_info': {'name': 'Lam', 'age': 35},
 'location': 'UK',
 'hobbies': ['Lifting', 'Running', 'Reading'],
 'joined': '2010-05-10'}
```

We could also write the RDD back to disk as a JSON file:

```
json_rdd.map(lambda x: json.dumps(x)).saveAsTextFile("data/output.json")
```

This again will be a directory. You can check the content of the files inside the directory (you can simply open them as text files) to better understand how the elements were divided into partitions and written to separate files.

CSV Files

We could load a CSV file and parse it like this:

```
import csv
from io import StringIO
def loadRecord(line):
    """Parse a CSV line"""
    input_data = StringIO(line)
    reader = csv.DictReader(input_data, fieldnames=["employee_id", "name",
                                                    "age", "location",
                                                    "hobbies", "joined"])
    return next(reader)

input_csv_rdd = sc.textFile("data/people.csv").map(loadRecord)
```

```
input_csv_rdd.take(2)
```

```
[{'employee_id': '8761',
  'name': 'Lam',
  'age': '35',
  'location': 'Vietnam',
  'hobbies': 'Lifting;Running;Reading',
  'joined': '2010-05-10'},
 {'employee_id': '12441',
  'name': 'Direnc',
  'age': '36',
  'location': 'Turkey',
  'hobbies': 'Triathlon;Running;Cycling',
  'joined': '2009-01-12'}]
```

And you can write things back to disk:

```
def writeRecords(records):
    """Write out CSV lines"""
    output = StringIO()
    writer = csv.DictWriter(output, fieldnames=["employee_id", "name",
                                                "age", "location",
                                                "hobbies", "joined"])
```

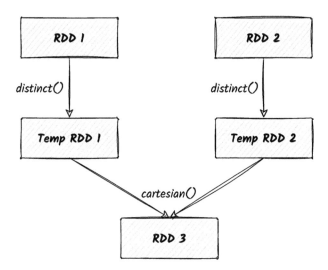

Figure 4.6 Example of RDD lineage. When applying `distinct()` to rdd1 and rdd2, we are somehow creating temporary RDD objects (with no name) that are later combined. The figure shows these RDDs as "Temp RDD1" and "Temp RDD2," respectively.

```
for record in records:
    writer.writerow(record)
return [output.getvalue()]

input_csv_rdd.mapPartitions(writeRecords)\
        .saveAsTextFile("data/output.csv")
```

4.3.8   RDD Lineage

Spark keeps track of all transformations used to provide tolerance to errors. To do so, it keeps a graph of all the transformations made to an RDD and creates a logical execution plan.

If we take one of the previous examples, for example, the cartesian product, first we applied the `distinct()` transformation to rdd1, and then we did the same for rdd2. If we were to allocate the results of the cartesian product to a variable rdd3...

```
rdd3 = rdd1.distinct().cartesian(rdd2.distinct())
```

... there would be a lineage graph that looks like Figure 4.6.

If the computation in one partition is lost (e.g., due to a hardware failure), the lineage graph allows Spark to backtrack, identify the dependencies of that partition, and reconstruct/rerun what is needed. For example, if there is an issue with the `cartesian()` call, Spark will be able to identify that this transformation depended on the two `distinct()` operations. Thus, it would quickly know that the origins of the cartesian product were rdd1 and rdd2. Those RDDs might be stored in HDFS, which would then need to be read and reconstructed to generate the lost partitions.

4.3.9 Cache Your RDDs

You may remember that we previously discussed a funny situation in which we created an RDD from a list, and then applied two different transformations plus a collect. In that case, we could see in the Spark WebUI that Spark parallelized the list twice.

RDDs are not cached by default; you need to tell Spark that you want that data structure to persist in main memory because it is going to be reused. Otherwise, each time you use an RDD it will be reconstructed from scratch (or from the last cached RDD in the lineage).

Let's load the book again:

```
quixote_rdd = sc.textFile("data/quixote.txt")
```

We'll first use flatMap() to get an RDD of all the words in the document:

```
words_quixote = quixote_rdd.flatMap(lambda line: line.split(' '))
```

Let's see the first five words:

```
words_quixote.take(5)
```

```
['', 'The', 'Project', 'Gutenberg', 'EBook']
```

We want to know how many times the words "blockhead" and "spear" appear in the text. Let's use filter() and count() for this.

```
words_quixote.filter(lambda line: "blockhead" in line).count()
```

```
17
```

```
words_quixote.filter(lambda line: "spear" in line).count()
```

```
13
```

In this case, both times we apply filter() and count(), the book is read from the drive, flat mapped, filtered, and then count. But both filtering operations start with the words_quixote RDD. So we should make sure that this RDD is cached in main memory by using cache() or persist():

```
words_quixote = quixote_rdd.flatMap(lambda line: line.split(" ")).cache()
```

Although we called cache() above, nothing has happened yet. It will be cached the first time that we run an action that involves the RDD that needs to be cached. If we now run the two filters. . .

```
words_quixote.filter(lambda line: "blockhead" in line).count()
```

```
17
```

```
words_quixote.filter(lambda line: "spear" in line).count()
```

```
13
```

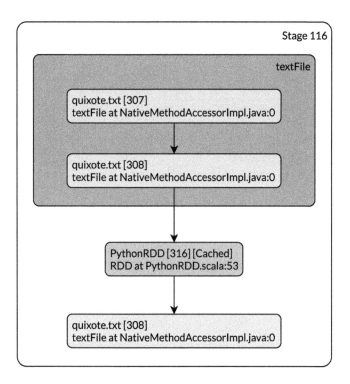

Figure 4.7 Spark WebUI: Caching an RDD to save computation.

... we will be able to see on the Spark WebUI that words_quixote was filtered. And hopefully you will also see that the runtime was lower in the second filter (Figure 4.7).

There are different persistence/caching levels in Spark, including memory only, memory and disk, disk only, and so on. For more information, check the Spark documentation.[4] In Python, all the objects are serialized using the pickle library, and apparently that means that indicating a persistence level doesn't really matter.

You can tell Spark that you will not need the cached RDD any more using unpersist(). Note that Spark will automatically unpersist old cached RDDs if it needs more memory to cache new RDDs.

4.4   Advanced Concepts

We now briefly cover a few advanced RDD topics, including shared variables, working with partitions, and numeric RDDs.

4.4.1   Shared Variables

As mentioned before, Spark sends functions and global variables to all executors for each task, and there is no communication between executors (Figure 4.8). This means

---

[4] https://spark.apache.org/docs/3.3.0/rdd-programming-guide.html#rdd-persistence

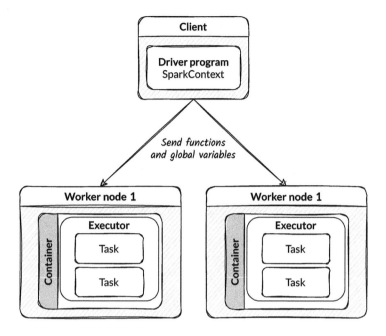

Figure 4.8 Shared variables are sent to worker nodes.

that any changes made in global variables by executors are not visible in the driver! This might also be a problem for jobs that share relatively large data structures because it is very inefficient to send large collections to each executor.

Is it possible to share some variables in Spark? Yes, Spark provides two advanced variable concepts:

- **Broadcast variables** are read-only variables that are sent efficiently to all executors and remain cached. They are stored in the executors (in main memory), so that they can be used by one or more Spark operations. They are only sent once, not for each task.
- **Accumulators** aggregate values from the executors in the driver. Only the driver can access the values of these variables. For the tasks (executors), accumulators are write-only. You can only add values. They are typically used to implement efficient counters and parallel additions.

Let's see some examples for both.

Broadcast Variables
Imagine that we need a relatively large lookup table in our program, but it is still possible to store it in main memory without distributing it. For example, a table to determine the postcode given an address. To simulate that, we will create a dictionary that we would like to be shared (efficiently) by all executors.

```
look_up_table = {1: "a", 2: "b", 3: "c", 4: "d"}
```

In addition to that lookup table, we have a big dataset that we parallelize using RDDs:

```
rdd = sc.parallelize([1, 2, 3, 4])
```

Without using broadcast variables, we could still do something like this:

```
rdd.map(lambda v: look_up_table[v]).collect()
```

```
['a', 'b', 'c', 'd']
```

This is because look_up_table is a global variable, and it is sent to all executors together with the lambda function. But when it is big, this becomes very inefficient. In these cases, you should broadcast the variable like this:

```
look_up_table_bc = sc.broadcast(look_up_table)
```

This uses peer-to-peer strategies to share those specific variables more efficiently than sending them one by one to each executor. Note, however, that this is again lazily evaluated, meaning that it won't be shared until needed by an executor to perform a task.

After creating the broadcast variable, we can use it in our map function, which we know will happen in parallel. Pay attention to the use of the attribute value to access the value of the broadcast variable:

```
rdd.map(lambda v: look_up_table_bc.value[v]).collect()
```

```
['a', 'b', 'c', 'd']
```

The result is obviously the same, but when large collections are involved, broadcast variables should be the preferred option.

Accumulator Variables

These are variables that are global to all the executors of our cluster. This means that every executor will write to the same variable, but the value is not readable at the executors. They may be useful as counters of operations that are happening. We can define an accumulator variable as:

```
accum = sc.accumulator(0)
```

If we have an RDD in which we want to apply a function f to each element, but it is not going to return anything, we could use an accumulator to count how many times this function is run.

```
rdd = sc.parallelize([1, 2, 3, 4])
```

We first define the function we want to apply to each element. In this case, simply add one to the accumulator, a global variable!

```
def f(x):
    global accum
    accum += 1
```

Now, we use the foreach() action to apply the function f to each element of rdd, and we will see it doesn't return anything:

```
rdd.foreach(f)
```

However, the value of accum, which is a global variable readable only at the driver, has been updated as expected:

```
accum.value
```

```
10
```

By the way, if you run the foreach() multiple times, the accumulator will keep increasing.

The previous example wasn't really useful, because we could do the same with a reduce, more efficiently and elegantly. But how about reading the *Don Quixote* book and doing two things at once: extracting the words and counting the number of blank lines.

```
quixote_rdd = sc.textFile("data/quixote.txt")
```

We could create a function that do both:

```
blank_lines = sc.accumulator(0)
def extract_words_blanklines(line):
    global blank_lines
    if line == "":
        blank_lines += 1
    return line.split(" ")
```

And use that function within the flatMap():

```
words_quixote = quixote_rdd.flatMap(extract_words_blanklines)
```

If we now trigger a count() action, we will get the word count of the book:

```
words_quixote.count()
```

```
437863
```

And the global accumulator variable blank_lines has counted the number of blank lines.

```
blank_lines.value
```

```
6820
```

It is important to be aware that using accumulators on transformations might not be ideal, and is maybe only good for debugging. If a task fails, we can't guarantee that it won't increment that global variable. In this example, the counter could be wrong. This won't happen if we use accumulators with actions.

4.4.2   Partitions

Instead of applying an operation to every single element of an RDD, we might want to use all the elements of a partition at once. To do so, Spark offers a few useful operations (see Table 4.7).

Table 4.7 Operations to manipulate RDDs by partitions.

Transformation/Action	Description
mapPartitions(func)	Applies the function func to each partition of the RDD; func receives an iterator and returns another iterator that can be of a different type.
mapPartitionsWithIndex(func)	Applies the function func to each partition of the RDD. func receives a tuple (⟨*integer*⟩, ⟨*iterator*⟩), where the integer represents the index of the partition, and iterator contains all the elements of the partitions.
foreachPartition(func)	Applies the function func to each partition of the RDD but doesn't return anything. func receives an iterator and returns nothing.

mapPartitions(func)

On many occasions we need to use entire data partitions to perform some operations. For example, in machine learning using mapPartitions() could be an obvious way to do a divide-and-conquer approach, so we learn a model for each subset of the data.

Let's see the difference between map() and mapPartitions() with an example. Let's say we want to compute the average of an RDD of integers.

```
rdd = sc.parallelize([1, 2, 3, 4, 5, 6, 7])
```

Similar to what we did before with MapReduce when computing averages, we will try to come up with a tuple (a, b), where a is the sum of all the elements, and b is the count of elements. The map could simply return the number as key and the value 1 to indicate you counted it once. The reduce could aggregate the elements of the tuple individually:

```
sum_count = rdd.map(lambda num: (num, 1))\
               .reduce(lambda x, y: (x[0] + y[0], x[1] + y[1]))

sum_count
```

```
(28, 7)
```

The average would be:

```
sum_count[0] / sum_count[1]
```

```
4.0
```

With mapPartitions(), we should probably define a function to determine how to compute the tuple in an entire partition of data (which contains multiple tuples). We have a number of partitions:

```
rdd.getNumPartitions()
```

```
12
```

```
def partition_counter(nums):
    """
    Input: `nums` is an iterator to the Integers
           of a given partition.
    Output: returns a list (i.e., an iterator) with
           the Word Count and the total length as a list
    """
    sum_count = [0, 0]
    for num in nums:
        sum_count[0] += num
        sum_count[1] += 1
    return [sum_count]
```

The reduce would be the same:

```
rdd.mapPartitions(partition_counter)\
   .reduce(lambda x, y: (x[0] + y[0], x[1] + y[1]))
```

```
(28, 7)
```

Which one is best? On a single computer, and for this very simple example, we won't see much difference. However, precomputing things in each partition before sending things away to the reducers may save a lot of overhead.

> **Challenge #4.2**
>
> In the first challenge we used the map() operation for the word count task. Does it make sense to use mapPartitions()?

```
mapPartitionsWithIndex(func)
```
This is almost the same as mapPartitions(), but we can figure out the index of each partition, which could be really useful.

```
rdd = sc.parallelize([1, 2, 3, 4, 5, 6, 7], 3)
```

In this case, the function we define must have two input parameters, the index and the iterator (which allows us to go through all the elements in the partition). Let's simply print out both the indexes and elements of each partition:

```
def show(index, iterator):
    return ["index: " + str(index) + " values: " + str(list(iterator))]
rdd.mapPartitionsWithIndex(show).collect()
```

```
['index: 0 values: [1, 2]',
 'index: 1 values: [3, 4]',
 'index: 2 values: [5, 6, 7]']
```

4.4.3 Operations with Numeric RDDs

Spark provides some built-in methods to generate some descriptive statistics of a numeric RDD, for example, stats(), count(), mean(), max(), and so on.

`stats()`

If you have an RDD of integers or real numbers, you can easily apply the `stats()` method to obtain some basic statistics for your RDD.

```
rdd = sc.parallelize([1, 2, 3, 4, 5, 6, 7])
```

```
results = rdd.stats()
```

```
results
```

```
(count: 7, mean: 4.0, stdev: 2.0, max: 7.0, min: 1.0)
```

```
type(results)
```

```
pyspark.statcounter.StatCounter
```

This method returns a `StatsCounter` object with all the statistics of the RDD. The main benefit of this method is that all the stats are computed in one single go over the data.

You could also apply specific operations like `count()`, `mean()`, `sum()`, `max()`, and so forth, but if you do it individually it will be less efficient than using `stats()` because every time we run one of these operations we iterate over the data. So the following print statement provides exactly the same output but it is more inefficient than `stats()`.

```
print(f"(count: {rdd.count()}, mean: {rdd.mean()}\
, stdev: {rdd.stdev()}, max: {rdd.max()}, min: {rdd.min()})")
```

```
(count: 7, mean: 4.0, stdev: 2.0, max: 7, min: 1)
```

> ### Challenge #4.3
>
> Before, we implemented the average of a list using `mapPartitions()`. The first challenge is to compute the standard deviation of that list without using `stats()`. You can initially assume you have the average (e.g., the result of `rdd.avg()` or by using the previous solution). As a second challenge, investigate whether you could apply some mathematical tricks to implement both the mean and the standard deviation in a single pass.

4.5   Internal Workings

To understand how Spark works internally and the optimizations it performs, we need to distinguish between two types of transformations:

- **Narrow dependencies:** Each partition will contribute to only one output partition. What does this mean? It means that the result is applied to each partition of an RDD, and to compute the output we don't need any other information. Imagine for example, a map function that multiplies each element of an RDD by two (e.g.,

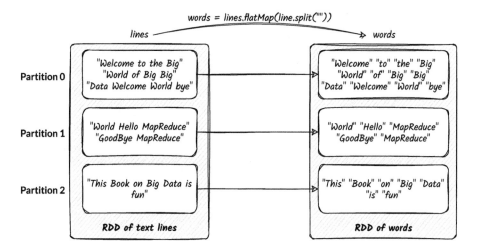

Figure 4.9 Example of a narrow transformation.

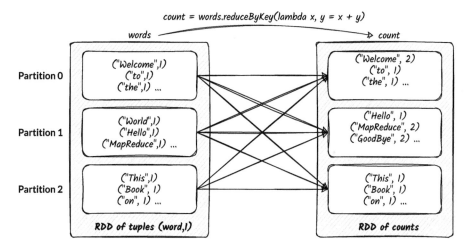

Figure 4.10 Example of a wide transformation.

`rdd.map(lambda x: x*2))`. The result depends only on the value of the particular elements in the partition, and no other (Figure 4.9).

- **Wide dependencies:** Multiple input partitions contributed to many output partitions. Here we are talking about transformations that will provoke a shuffle, and therefore traffic over the network, because the result depends on more than one partition and is not predefined. For example, `rdd.reduceByKey()` is a wide dependency, because it will require data from different nodes to create the list of values for each key (Figure 4.10).

We already suggested that Spark performs some optimizations. The interesting thing about this distinction here is that narrow dependencies can be optimized (e.g., a `map()`

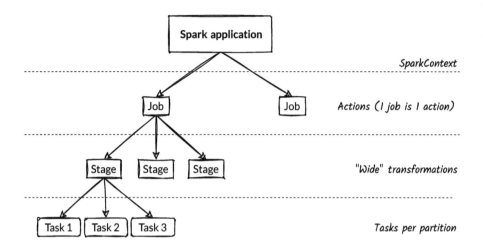

Figure 4.11 Anatomy of a Spark application.

or a filter() after a flatMap()), while wide dependencies somehow mark the end of a stage in Spark.

> **Coding tip:** On many occasions you will have to perform various transformations to the elements of an RDD (e.g., split a string by blank space, then convert it to a tuple (⟨*word*⟩, 1)). While you will be able to do that with a single map that uses a function to compute all of those operations, we recommend you concatenate multiple maps, filters, and other narrow transformations with simpler (lambda) functions, for example rdd.flatMap(lambda line: line.split(' ')).map(lambda x: (x, 1)).

4.5.1   Anatomy of a Spark Application

Let's look at the anatomy of a Spark application (Figure 4.11). Spark creates a directed acyclic graph to optimize the execution of an application. An action defines a new **job** (e.g., a count(), collect(), etc.). A job is split into a number of **stages** that are defined by the appearance of wide transformations (that can't be further optimized). Each stage is composed of a number of **tasks**, which basically apply an operation to each partition of an RDD.

We are going to investigate one simple example. We have some data, on which we are going to perform a number of operations (several transformations and one final action):

```
rdd = sc.parallelize([1, 2, 3, 4, 5, 6, 7, 8, 9])

rdd.filter(lambda x : x<5)\
    .map(lambda x: (x, x))\
        .groupByKey()\
        .map(lambda k_v : (sum(k_v[1]),k_v[0]))\
        .sortByKey()\
        .count()
```

```
4
```

In the code above we have one action, `count()`, at the end, that defines a job, and we have two wide transformations, `groupByKey()` and `sortByKey()`, that split the processing into three stages.

In the first two lines, we first remove those elements greater than or equal to 5, and then we transform each element into a tuple of (⟨*element*⟩, ⟨*element*⟩). Both `filter()` and `map()` are narrow transformations, and we could do both in one single pass through the data!

```
rdd.filter(lambda x : x<5)\
    .map(lambda x: (x,x))\
```

The next instruction is a `groupByKey()`, which is a wide transformation, and requires shuffling data around. So the previous two instructions formed a stage that is optimized and can be applied in one single go. Then, we don't have a wide transformation until we get to the `sortByKey()`, so the next two lines form a different stage:

```
.groupByKey()\
.map(lambda k_v : (sum(k_v[1]),k_v[0]))\
```

Here, we group the tuples by key, and then `map()` is used to apply an operation to each key. Finally, the last wide transformation is put together as a final stage, with the action to complete the job.

```
.sortByKey()\
.count()
```

Hopefully, this helps us understand the complexity of our program and how Spark processes it.

4.6   Take-Home Message

In this chapter we have learned that Spark RDDs are great distributed data structures that extend the MapReduce paradigm, allowing us to perform efficient interactive, iterative, and streaming processing. To use Spark RDDs effectively, you will have to play with the API and solve some problems to gain some experience with it. The key take-away messages are:

- An RDD is a distributed data abstraction. In essence, RDDs are Python lists that are distributed across the computing nodes and can be operated in parallel. They are immutable, so we can't modify an existing RDD but we can create a new one.
- There are two distinct operations: transformations and actions. Transformations are lazy and are not executed until an action is invoked.
- Some transformations may have similar behavior, but they may be quite different in terms of what they actually output or their performance; for example, `map()` vs. `flatMap()`, `groupByKey()` vs. `reduceByKey()`.
- Every operation over RDDs happens in parallel (in the workers); the code and global variables are sent to the executors. When global variables are big, Spark offers advanced operations to broadcast them efficiently.

- When reusing RDDs, we should use the `cache()` (or `persist()`) function to maintain the RDD in the main memory of the executors, therefore using it more efficiently.
- Understanding the anatomy of a Spark application and identifying the different kinds of transformations and the movement across the network is very important. We have seen that when working with an RDD, we perform a series of transformations to this distributed data structure, establishing dependencies between the different RDDs we create. In other words, a new partition of the data depends on other, previous, partitions. There are therefore two types of transformation: narrow, which depends on one partition, or wide, which depends on several partitions (and has an impact in several partitions).

The Spark RDD API performs some optimizations under the hood when there are multiple narrow transformations happening consecutively. In the next chapter we move on to the Spark SQL API, which was developed to improve upon the RDD API to enable further optimizations.

4.7   To Learn More

Are you willing to learn more about Spark and RDDs?

Damji et al. (2020) is one of the main books on Apache Spark, and contains more details on Spark's architecture and programming with Scala.

This chapter is focused on the RDD API, and we suggest you keep the Spark RDD programming guide[5] close by to find out about all the latest additions.

As we said for Hadoop, it is important to keep up to date with the latest changes in the platform. See the Apache Spark website[6] to find out about all the latest additions.

If you want to look at other promising big data frameworks, we suggest you investigate Flink[7] (particularly interesting for data streaming tasks) and Dask[8] (parallel computing with Python).

4.8   Solutions to Challenges

Challenge #4.1

Compute the word count of a list of strings using `groupByKey()` and `reduceByKey()`. Which one do you prefer?

---

[5] https://spark.apache.org/docs/latest/rdd-programming-guide.html
[6] https://spark.apache.org/
[7] https://flink.apache.org/
[8] https://www.dask.org/

```
lst = [
    "Welcome to the Big World of Big Big Data Welcome World bye",
    "World Hello MapReduce GoodBye MapReduce",
    "This Book on Big Data is fun",
]
```

```
rdd = sc.parallelize(lst)
```

First, we need to get all the words of that list by breaking it down by blank spaces. So, we could transform the RDD to get what we want. If you remember, we did something similar before using flatMap()!

> For the sake of space, we shorten the outputs to five elements. If you are testing this, you'd better remove the slicing ([:5]).

```
# use collect to visualize the output - we only show the first 5 elements
rdd.flatMap(lambda line: line.split(" ")).collect()[:5]
```

```
['Welcome', 'to', 'the', 'Big', 'World']
```

Following what we did before for Word Count with MapReduce, for each word we now want to create a tuple (*word*, 1), right?

```
rdd.flatMap(lambda line: line.split(" "))\
    .map(lambda word : (word, 1)).collect()[:5]
```

```
[('Welcome', 1), ('to', 1), ('the', 1), ('Big', 1), ('World', 1)]
```

Now we want to group together the same keys and add up the list of ones. We could do it with groupByKey(), maybe something like this:

```
rdd.flatMap(lambda line: line.split(" "))\
    .map(lambda word : (word, 1))\
    .groupByKey().map(lambda x : (x[0], len(list(x[1]))))\
    .collect()[:5]
```

```
[('Welcome', 2), ('of', 1), ('bye', 1), ('MapReduce', 2), ('GoodBye', 1)]
```

But, as stated before, that will be very slow; we should normally use reduceByKey() to be more efficient and exploit local optimizations:

```
rdd.flatMap(lambda line: line.split(" "))\
    .map(lambda word : (word, 1))\
    .reduceByKey(lambda a, b: a + b).collect()[:5]
```

```
[('Welcome', 2), ('of', 1), ('bye', 1), ('MapReduce', 2), ('GoodBye', 1)]
```

Challenge #4.2

In the first challenge we used the map() operation for the word count task. Does it make sense to use mapPartitions()?

Instead of using the second map in the above code, we could replace it with mapPartitions(). To do this, we need to implement a function that will do the word count in each single partition. This function will use Python dictionaries to count each word, but it has to return a list of key–value pairs for the following reduce.

```python
from collections import defaultdict
def partition_count(words):
    kv_dict = defaultdict(lambda: 0)
    for word in words:
        kv_dict[word] += 1
    # returning a list of key-value pairs
    return list(kv_dict.items())
```

```python
# we only show the first 5 elements [:5]
rdd.flatMap(lambda line: line.split(" "))\
   .mapPartitions(partition_count)\
   .reduceByKey(lambda a, b: a + b).collect()[:5]
```

```
[('Welcome', 2), ('of', 1), ('bye', 1), ('MapReduce', 2), ('GoodBye', 1)]
```

While it makes sense to use mapPartitions() to do the word count, and it might help to a certain extent, is it really better than map()? Well, in the original solution with map(), Spark automatically uses combiners, so it is already reducing the amount of data that goes across the network. Thus, the benefits of using mapPartitions() over map() in this example are not really clear.

Challenge #4.3

Before, we implemented the average of a list using mapPartitions(). The first challenge is to compute the standard deviation of that list without using stats(). You can initially assume you have the average (e.g., the result of rdd.avg() or by using the previous solution). As a second challenge, investigate whether you could apply some mathematical tricks to implement both the mean and the standard deviation in a single pass.

```python
rdd = sc.parallelize([1, 2, 3, 4, 5, 6, 7])
```

The simplest way of doing this is to first compute the mean value of the list, either with our solution based on mapPartitions() or using Spark numerical operations.

```python
avg = rdd.mean()
```

```python
avg
```

```
4.0
```

Using avg as a global variable, we could use mapPartitions() to compute the total number of elements in the partition and the squared differences with respect to the mean value.

```
def std(nums):
    sum_count = [0, 0]
    for num in nums:
        diff = num - avg
        sum_count[0] += diff * diff
        sum_count[1] += 1
    return [sum_count]

result = rdd.mapPartitions(std)\
    .reduce(lambda x, y: (x[0] + y[0], x[1] + y[1]))

result
```

```
(28.0, 7)
```

Of course, we still have to divide these two numbers and compute the square root (but we can do this easily in the driver):

```
import math
math.sqrt(result[0] / result[1])
```

```
2.0
```

```
rdd.stdev()
```

```
2.0
```

Here, we needed to first compute the mean value and then the standard deviation. Alternatively, you could try to do this faster if you know how to compute the standard deviation in one single pass.

```
def fast_std(nums):
    sum_count = [0, 0, 0]
    for num in nums:
        sum_count[0] += num
        sum_count[1] += num * num
        sum_count[2] += 1
    return [sum_count]

result = rdd.mapPartitions(fast_std)\
    .reduce(lambda x, y: (x[0] + y[0], x[1] + y[1], x[2] + y[2]))

result
```

```
(28, 140, 7)
```

```
avg = result[0] / result[2]
```

```
variance = result[1] / result[2] - avg * avg
```

```
variance
```

```
4.0
```

```
math.sqrt(variance)
```

```
2.0
```

4.9   Exercises

4.1 Indicate whether the following statements about Spark are true or false:
  (a) Spark is not just a data processing engine as it comes with its own distributed file system.
  (b) Spark extended the MapReduce programming model with additional operations.
  (c) Spark aims to mitigate the data serialization to disk problems that Hadoop MapReduce suffers.
  (d) Spark needs YARN to run its applications on a cluster.

4.2 Both Hadoop and Spark are big data frameworks that implement the MapReduce paradigm. Briefly explain why Spark is usually preferred over Hadoop MapReduce. If your MapReduce application consists of a single stage, would you still expect Spark to be faster than Hadoop MapReduce? Explain your answer.

4.3 Spark does not necessarily need to use HDFS to run an application. However, most clusters of computing nodes will use HDFS. Briefly explain why this is the case.

4.4 You are using your own laptop to develop a Spark application and you test it in local mode using multiple threads (i.e., option local[*]). You test the runtime of your application and you are happy with how much you have accelerated the processing. Would you expect this improvement to be kept when using a "real" cluster of computing nodes? Briefly explain your answer.

4.5 Indicate whether the following statements about RDDs are true or false:
  (a) RDDs are not fault tolerant.
  (b) An RDD can be created from existing collections like a Python list.
  (c) We can create RDDs by reading a file from our local hard drive.
  (d) RDDs are not partitioned by default.

4.6 Without using a computer, what is the output of the following pyspark program?
```
rdd = sc.parallelize([1, 2, 3, -1, -2, -3])
rdd.filter(lambda x: x >= 0)\
    .map(lambda x: (1, x) if x % 2 == 0 else (2, x))\
    .reduceByKey(lambda x, y: x + y).collect()
```

4.7 Indicate whether or not the following instructions are lazy:
  (a) rdd = sc.parallelize([[('COMP4103', 54), ('COMP4103', 64),('COMP4008',87)])
  (b) print(rdd.collect())
  (c) rdd.filter(lambda x: x[1] < 10)
  (d) rdd.mapPartitions(lambda x : x)

4.8 We have the following rdd that contains tuples with names and exam marks for our lab helpers.
```
rdd = sc.parallelize([('Lam', 45),
                      ('Khiv', 64),
                      ('Alexi',69),
                      ('Kavan', 87),
                      ('Rebecca',95)])
```
Using RDDs, write a Spark program that will transform rdd, converting the numerical marks into degree classifications. That is, anything less than 50 is a Fail; anything in the [50, 59] interval is a Pass; anything in the [60, 69] interval is a Merit; and anything in the [70, 100] interval is a Distinction. When collecting the new RDD, it should return a list like this:
```
[('Lam', 'Fail'),
 ('Khiv', 'Merit'),
 ('Alexi', 'Merit'),
 ('Kavan', 'Distinction'),
 ('Rebecca', 'Distinction')]
```

4.9 When working with key–value RDDs, briefly explain why groupByKey() may be more inefficient than reduceByKey().

4.10 The following code aims to efficiently analyze big log files. Do you see a problem with it? If yes, describe what you would do differently. Briefly explain your answer.
```
lines = spark.textFile("hdfs://...")
errors = lines.filter(lambda s: s.startswith("ERROR"))
messages = errors.map(lambda s: s.split("\t")[2])
print(messages.filter(lambda s: "Failed" in s).count())
print(messages.filter(lambda s: "Memory" in s).count())
```

4.11 Indicate whether the following statements about Spark and RDDs are true or false:
   (a) RDD lineage is simply a graph representation of the operations performed on an RDD for visualization purposes only.
   (b) Global variables in a driver program are not accessible in the worker nodes.
   (c) Large objects can be broadcast efficiently to all the worker nodes in a cluster.
   (d) mapPartitions() can only be applied to key–value RDDs.

4.12 We have written the following code to add 1 to each element of an RDD, but it doesn't seem to work. Briefly explain why it fails and suggest how to amend it. We would like to still work by partitions rather single elements.
```
rdd = sc.parallelize([1, 2, 3, 4, 5, 6, 7])
rdd.mapPartitions(lambda x: x + 1).collect()
```

4.13 Spark distinguishes between narrow and wide transformations. Briefly explain why Spark can only optimize narrow transformations.

4.14 You are given a file containing numbers on each line. We have to perform three transformations: (i) filter negative numbers; (ii) multiply each element by two; (iii) group them by key (e.g., to differentiate between odd and even numbers). Indicate and explain what kinds of dependencies are associated with these three transformations.

4.15 Spark distinguishes between jobs, stages, and tasks to define the execution of an application. Identify the **stages** that happen in the execution of the following code:

```
input = sc.parallelize([1, 2, 3, 4, 5, 6, 7, 8, 9]
input\
 .filter(lambda x: x < 2)\
 .map(lambda x: (x, x))\
 .groupByKey()\
 .map(lambda (x, y): (sum(y), x))\
 .sortByKey()\
 .count()
```

5   Spark SQL and DataFrames

Learning Outcomes

[KU]	The importance of structured data to optimize big data processing
[KU]	The concept of DataFrames to work with structured data in Spark
[KU, IS, PPS]	How to operate with DataFrames: understanding the differences from RDDs
[IS, PPS]	How to use DataFrames in practice for problem solving

We have learned that Spark optimizes the execution of the parallel tasks on RDDs, but this is only possible for *narrow transformations* that do not cause data movement across nodes (i.e., a shuffle). In this way, consecutive transformations can be applied together, increasing performance.

Spark cannot optimize RDD executions further because transformations are "black boxes." We create a function that is applied to a partition of the data (either elementwise or to the partition as a whole), returning another partition as an iterator (`Partition => Iterator[T]`). Here, since the function is opaque to Spark, the resulting data type (`T`) could be anything (which needs to be serialized when sending it to other nodes). That is a great thing because it provides lots of flexibility, but at the same time it makes it very difficult to optimize, since Spark doesn't know what is going on in the transformation itself. In Spark SQL, the idea is to gain knowledge about the data being processed in the form of a structure, so that further optimizations can be performed.

> If you like the world of big data, you will soon realize that one of the main challenges is to keep up with the latest advances in the available frameworks. Spark is a great example of this, as it continues to evolve very rapidly. For example, the Spark SQL module aims to improve the performance of RDDs with structured data, and several new structures have been developed for this purpose in a few years.

5.1   What Is Spark SQL?

Spark SQL is a module in Spark for structured data processing. The key idea of this module is to impose structure on the data so that Spark can perform further optimizations by knowing more about the underlying data.

When we talk about structured data, we are talking about organizing the data, assigning "names" and specific data types to the columns that define our data, similar to pandas in Python. If you have previous experience with databases, this new structured data API for parallel processing will also remind you of relational databases and Structured Query Language (SQL), which is why they used this name for the module. In fact, we will be able to directly apply SQL queries! Don't worry if you are not very familiar with SQL; although it is common to find more difficulties getting used to it, you will still get better at it after you see a few examples.

> You may be wondering whether RDDs will become deprecated with Spark SQL? No! They are still being used underneath, and we will be able to move from Spark SQL to RDDs and vice versa.

However, you should probably focus on the Spark SQL API as long as possible due to its superior performance. Spark RDD performance is highly dependent on the programming language. For example, Scala code tends to be much faster than Python code. In Spark SQL, this difference completely disappears since the actual code that is finally executed becomes the same (Java code!). Thus, the optimizations provided in Spark SQL are equally beneficial independent of the programming language used.

5.2   Basic Concepts: From RDDs to Structured Data

Without going into too much detail about what these optimizations are and how they work, we wanted to give you a quick overview of how the different Spark APIs have evolved.

5.2.1   DataFrame and Dataset APIs

In Spark 1.0, when the RDD API was released, two additional APIs were introduced: DataFrames and Datasets; they were later fused in Spark 2.0. Two key projects, Catalyst and Tungsten (for execution and memory optimization, respectively), were responsible for this shift from unstructured data (RDDs) to structured data. The key idea again is that imposing limits on what you can express allows Spark to perform optimizations.

Although RDDs do reduce the I/O overhead compared with Hadoop, when Spark needs to write something to disk or distribute it over the network, it does this using Java serialization[1] (and sometimes something called Kryo[2] for quicker serialization). The overhead of serializing individual Java and Scala objects is expensive and requires

---

[1] https://en.wikipedia.org/wiki/Serialization
[2] https://github.com/EsotericSoftware/kryo

storing additional information with the data itself. There is also the overhead of the garbage collector that results from creating and destroying individual objects. In *pyspark*, it is even more expensive when all data is double-serialized/deserialized to Java/Scala and then to Python (using `cloudpickle`) and back.

To deal with this issue, the Tungsten[3] project implemented a way of reducing overhead and making serialization faster using the off-heap memory (memory outside the Java Virtual Machine). This also allowed them to greatly reduce the amount of memory occupied by data and remove the dependency on the garbage collector for data management.

The other key project driving Spark SQL was Catalyst.[4] The main thing about the Catalyst optimizer is that it is able to represent the operations to be performed in the same way regardless of the programming language used (Scala, Java, Python, or R). Subsequently, it performs logical and physical optimizations based on a series of rules. Finally, the solution to be executed is compiled to Java bytecode in real time, which makes its execution really fast and independent of the programming language used.

The DataFrame API (introduced in Spark 1.3) was originally quite different from the RDD API because it builds a relational query plan, so it was more intuitive for database developers and did not follow an object-oriented programming (OOP) style. The DataFrame API introduced the concept of a schema to describe the data, which was exploited in the Tungsten and Catalyst projects to accelerate the data processing. Nevertheless, DataFrames came with an additional drawback: since they were interpreted at run time, some types of errors such as wrongly referring to the name of a column in the DataFrame were not detected until the application was launched. That is, they did not provide compile-time type safety. This was obviously not very relevant for Python as it is an interpreted language, but can be very inconvenient for compiled languages such as Scala and Java.

Later (from version 1.6) the Dataset API emerged to bring the best of both RDD and DataFrame worlds, allowing for functional transformations (e.g., `map`, `reduce`, ...) and compile-time type safety, but only for Scala and Java. The key idea was to provide strongly typed RDDs with the optimized execution engine of DataFrames.

From Spark 2.0 the Dataset and DataFrame APIs were fused, so that a DataFrame became simply a Dataset of Rows (where a `Row` is a new data type in Spark to enable the Tungsten and Catalyst optimizations; see the next section). However, in Python, *we don't have Datasets* and obviously not compile-time type safety, as this is an interpreted language. This is a little bit inconvenient because Datasets provide functional transformations that are very useful for many machine learning problems, and we will have to use RDDs in this case when using Python.

5.2.2   Optimizations: DataFrames and Datasets versus RDDs

The key point in understanding the optimizations that Spark SQL provides is that we will be working with columns of a specific data type (defined by the schema). When

---

[3] https://databricks.com/blog/2015/04/28/project-tungsten-bringing-spark-closer-to-bare-metal.html
[4] https://databricks.com/blog/2015/04/13/deep-dive-into-spark-sqls-catalyst-optimizer.html

operating with columns we know much more about the operation that is going to be done in comparison to what we understand from a `lambda` function with RDDs.

For example, with `lambda` functions, when we type `lambda x: x==1`, Spark internally understands it as . . .

```
class $anonfun$1 {
    def apply(Int):  Boolean
}
```

. . . a function that takes an integer and returns a boolean (Spark doesn't really know what's going on inside). Working with columns, when we type something like `col["x"] == 1`, Spark understands it as . . .

```
EqualTo(x, Lit(1))
```

. . . a comparison between the value of a specific variable/attribute (x) and a literal one (1). So, Spark knows exactly what is going on, making it optimizable!

To allow for optimizations at that level, Spark SQL includes more than 100 functions that are highly optimized (e.g., to manipulate strings, math functions, dates and times, etc.) and its own SQL types. We will always try to use those functions[5] and data types[6] provided in PySpark SQL.[7] We will work with a number of them throughout this chapter. To make use of these functions, we need to import them from `pyspark`.

```
from pyspark.sql.types import * # import data types from Spark
import pyspark.sql.functions as sql_f # import SQL functions
```

> Note that we imported the `sql.functions` with the alias `sql_f`. We do this to avoid potential name clashes with other functions available in Python (e.g., `max()`, `min()`, etc).

In summary, RDDs allow us to decide "how" to do operations, but this limits the optimizations that Spark can do. However, Datasets and Dataframes allow us to define "what" we want to do, and Spark decides how to do it.

> Due to its superior performance over RDDs, DataFrames has become the primary API for the machine learning library of Apache Spark. That doesn't mean that the actual implementations are always done using DataFrames, but to interact with them we will use DataFrames.

5.2.3   Spark Session: A New Entry Point to Spark

To enable the Spark SQL module, we need to use a new entry point to Spark. Rather than using the `SparkContext` we used for RDDs, we will use a new access point called `SparkSession`. This unifies all the different Spark contexts (i.e., `sqlContext`, `SparkContext`, `StreamingContext`, and `HiveContext`). You can still access the `SparkContext`; we allocate it to `sc` below, so you can still use RDDs.

---

[5] https://spark.apache.org/docs/3.3.0/api/python/reference/pyspark.sql/functions.html
[6] https://spark.apache.org/docs/3.3.0/api/python/reference/pyspark.sql/data_types.html
[7] https://spark.apache.org/docs/3.3.0/api/python/reference/pyspark.sql/index.html

```
from pyspark.sql import SparkSession
spark = SparkSession \
    .builder \
    .master("local[*]") \
    .appName("Chapter 5: pyspark SQL") \
    .getOrCreate()
sc = spark.sparkContext
```

Check the content of spark:

```
spark
```

```
SparkSession - in-memory SparkContext Spark UI: http://localhost:4040/
 ↪Version v3.3.0 Master local[*] AppName Chapter 5: pyspark SQL
```

If you have initiated multiple SparkSessions, you may get a different URL every time (a different port, as shown in the output above). We will see the same user interface as with RDDs.

5.3   DataFrames

As with RDDs, we are just going to show you some examples. For a thorough list of operations with Spark DataFrames in Python, please consult the official documentation.[8] Let's get started.

A DataFrame is a two-dimensional data structure (a table) organized by columns that are defined in a schema indicating their types (e.g., integer, string, float, etc.). Column names can be used to refer to the content of a column and perform operations with it.

In Spark, a DataFrame is a distributed collection of elements of type Row. You can think of a Row as an array that can be indexed by name (like a dictionary). Obviously, all the Row elements in a DataFrame will share the same index names, which are referred to as columns, and the same types. Like RDDs, DataFrames are immutable.

Let's create our first Row:

```
from pyspark.sql import Row
row = Row(name="Isaac", age=36)
row
```

```
Row(name='Isaac', age=36)
```

We can access the fields as if they are "attributes" (OOP style), or like the values of a dictionary:

```
row.name
```

```
'Isaac'
```

```
row["name"]
```

```
'Isaac'
```

---

[8] https://spark.apache.org/docs/3.3.0/api/python/reference/pyspark.sql/index.html

> It is recommended to use the latter option to avoid conflicts with potential method names of the class Row.

There are a few operators you can use with this data type.

```
"name" in row
```

```
True
```

```
"surname" in row
```

```
False
```

The order of the columns (indexes) in the Row type is relevant, for example if you try to interoperate with Python tuples (which is possible):

```
("Isaac", 36) == row
```

```
True
```

```
(36, "Isaac") == row
```

```
False
```

Although they can be more like a dictionary, they do not interoperate well.

```
{'name': "Isaac", 'age': 36} == row
```

```
False
```

Alternatively, you can also define a Row with the indexes only, which will work as a constructor, and then add the data:

```
person = Row('name','age')
```

```
person
```

```
<Row('name', 'age')>
```

For now, person doesn't have any values, but you can allocate them:

```
person("Isaac", 36)
```

```
Row(name='Isaac', age=36)
```

In a DataFrame the indexes of the Row become the columns. Now we focus on how to create DataFrames, how to transform them, and more about the Column concept in Spark SQL.

> Are you wondering if the Row objects we have created are distributed? No: Row elements will be distributed when they are part of a DataFrame.

5.3.1 Creating a DataFrame

To create a DataFrame we need to provide a schema, which means we need to indicate column names, types, and whether they can contain null values. We can create a DataFrame following different strategies:

- *Inferring the schema automatically from the data (e.g., JSON files, RDDs of Rows).* Spark SQL will try to infer the schema based on the data. This option is very useful for fast prototyping, but it may not be the most efficient way if a lot of data is required to infer the schema (e.g., columns with many missing values may prevent us from inferring the schema from a subset of the data).
- *Inferring the schema automatically from metadata (e.g., JDBC, JavaBeans).* When reading data from structured data sources like relational databases, Spark SQL can directly use the existing schema. In this way, getting the schema comes at no cost. We will not discuss this approach in further detail as it requires a database connection.
- *Explicitly defining the schema if you know it.* This avoids the need to infer the schema, making the process faster, but it requires you to detail it exactly.

Similar to RDDs, we can create DataFrames from several data sources such as an existing collection or a number of storage systems.

Inferring the Schema from the Data

Let's start creating our first DataFrame by inferring the schema from a list of tuples:

```
tuples = [('Celine', 16), ('Meng', 14), ('John', 10),\
          ('Debbi', 25), ('Zijian', 36), ('Qian', 40)]
```

Using the `SparkSession` variable called `spark`, we can create a DataFrame using the `createDataFrame()` method:

```
df = spark.createDataFrame(tuples)
```

Let's check the type and what is inside:

```
type(df)
```

```
pyspark.sql.dataframe.DataFrame
```

```
df
```

```
DataFrame[_1: string, _2: bigint]
```

You can see that it has inferred the type of the data automatically. You can get the details of the schema using the function `printSchema()`. This tells you the types and that the values could be `null`.

```
df.printSchema()
```

```
root
 |-- _1: string (nullable = true)
 |-- _2: long (nullable = true)
```

But if you really want to see the content, you need to do a `collect()` or `show()`, as we did with RDDs. Both of them are actions and take data to the driver, so remember to be careful using them, although `show()` limits the data displayed by default.

```
df.collect()
```

```
[Row(_1='Celine', _2=16),
 Row(_1='Meng', _2=14),
 Row(_1='John', _2=10),
 Row(_1='Debbi', _2=25),
 Row(_1='Zijian', _2=36),
 Row(_1='Qian', _2=40)]
```

```
df.show()
```

```
+------+---+
|    _1| _2|
+------+---+
|Celine| 16|
|  Meng| 14|
|  John| 10|
| Debbi| 25|
|Zijian| 36|
|  Qian| 40|
+------+---+
```

> The output from `show()` is much nicer, showing the information as a table with column names in the first row. This can be done with DataFrames because Spark understands the data behind thanks to the schema, but couldn't be done with RDDs.

The above DataFrame does not have any name for the columns, so `_1` and `_2` are used to refer to them (this notation is typical in Scala to name the elements of a tuple). In these cases, we can explicitly specify the column names when creating the DataFrame:

```
df_names = spark.createDataFrame(tuples, ['name', 'age'])
```

```
df_names.show()
```

```
+------+---+
|  name|age|
+------+---+
|Celine| 16|
|  Meng| 14|
|  John| 10|
| Debbi| 25|
|Zijian| 36|
|  Qian| 40|
+------+---+
```

If `tuples` was to be an RDD (i.e., you parallelized it), you can still use `spark.createDataFrame()` for that RDD, and obtain the same DataFrame. Let's create an RDD with the content of `tuples`:

```
rdd = sc.parallelize(tuples) # we use `sc` to create an RDD!
```

```
df_rdd = spark.createDataFrame(rdd, ['name','age'])

df_rdd.show(2) # you can indicate the number of elements to show.
```

```
+------+---+
|  name|age|
+------+---+
|Celine| 16|
|  Meng| 14|
+------+---+
only showing top 2 rows
```

But probably the most natural way of getting a DataFrame from an RDD would be using the function `to_DF()`.

```
df_rdd2 = rdd.toDF(['name', 'age']) # column names not required

df_rdd2.show(2)
```

```
+------+---+
|  name|age|
+------+---+
|Celine| 16|
|  Meng| 14|
+------+---+
only showing top 2 rows
```

If you ever need to carry out RDD-based operations (like `map` or `flatMap` transformations), you can always access the underlying RDD from the DataFrame as follows:

```
row_rdd = df_rdd2.rdd
row_rdd.collect()
```

```
[Row(name='Celine', age=16),
 Row(name='Meng', age=14),
 Row(name='John', age=10),
 Row(name='Debbi', age=25),
 Row(name='Zijian', age=36),
 Row(name='Qian', age=40)]
```

And you could apply any operation you like on that RDD, assuming that each element is of type Row:

```
row_rdd.map(lambda x: x.name).collect()
```

```
['Celine', 'Meng', 'John', 'Debbi', 'Zijian', 'Qian']
```

By the way, if you try to create a DataFrame as we did above with a list of integers or floats, you might be disappointed because it won't work! Spark SQL expects a collection of tuples, lists, or dictionaries as inputs. Otherwise, it can't infer any schema. For example:

```
numbers_rdd = sc.parallelize([1, 2, 3])
```

```
spark.createDataFrame(numbers_rdd, ["number"])
```

```
TypeError Traceback (most recent call last)
Input In [7], in <cell line: 1>() ----> 1 spark.createDataFrame (numbers_rdd,
["number"])
...
```

Whenever you have unstructured data in an RDD (not Row elements), you can first transform it to an RDD of Row elements and then proceed with the DataFrame. As before, we create that `Person`:

```
Person = Row('name', 'age')
```

Now we use map to access each element of the `rdd` and create an RDD of Rows:

```
person = rdd.map(lambda r: Person(*r))
```

> If you wonder what the asterisk in `Person(*r)` means, it is a way to tell Python that we want to unpack the elements of the tuple `r` and use them as independent parameters to `Person()`.

Now we use the `createDataFrame()` method:

```
df2 = spark.createDataFrame(person)
df2.show()
```

```
+------+---+
|  name|age|
+------+---+
|Celine| 16|
|  Meng| 14|
|  John| 10|
| Debbi| 25|
|Zijian| 36|
|  Qian| 40|
+------+---+
```

It would also work for the numbers if you create a Row with a single element.

```
nums = Row("numbers")
numbers_df = spark.createDataFrame(numbers_rdd.map(lambda n: nums(n)))
numbers_df.show()
```

```
+-------+
|numbers|
+-------+
|      1|
|      2|
|      3|
+-------+
```

You can also transform your Spark DataFrame into a pandas DataFrame, and vice versa. Note, however, that this is an action like `collect()`, which sends all the data to the driver node. Hence, you must be sure that it will fit in its main memory.

```
df2.toPandas()
```

```
     name  age
0  Celine   16
1    Meng   14
2    John   10
3   Debbi   25
4  Zijian   36
5    Qian   40
```

We can create a pandas DataFrame from `tuples`.

```
import pandas as pd
panda_df = pd.DataFrame(data=tuples, columns=['name', 'age'])
panda_df
```

```
     name  age
0  Celine   16
1    Meng   14
2    John   10
3   Debbi   25
4  Zijian   36
5    Qian   40
```

And now we parallelize it:

```
parallel_df = spark.createDataFrame(panda_df)
```

```
parallel_df.show()
```

```
+------+---+
|  name|age|
+------+---+
|Celine| 16|
|  Meng| 14|
|  John| 10|
| Debbi| 25|
|Zijian| 36|
|  Qian| 40|
+------+---+
```

```
parallel_df.printSchema()
```

```
root
 |-- name: string (nullable = true)
 |-- age: long (nullable = true)
```

In all the cases above, the schema has been automatically inferred from the data without indicating the data types of each column.

Manually Specifying the Schema

Typically you would try to infer the schema automatically from the data, but sometimes you might want to specify it manually. This may be the case if you need to go through the whole dataset to infer the schema appropriately. Although we have overlooked it until now, the createDataFrame() method has a samplingRatio parameter that indicates the number of rows (as a percentage) used to infer the schema. If not set, only the first row is used, working very fast. However, depending on where your data comes from, you may need to inspect a larger portion of the data to infer the schema or may lose information for columns that did not appear in the first element (which will be ignored if not present in the schema).

If we want to avoid that, we can manually specify the schema using a StructType. We will also need to access the different data types from Spark[9] that we imported earlier.

```
schema = StructType([
    # False: indicates it can't be null
    StructField("name", StringType(), False),
    # True: indicates it can be null
    StructField("age", IntegerType(), True)])
```

Then, we simply create the DataFrame as before, but now we indicate the schema created.

```
df3 = spark.createDataFrame(rdd, schema)
df3.show()
```

```
+------+---+
|  name|age|
+------+---+
|Celine| 16|
|  Meng| 14|
|  John| 10|
| Debbi| 25|
|Zijian| 36|
|  Qian| 40|
+------+---+
```

```
df3.printSchema()
```

```
root
 |-- name: string (nullable = false)
 |-- age: integer (nullable = true)
```

Alternatively, you could also do it like this:

```
spark.createDataFrame(rdd, "name: string, age: int").collect()
```

```
[Row(name='Celine', age=16),
 Row(name='Meng', age=14),
 Row(name='John', age=10),
 Row(name='Debbi', age=25),
 Row(name='Zijian', age=36),
 Row(name='Qian', age=40)]
```

---

[9] https://spark.apache.org/docs/3.3.0/api/python/reference/pyspark.sql/data_types.html

Schema when Reading/Writing from/to Files

You can also read data in different data types (e.g., JSON and CSV formats) and automatically infer their schema. Let's try it with the following JSON file.

```
open('data/data.json', 'r').readlines()
```

```
['{"employee_id":8761,"personal_info":{"name":"Lam","age":35},"location":"UK"
,"hobbies":["Lifting","Running","Reading"],"joined":"2010-05-10"}\n',
 '{"employee_id":12441,"personal_info":{"name":"Direnc","age":36},"location":
"Spain","hobbies":["Triathlon","Running","Cycling"],"joined":"2009-01-12"}\n'
, '{"employee_id":5646,"personal_info":{"name":"Rebecca","age":42},"location":
"USA","hobbies":["Singing","Dancing"],"joined":"2002-10-25"}\n',
 '{"employee_id":1233,"personal_info":{"name":"Grazziela","age":46},"location
":"UK","joined":"2018-08-14"}\n',
 '{"employee_id":3242,"personal_info":{"name":"Edwina","age":22},"location":"
Australia","hobbies":["Running","Music"],"joined":"2018-08-14"}\n']
```

Reading JSON and CSV files is just as simple as with text files. You can use either of the following two ways:

$$\texttt{spark.read.}\langle \textit{filetype}\rangle(\langle \textit{filename}\rangle)$$
$$\texttt{spark.read.format}(\langle \textit{filetype}\rangle)\texttt{.options}(\langle \textit{options}\rangle)\texttt{.load}(\langle \textit{filename}\rangle)$$

where ⟨*filetype*⟩ can be json, csv, or text, respectively.

We can now read our JSON file.

```
json_df = spark.read.json("data/data.json")
json_df.printSchema()
```

```
root
 |-- employee_id: long (nullable = true)
 |-- hobbies: array (nullable = true)
 |    |-- element: string (containsNull = true)
 |-- joined: string (nullable = true)
 |-- location: string (nullable = true)
 |-- personal_info: struct (nullable = true)
 |    |-- age: long (nullable = true)
 |    |-- name: string (nullable = true)
```

```
json_df.show()
```

```
+-----------+--------------------+----------+---------+---------------+
|employee_id|             hobbies|    joined| location|  personal_info|
+-----------+--------------------+----------+---------+---------------+
|       8761|[Lifting, Running...|2010-05-10|       UK|     {35, Lam}|
|      12441|[Triathlon, Runni...|2009-01-12|    Spain|  {36, Direnc}|
|       5646|  [Singing, Dancing]|2002-10-25|      USA|  {42, Rebecca}|
|       1233|                null|2018-08-14|       UK|{46, Grazziela}|
|       3242|    [Running, Music]|2018-08-14|Australia|   {22, Edwina}|
+-----------+--------------------+----------+---------+---------------+
```

In the above show(), you could used truncate=False inside of the show() to see all the data in each column despite its length.

However, if the (JSON) file is too big, inferring the schema could take quite some time because Spark needs two passes through the data, first to infer the schema and then to read and structure the data following that schema. As with the `createDataFrame()` method, here we also have a `samplingRatio` parameter, telling Spark what portion of the data it should look at to infer the schema. However, in this case, by default, this ratio is set to `1.0`, that is, 100% of the data. If you are confident that you won't need to inspect all the data to infer the schema, you can tell Spark to use only a portion:

```
json_df = spark.read.json("data/data.json", samplingRatio=0.1)
json_df.printSchema()
```

```
root
 |-- employee_id: long (nullable = true)
 |-- joined: string (nullable = true)
 |-- location: string (nullable = true)
 |-- personal_info: struct (nullable = true)
 |    |-- age: long (nullable = true)
 |    |-- name: string (nullable = true)
```

```
json_df.show(truncate=False)
```

```
+-----------+----------+---------+---------------+
|employee_id|joined    |location |personal_info  |
+-----------+----------+---------+---------------+
|8761       |2010-05-10|UK       |{35, Lam}      |
|12441      |2009-01-12|Spain    |{36, Direnc}   |
|5646       |2002-10-25|USA      |{42, Rebecca}  |
|1233       |2018-08-14|UK       |{46, Grazziela}|
|3242       |2018-08-14|Australia|{22, Edwina}   |
+-----------+----------+---------+---------------+
```

> Be careful with this, because you may notice that we have lost "hobbies" information from our data as Spark has used the only entries without hobbies to infer the schema.

Alternatively, you could also provide the schema manually as explained above. If you do so, we can load the data faster.

```
schema = StructType(
    [
        StructField("employee_id", IntegerType(), True),
        StructField("hobbies", ArrayType(StringType(), True), True),
        StructField("joined", DateType(), True),
        StructField("location", StringType(), True),
        StructField("personal_info", StructType(
                [StructField("name", StringType(), True),
                StructField("age", IntegerType(), True)]
        ), True)
    ]
)
json_df = spark.read.json("data/data.json", schema)
json_df.printSchema()
```

```
root
 |-- employee_id: integer (nullable = true)
 |-- hobbies: array (nullable = true)
 |    |-- element: string (containsNull = true)
 |-- joined: date (nullable = true)
 |-- location: string (nullable = true)
 |-- personal_info: struct (nullable = true)
 |    |-- name: string (nullable = true)
 |    |-- age: integer (nullable = true)
```

```
json_df.show()
```

```
+-----------+--------------------+----------+---------+---------------+
|employee_id|             hobbies|    joined| location|  personal_info|
+-----------+--------------------+----------+---------+---------------+
|       8761|[Lifting, Running...|2010-05-10|       UK|      {Lam, 35}|
|      12441|[Triathlon, Runni...|2009-01-12|    Spain|   {Direnc, 36}|
|       5646| [Singing, Dancing]|2002-10-25|      USA|  {Rebecca, 42}|
|       1233|                null|2018-08-14|       UK|{Grazziela, 46}|
|       3242|   [Running, Music]|2018-08-14|Australia|   {Edwina, 22}|
+-----------+--------------------+----------+---------+---------------+
```

> Working with CSV files is as simple as with JSON. You can also read from text files, although the schema will always be a single String column named value.

In the same way that Spark SQL makes reading data more comfortable than with RDDs, it also makes it easier to write to the same formats using either of the following two ways:

```
DataFrame.write.⟨filetype⟩(⟨filename⟩)
DataFrame.write.format(⟨filetype⟩).options(⟨options⟩).load(⟨filename⟩)
```

```
json_df.write.json("data/json_file.json")
```

> **Important:** As happened with RDDs, the output file will be a directory, since each data partition will be written to a data block (a file in our filesystem).

For additional information on how to read and write DataFrames from/to files, you can check the Spark SQL input/output documentation.[10]

The Columns of a DataFrame and the Column Object

As we saw with printSchema(), Spark gives names and types to the columns that comprise the DataFrame. Hence, a DataFrame is composed of a distributed set of Row objects that share indices and data types, comprising the columns of the DataFrame.

```
df2.printSchema()
df2.show()
```

---

[10] https://spark.apache.org/docs/3.3.0/api/python/reference/pyspark.sql/io.html

```
root
 |-- name: string (nullable = true)
 |-- age: long (nullable = true)
+------+---+
|  name|age|
+------+---+
|Celine| 16|
|  Meng| 14|
|  John| 10|
| Debbi| 25|
|Zijian| 36|
|  Qian| 40|
+------+---+
```

As we did with the Row objects, we can access a column like an attribute or like a dictionary:

```
df2.name
```

```
Column<'name'>
```

```
df2["name"]
```

```
Column<'name'>
```

But perhaps you're a bit disappointed with the above outputs because we didn't get the column of data, but just the name of the column (an object of class Column in Spark). So, how do we get the actual content? You should understand the Column object as an *SQL expression* that needs to be evaluated to get the actual content (we will also refer to them as Column expressions). So, you need to perform an operation like select() with that Column. We will see this in the next section, but let's illustrate it with an example.

```
df2.select(df2["name"]).show()
```

```
+------+
|  name|
+------+
|Celine|
|  Meng|
|  John|
| Debbi|
|Zijian|
|  Qian|
+------+
```

> Don't expect to get the actual content of a column as a Python list unless you collect the DataFrame. Row elements are still distributed even if you decide to work with a single column.

That was a very simple Column object, but these objects can be more complex expressions than just a column name. Now we will deep dive into DataFrame operations and Column expressions.

5.3.2   Operations with DataFrames

As we have just anticipated with `select()`, there are different operations that can be carried out with DataFrames. Similar to RDDs, we distinguish two types of operations with DataFrames:

- A **transformation** creates a new DataFrame using lazy evaluation, i.e., there is no computation until an action is triggered.
- An **action** uses a DataFrame to return a result to the driver (or to save it to disk).

> In Spark SQL there are various ways to perform the same operations, some with a more OOP style, others more like SQL. Use the style you feel more comfortable with.

> Many of the things we learned about RDDs (fault tolerance through a lineage, lazy evaluations, immutable objects) are true for DataFrames.

5.3.3   Transformations

The transformations that can be applied to DataFrames look similar to SQL operations, but they still behave in a similar way, building a new DataFrame when an action is triggered. That is, DataFrames remain immutable (transformations don't change their content but create new ones). Let's start by understanding the most basic transformations we can perform.

Basic Transformations

Table 5.1 provides a list of the most basic transformations with DataFrames and their descriptions. Let's investigate these transformations using the same sample Data Frame:

```
tuples = [('Celine', 16), ('Meng', 14), ('John', 10),\
          ('Debbi', 25), ('Zijian', 36), ('Qian', 40)]
df = spark.createDataFrame(tuples, ['name', 'age'])
```

select(*cols)

Use `select()` to create a new DataFrame with the content of another DataFrame.

```
df.select('*').show() # select all columns
```

```
+------+---+
|  name|age|
+------+---+
|Celine| 16|
|  Meng| 14|
|  John| 10|
| Debbi| 25|
|Zijian| 36|
|  Qian| 40|
+------+---+
```

Table 5.1 Basic DataFrame transformations.

Transformation	Description
select(*cols)	Returns a new DataFrame using a series of expressions that could be column names or Column objects. If * is used, all the columns of the DataFrame are returned.
selectExpr(*expr)	Variation of select to allow for SQL expressions in String format.
filter(condition) where(condition)	Filter the rows according to a condition.
orderBy(*cols,**kwargs) sort(*cols,**kwargs)	Returns a new DataFrame sorted by the specified columns (in ascending order by default).

> Remember that we are applying the show() action just to understand what the transformation is doing, otherwise it wouldn't be executed.

You can select a particular column in different, though equivalent, ways:

```
df.select('age').show(2)
```

```
+---+
|age|
+---+
| 16|
| 14|
+---+
only showing top 2 rows
```

```
df.select(df.age).show(2)
```

```
+---+
|age|
+---+
| 16|
| 14|
+---+
only showing top 2 rows
```

```
df.select(df['age']).show(2)
```

```
+---+
|age|
+---+
| 16|
| 14|
+---+
only showing top 2 rows
```

Sometimes it may be very useful to refer to a column you have just created by its name but not referring to the DataFrame. You can use the SQL function col() for this. To access this function, we will use the alias sql_f.

```
df.select(sql_f.col('age')).show(2)
```

```
+---+
|age|
+---+
| 16|
| 14|
+---+
only showing top 2 rows
```

With `select()` we can alter a column by applying an operation to it. This example adds 10 years to everybody's age:

```
df.select(df.name, (df.age + 10)).show()
```

```
+------+----------+
|  name|(age + 10)|
+------+----------+
|Celine|        26|
|  Meng|        24|
|  John|        20|
| Debbi|        35|
|Zijian|        46|
|  Qian|        50|
+------+----------+
```

If you wish to change the name (currently age+10) while creating this new DataFrame, you could use the `alias()` method.

```
df.select(df.name, (df.age + 10).alias('age')).show()
```

```
+------+---+
|  name|age|
+------+---+
|Celine| 26|
|  Meng| 24|
|  John| 20|
| Debbi| 35|
|Zijian| 46|
|  Qian| 50|
+------+---+
```

> You can understand `select()` as the `map()` equivalent in DataFrames. It works completely in parallel taking each Row and applying the necessary operations to generate a new Row, which can contain a subset of columns, but also additional columns obtained by transforming existing ones.

`selectExpr(*expr)`

This is the same as `select()` but allowing for SQL expressions directly written as strings. This might look a bit funny:

```
df.selectExpr("age * 2 as twice", "abs(age)").show()
```

```
+-----+--------+
|twice|abs(age)|
+-----+--------+
|   32|      16|
|   28|      14|
|   20|      10|
|   50|      25|
|   72|      36|
|   80|      40|
+-----+--------+
```

filter(condition) ≡ where(condition)

filter() and where() are the same transformation and they are very similar to what we did with RDDs. Remember that we can follow two different styles. In OOP style we can write:

```
df.filter(df.age > 18).show()
```

```
+------+---+
|  name|age|
+------+---+
| Debbi| 25|
|Zijian| 36|
|  Qian| 40|
+------+---+
```

```
df.where(df.age == 14).show()
```

```
+----+---+
|name|age|
+----+---+
|Meng| 14|
+----+---+
```

And in SQL style:

```
df.filter("age > 18").show()
```

```
+------+---+
|  name|age|
+------+---+
| Debbi| 25|
|Zijian| 36|
|  Qian| 40|
+------+---+
```

```
df.where("age = 14").show()
```

```
+----+---+
|name|age|
+----+---+
|Meng| 14|
+----+---+
```

Both styles do the same; choose the one you feel more comfortable with!

orderBy(*cols, ascending) ≡ sort(*cols, **kwargs)
Again, both transformations do the same and share parameters. We first indicate the columns that will be used to sort the DataFrame. Then, there are different ways to tell Spark how we want to sort them (ascending or descending).

Let's do it in descending order by age:

```
df.sort(df.age.desc()).show()
```

```
+------+---+
|  name|age|
+------+---+
|  Qian| 40|
|Zijian| 36|
| Debbi| 25|
|Celine| 16|
|  Meng| 14|
|  John| 10|
+------+---+
```

We just used the OOP style to access the age attribute and the function desc() to sort it. The SQL-style counterpart would be:

```
df.sort("age", ascending=False).show()
```

```
+------+---+
|  name|age|
+------+---+
|  Qian| 40|
|Zijian| 36|
| Debbi| 25|
|Celine| 16|
|  Meng| 14|
|  John| 10|
+------+---+
```

Alternatively, you could do the very same thing using orderBy():

```
df.orderBy(df.age.desc()).show()
```

```
+------+---+
|  name|age|
+------+---+
|  Qian| 40|
|Zijian| 36|
| Debbi| 25|
|Celine| 16|
|  Meng| 14|
|  John| 10|
+------+---+
```

There are other alternatives using SQL functions. For example, ascending order by age:

```
df.sort(sql_f.asc("age")).show()
```

```
+------+---+
|  name|age|
+------+---+
|  John| 10|
|  Meng| 14|
|Celine| 16|
| Debbi| 25|
|Zijian| 36|
|  Qian| 40|
+------+---+
```

Or sorting it in descending order by age but ascending by name:

```
df.orderBy(sql_f.desc("age"), "name").show()
```

```
+------+---+
|  name|age|
+------+---+
|  Qian| 40|
|Zijian| 36|
| Debbi| 25|
|Celine| 16|
|  Meng| 14|
|  John| 10|
+------+---+
```

Alternatively:

```
df.orderBy(["age", "name"], ascending=[False, True]).show()
```

```
+------+---+
|  name|age|
+------+---+
|  Qian| 40|
|Zijian| 36|
| Debbi| 25|
|Celine| 16|
|  Meng| 14|
|  John| 10|
+------+---+
```

Additional Transformations

Let's investigate some additional transformations one by one (Table 5.2).

distinct() and dropDuplicates(*cols)

The difference between these two operations is that in dropDuplicates() we can specify the fields to consider if two rows are duplicated.

We create a DataFrame from an RDD of Rows with attributes name, profession, and age:

Table 5.2 Additional DataFrame transformations.

Transformation	Description
distinct()	Returns a new DataFrame with the unique rows of the original one.
dropDuplicates(*cols)	Returns a new DataFrame without duplicates, only considering the columns specified.
withColumn(colName,col)	Returns a new DataFrame, adding a new column or replacing an existing column with the given name.
withColumnRenamed (<existing>, <new>)	Returns a new DataFrame renaming an existing column.
drop(col)	Returns a new DataFrame without the specified column.
limit(num)	Limits the number of rows obtained as a result.
cache()	Keeps the DataFrame cached for future reuse.

```
from pyspark.sql import Row
df2 = sc.parallelize([ \
    Row(name='Isaac', profession='lecturer', age=36), \
    Row(name='Mikel', profession='lecturer', age=36), \
    Row(name='Isaac', profession='lecturer', age=36)]).toDF()
```

```
df2.show()
```

```
+-----+----------+---+
| name|profession|age|
+-----+----------+---+
|Isaac|  lecturer| 36|
|Mikel|  lecturer| 36|
|Isaac|  lecturer| 36|
+-----+----------+---+
```

If we apply distinct() or dropDuplicates() directly, we see the same output:

```
df2.distinct().show()
```

```
+-----+----------+---+
| name|profession|age|
+-----+----------+---+
|Isaac|  lecturer| 36|
|Mikel|  lecturer| 36|
+-----+----------+---+
```

```
df2.dropDuplicates().show()
```

```
+-----+----------+---+
| name|profession|age|
+-----+----------+---+
|Isaac|  lecturer| 36|
```

```
|Mikel|  lecturer| 36|
+-----+----------+---+
```

Above, `dropDuplicates()` and `distinct()` had exactly the same behavior; however, we can tell `dropDuplicates()` to only consider two of the fields:

```
df2.dropDuplicates(['profession', 'age']).show()
```

```
+-----+----------+---+
| name|profession|age|
+-----+----------+---+
|Isaac|  lecturer| 36|
+-----+----------+---+
```

According to `profession` and age, all of the Rows were redundant, so we end up with only one row.

drop(col)

This transformation removes the column but doesn't modify the input DataFrame (as they are immutable). It returns the DataFrame without a column.

Let's remove the age column in `df`:

```
df.drop('age').show()
```

```
+------+
|  name|
+------+
|Celine|
|  Meng|
|  John|
| Debbi|
|Zijian|
|  Qian|
+------+
```

And in OOP style:

```
df.drop(df.age).show()
```

```
+------+
|  name|
+------+
|Celine|
|  Meng|
|  John|
| Debbi|
|Zijian|
|  Qian|
+------+
```

`df` remains unchanged!

```
df.show()
```

```
+------+---+
|  name|age|
+------+---+
|Celine| 16|
|  Meng| 14|
|  John| 10|
| Debbi| 25|
|Zijian| 36|
|  Qian| 40|
+------+---+
```

limit(num)

You can indicate the number of Rows you want to get before applying an action:

```
df.limit(1).show()
```

```
+------+---+
|  name|age|
+------+---+
|Celine| 16|
+------+---+
```

```
df.limit(0).show()
```

```
+----+---+
|name|age|
+----+---+
+----+---+
```

withColumn(colName, col)

Similarly to what we did before with select(), we can add a column indicating a name and a Column expression to create the new column.

```
df.withColumn('after birthday', df.age + 1).show()
```

```
+------+---+--------------+
|  name|age|after birthday|
+------+---+--------------+
|Celine| 16|            17|
|  Meng| 14|            15|
|  John| 10|            11|
| Debbi| 25|            26|
|Zijian| 36|            37|
|  Qian| 40|            41|
+------+---+--------------+
```

We may be interested in creating a column with a value for the entire column. We can use this transformation with lit() (from pyspark.sql.functions) to indicate this.

```
df.withColumn('all ones', sql_f.lit(1)).show()
```

```
+------+---+--------+
|  name|age|all ones|
+------+---+--------+
|Celine| 16|       1|
|  Meng| 14|       1|
|  John| 10|       1|
| Debbi| 25|       1|
|Zijian| 36|       1|
|  Qian| 40|       1|
+------+---+--------+
```

withColumnRenamed(existing, new)
You can rename the columns:

```
df.withColumnRenamed('age', 'age renamed').show()
```

```
+------+-----------+
|  name|age renamed|
+------+-----------+
|Celine|         16|
|  Meng|         14|
|  John|         10|
| Debbi|         25|
|Zijian|         36|
|  Qian|         40|
+------+-----------+
```

Transformations: Column Operations

We have already given you a hint of what Column objects are: SQL expressions that can be applied to DataFrames inside a transformation. Spark SQL provides us with several functions/operations that can be applied to Column objects that only return another Column, that is, an SQL expression. The key here is that to apply a Column operation to a DataFrame, *they must be used in conjunction with another transformation* such as select(). Note that they are not applied on a DataFrame directly either; for example, df.alias() wouldn't work.

Let's check a few important methods from the Column API.[11] Table 5.3 describes some of these methods.

alias(*alias)
With alias() we can change the name of a column:

```
df.name.alias("Hello")
```

```
Column<'name AS Hello'>
```

This hasn't done anything at all in df, nor has it returned a new DataFrame. It only returns that Column expression that can be used to modify the name. So we must apply this inside a transformation.

[11] https://spark.apache.org/docs/3.3.0/api/python/reference/pyspark.sql/column.html

Table 5.3 Some relevant Column operations.

Operation	Description
alias(*alias)	Returns a column with a new name.
between (<lowerBound>, <upperBound>)	Returns true if the value is in the range specified.
isNull()	Returns true if the value is null.
isNotNull()	Returns true if the value is not null.
when(condition,value) otherwise(value)	Evaluate a list of conditions and perform a transformation based on those.
length(col)	Returns the length of the column.
substring(startPos,len) like(other) startswith(other) endswith(other)	These functions operate on strings.
expr(str)	Parses the input string into the column that it represents.
isin(*cols)	Returns true if the value is in the list of arguments.
lit(value)	Creates a column with the value provided.
explode(col)	Returns a new row for each element of the array.

```
df.select(df.name.alias("Hello")).show()
```

```
+------+
| Hello|
+------+
|Celine|
|  Meng|
|  John|
| Debbi|
|Zijian|
|  Qian|
+------+
```

Again, df is not modified, but a new DataFrame is returned with the column name changed to Hello.

> Column operations follow an OOP style. If you want to use SQL style, you can write the SQL expression.

```
df.selectExpr("name as Hello").show()
```

```
+------+
| Hello|
+------+
|Celine|
```

```
|  Meng|
|  John|
| Debbi|
|Zijian|
|  Qian|
+------+
```

between(lowerBound, upperBound)

Let's get the people with ages between 18 and 65. We could use a Column expression like this . . .

```
df.age.between(18, 65)
```

```
Column<'((age >= 18) AND (age <= 65))'>
```

. . . and use it as part of a transformation (i.e., select()):

```
df.select(df.name, df.age.between(18, 64)).show()
```

```
+------+----------------------------+
|  name|((age >= 18) AND (age <= 64))|
+------+----------------------------+
|Celine|                       false|
|  Meng|                       false|
|  John|                       false|
| Debbi|                        true|
|Zijian|                        true|
|  Qian|                        true|
+------+----------------------------+
```

This operation has returned a DataFrame with a new column that checks the condition and returns true or false. But we could also use that Column expression to filter those that are false instead:

```
df.filter(df.age.between(18, 64)).show()
```

```
+------+---+
|  name|age|
+------+---+
| Debbi| 25|
|Zijian| 36|
|  Qian| 40|
+------+---+
```

isNull() / isNotNull()

Similarly, we can check whether the values in a column are null or not:

```
df.age.isNull()
```

```
Column<'(age IS NULL)'>
```

```
df.age.isNotNull()
```

```
Column<'(age IS NOT NULL)'>
```

Using this operation in combination with a transformation, for example `filter()`, we can get those rows with null values in a specific column . . .

```
df.filter(df.age.isNull()).show()
```

```
+----+---+
|name|age|
+----+---+
+----+---+
```

. . . which is an empty DataFrame because all Rows of `df` have values for the `age` column.

`when(condition, value)` / `otherwise(value)`
This is similar to an if–else structure. In this case, we need to start the first condition with the function `when()` from `pyspark.sql.functions`.

We could define a condition that says that a person is an adult if their age is greater than 18, and a kid otherwise:

```
sql_f.when(df.age > 18, "Adult").otherwise("Kid")
```

```
Column<'CASE WHEN (age > 18) THEN Adult ELSE Kid END'>
```

Again, you use this in conjunction with a transformation:

```
df.select(df.name, sql_f.when(df.age > 18, 'Adult')\
                 .otherwise('Kid').alias('category')).show()
```

```
+------+--------+
|  name|category|
+------+--------+
|Celine|     Kid|
|  Meng|     Kid|
|  John|     Kid|
| Debbi|   Adult|
|Zijian|   Adult|
|  Qian|   Adult|
+------+--------+
```

You can concatenate multiple conditions:

```
df.select(df.name, df.age, sql_f.when(df.age > 18, 'Adult')\
                    .when(df.age < 12, 'Kid')\
                    .otherwise('Teenager').alias('category')).show()
```

```
+------+---+--------+
|  name|age|category|
+------+---+--------+
|Celine| 16|Teenager|
|  Meng| 14|Teenager|
|  John| 10|     Kid|
| Debbi| 25|   Adult|
|Zijian| 36|   Adult|
|  Qian| 40|   Adult|
+------+---+--------+
```

length(col)

You can use the length() on a column of strings to compute their lengths (again using sql_f to access the function):

```
sql_f.length(df.name)
```

```
Column<'length(name)'>
```

```
df.select(sql_f.length(df.name).alias('len')).show()
```

```
+---+
|len|
+---+
|  6|
|  4|
|  4|
|  5|
|  6|
|  4|
+---+
```

substring(startPos, len), like(other), startswith(other), endswith(other)

These are common operations for working with strings, but are implemented in Spark so that you can take advantage of the optimizations. Let's test some them:

```
df.withColumn('Abbr', sql_f.substring(df.name,1, 3)).show()
```

```
+------+---+----+
|  name|age|Abbr|
+------+---+----+
|Celine| 16| Cel|
|  Meng| 14| Men|
|  John| 10| Joh|
| Debbi| 25| Deb|
|Zijian| 36| Zij|
|  Qian| 40| Qia|
+------+---+----+
```

```
df.filter(df.name.like('J%')).show()
```

```
+----+---+
|name|age|
+----+---+
|John| 10|
+----+---+
```

expr(str)

This function parses a string into the column it represents. For example, instead of using the length() function as before, we could do it like this:

```
df.select(sql_f.expr("length(name)")).show()
```

```
+------------+
|length(name)|
+------------+
|           6|
|           4|
|           4|
|           5|
|           6|
|           4|
+------------+
```

This doesn't seem very useful, right? Well, it may come in handy on some occasions. Let us show you an example.

We want to use the previous substring() function to remove the first letter of all the names. This function requires the start position (i.e., the character index, which would be 2 for us to remove the first one), and the length of that substring (both should be Integer!). However, the length of the string depends on each name; should we try to use the Column operation length() inside?

```
df.withColumn('Without first letter',
              sql_f.substring(df.name,2, sql_f.length(df.name)))\
  .show()
```

```
TypeError Traceback (most recent call last)
Input In [284], in <cell line: 1>()  1 df.withColumn('Without first letter',\
----> 2 sql_f.substring(df.name,2, sql_f.length(df.name)))\  3 .show()
...
```

That didn't quite work! Why? well, the parameter len of the function substring was meant to be an integer and not a Column object. In this case, using expressions would be useful as it would allow us to use Column values as input to these functions.

```
df.withColumn('Without first letter',\
              sql_f.expr("substring(name, 2, length(name))"))\
  .show()
```

```
+------+---+--------------------+
|  name|age|Without first letter|
+------+---+--------------------+
|Celine| 16|               eline|
|  Meng| 14|                 eng|
|  John| 10|                 ohn|
| Debbi| 25|                ebbi|
|Zijian| 36|               ijian|
|  Qian| 40|                 ian|
+------+---+--------------------+
```

isin(*cols)
This allows us to check whether specific values are in the DataFrame. For example, we can see if our names or our friend Jack's name are in the DataFrame:

```
df.name.isin("Márcio", "Grazziela", "Celine")
```

```
Column<'(name IN (Márcio, Grazziela, Celine))'>
```

We could use filter() or select().

```
df.filter(df.name.isin("Márcio", "Grazziela", "Celine")).show()
```

```
+------+---+
|  name|age|
+------+---+
|Celine| 16|
+------+---+
```

Or alternatively, you can use square brackets [] (more similar to pandas).

```
df[df.name.isin("Márcio", "Grazziela", "Celine")].show()
```

```
+------+---+
|  name|age|
+------+---+
|Celine| 16|
+------+---+
```

lit(value)

As we introduced earlier, it can be helpful to produce a column of literal values:

```
sql_f.lit(0)
```

```
Column<'0'>
```

What is that useful for? Maybe to add a new column (that we rename as "balance")
with zeros:

```
df.select("*", sql_f.lit(0).alias("balance")).show()
```

```
+------+---+-------+
|  name|age|balance|
+------+---+-------+
|Celine| 16|      0|
|  Meng| 14|      0|
|  John| 10|      0|
| Debbi| 25|      0|
|Zijian| 36|      0|
|  Qian| 40|      0|
+------+---+-------+
```

explode(col)

This is an important operation that can simulate the use of flatMap() in RDDs because
it creates as many rows as values that are contained in an array, or a dictionary inside
a column.

It basically *expands* a list, tuple, or dictionary into rows. Let's follow our hobbies
example.

```
df3 = spark.createDataFrame([
    Row(name='Direnc', hobbies=["Lifting", "Running", "Reading"],
        avatar={"hair": "black","hair_length": "short"}),
    Row(name='Lam', hobbies=["Triathlon", "Running", "Cycling"],
        avatar={"hair": "blond","hair_length": "very short"}),
    Row(name='Rebecca', hobbies=["Singing", "Dancing"],
        avatar={"hair": "brown","hair_length": "large"}),
    Row(name='Edwina', hobbies=["Running", "Music"],
        avatar={"hair": "red","hair_length": "middle"})
])
df3.show()
```

```
+-------+------------------+------------------+
|   name|           hobbies|            avatar|
+-------+------------------+------------------+
| Direnc|[Lifting, Running...|{hair_length -> s...|
|    Lam|[Triathlon, Runni...|{hair_length -> v...|
|Rebecca|  [Singing, Dancing]|{hair_length -> l...|
| Edwina|     [Running, Music]|{hair_length -> m...|
+-------+------------------+------------------+
```

To expand the list hobbies as rows, that is, having a row for each hobby:

```
df3.select("*", sql_f.explode("hobbies")).show()
```

```
+-------+------------------+------------------+---------+
|   name|           hobbies|            avatar|      col|
+-------+------------------+------------------+---------+
| Direnc|[Lifting, Running...|{hair_length -> s...|  Lifting|
| Direnc|[Lifting, Running...|{hair_length -> s...|  Running|
| Direnc|[Lifting, Running...|{hair_length -> s...|  Reading|
|    Lam|[Triathlon, Runni...|{hair_length -> v...|Triathlon|
|    Lam|[Triathlon, Runni...|{hair_length -> v...|  Running|
|    Lam|[Triathlon, Runni...|{hair_length -> v...|  Cycling|
|Rebecca|  [Singing, Dancing]|{hair_length -> l...|  Singing|
|Rebecca|  [Singing, Dancing]|{hair_length -> l...|  Dancing|
| Edwina|     [Running, Music]|{hair_length -> m...|  Running|
| Edwina|     [Running, Music]|{hair_length -> m...|    Music|
+-------+------------------+------------------+---------+
```

As we used the *, columns name, hobbies, and avatar remain the same but are duplicated in each row. There is now a new column col that contains the elements of hobbies exploded (just one element in each row). We could actually give it a new name with alias:

```
df3.select("*", sql_f.explode("hobbies").alias("new_explode")).show()
```

```
+-------+------------------+------------------+-----------+
|   name|           hobbies|            avatar|new_explode|
+-------+------------------+------------------+-----------+
| Direnc|[Lifting, Running...|{hair_length -> s...|    Lifting|
| Direnc|[Lifting, Running...|{hair_length -> s...|    Running|
| Direnc|[Lifting, Running...|{hair_length -> s...|    Reading|
|    Lam|[Triathlon, Runni...|{hair_length -> v...|  Triathlon|
|    Lam|[Triathlon, Runni...|{hair_length -> v...|    Running|
|    Lam|[Triathlon, Runni...|{hair_length -> v...|    Cycling|
```

```
|Rebecca|   [Singing, Dancing]|{hair_length -> l...|      Singing|
|Rebecca|   [Singing, Dancing]|{hair_length -> l...|      Dancing|
| Edwina|     [Running, Music]|{hair_length -> m...|      Running|
| Edwina|     [Running, Music]|{hair_length -> m...|        Music|
+-------+--------------------+--------------------+-----------+
```

If we just wanted to get the list of hobbies in a column, to measure their popularity:

```
df3.select(sql_f.explode(df3.hobbies).alias("hobbies")).show()
```

```
+---------+
|  hobbies|
+---------+
|  Lifting|
|  Running|
|  Reading|
|Triathlon|
|  Running|
|  Cycling|
|  Singing|
|  Dancing|
|  Running|
|    Music|
+---------+
```

This will be very useful to perform our favorite big data exercise, Word Count!

We can also apply `explode()` to dictionaries like the one in `avatar`:

```
df3.select("name", sql_f.explode(df3.avatar).alias("key", "value")).show()
```

```
+-------+-----------+----------+
|   name|        key|     value|
+-------+-----------+----------+
| Direnc|hair_length|     short|
| Direnc|       hair|     black|
|    Lam|hair_length|very short|
|    Lam|       hair|     blond|
|Rebecca|hair_length|     large|
|Rebecca|       hair|     brown|
| Edwina|hair_length|    middle|
| Edwina|       hair|       red|
+-------+-----------+----------+
```

> Many of the operations that we have shown here with Column expressions could be performed by Python functions working with RDDs, and you know how to get the RDD from a DataFrame. However, you should stick to the DataFrame API and Column expressions as much as you can so that Spark can perform its optimizations. Moving back to RDDs will make you lose the performance gains.

Transformations with Pseudo-Sets

Similar to RDDs, you can do set-like operations with a DataFrame (Table 5.4). Let's try them with the same example from the previous chapter.

Table 5.4 Transformations with pseudo-sets.

Transformation	Description
distinct()	Returns a new DataFrame with the unique rows of the original one.
union(df)	Returns the union of the elements of two DataFrames (keeping duplicates).
intersect(df)	Returns the union of the elements of two DataFrames (removing duplicates). **Warning:** This requires a shuffle!
subtract(df)	Returns a DataFrame with the elements present in the first DataFrame but not in the second one. **Warning:** This requires a shuffle!
crossJoin(df)	Returns a DataFrame with the cartesian product of both DataFrames (all possible pairs of rows of both).

```
df1 = spark.createDataFrame(["water", "wine", "beer",\
                    "water", "water", "wine"], "string")
df2 = spark.createDataFrame(["beer", "beer", "water", "water",\
                    "wine", "coca-cola", "lemonade"], "string")
```

As we have already seen `distinct()` can remove duplicates from DataFrames.

```
df1.distinct().show()
```

```
+-----+
|value|
+-----+
|water|
| wine|
| beer|
+-----+
```

With `union()`, we can concatenate the rows of two DataFrames into a single one (they need to have compatible schemas). Similarly, `intersect()` will just retain Row elements present in both DataFrames, whereas `substract()` will only get those present in the first DataFrame.

```
df1.union(df2).show()
```

```
+---------+
|    value|
+---------+
|    water|
|     wine|
|     beer|
|    water|
|    water|
|     wine|
|     beer|
```

```
|     beer|
|    water|
|    water|
|     wine|
|coca-cola|
| lemonade|
+---------+
```

```
df1.intersect(df2).show()
```

```
+-----+
|value|
+-----+
|water|
| wine|
| beer|
+-----+
```

```
df1.subtract(df2).show()
```

```
+-----+
|value|
+-----+
+-----+
```

As with RDDs, both `substract()` and `intersect()` remove duplicates and require a shuffle (like `distinct()`), so they can have performance issues.

We can also get the cartesian product of the rows in two DataFrames with `crossJoin()`. This is not really recommended if you can avoid it as it generates lots of data.

```
df1.distinct().crossJoin(df2.distinct()).show()
```

```
+-----+---------+
|value|    value|
+-----+---------+
|water|     beer|
| wine|     beer|
| beer|     beer|
|water|    water|
| wine|    water|
| beer|    water|
|water|     wine|
| wine|     wine|
| beer|     wine|
|water|coca-cola|
| wine|coca-cola|
| beer|coca-cola|
|water| lemonade|
| wine| lemonade|
| beer| lemonade|
+-----+---------+
```

Table 5.5 Transformations to perform aggregations.

Transformation	Description
agg(*exprs)	Performs aggregations over the entire DataFrame; exprs can be a dictionary or a list of expressions.
groupBy(*cols)	Groups a DataFrame using the specified columns (GroupedData) to perform aggregations over those groups.

Transformations to Perform Aggregations

We will now see how to perform aggregations for numerical data in a DataFrame and how to perform these aggregations on data that has previously been grouped together (Table 5.5).

agg(*exprs)

With this method we can perform aggregations over the entire DataFrame. This means that we can, for example, compute the average or sum of values over a column. The aggregations we can compute are avg, max, min, sum, and count.

The argument *exprs can be either a key–value dictionary in which the key is the name of a column and the value an aggregation function, or a list of Column expressions with aggregations.

With a dictionary we can do something like:

```
df.agg({"age": "max"}).show()
```

```
+--------+
|max(age)|
+--------+
|      40|
+--------+
```

Or we can use a Column expression with the function max() from Spark SQL (be careful not to use the one from Python!):

```
df.agg(sql_f.max(df.age)).show()
```

```
+--------+
|max(age)|
+--------+
|      40|
+--------+
```

If we wanted to get different aggregations, for example, min and max for age, a dictionary wouldn't quite work:

```
df.agg({"age": "max", "age": "min"}).show()
```

```
+--------+
|min(age)|
+--------+
|      10|
+--------+
```

We should use a list of expressions:

```
df.agg(sql_f.min(df.age), sql_f.max(df.age),\
       sql_f.mean(df.age)).show()
```

```
+--------+--------+--------+
|min(age)|max(age)|avg(age)|
+--------+--------+--------+
|      10|      40|    23.5|
+--------+--------+--------+
```

groupBy(*cols)

This operation groups together the rows of a DataFrame with the same values in the specified columns. It creates a `GroupedData`[12] object that can later be used to compute aggregations by groups, using, for example, the previous function `agg()`.

For example, we can group our DataFrame by name, and for each name we can count the number of repetitions and the average age. Let us first get a more complete DataFrame:

```
df.show()
```

```
+------+---+
|  name|age|
+------+---+
|Celine| 16|
|  Meng| 14|
|  John| 10|
| Debbi| 25|
|Zijian| 36|
|  Qian| 40|
+------+---+
```

```
tuples2 = [('Nasser', 25), ('Nasser', 45),('Debbi', 20),\
           ('Grazziela', 12), ('Khivishta', 10)]
df2 = spark.createDataFrame(tuples2, ['name', 'age'])
df3 = df.union(df2)
df3.show()
```

```
+---------+---+
|     name|age|
+---------+---+
|   Celine| 16|
|     Meng| 14|
|     John| 10|
|    Debbi| 25|
|   Zijian| 36|
|     Qian| 40|
|   Nasser| 25|
|   Nasser| 45|
|    Debbi| 20|
|Grazziela| 12|
|Khivishta| 10|
+---------+---+
```

---

[12] https://spark.apache.org/docs/3.3.0/api/python/reference/pyspark.sql/grouping.html

```
df3.groupBy('name')
```

```
<pyspark.sql.group.GroupedData at 0x7fb1154fec10>
```

This data type cannot be collected:

```
df3.groupBy('name').collect()
```

```
AttributeError Traceback (most recent call last)
Input In [355], in <cell line: 1>() ----> 1 df3.groupBy ('name').collect()
...
```

There are different transformations that can be applied for this data type. For example, we can directly use count() or avg(), but we can also perform aggregations using agg():

```
df3.groupBy('name').count().show()
```

```
+---------+-----+
|     name|count|
+---------+-----+
|   Celine|    1|
|     Meng|    1|
|     John|    1|
|    Debbi|    2|
|   Zijian|    1|
|     Qian|    1|
|   Nasser|    2|
|Grazziela|    1|
|Khivishta|    1|
+---------+-----+
```

Note that we had to use show() after count(), because that count() function on GroupedData is *not* an action!

```
df3.groupBy("name").agg(sql_f.mean(df3.age), sql_f.count(df3.age)).show()
```

```
+---------+--------+----------+
|     name|avg(age)|count(age)|
+---------+--------+----------+
|   Celine|    16.0|         1|
|     Meng|    14.0|         1|
|     John|    10.0|         1|
|    Debbi|    22.5|         2|
|   Zijian|    36.0|         1|
|     Qian|    40.0|         1|
|   Nasser|    35.0|         2|
|Grazziela|    12.0|         1|
|Khivishta|    10.0|         1|
+---------+--------+----------+
```

> Using count() or agg() will depend on whether or not you need to calculate more than one aggregation at a time. If yes, you need to stick to agg().

Table 5.6 Transformations for `GroupedData`.

Transformation	Description
`avg(*cols)` `mean(*cols)`	Calculate the average value for each group in each numeric column.
`count()`	Counts the number of rows for each group.
`max(*cols)`	Calculates the maximum for each group in each numeric column specified.
`min(*cols)`	Calculates the minimum for each group in each numeric column specified.
`sum(*cols)`	Calculates the sum for each group in each numeric column specified.
`pivot(pivot_col,values)`	Pivots over a column of the DataFrame to perform a specific aggregation.
`agg(*exprs)`	As before, but for each group of the DataFrame.

Table 5.6 presents descriptions of the different transformations you can use for `GroupedData`. Most of them are straightforward to apply based on their description, but we want to show you an example with `pivot()`.

`pivot(pivot_col, values)`
This transformation allows you to pivot over a column to then perform an aggregation. This is similar to a pivot table in pandas (if you are familiar with it). The `pivot_col` argument indicates the column in which we want to pivot. Pivoting means that the unique or indicated values of the column will be used to create new columns in the resulting DataFrame. The `values` argument specifies which values will appear in the columns of the resulting DataFrame. If not provided, Spark computes it automatically (though this is less efficient!).

If you are not familiar with pivot tables, you will understand them better with an example. Let's say we have a big table of marks for each student that looks like this:

```
data = [(2021,'Nasser', 67, 60, 'COMP4008'),
        (2021,'Nasser', 67, 25, 'COMP4103'),
        (2021,'Khivishta', 34, 70, 'COMP4008'),
        (2021,'Khivishta', 34, 95, 'COMP4103'),
        (2022,'Heda Song', 67, 60, 'COMP4008'),
        (2022,'Heda Song', 67, 25, 'COMP4103'),
        (2022,'Selvi', 34, 70, 'COMP4008'),
        (2022,'Selvi', 34, 95, 'COMP4103') ]

df = spark.createDataFrame(data, ['year', 'name', 'age',\
                                  'grade', 'module_name'])

df.show()
```

```
+----+---------+---+-----+-----------+
|year|     name|age|grade|module_name|
+----+---------+---+-----+-----------+
|2021|   Nasser| 67|   60|   COMP4008|
|2021|   Nasser| 67|   25|   COMP4103|
|2021|Khivishta| 34|   70|   COMP4008|
|2021|Khivishta| 34|   95|   COMP4103|
|2022|Heda Song| 67|   60|   COMP4008|
|2022|Heda Song| 67|   25|   COMP4103|
|2022|    Selvi| 34|   70|   COMP4008|
|2022|    Selvi| 34|   95|   COMP4103|
+----+---------+---+-----+-----------+
```

How could we compute the average mark for each year in each module? You will be thinking that you could do this with just a `groupBy()`. That's true:

```
df.groupBy("year", "module_name").avg("grade").show()
```

```
+----+-----------+----------+
|year|module_name|avg(grade)|
+----+-----------+----------+
|2021|   COMP4008|      65.0|
|2021|   COMP4103|      60.0|
|2022|   COMP4008|      65.0|
|2022|   COMP4103|      60.0|
+----+-----------+----------+
```

However, if we want to get a table that's easier to interpret, where the different columns contain the module names while the rows are used for the years, we can use a pivot table. We indicate that we want to pivot with respect to the module name:

```
df.groupBy("year").pivot("module_name").avg("grade").show()
```

```
+----+--------+--------+
|year|COMP4008|COMP4103|
+----+--------+--------+
|2021|    65.0|    60.0|
|2022|    65.0|    60.0|
+----+--------+--------+
```

Remember that if you don't specify the values in the pivoting column, Spark will need to scan the column looking for unique values before computing the aggregation, and is thus less efficient. For this reason, we can also indicate the module names we want to consider for pivoting:

```
df.groupBy("year").pivot("module_name", ["COMP4008", "COMP4103"])\
                  .avg("grade").show()
```

```
+----+--------+--------+
|year|COMP4008|COMP4103|
+----+--------+--------+
|2021|    65.0|    60.0|
|2022|    65.0|    60.0|
+----+--------+--------+
```

Table 5.7 Join-like transformations with DataFrames.

Transformation	Description
join(other,on,how)	Joins two DataFrames.

Join-Like SQL Transformations

It may be obvious that in Spark SQL we are able to perform SQL join operations. As we showed in the previous chapter, SQL joins combine two tables (DataFrames in this case) based on a related column (or a set of related columns). With DataFrames, we just need to indicate the columns on which we want to do the join and the type of join (Table 5.7).

As far as the parameters of this transformation are concerned, other is the other DataFrame for the join; on is the name of the column on which to perform the join (it can also be a list of columns or a Column expression); and how is the type of join. The most common types are 'inner' (default), 'outer', 'left_outer', and 'right_outer'.

We will reuse our example from RDDs to test the different joins.

```
people = sc.parallelize([("Lam", 35), ("Direnc", 35),\
                        ("Rebecca", 24), ("Edwina", 25)])
hobbies = sc.parallelize([("Lam", ["Triathlon", "Running", "Cycling"]),
                        ("Direnc", ["Lifting", "Running", "Reading"]),
                        ("Rebecca", ["Singing", "Dancing"]),
                        ("Grazziela", ["Running", "Music"])])
people_df = spark.createDataFrame(people, ["name", "age"])
hobbies_df = spark.createDataFrame(hobbies, ["name", "hobbies"])
```

'inner' join

With this type of join, we combine the rows of two DataFrames that have matching values in the indicated columns. For example, we can get the age and hobbies of the people together in the same DataFrame. Note that 'inner' is the value for how by default, so we don't need to indicate it.

```
people_df.join(hobbies_df, 'name').show(truncate=False)
```

```
+-------+---+-----------------------------+
|name   |age|hobbies                      |
+-------+---+-----------------------------+
|Direnc |35 |[Lifting, Running, Reading]  |
|Lam    |35 |[Triathlon, Running, Cycling]|
|Rebecca|24 |[Singing, Dancing]           |
+-------+---+-----------------------------+
```

With 'inner', if there are rows in either of the DataFrames that don't match, they won't appear in the resulting DataFrame (we have lost Edwina's age and also Grazziela's hobbies).

'left_outer' join

This works like 'inner' except that we also get the rows from the first DataFrame that don't match with any from the second one. A null value is given to the columns of the second DataFrame. In this way, we get Edwina in our resulting DataFrame despite not having their hobbies.

```
people_df.join(hobbies_df, "name", "left_outer").show(truncate=False)
```

```
+-------+---+---------------------------+
|name   |age|hobbies                    |
+-------+---+---------------------------+
|Lam    |35 |[Triathlon, Running, Cycling]|
|Direnc |35 |[Lifting, Running, Reading]  |
|Rebecca|24 |[Singing, Dancing]           |
|Edwina |25 |null                         |
+-------+---+---------------------------+
```

'right_outer' join

This is just the same as 'left_outer', but the other way around: we maintain those rows in the second DataFrame not matching with any of the first one. In this case, we maintain Grazziela in our resulting DataFrame with a null value for the age column.

```
people_df.join(hobbies_df, "name", "right_outer").show(truncate=False)
```

```
+---------+----+---------------------------+
|name     |age |hobbies                    |
+---------+----+---------------------------+
|Lam      |35  |[Triathlon, Running, Cycling]|
|Direnc   |35  |[Lifting, Running, Reading]  |
|Rebecca  |24  |[Singing, Dancing]           |
|Grazziela|null|[Running, Music]             |
+---------+----+---------------------------+
```

'outer' join

This is like doing both 'left_outer' and 'right_outer' simultaneously, getting all the rows of the input DataFrames that don't match one way or the other with null values in the corresponding unmatched columns.

```
people_df.join(hobbies_df, "name", "outer").show(truncate=False)
```

```
+---------+----+---------------------------+
|name     |age |hobbies                    |
+---------+----+---------------------------+
|Direnc   |35  |[Lifting, Running, Reading]  |
|Edwina   |25  |null                         |
|Grazziela|null|[Running, Music]             |
|Lam      |35  |[Triathlon, Running, Cycling]|
|Rebecca  |24  |[Singing, Dancing]           |
+---------+----+---------------------------+
```

Table 5.8 Actions with DataFrames.

Action	Description
show(n=20,truncate=True)	Prints n rows of the DataFrame; truncate indicates whether strings should be cut if too long.
count()	Returns the number of rows in the DataFrame.
collect()	Returns all the rows of the DataFrame as a list of Rows. **Warning:** Should fit in the driver's main memory.
first()	Returns the first Row of the DataFrame.
take(n)	Returns the first n rows of the DataFrame as a list of Row elements.
toPandas()	Returns the content of the DataFrame as a pandas.DataFrame. **Warning:** Should fit in the driver's main memory.
columns	Returns the column names of the DataFrame as a list.
describe(*cols)	Provides some statistics for numeric columns (count, mean, standard deviation, minimum, and maximum.
explain(extended=False)	Prints out the physical and logical plans for debugging.

> With Spark SQL, we can perform joins using more than one column and also with Column expressions. Check the pyspark documentation[13] for more examples.

5.3.4   Actions on DataFrames

We have already been using some actions like show() and collect() to test transformations. We will now get to know some additional basic actions available in Spark SQL (Table 5.8).

You may have noticed that show() prints out the results but does not return anything. So, if you wanted to use its output for further calculations, it won't work. For example:

```
res = df.show()
print('res = ', res)
```

```
+----+---------+---+-----+-----------+
|year|     name|age|grade|module_name|
+----+---------+---+-----+-----------+
|2021|   Nasser| 67|   60|   COMP4008|
|2021|   Nasser| 67|   25|   COMP4103|
|2021| Khivishta| 34|   70|   COMP4008|
|2021| Khivishta| 34|   95|   COMP4103|
|2022| Heda Song| 67|   60|   COMP4008|
```

[13] spark.apache.org/docs/3.3.0/api/python/reference/pyspark.sql/api/pyspark.sql.DataFrame.join.html

```
|2022|Heda Song| 67|    25|    COMP4103|
|2022|    Selvi| 34|    70|    COMP4008|
|2022|    Selvi| 34|    95|    COMP4103|
+----+---------+---+-----+-----------+
res =   None
```

Therefore, if we need to work with a few rows, we suggest using take(), as we did with RDDs.

```
df.take(2)
```

```
[Row(year=2021, name='Nasser', age=67, grade=60, module_name='COMP4008'),
 Row(year=2021, name='Nasser', age=67, grade=25, module_name='COMP4103')]
```

If we just need a row, we can use first().

```
df.first()
```

```
Row(year=2021, name='Nasser', age=67, grade=60, module_name='COMP4008')
```

Remember that we can also collect the entire DataFrame, but we must be sure that it will fit in the main memory of the driver. This may be common after performing some group transformations followed by aggregations. We can use collect() as in RDDs, or toPandas() to get the Spark DataFrame as a pandas DataFrame.

```
df.collect()
```

```
[Row(year=2021, name='Nasser', age=67, grade=60, module_name='COMP4008'),
 Row(year=2021, name='Nasser', age=67, grade=25, module_name='COMP4103'),
 Row(year=2021, name='Khivishta', age=34, grade=70, module_name='COMP4008'),
 Row(year=2021, name='Khivishta', age=34, grade=95, module_name='COMP4103'),
 Row(year=2022, name='Heda Song', age=67, grade=60, module_name='COMP4008'),
 Row(year=2022, name='Heda Song', age=67, grade=25, module_name='COMP4103'),
 Row(year=2022, name='Selvi', age=34, grade=70, module_name='COMP4008'),
 Row(year=2022, name='Selvi', age=34, grade=95, module_name='COMP4103')]
```

```
df.toPandas()
```

```
    year        name  age  grade module_name
0   2021      Nasser   67     60    COMP4008
1   2021      Nasser   67     25    COMP4103
2   2021   Khivishta   34     70    COMP4008
3   2021   Khivishta   34     95    COMP4103
4   2022   Heda Song   67     60    COMP4008
5   2022   Heda Song   67     25    COMP4103
6   2022       Selvi   34     70    COMP4008
7   2022       Selvi   34     95    COMP4103
```

Counting the number of rows in the DataFrame is also useful for debugging:

```
df.count()
```

```
8
```

Getting the column names is also considered an action. It may not be obvious why this is an action, and not simply an attribute of the DataFrame, but remember that even creating a DataFrame is a lazy transformation, so if we wanted to get its columns we need to trigger this as an action.

```
df.columns
```

```
['year', 'name', 'age', 'grade', 'module_name']
```

describe(*cols)

This function allows us to compute some statistics (similar to `stats()` for RDDs). If you run it and check the Spark Web UI, you will see that this is certainly an action (it triggers the computation). However, it doesn't return anything:

```
df.describe(['age'])
```

```
DataFrame[summary: string, age: string]
```

It has created a new DataFrame, and we need to show it:

```
df.describe(['age']).show()
```

```
+-------+-----------------+
|summary|              age|
+-------+-----------------+
|  count|                8|
|   mean|             50.5|
| stddev|17.63924196622001|
|    min|               34|
|    max|               67|
+-------+-----------------+
```

With `explain()` we can get some low-level information from the physical and logical plans of Spark's optimization pipeline:

```
df.filter(df.age > 10).select(df.age).explain(True)
```

```
== Parsed Logical Plan ==
Project [age#3456L]
+- Filter (age#3456L > cast(10 as bigint))
   +- LogicalRDD [year#3454L, name#3455, age#3456L, grade#3457L,
module_name#3458], false
== Analyzed Logical Plan ==
age: bigint
Project [age#3456L]
+- Filter (age#3456L > cast(10 as bigint))
   +- LogicalRDD [year#3454L, name#3455, age#3456L, grade#3457L,
module_name#3458], false
== Optimized Logical Plan ==
Project [age#3456L]
+- Filter (isnotnull(age#3456L) AND (age#3456L > 10))
   +- LogicalRDD [year#3454L, name#3455, age#3456L, grade#3457L,
module_name#3458], false
== Physical Plan ==
*(1) Project [age#3456L]
+- *(1) Filter (isnotnull(age#3456L) AND (age#3456L > 10))
   +- *(1) Scan
ExistingRDD[year#3454L,name#3455,age#3456L,grade#3457L,module_name#3458]
```

5.3.5   Caching DataFrames

Similar to RDDs, we need to explicitly cache a DataFrame if we are going to reuse it. Otherwise, the data and all the transformations required to yield the current DataFrame would be run each time the DataFrame is used.

To illustrate the need for caching we implement a simple example counting how many times the words "blockhead" and "spear" appear in our favorite book using two different filter transformations (which may not be very efficient, but serve our purpose).

```
lines_df = spark.read.text("data/quixote.txt")
```

We get a DataFrame with a single Column where each row is a line of the book.

```
lines_df.show(2)
```

```
+--------------------+
|               value|
+--------------------+
|                    |
|The Project Guten...|
+--------------------+
only showing top 2 rows
```

With RDDs, we performed a `flatMap()` to obtain an RDD of words, and we need to do something similar to get a DataFrame of words before filtering and counting. To do so, we will make use of `explode()` together with the function `split()` from `pyspark.sql.functions`; `split()` takes an existing column of a DataFrame as a first argument and a pattern to split on as the second argument (this is usually a delimiter). This function returns an array of Column type that can be exploded.

> You should differentiate between the `split()` function of Spark SQL and the commonly used `split()` method of the `str` class, which does the same for strings in pure Python. The latter is not optimizable for Spark.

Putting everything together, we can create a DataFrame `words_df`, which we are going to cache, as follows:

```
words_df = lines_df.select(sql_f.explode(sql_f.split('value', ' '))\
                    .alias('word')).cache()

words_df.show(4)
```

```
+---------+
|     word|
+---------+
|         |
|      The|
|  Project|
|Gutenberg|
+---------+
only showing top 4 rows
```

We can now count words in that DataFrame very efficiently, as we have cached `words_df`.

```
words_df.where(words_df["word"].like("%blockhead%")).count()
```

```
17
```

```
words_df.where(words_df["word"].like("%spear%")).count()
```

```
13
```

> If you are working on your PC with Spark in local mode, don't try to check whether you are really getting an advantage from `cache()`. The Quixote book is probably not big enough for that. You should try with bigger datasets to see a real difference. You will notice this in the lab assignment.

> **Challenge #5.1**
>
> You have now learned all the necessary functions to implement the entire Word Count example with Spark SQL. Implement a function that would compute the word count using DataFrames.

5.4   Advanced Concepts

User-Defined Functions

Although most of the functionality you might want to work with Spark columns is already implemented as functions within Spark SQL (and the Spark development team keeps adding new ones), you may need to perform an operation that is unavailable. For this, there are user-defined functions, also known as UDFs.

> We include this to mention that it is possible, but we wouldn't advise using it unless strictly necessary. Native functions are highly optimized, while your function won't work as fast on Spark (especially on Python as it would involve double serialization).

Here is an example using the `udf()` function. You could define a transformation to compute the length of a string in a column. You just need to indicate the function to be applied and the type of data being returned.

```
slen = sql_f.udf(lambda s: len(s), IntegerType())
```

Then, you use it as if it were any other Column operation, for example within a `select()`.

> We are going to measure the run time ("wall time") using `%time` at the beginning of the instruction. We could also use `%timeit` to get a more accurate estimation of the running time (which gives us an average by running the instruction multiple times). Note that if you use `'%%time` or `'%%timeit` in the first line of the code cell, you can also measure the run time for all the instructions in the cell.

```
%time words_df.select(slen(words_df.word).alias('slen')).show(5)
```

```
+----+
|slen|
+----+
|   0|
|   3|
|   7|
|   9|
|   5|
+----+
only showing top 5 rows
CPU times: user 1.72 ms, sys: 409 µs, total: 2.13 ms
Wall time: 84.2 ms
```

You could do the same more efficiently using the Spark function length():

```
%time words_df.select(sql_f.length(words_df.word).alias('length')).show(5)
```

```
+------+
|length|
+------+
|     0|
|     3|
|     7|
|     9|
|     5|
+------+
only showing top 5 rows
CPU times: user 483 µs, sys: 1.39 ms, total: 1.87 ms
Wall time: 48.1 ms
```

These UDFs are the basic ones initially introduced by Spark, which are applied element by element and whose overhead is very high. In the latest versions of Spark (2.3[14] and 3.0[15]), improvements in this area have been introduced with the aim of applying vectorized operations on the basis of Apache Arrow[16] to reduce the overhead of converting data from Java to Python.

> Apache Arrow defines a columnar memory format that can be efficiently shared across programming languages to perform faster operations and avoid serialization overhead. You will need to install the pyarrow library to run the following examples.

Let's see a simple example with string length. We previously used a udf() function; in this case we should use the pandas_udf() function. However, it is also common to use a decorator (@pandas_udf()) when defining our pandas UDF function, which is equivalent to using pandas_udf() with the defined function.

---

[14] https://databricks.com/blog/2017/10/30/introducing-vectorized-udfs-for-pyspark.html
[15] https://databricks.com/blog/2020/05/20/new-pandas-udfs-and-python-type-hints-in-the-upcoming-release-of-apache-spark-3-0.html
[16] https://arrow.apache.org/

> Decorators in Python allow you to add new functionalities to existing code without explicit modification of that code.

```
import pandas as pd
@sql_f.pandas_udf('int')
def pandas_len(s: pd.Series) -> pd.Series:
    return s.str.len()
%time words_df.select(pandas_len(words_df.word).alias('length')).show(5)
```

```
+------+
|length|
+------+
|     0|
|     3|
|     7|
|     9|
|     5|
+------+
only showing top 5 rows
CPU times: user 2.82 ms, sys: 0 ns, total: 2.82 ms
Wall time: 436 ms
```

> Although we may not see an improvement with this example, it is again related to the dataset size. You can check the pandas UDF benchmark from Databricks[17] for additional performance comparisons.

More information on how to define efficient UDFs can be found in the Spark SQL documentation,[18] and also in a blog post.[19]

Challenge #5.2

> Given a DataFrame with a single column of words (e.g., the previous words_df), add an additional column with the words "rotated." For example, with the string "Mikel" it would output "lMike." If you apply your solution to words_df, you should get the following output:

```
+---------+---------+
|     word|   rotate|
+---------+---------+
|         |         |
|      The|      heT|
|  Project|  rojectP|
|Gutenberg|utenbergG|
|    EBook|    BookE|
|       of|       fo|
|      The|      heT|
```

---

[17] https://docs.databricks.com/_static/notebooks/pandas-udfs-benchmark.html

[18] https://spark.apache.org/docs/3.3.0/api/python/reference/pyspark.sql/api/pyspark.sql.functions.pandas_udf.html#pyspark.sql.functions.pandas_udf

[19] https://databricks.com/blog/2020/05/20/new-pandas-udfs-and-python-type-hints-in-the-upcoming-release-of-apache-spark-3-0.html

```
|  History|  istoryH|
|      of|       fo|
|     Don|      onD|
+---------+---------+
```

Explore two different options: (a) defining your own UDF function `rotate`, and (b) using Spark SQL functions. Compare the required time for both of them.

SQL in Spark

If you are familiar with SQL and its syntax, Spark also allows you to directly use SQL queries on a DataFrame. To do so, you have to "register" the DataFrame as a SQL temporary view and give a name to it. We'll reuse the people and hobbies DataFrames from before to show you an example:

```
people_df.createOrReplaceTempView("people")
hobbies_df.createOrReplaceTempView("hobbies")
```

Now you can use the `sql()` function to make a query and get the resulting DataFrame.

```
sql_df = spark.sql("SELECT * FROM people")
sql_df.show()
```

```
+-------+---+
|   name|age|
+-------+---+
|    Lam| 35|
| Direnc| 35|
|Rebecca| 24|
| Edwina| 25|
+-------+---+
```

You can also perform more complex queries.

```
spark.sql("SELECT * FROM people INNER JOIN hobbies ON\
          people.name=hobbies.name WHERE age > 34").show()
```

```
+------+---+------+--------------------+
|  name|age|  name|             hobbies|
+------+---+------+--------------------+
|Direnc| 35|Direnc|[Lifting, Running...|
|   Lam| 35|   Lam|[Triathlon, Runni...|
+------+---+------+--------------------+
```

The main difference with respect to pure SQL is that we cannot use the `DELETE FROM` clause, since DataFrames are immutable. To remove rows, you should use `where()`/`filter()` transformations.

pandas on Spark

We have seen before that is possible to move back and forth from Spark DataFrames to pandas DataFrames (e.g., using `toPandas()`, or creating a Spark DataFrame directly from a pandas one). While that may be useful in some cases, many data scientists who are very familiar with pandas have found the Spark SQL API a little confusing, but they wanted to use its big data capabilities. For this reason, there has been an initiative to implement the pandas DataFrame API on top of Spark (initially known as "Koalas"). This project has now been seamlessly integrated with Spark from version 3.2; see the pandas API on Spark.[20]

> The pandas API on Spark often outperforms pandas even on a single machine thanks to the Catalyst optimizations and the use of multiple threads. Thus, if you are a pandas user, you may want to use pandas-on-Spark even if you are not considering "pure" big data scenarios.

To use the pandas-on-Spark API we need to import it.

```
import pyspark.pandas as ps
```

Then, you can easily move from Spark DataFrames to pandas-on-Spark DataFrames and also to traditional pandas. For clarity, we will add a suffix to the names of our variables: df for Spark DataFrames, pd for standard pandas, and ps for pandas-on-Spark.

If we use the previous people_df Spark DataFrame as an example, we can convert it to standard pandas with the function toPandas(), as we showed before.

```
type(people_df)
```

```
pyspark.sql.dataframe.DataFrame
```

```
people_pd = people_df.toPandas()
```

```
people_pd
```

```
      name  age
0      Lam   35
1   Direnc   35
2  Rebecca   24
3   Edwina   25
```

We can convert the Spark DataFrame into a pandas-on-Spark DataFrame using the pandas_api function:

```
people_ps = people_df.pandas_api()
```

```
type(people_ps)
```

```
pyspark.pandas.frame.DataFrame
```

> A pandas-on-Spark DataFrame and a pandas DataFrame are very similar. So, operating with people_pd or with people_ps may be extremely similar. However,

---

[20] https://spark.apache.org/docs/3.3.0/api/python/reference/pyspark.pandas/index.html

> as `people_pd` is a standard pandas DataFrame, there won't be any parallelization when using it.

There is no `to_spark` function in pandas (at least yet); so, to convert a pandas DataFrame into a pandas-on-Spark DataFrame, we need to use the function `from_pandas`:

```
people_ps = ps.from_pandas(people_pd)
```

A pandas-on-Spark DataFrame and a Spark DataFrame are virtually interchangeable, but they operate differently. For example, you may remember that if we try to inspect the content of a Spark DataFrame, we needed to use `show()` or `collect()`, otherwise we don't see the content because it is a distributed structured. With a pandas-on-Spark DataFrame, it will automatically take part of the data and show it as if it was a standard pandas DataFrame.

```
people_df
```

```
DataFrame[name: string, age: bigint]
```

```
people_ps
```

```
     name   age
0     Lam    35
1   Direnc   35
2  Rebecca   24
3   Edwina   25
```

To cover all the available transformations, we can also go from pandas-on-Spark to standard pandas.

```
people_pd = people_ps.to_pandas()
```

```
people_pd
```

```
     name   age
0     Lam    35
1   Direnc   35
2  Rebecca   24
3   Edwina   25
```

```
type(people_pd)
```

```
pandas.core.frame.DataFrame
```

> *Remember*: when converting between either pandas-on-Spark or Spark DataFrames and standard pandas, the data will have to be transferred between multiple machines and the driver.

Now we can work with pandas-on-Spark in a distributed manner like Spark DataFrames and also plot the results as if they were standard pandas. We are not aiming to cover all the functionality, but we will show a few operations with a simple example.

If we only want to select the column name from `people_df`, we should use `select()` and an action like `show()`:

```
people_df.select("name").show()
```

```
+-------+
|   name|
+-------+
|    Lam|
| Direnc|
|Rebecca|
| Edwina|
+-------+
```

In the pandas-on-Spark API, we can simply name the attribute:

```
people_ps['name']
```

```
0        Lam
1      Direnc
2      Rebecca
3      Edwina
Name: name, dtype: object
```

To filter those people who are below 30, we could use the filter transformation with the Spark SQL:

```
people_df.filter(people_df.age < 30).show()
```

```
+-------+---+
|   name|age|
+-------+---+
|Rebecca| 24|
| Edwina| 25|
+-------+---+
```

Or apply the `loc` function on the pandas DataFrame:

```
people_ps.loc[people_ps.age < 30]
```

```
      name  age
2  Rebecca   24
3   Edwina   25
```

As we said before, pandas-on-Spark and Spark DataFrames are almost interchangeable. To change the way we operate on a pandas-on-Spark DataFrame to the Spark DataFrame style, we have to use the function `to_spark()`:

```
people_ps.to_spark().filter("age < 30").show()
```

```
+-------+---+
|   name|age|
+-------+---+
|Rebecca| 24|
| Edwina| 25|
+-------+---+
```

As we do commonly with pandas DataFrames, we can visualize its content. For example, we can plot a histogram of the ages on `people_ps`.

> By default, pandas-on-Spark DataFrames use the `plotly`[21] library to provide interactive plots instead of `matplotlib`, which is used by default in pandas DataFrames. You will need to have `plotly` installed or change the plotting backend using `ps.set_option("plotting.backend", "matplotlib")`.

```
ps.set_option("plotting.backend", "matplotlib")
people_ps['age'].hist(cmap="Set1_r");
```

By the way, if we are using `people_ps` multiple times, we may as well cache it (as with a standard Spark DataFrame). We need to use the `DataFrame.spark`[22] package that provides features that exist in Spark but not in pandas.

```
people_ps.spark.cache()
```

```
       name  age
0       Lam   35
1    Direnc   35
2   Rebecca   24
3    Edwina   25
```

> **Challenge #5.3**
>
> Implement Word Count using the pandas-on-Spark API, and plot a word frequency histogram.

5.5   Take-Home Message

This chapter has introduced the SQL module of Spark, covering its key features for processing big data. The most important concepts to keep in mind about this module are:

- RDDs are black boxes to Spark and that limits the optimizations that can be done with them.

---

[21] https://github.com/plotly/plotly.py

[22] https://spark.apache.org/docs/3.3.0/api/python/reference/pyspark.pandas/api/pyspark.pandas.DataFrame.spark.cache.html

- This module features a new distributed data structure called a *DataFrame* (Datasets are even more flexible but are only available in strongly typed languages like Java and Scala), which is based on the idea of imposing structure on the data to further accelerate big data processing.
- DataFrames improved upon RDDs by means of the Tungsten and Catalyst projects of Spark, allowing for enhanced performance independent of the programming language used.
- DataFrames have a schema, which means that each column of the data has a name and a type (e.g., Integer, String), and can be accessed and manipulated individually. The schema may be indicated manually or inferred from the data.
- Operating with DataFrames may feel more natural for SQL developers, but the ideas we learned with RDDs remain the same. That is, two types of (parallel) operation exist, transformations and actions; and caching is needed when reusing data.
- With the Spark SQL module, you can work either in SQL or OOP style in most cases. You can use the one that best fits your development style, also considering what can be more expressive for others who might make use of that code.
- As we can manipulate DataFrames by column, we gain the concepts of a Column object and operation. A Column is a SQL expression that will be applied to a given column when this expression is used in conjunction with a transformation.
- DataFrames can be grouped by the value of a given column. This is commonly used to later perform some aggregations (e.g., counting word repetition).
- This module contains a large set of highly optimized functions that can be used when processing Spark DataFrames. It is certainly difficult not to find a Spark function that would help solve most of the data processing you may need! Alternatively, you may be able to define your own functions, but that will not exploit Spark optimizations and will certainly be slower (although some improvements are being made in this direction, e.g., pandas UDFs).
- Recent advances in this module include pandas-on-Spark, which is an effort to provide a pandas-like API for Spark DataFrames, making them easier to use for those familiar with pandas.

In summary, the Spark SQL API is extremely powerful and will continue to evolve to allow for even faster big data processing. Working with this module, we only need to specify "what" we want to do, and Spark will take care of delivering such operations in an optimized fashion. Spark SQL has become the primary API for machine learning with Spark, as we see in the next chapter.

5.6   To Learn More

Are you eager to know more about the Spark SQL module? The following resources may be of interest:

> Watch "A Tale of Three Apache Spark APIs"[23] to find out more about the history of the different APIs.

> Spark "SQL: Relational Data Processing in Spark"[24] introduces in detail the motivation for and functioning of Spark SQL.

> If you are familiar with Scala, we suggest you look into its Dataset API.[25]

> More about UDFs:[26] UDFs keep improving and may be very useful.

> We also touched on a few Python concepts you may not be familiar with. You might find the pandas tutorial[27] useful.

> You may also want to find some resources online about decorators in Python.

5.7   Solutions to Challenges

> ### Challenge #5.1
>
> You have now learned all the necessary functions to implement the entire Word Count example with Spark SQL. Implement a function that would compute the word count using DataFrames.

We first summarize the complete solution and then go through it step by step. You will get some insights that you can use to develop the solutions in the lab assignment.

```
df_text = spark.read.format("text").load("data/quixote.txt")
df_text.select(sql_f.explode(sql_f.split(df_text["value"], " "))\
               .alias("word")) \
    .filter("word != ''") \
    .groupBy("word").count() \
    .sort(sql_f.desc("count")) \
    .show(5)
```

```
+----+-----+
|word|count|
+----+-----+
| the|20923|
| and|16606|
|  to|13492|
|  of|12866|
|that| 7164|
+----+-----+
only showing top 5 rows
```

[23] https://youtu.be/Ofk7G3GD9jk
[24] https://people.csail.mit.edu/matei/papers/2015/sigmod_spark_sql.pdf
[25] https://spark.apache.org/docs/3.3.0/api/scala/org/apache/spark/sql/Dataset.html
[26] https://spark.apache.org/docs/3.3.0/api/python/reference/api/pyspark.sql.functions.pandas_udf.html
[27] www.w3schools.com/python/pandas/default.asp

These are the steps we have followed:

1 Apply the `split()` and `explode()` functions inside `select()` to get a DataFrame of words (equivalent to the `flatMap()` operation we used with RDDs). We will use `'word'` as an alias for the new column.
2 Filter empty words.
3 Group by word and count how many times each one is repeated.
4 Order by counts, in descending order.
5 Show the result.

Recall that the *value* is by default the name of the column when reading text data.

Let's now go through step by step how you should achieve this solution. We start by reading and caching the text file.

```
df_text = spark.read.format("text").load("data/quixote.txt")
df_text.cache()
```

```
DataFrame[value: string]
```

We can check the content of our DataFrame.

```
df_text.select("*").show(5)
```

```
+--------------------+
|               value|
+--------------------+
|                    |
|The Project Guten...|
|                    |
|This eBook is for...|
|almost no restric...|
+--------------------+
only showing top 5 rows
```

So, we have the text lines in each row. The column name is the *value*. We can now split the lines into words using the Spark `split()` function:

```
df_text.select(sql_f.split("value", " ")).show(5)
```

```
+--------------------+
|  split(value,  , -1)|
+--------------------+
|                  []|
|[The, Project, Gu...|
|                  []|
|[This, eBook, is,...|
|[almost, no, rest...|
+--------------------+
only showing top 5 rows
```

We now have a DataFrame of arrays composed of words. We can use `explode()` to generate a new row with each element of the arrays.

```
df_text.select(sql_f.explode(sql_f.split("value", " "))).show(5)
```

```
+---------+
|      col|
+---------+
|         |
|      The|
|  Project|
|Gutenberg|
|    EBook|
+---------+
only showing top 5 rows
```

The default name for this column is `col`; we use `alias()` to rename it to `word`.

```
df_text.select(sql_f.explode(sql_f.split("value", " ")).alias("word"))\
     .show(5)
```

```
+---------+
|     word|
+---------+
|         |
|      The|
|  Project|
|Gutenberg|
|    EBook|
+---------+
only showing top 5 rows
```

You may notice that some empty words have been generated. We will filter them.

```
df_text.select(
    sql_f.explode(sql_f.split("value", " ")).alias("word")
).filter("word != ''").show(5)
```

```
+---------+
|     word|
+---------+
|      The|
|  Project|
|Gutenberg|
|    EBook|
|       of|
+---------+
only showing top 5 rows
```

Now it's time to group by word and count the number of occurrences of each word.

```
df_text.select(
    sql_f.explode(sql_f.split("value", " ")).alias("word")
).filter("word != ''").groupBy("word").count().show(5)
```

```
+------+-----+
|  word|count|
+------+-----+
|online|    4|
|  July|    1|
|CASTLE|    8|
```

```
|  XVII|    2|
|  AWAY|    2|
+------+-----+
only showing top 5 rows
```

Finally, we can order by count, in descending order.

```
df_text.select(sql_f.explode(sql_f.split("value", " ")).alias("word"))\
       .filter("word != ''").groupBy("word").count() \
       .sort(sql_f.desc("count")).show(5)
```

```
+----+-----+
|word|count|
+----+-----+
| the|20923|
| and|16606|
|  to|13492|
|  of|12866|
|that| 7164|
+----+-----+
only showing top 5 rows
```

> It is very helpful to develop the solutions to these kinds of problems step by step, so that you can be sure that you are obtaining what you expect. Otherwise, it may be difficult to locate the error in your code.

Challenge #5.2

Given a DataFrame with a single column of words (e.g., the previous words_df), add an additional column with the words "rotated." For example, with the string "Mikel" it would output "lMike." If you apply your solution to words_df, you should get the following output:

```
+---------+---------+
|     word|   rotate|
+---------+---------+
|         |         |
|      The|      heT|
|  Project|  rojectP|
|Gutenberg|utenbergG|
|    EBook|    BookE|
|       of|       fo|
|      The|      heT|
|  History|  istoryH|
|       of|       fo|
|      Don|      onD|
+---------+---------+
```

Explore two different options: (a) defining your own UDF function rotate, and (b) using Spark SQL functions. Compare the required time for both of them.

Let's start from a DataFrame of words:

```
words_df = df_text.select(
    sql_f.explode(sql_f.split("value", " ")).alias("word")
)
words_df.show(5)
```

```
+---------+
|     word|
+---------+
|         |
|      The|
|  Project|
|Gutenberg|
|    EBook|
+---------+
only showing top 5 rows
```

We can create a function `rotating` that will rotate a string, and then use `udf()` to define a Column operation:

```
def rotating(x) :
    return x[1:] + x[0:1]
rotate = sql_f.udf(rotating, StringType())
```

```
%time words_df.withColumn('rotate',rotate(words_df.word)).show(5)
```

```
+---------+---------+
|     word|   rotate|
+---------+---------+
|         |         |
|      The|      heT|
|  Project|  rojectP|
|Gutenberg|utenbergG|
|    EBook|    BookE|
+---------+---------+
only showing top 5 rows
CPU times: user 3.07 ms, sys: 1 ms, total: 4.07 ms
Wall time: 71.5 ms
```

Alternatively, we may try to use a Spark SQL function. One function that could be particularly useful is `substring`, as this would be the equivalent of slicing in Python. The main problem is that we can't do an alternative to `x[1:]` (from the second character to the end) because the `substring()` function requires the length of the string as a parameter. You could do something a little "funny" like this:

```
%time words_df.\
withColumn('rotate', sql_f.\
           concat(sql_f.substring(words_df.word, 2, 50),\
                  sql_f.substring(words_df.word, 1, 1))).show(5)
```

```
+---------+---------+
|     word|   rotate|
+---------+---------+
|         |         |
|      The|      heT|
|  Project|  rojectP|
```

```
|Gutenberg|utenbergG|
|   EBook|   BookE|
+---------+---------+
only showing top 5 rows
CPU times: user 246 µs, sys: 1.84 ms, total: 2.09 ms
Wall time: 41.6 ms
```

This assumes there is no word longer than 50 characters. That's certainly not ideal; we should use the length of the words. If you try this . . .

```
%time words_df.\
withColumn('rotate',\
        sql_f.concat(sql_f.\
              substring(words_df.word, 2, sql_f.length(words_df.word)),\
              sql_f.substring(words_df.word, 1, 1))).show(5)
```

```
TypeError Traceback (most recent call last)
File <timed eval>:1, in <module>
 . . .
```

. . . it fails as we explained earlier. The solution is to use `expr()`:

```
%time words_df\
.withColumn('length',\
        sql_f.concat(sql_f.\
                    expr("substring(word, 2, length(word))"),\
                    sql_f.substring(words_df.word, 1, 1))).show(5)
```

```
+---------+---------+
|     word|   length|
+---------+---------+
|         |         |
|      The|      heT|
|  Project|  rojectP|
|Gutenberg|utenbergG|
|    EBook|    BookE|
+---------+---------+
only showing top 5 rows
CPU times: user 1.16 ms, sys: 994 µs, total: 2.16 ms
Wall time: 61.2 ms
```

Challenge #5.3

Implement Word Count using the pandas-on-Spark API, and plot a word frequency histogram.

We can read the `'quixote.txt'` file as if it were a CSV file using the classic `read_csv()` function of pandas:

```
# Be careful with the separator, using the default
# will drop anything after a comma
ps_text = ps.read_csv("data/quixote.txt",\
                    header = None, names=["word"], sep='\n')
```

We can inspect the content of a few rows:

```
ps_text.head(3)
```

```
   word
0  The Project Gutenberg EBook of The History of Don Quixote by Miguel de
Cervantes
1                         This eBook is for the use of anyone anywhere at no cost
and with
2                         almost no restrictions whatsoever.  You may copy it, give it
away or
```

We will access the word attribute and split it by blank space, and later explode it:

```
new_ps = ps_text.word.str.split().explode().reset_index(drop=True)
```

Finally, we can use the value_counts() function to do the counting for us:

```
new_ps.value_counts().head(5)
```

```
the      20923
and      16606
to       13492
of       12866
that      7164
Name: word, dtype: int64
```

```
ps.set_option("plotting.backend", "matplotlib")
new_ps.value_counts().head(10).plot.bar(cmap="Set1_r");
```

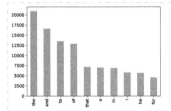

5.8   Exercises

5.1 Indicate whether the following statements about Spark SQL are true or false:
  (a) RDDs are now deprecated and Spark SQL is the de facto API.
  (b) Spark SQL is generally faster when using the Scala API compared to the
      Python API.
  (c) Spark provides a fault tolerance mechanism for RDDs but not for DataFrames.
  (d) The Dataset API is not yet available for Python, but it may be soon.

5.2 Briefly explain why Spark RDDs can't be further optimized, and how the Spark
     SQL API improves upon them.

5.3 A DataFrame is formed of Row objects. If we create the Row object
     row = Row(name = "Isaac", age = 36)
     is row a distributed data structure?

5.4 Briefly explain what the schema of a DataFrame is and its purpose.

5.5 Indicate whether the following statements about DataFrames are true or false:
   (a) DataFrames are immutable.
   (b) A DataFrame can be created from any existing collections like a list of integers.
   (c) You can access the underlying RDD of a DataFrame and apply transformations like `map()`.
   (d) When inferring the schema automatically, Spark will be able to load the data faster than when specifying it manually.

5.6 We can refer to a column of a DataFrame as `df['name']`; however, we wouldn't see any content if we ran that. How could we get to see the content of an entire column?

5.7 Indicate whether or not the following instructions are *lazy*:
   (a) `df = rdd.toDF(['module', 'mark'])`
   (b) `df.count()`
   (c) `print(df.collect())`
   (d) `df2 = df.groupBy('module').count()`

5.8 Similar to what we did in the previous chapter, we want to transform numerical marks into degree classifications. In this case, we have the following DataFrame that contains tuples with names and exam marks for our lab helpers.

```
df = spark.createDataFrame([('Lam', 45),
                            ('Khiv', 64),
                            ('Alexi', 69),
                            ('Kavan', 87),
                            ('Rebecca', 95)], ['name', 'mark'])
```

Using Spark SQL functions, write a Spark program that will add a new column `'Classification'` to df, converting the numerical marks into degree classifications. That is, anything less than 50 is a fail; anything in the [50, 59] interval is a Pass; anything in the [60, 69] interval is a Merit; and anything in the [70,100] interval is a Distinction. When showing the content of the new DataFrame, we should see a table like this:

```
+-------+----+--------------+
|   name|mark|Classification|
+-------+----+--------------+
|    Lam|  45|          Fail|
|   Khiv|  64|         Merit|
|  Alexi|  69|         Merit|
|  Kavan|  87|   Distinction|
|Rebecca|  95|   Distinction|
+-------+----+--------------+
```

Note: you are asked to use only Spark SQL functions.
Hint: Column operations like `when()` may come in handy.

5.9 Instead of using SQL functions, implement a solution for the previous exercise based on UDFs. Which one is faster? Briefly explain why.

5.10 We have a DataFrame with the output of the previous exercise:

```
df.show()
+-------+----+--------------+
|   name|mark|Classification|
+-------+----+--------------+
|    Lam|  45|          Fail|
|   Khiv|  64|         Merit|
|   Alexi|  69|        Merit|
|   Kavan|  87|   Distinction|
|Rebecca|  95|   Distinction|
+-------+----+--------------+
```

We are trying to group the data by degree classification with

```
df.groupBy('Classification').collect()
```

However, that doesn't seem to work. Briefly explain what we may be doing wrong.

5.11 Write the necessary code to calculate the number of students in each degree classification. The output should be like this:

```
+--------------+-----+
|Classification|count|
+--------------+-----+
|          Fail|    1|
|         Merit|    2|
|   Distinction|    2|
+--------------+-----+
```

5.12 We learned that we could compute statistics of numerical RDDs with the function `stats()`. With the Spark SQL API we can perform aggregations in different columns. Following the previous example, if we run

```
df.agg({'mark':'max'}).show()
```

it would return:

```
+---------+
|max(mark)|
+---------+
|       95|
+---------+
```

Investigate the Spark SQL API to obtain statistics of the column 'mark'. The output should be:

```
+-------+-----------------+
|summary|             mark|
+-------+-----------------+
|  count|                5|
|   mean|             72.0|
| stddev|19.72308292331602|
|    min|               45|
|    max|               95|
+-------+-----------------+
```

5.13 We have the following two DataFrames with marks for different students:

```
df = spark.createDataFrame([('Lam', 45),
                            ('Khiv', 64),
                            ('Alexi', 69),
                            ('Kavan', 87),
                            ('Rebecca', 95)], ['name', 'Big Data mark'])
```

```
df2 = spark.createDataFrame([('Lam', 95),
                             ('Khiv', 44),
                             ('Alexi', 89),
                             ('Kavan', 47),
                             ('Julie', 75)], ['name', 'Programming mark'])
```
Write the code to create a DataFrame df3 with the following content:
```
+-----+----------------+-------------+
| name|Programming mark|Big Data mark|
+-----+----------------+-------------+
|  Lam|              95|           45|
| Khiv|              44|           64|
|Alexi|              89|           69|
|Kavan|              47|           87|
|Julie|              75|         null|
+-----+----------------+-------------+
```

5.14 We want to compute some statistics on a binary classification dataset, and we came up with the following code:
```
df = spark.read.csv("huge_file.data")
df2 = df.groupBy('class').cache()
print("Some stats of my dataset")
df2.count().show()
for feature in df.columns:
    df.select(feature).mean()
```
Is there any issue with this code? If yes, how would you make it more efficient?

5.15 Indicate whether the following statements about Spark and DataFrames are true or false:

(a) UDFs are the preferred choice to operate with DataFrame columns because in that way we can be sure how the operation will take place.

(b) Column operations need to be used in conjunction with a transformation. However, you can design a UDF that works directly on the DataFrame.

(c) Although there is no transformation for deleting content from a DataFrame, we can use the DELETE FROM clause with spark.sql to do so.

(d) pandas-on-Spark may be faster than using the standard pandas library, even if we use a single computer.

Part III

Machine Learning for Big Data

6 Machine Learning with Spark

Learning Outcomes

[KU]	Understanding the need for machine learning in big data
[KU, PPS]	How to use the Spark machine learning library as a tool: defining machine learning pipelines
[KU]	Understanding the differences between standard machine learning and machine learning for big data
[KU]	Understanding the limitations of distributed machine learning in big data

So far, we have been studying Apache Spark as a big data framework, that is, a platform that allows us to process big data efficiently. We have seen that the key benefit of this platform is that its distributed data structures (RDDs or DataFrames) allow us to iterate multiple times through the data, query it interactively, or process streams of data efficiently.

We are going to focus now on how to do machine learning when we have big data. Although we expect the reader to be familiar with machine learning, we will start with a brief recap of the concepts and the key terminology that we will be using in the following chapters. Next, we will discuss the challenges of doing machine learning with big data and the motivation for using big data frameworks like Spark in this scenario. To get started with this topic, in this chapter we will focus directly on how to use the machine learning library of Apache Spark. Then, in the next two chapters, we will dig a bit more into how to design and implement machine learning algorithms scalable to big data.

> For those readers who are not familiar with machine learning, we provide some useful resources in Section 6.5.

6.1 Machine Learning Basics and Key Terminology

Machine learning is all about machines that learn from experience. It is common to refer to it as learning from examples, since we usually focus on learning from previous *examples* or *instances* of the problem we are trying to solve. For example, a typical machine learning problem would be to make the machine learn to detect defects in manufacturing, that is, differentiate between correct and faulty components. Let's think of a car rim (wheel) factory. In this case, the car rims, the examples, are characterized by some *features* or *attributes*, which could be the pixels of images of the rims or some telemetry information about them (e.g., eddy currents). We would usually have to provide the machine with lots of *training examples*, for example, images or telemetry data, indicating for each rim whether it is faulty or not (*labeled examples*). With this information, the machine will learn a *model* (also referred to as "training a model") that should be capable of correctly classifying future, previously unseen, examples (images or telemetry data) whose status (faulty or not) we don't know. This would mean that the model has good *generalization* capabilities. This simple example falls within the category of supervised classification, which is a specific type of machine learning. We commonly distinguish between three main machine learning paradigms:

- **Supervised learning**: Learning that is based on labeled examples, as for defect detection we have mentioned. Each example has a desired output associated with it that the model can use to learn.
- **Unsupervised learning**: In this case the examples are not labeled, and therefore the desired output is unknown. However, we can still perform learning. This can focus either on automatically reducing the stored information while keeping valuable information in the data (dimensionality reduction) or grouping sets of similar examples together to find hidden patterns in the data (clustering).
- **Reinforcement learning**: The machine acts and receives rewards depending on whether its actions are appropriate or not. This type of learning is the most similar to human learning, as the machine adapts itself to the environment, but it is also the most complex to adopt in real environments, although this may change very rapidly.

In this book we focus on the first two types of learning, and especially on the first one, although most of the concepts are common to all of them.

6.1.1   Supervised Learning: Classification and Regression

In supervised learning, machine learning algorithms aim to find the relationship between the features of the training examples (i.e., input features) and their labels (usually called the output or target label). Depending on the nature of the output label, we talk about:

- **Classification**: The output label is a discrete value, for example, differentiating between faulty and non-faulty components in manufacturing (our car rim defect prediction), or distinguishing between cats and dogs in images.
- **Regression**: The output label is a real value, for example, estimating the next day's temperature or predicting future gas prices.

There are also variants within these general categories that refer to problems where we have more than one target (multi-target or multi-task problems), and also other cases such as multi-label where each example can be of more than one class at a time.

Different methods have been developed to establish such relationships between input and output features, following different learning strategies and assumptions. Among the most distinctive supervised machine learning methods, we find linear and logistic regression, naïve Bayes, decision trees, k-nearest neighbors, support vector machines (SVMs), neural networks, and ensembles as the most well-known and most commonly used.

6.1.2 Unsupervised Learning: Dimensionality Reduction and Clustering

Conversely, in unsupervised learning we don't aim to find that relationship, as the output labels don't exist, or are unknown. Instead, the goal is usually to describe and understand the structure and patterns within the data. Depending on the objective, we talk about:

- **Dimensionality reduction**: The aim is to summarize the data by reducing the number of dimensions (features), while preserving the largest amount of information possible. For example, it is common to use these techniques to visualize complex high-dimensional biological data in two dimensions.
- **Clustering**: The goal is to group similar examples into clusters. Market and customer segmentations are well-known examples of clustering, where customers are grouped in order to create advertising campaigns tailored to each group.

Among others, frequently used techniques in this category include principal component analysis (PCA), t-distributed stochastic neighbor embedding (t-SNE), or singular value decomposition (SVD) for dimensionality reduction, and k-means clustering, density-based clustering, or Gaussian mixture models for clustering.

6.1.3 Machine Learning Life Cycle

For a machine to learn something meaningful, we cannot just simply expect to feed it some raw data (e.g., a random spreadsheet with numbers) and expect some magic to happen. We first need to know what we are aiming to achieve, and what actual problem we are trying to solve (e.g., the *business needs*, what needs to be automatized or predicted). When that is clear, we need to either put in place a *data collection* process and/or explore any existing data that may be related to the end goal. After exploring the data and deciding which information may be useful, we may have to *preprocess* the data to shape it in a way that machine learning algorithms will be able to exploit. Once that's done, we don't have a single algorithm that will always yield the best solution, and that means that we need to find out which model (and its configurations/parameters) would work best for a given dataset (although there are recent automated machine learning strategies that help to solve this automatically). For us to be able to *choose a model*, we need to know how to evaluate the success of a solution with respect to the original goal, and so we require a *validation mechanism*, defining appropriate *metrics*. This process will provide us with some results that need to be *analyzed and interpreted*. Finally, once we are satisfied with the results, we can *deploy* the model into production

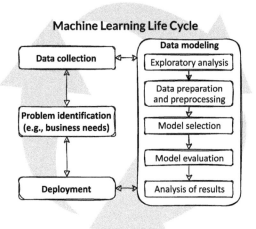

Figure 6.1 Key stages of the machine learning life cycle.

and continuously monitor it to detect possible inconsistencies. Both the analysis of the results and the behavior of the model in production may change what we originally understood about the original goal and require us to tailor the definition of the problem and repeat the same process from the beginning. Some may define more (or different) stages in the literature. In any case, the key point is that this is an iterative process in which we can go back and forth through the different steps depending on the results we get.

All of these stages (roughly) compose what has become referred to as the *machine learning life cycle* (also referred to as the data science life cycle). This is also where the term *MLOps* (machine learning operations) comes into play, which is the set of procedures and practices that help carry out this process efficiently and reliably from the lab, where the models are developed by data scientists, to production, where models are deployed and monitored by a mix of software and machine learning engineers. Figure 6.1 presents a graphical visualization of some of the most common stages of a machine learning life cycle. We now briefly describe the key ones that we will be using in this book.

6.1.4   Data Preparation and Preprocessing

As we just mentioned, once the problem at hand has been appropriately identified and the data has been collected, we need to decide which data to use and shape it in a way that is manageable and useful for the downstream machine learning algorithm. This may involve transformations to *extract features from raw data*, *feature engineering*, including feature selection and feature generation from existing features, and *feature normalization* to ease the correct training of the subsequent machine learning model.

Of these tasks, the first is the most problem dependent. Continuing with our car rim defect prediction example, we may need to extract features from images or telemetry data, especially if we are not considering deep learning models that may work directly with raw data. We could get the histogram of oriented gradients (HOG) features from images or process time-series telemetry data to get window statistics (such as minimum, maximum, or average values, among others). Determining the feature extractor that works best will be highly dependent on the application at hand, and specific feature extractors would be needed for different problems. However, some of them may be adequate for a variety of problems, like the TF–IDF (term frequency–inverse document frequency) feature extractor to encode text data.

Although extracting features can also be considered part of the feature engineering process, we like to assume that we already have some features to work with in this phase. With them, the goal is now to transform them to generate more relevant features, also dropping those that may be irrelevant to the problem (feature selection). For example, we may have information from our car rims like the rim id, which will obviously be irrelevant, since it is unique among all rims and should not be used as a pattern. On the other hand, the timestamp when the rim was analyzed may seem irrelevant, but it could be used to know whether previous car rims were defective, which may be indicative of a machine malfunction that is causing faulty rims.

Once relevant features are identified and ready for our machine learning algorithm, we may still need to ensure that they are in the proper shape for exploiting them. This is where data normalization is required. But, what is the data normalization about? Let's recall some well-known examples in which we need it. It is common for gradient- and distance-based learning algorithms to require feature normalization (or standardization), so that all features are weight equally independently of the magnitude in which their values lie. The most common way to solve this is by applying the standard scaler, which makes all features have the same mean and variance. Some features could also be categorical, for example, the material of the car rims (steel, aluminum, chrome, carbon fiber, ...). These features can't be codified with numbers as there is no order relation among them, so we need to encode them differently. The simplest way is to use *one-hot encoding*, although other methods also exist. In one-hot encoding, we generate a new feature for each value of the original feature and set it to one if the example has that value and zero otherwise.

Some of these tasks may seem rather manual, especially those regarding feature extraction and feature engineering, which in many cases are specific to the problem at hand. However, there are a number of machine learning methods that are useful and applicable independently of the problem, like the data normalization we just introduced. Other preprocessing techniques you may hear of are feature selection, dimensionality reduction, instance reduction, or missing value imputation. In this book we are interested in preprocessing techniques that are general and could be made available in frameworks such as Spark.

All of the prepreprocessing methods mentioned may be relevant to improving the performance of machine learning models. Not performing the appropriate data preparation and preprocessing can simply end with a model that is not useful, while doing it properly, even for the same problem, can really make a difference.

6.1.5   Model Evaluation and Selection

When it comes to selecting an algorithm for our problem, the range of possibilities increases rapidly. It is not only that there are an infinite number of machine learning methods out there, but also because the models are typically accompanied by a number of *hyperparameters* which will normally influence and govern their behavior, and therefore their ability to learn from the data. This means that we need ways to decide which hyperparameters are more promising.

For the sake of simplicity and clarity, we are going to distinguish between parameters and hyperparameters.

- When talking about parameters, we will refer to those parameters that must be learned in a model. For example, for a neural network that would be the weights that a model learns to establish the relationships between input features and the output label.
- Hyperparameters allude to those configuration parameters of a learning algorithm that govern its behavior. For example, this could be the number of layers of a neural network, or the number of neighbors for the nearest neighbor rule.

Therefore, a machine learning algorithm may learn the parameters, but we have to establish the hyperparameters. To do this, we need to find ways to evaluate the success in learning, by measuring, for example, the classification or error rate. However, as we are only provided with a limited set of labeled data, we need to use a *validation strategy*. A classical way of doing this is to split the data provided into three subsets:

- **Training set**: This subset is used to teach a machine learning model with a given set of hyperparameters.
- **Validation set**: When a model has been taught, the error/success rate is checked against this validation set. We can train various combinations of a machine learning algorithm plus a set of hyperparameters and check their performance against the validation set to make an informed choice of the best combination.
- **Test set**: This subset is left until the end, and is used to evaluate the behavior of the final chosen model and its configuration. That final choice is normally trained using training plus validation sets, and its behavior is evaluated against the test set. Obviously, we can't use the test set to select the best model and configuration pair, as that would be unrealistic and overly optimistic. The test set gives us a hint of how the model will perform in production.

The need for this split lies in the trade-off between *bias* and *variance* (underfitting and overfitting) of a model. Generally, a machine learning algorithm may adjust its parameters well to the training data, and, depending on the hyperparameters, it could even "memorize" them (known as *overfitting* or *high variance*). However, that doesn't mean they are going to be good models as they may not perform well when unseen data (like the validation) is used to evaluate their performance. This is usually referred to as *lack of generalization* abilities. Using the validation set to make a decision on the best combination of model and hyperparameters allows us to reduce overfitting. Inversely, we could end up experiencing *underfitting* or *high bias*, which means that the model is not able to find a relationship between input and output features, even in the training set. As we use the validation set to discover the best hyperparameters by analyzing the bias–variance trade-off (*model selection* or *hyperparameter tuning*), the test set serves as a realistic way to evaluate the expected performance of the selected model and hyperparameters when previously unseen data is used. Given that the validation is being used to select ("train") the hyperparameters, it won't give us a good estimation of the performance on unseen data.

There are more advanced validation techniques, such as k-fold cross-validation. These are typically applied to get a better estimate of the validation performance, although they could also be applied for the test. In k-fold cross-validation, we divide the dataset into k partitions and then train a model with every combination of $k - 1$ partitions and validate the model in the remaining partition each time. Consequently, we get k estimates of the performance that can be averaged. This allows us to obtain more accurate measurements since we make sure that all the examples go through validation. There are other validation techniques that need to be taken into account depending on the properties of the problem: stratified partitioning, grouped partitioning, leave one out, or special cases like time series partitioning.

6.1.6   Machine Learning Pipelines

The machine learning life cycle follows an iterative workflow from data capture to model deployment. The stages may differ depending on the problem at hand, but the idea of coding and automating part of this workflow is what is usually known as a *pipeline*. Thus, pipelines are not a step of the machine learning life cycle, but they are a useful MLOps tool that ensures best practice is applied to develop and deploy machine learning models. It is not so rare to mistakenly carry out different processes on data in the different sets (training, validation, and test), or even in production. For example, a data scientist may have deemed it necessary to apply data standardization. However, the machine learning engineer who is in charge of putting this into production might skip this step (e.g., it wasn't correctly documented), which will provoke the model to make meaningless predictions.

Machine learning pipelines are software elements designed to avoid this kind of mistake, reducing the amount of code required and simplifying the whole process. This programming construct will help us group together a set of preprocessing and transformation techniques needed prior to teaching and evaluating models, avoiding potential mistakes, since the same pipeline will be applied to any data that goes into the model. In machine learning libraries, such as the scikit-learn library for Python and the Spark MLlib library, this concept is already provided.

> Note that a pipeline may implement and automate part of the machine learning life cycle, for example, data preprocessing to model evaluation and even deployment, but the machine learning life cycle involves additional tasks, such as data collection, which may require human intervention.

6.2   Machine Learning with Big Data

When dealing with big data, all the stages of the machine learning life cycle may be affected. From data collection and storage to model deployment, all steps may encounter scalability problems due to the intrinsic characteristics of a big data problem. One may think that data preprocessing techniques such as feature selection, dimensionality reduction, or instance reduction may alleviate the issues with the volume of big data for teaching machine learning models. While that may be true to an extent, the main problem is that those data preprocessing techniques will also be negatively influenced by the size and complexity of the data, which may limit their role if they are not well designed for this scenario. Conversely, it could also happen that we don't find any problems in training a model, but we may encounter scalability issues deploying it. Hence, not all stages will always be affected at once, and this will depend on the problem itself.

So, what's the problem with these techniques in the context of big data? Let's start off with an example. Imagine you are tasked to analyze a huge dataset with millions of examples, and you want to perform some clustering using the k-means algorithm. What's going to be the bottleneck? For starters, if the dataset is way too big, it might simply not fit in the main memory of a single computer. Additionally, if you remember how k-means works, it will kick off with some random data centroids that will define the clusters found, and those are refined by iterating multiple times through the data and computing distances against *all* instances in the data. That will be a very time-consuming operation that will require keeping the dataset in the main memory, and distributed computing will be a must to provide an answer in a reasonable amount of time.

Therefore, standard machine learning techniques are not always appropriate to deal with massive datasets because they are confronted with those Vs that define big data:

- increasing scale of the data at different levels: instances/examples and features;
- the velocity at which the data arrives;
- the variety/complexity of the data as it may come from many varied sources.

You might now be thinking that all we need to do is reimplement machine learning algorithms using distributed data structures like RDDs or, even better, with DataFrames, instead of traditional sequential data structures. And yes, you're right. So, is there any "science" in doing machine learning on big datasets? Or does it only involve learning how to program with distributed data structures? The science of it lies in how to distribute the computation (reducing data movement) to maximize what you can learn from the data in a reasonable amount of time, and sometimes adapt or redesign specific steps that may be intractable with large datasets.

To do this, we need to bear in mind some of the key properties of machine learning algorithms in developing scalable distributed solutions. For example:

- Some algorithms may require long runs, so hardware or software failures may be catastrophic. Consequently, *fault tolerance* mechanisms will be invaluable in ensuring that a hardware failure in a single node of a cluster does not jeopardize the analysis of a huge dataset.
- Prior to running a machine learning model, we may require a set of preprocessing techniques that may transform the data multiple times. This means that these *transformations* will have to happen in parallel.
- Many algorithms may require to perform several *iterations* through the data to build and optimize a model, keeping transformed datasets *in main memory*.

Here, we have highlighted *fault tolerance*, *transformations*, *iterations*, and *in main memory*, which have been terms we have been introducing repeatedly in this book. Apart from those general properties of machine learning, we will (usually) need to know the nitty-gritty detail of the algorithm we are aiming to apply to big data to design how to effectively parallelize its operations. We will also have to think differently, as some of the operations and intrinsic ideas of some algorithms may just simply not work well in this context or may turn out to be unviable or unnecessary.

With this in mind, we hope you can see why the use of big data frameworks will be inevitable, and we will now lay the foundations for designing efficient big data solutions for machine learning. But, why are we using Apache Spark? As well as Hadoop and Spark, there are other frameworks and programming paradigms such as Flink or Dask. Each one has distinct technical innovations, and we need to choose the most appropriate to do the processing. Ultimately, this was simply a choice we had to make, but in our view, the efficiency to perform (scale-out) iterative computing (in memory) is key in machine learning, and this is the main advantage of Spark, which together with the integration with structured data processing, highly efficient data transformations tools, streaming, and graphs, makes it very appealing. Last, but not least, Spark has now consolidated globally as one of the key big data frameworks and has been adopted by major cloud providers.

6.3 The Spark Machine Learning Library

Many end users of machine learning do not know much about the details of the existing techniques, and they use machine learning as *off-the-shelf* tools. To do this, they usually rely on existing machine learning libraries, many of which are open source, to perform analyses on their datasets.

Even using off-the-shelf techniques requires some minimum knowledge of machine learning: understanding the behavior of the techniques, appropriateness for your problem, how to find the best hyperparameters, and how to validate your analysis. In the most extreme scenario, the user may not know anything at all about machine learning, and they usually go for automated machine learning (AutoML) libraries such as auto-sk-learn,[1] TPOT,[2] or AutoGluon.[3] Unfortunately, there is little for dealing with big data with AutoML as it could be extremely time/resource-consuming, but some, like H2O[4], are heading in that direction.

The machine learning library landscape has evolved quickly over the past few years. From a scalability perspective, we find those with only vertical scalability and those which are based on horizontal scalability. Traditional machine learning libraries such as Weka, KEEL, or the scikit-learn library in Python are designed for sequential processing, and provide a huge collection of algorithms (mostly anything you might look for). The main problem for these libraries is that they don't scale, and therefore don't cope well with big data, as well as not offering any fault tolerance. With the appearance of Hadoop, a library called Mahout[5] featured some classical algorithms such as k-means, random forest, or logistic regression based on the MapReduce programming model. As you may have guessed already, Mahout was soon deemed obsolete with the emergence of new big data frameworks such as Spark that went beyond Hadoop, providing more effective frameworks for performing iterative processing.

The Spark machine learning library is MLlib.[6] It includes a limited set of distributed algorithms, including some of the classical machine learning algorithms, for example, linear and logistic regression, decision trees, SVMs, k-means, and many more. As we will soon learn, their functionality may not be as flexible as their sequential counterparts due to the complexity of developing distributed solutions.

The MLlib library was first developed using the RDD API, but with the appearance of DataFrames it soon adopted this new API. The RDD-based MLlib API has been in maintenance mode since Spark 2.0. In a quick summary, it offers some high-level tools:

- traditional algorithms for classification, regression, clustering, and collaborative filtering;
- feature transformation methods such as feature extraction, dimensionality reduction, feature selection, etc.;
- pipeline tools to construct and evaluate ML pipelines;
- other utilities such as persistence tools to save and load models, compute statistics, or for data handling.

> You may be wondering: *Why does Spark MLlib not have all the algorithms provided in the scikit-learn?* The scikit-learn library is only adequate for sequential computation, while MLlib is focused on scale-out. Thus, scikit-learn provides almost any preprocessing and machine learning algorithm you could think of. However, "translating"/designing them to a scale-out approach is not straightforward. There are limitations that may imply changes in the learning procedures and adaptations to make the algorithms capable of handling large datasets.

[1] https://automl.github.io/auto-sklearn/master/
[2] http://epistasislab.github.io/tpot/
[3] https://auto.gluon.ai/
[4] https://docs.h2o.ai/h2o/latest-stable/h2o-docs/automl.html
[5] https://mahout.apache.org/
[6] https://spark.apache.org/docs/latest/ml-guide.html

6.3.1   Basic Concepts: Transformers, Estimators, and Pipelines

Before, we briefly mentioned the idea of a *pipeline* as a programming construct that allows us to automate part of the machine learning life cycle. In addition to everything we have learned so far about DataFrames, to use MLlib and its pipelines effectively we need to understand two main concepts, Transformer and Estimator, and how they are applied to our DataFrames. To put it simply, these concepts revolve around the two main types of operations you may want to do with your data in machine learning. Either you need to transform/preprocess your data for the subsequent machine learning algorithm (e.g., apply one-hot encoding to categorical variables), which will be done by a Transformer, or you use your data to learn the parameters of a model that can then be used for prediction, which will be the job of an Estimator that will create a Transformer (to add the predictions to unseen data as additional columns). Let's be a little bit more technical:

- A *Transformer* is an algorithm that transforms a DataFrame into a new one, generally by adding one or more columns. Basically, this is anything that can take a DataFrame and transforms it into a new one without needing to fit parameters because either the processing has no parameters or they have previously been fitted (with an Estimator that produces a Transformer with fitted parameters). Therefore, it could be any preprocessing method that won't require any parameter such as one-hot encoding, some preprocessing method with fitted parameters (e.g., a max–min scaler), or a previously created machine learning model that is capable of transforming an input DataFrame with features into a DataFrame with predictions. *Transformers implement the* `transform()` *method.*
- An *Estimator* can be any machine learning process or algorithm requiring some parameters to be fitted based on data. It takes a DataFrame as input and fits the required parameters based on the data, returning a `Transformer` object. It will typically be a learning algorithm whose output is a model that can be used to make predictions on a DataFrame, but it can also be a simple max–min scaler that needs the maximum and minimum values of each feature to be computed before being used as a Transformer to prepare the data for the learning algorithm. *Estimators implement the* `fit()` *method.*

To define a machine learning pipeline, it is common to chain multiple Transformers and Estimators sequentially. For example, before learning a linear regression, we may want to transform categorical features using one-hot encoding, while normalizing numerical ones with the standard scaler. In this case, we would need to create a Transformer to apply one-hot encoding, and an Estimator to normalize numerical features using the standard scaler, since the mean and variance for each feature need to be computed. Finally, an Estimator would be needed to learn the linear regression.

A Spark *Pipeline* allows us to concatenate multiple Transformer and Estimator objects. Interestingly, a Pipeline is an Estimator, and therefore it has a `fit()` method. The result of fitting a Pipeline is a Transformer, named *PipelineModel*, whose components are all Transformers, as the parameters of the Estimators in the Pipeline are fitted to

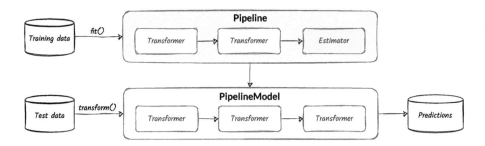

Figure 6.2 Typical pipeline of Transformers and Estimators.

the data. Figure 6.2 presents a schematic view of Pipeline and PipelineModel and their relationship with the training and test datasets.

> As a Pipeline is an Estimator, one could expect that the last stage of a pipeline should also be an Estimator, as it has implemented a fit() method. However, Spark doesn't enforce that, and you could have a Transformer as the last step of the pipeline.

We have given you a high-level definition of what an Estimator and a Transformer are, but there are a few more details we would like to delve into. To do this, we need to elaborate with an example.

6.3.2   An Example with Linear Regression

One thing we would like to know as lecturers is how well our students will perform in the exam after assessing their coursework. So, the question we would like to answer is ... could we predict the exam mark of a student based on their coursework marks? Such a prediction could be of use for both students and lecturers.

We are going to try to answer that question by using a supervised regression approach. As mentioned before, regression[7] is a kind of supervised learning, which aims to learn a function that maps a number of input features to a target output (which is a real number). As this is supervised learning, we assume that we have some initial data from which we can learn that mapping between the features. In this case, we have the data from 61 students, and what we want to learn is the relation between the exercise marks and the exam mark the students obtained. This is obviously not big data, but the goal is to provide a very simple example to understand how to use MLlib before using really big datasets.

Let's start by initializing our SparkSession:

```
from pyspark.sql import SparkSession
spark = SparkSession \
    .builder \
    .master("local[*]") \
    .appName("MLSpark") \
```

---

[7] https://en.wikipedia.org/wiki/Regression_analysis

```
    .getOrCreate()
sc = spark.sparkContext
```

We also need to import all the SQL functions:

```
import pyspark.sql.functions as sql_f
```

We are now going to load the historical data we have for 61 students we had a few years back. Completely anonymized, we have created a table with the marks that these students obtained for all the assessments, including coursework and exam marks. In particular, the coursework was composed of four exercises (Ex01 to Ex04) linked to different topics (MapReduce, Spark, SparkSQL, MLlib) and a group project to implement a big data solution for a real problem. The exam was also made up of four parts (Questions 1 to 4) associated with the same topics. The column 'Exam' is just the addition of the marks obtained for Questions 1–4. Finally, we have a column with the final 'Total' mark for each student. The idea is then to figure out the relationship between the coursework marks (Ex01 to Ex04, and the group project), and the exam mark.

The data is in CSV format, so we are going to use the DataFrame API to read the data and infer the schema:

```
df = spark.read.format("csv").option("header", "true").load("data/marks.csv")
```

Note that we used the option header here, because the CSV file has the names of each column in the first row. As we will be using this DataFrame quite often, it will be quite useful to cache it:

```
df.cache()
```

```
DataFrame[Ex01: string, Ex02: string, Ex03: string, Ex04: string, Project:
string, Question 1: string, Question 2: string, Question 3: string, Question
4: string, Exam: string, Total: string]
```

Wait! Has Spark inferred the data correctly? Doesn't it say string types?

```
df.printSchema()
```

```
root
 |-- Ex01: string (nullable = true)
 |-- Ex02: string (nullable = true)
 |-- Ex03: string (nullable = true)
 |-- Ex04: string (nullable = true)
 |-- Project: string (nullable = true)
 |-- Question 1: string (nullable = true)
 |-- Question 2: string (nullable = true)
 |-- Question 3: string (nullable = true)
 |-- Question 4: string (nullable = true)
 |-- Exam: string (nullable = true)
 |-- Total: string (nullable = true)
```

We could have defined the schema explicitly before reading the CSV file. Instead, we are going to transform those columns to float or double! How do we do this? We can use the SQL function col to access each column by its name and then cast each column to float. To do this with all columns, we can use list comprehension from Python.

```
df = df.select([sql_f.col(c).cast("float").alias(c) for c in df.columns])
df.printSchema()
```

```
root
 |-- Ex01: float (nullable = true)
 |-- Ex02: float (nullable = true)
 |-- Ex03: float (nullable = true)
 |-- Ex04: float (nullable = true)
 |-- Project: float (nullable = true)
 |-- Question 1: float (nullable = true)
 |-- Question 2: float (nullable = true)
 |-- Question 3: float (nullable = true)
 |-- Question 4: float (nullable = true)
 |-- Exam: float (nullable = true)
 |-- Total: float (nullable = true)
```

Let's see how the content looks:

```
df.show(2)
```

```
+-----+----+----+----+-------+----------+----------+----------+----------+---
-+-----+
| Ex01|Ex02|Ex03|Ex04|Project|Question 1|Question 2|Question 3|Question
4|Exam|Total|
+-----+----+----+----+-------+----------+----------+----------+----------+---
-+-----+
|100.0|85.0|80.0|70.0|   80.0|      18.0|      16.0|      23.0|
22.0|79.0| 81.0|
|100.0|85.0|80.0|90.0|   93.0|      20.0|      13.0|      11.0|
22.0|66.0| 79.0|
+-----+----+----+----+-------+----------+----------+----------+----------+---
-+-----+
only showing top 2 rows
```

Our aim is to predict the exam mark, which is calculated as the sum of the exam's questions (Questions 1 to 4). Obviously, we are trying to do this before the exam takes place. Since questions are part of the exam, we can't use them as input features, so we'd better remove them. The 'Total' mark is computed using the 'Exam' mark together with the coursework and the project. Therefore, we should not use it either, since it has information about the exam, which we are trying to predict. So, let's drop these columns and use only the exercise and project marks to predict the exam mark:

```
df = df.drop('Question 1').drop('Question 2').drop('Question 3')\
       .drop('Question 4').drop('Total')
```

```
df.show(2)
```

```
+-----+----+----+----+-------+----+
| Ex01|Ex02|Ex03|Ex04|Project|Exam|
+-----+----+----+----+-------+----+
|100.0|85.0|80.0|70.0|   80.0|79.0|
|100.0|85.0|80.0|90.0|   93.0|66.0|
+-----+----+----+----+-------+----+
only showing top 2 rows
```

Okay, so in machine learning, it is important that we use our data sensibly. And that means that we need to make sure that if we learn such a mapping function, we need to be able to test that it works on unseen data. As discussed before, there are different validation approaches for machine learning, but here we are going to simply split the data; we create a training partition containing 70% of the data, and the remainder will be used as test data to check whether we have learned the mapping correctly or not. We don't need a validation set, as we are not interested in optimizing the hyperparameters just yet.

Let's use the transformation `randomSplit()` to create two different DataFrames:

```
train_df, test_df = df.randomSplit([0.7, 0.3], seed=123456)
```

```
train_df.count()
```

```
39
```

```
test_df.count()
```

```
22
```

> Did you notice the use of a `seed` when splitting the data? This is typically used to ensure that the random split is "not so random," and therefore we always get the same random split even if we run this notebook multiple times. However, we must admit that we have seen differences when running this notebook on different computers with different operating systems. We are still looking for an answer as to why this really happens.

With the problem defined and the data already partitioned, we can now try to learn our first model.

Learning a Linear Regression Model

Spark has multiple regression algorithms available, but let's use a simple one like linear regression. We need to import the module:

```
from pyspark.ml.regression import LinearRegression
```

Let's create an instance of `LinearRegression`:

```
lr = LinearRegression(maxIter=10, regParam=0.3)
```

This is an Estimator because we are referring to the learning algorithm that will generate the model. We have directly indicated a few hyperparameters for that instance of the linear regression. Do you want to know more about these hyperparameters? We can use the object `lr` to figure out more about it, using the function `explainParams()`. For simplicity, we only show the first 200 characters of the output of that function.

```
lr.explainParams()[:200]
```

```
'aggregationDepth: suggested depth for treeAggregate (>= 2). (default:
2)\nelasticNetParam: the ElasticNet mixing parameter, in range [0, 1]. For
alpha = 0, the penalty is an L2 penalty. For alpha = 1, '
```

So far, we haven't trained the model, we just created an instance of it with some hyperparameters. We need to fit a model with the data we have in `train_df`. However, if you think we can just feed the data directly, well you will find some errors:

```
model = lr.fit(df)
```

```
IllegalArgumentException Traceback (most recent call last)
Input In [16], in <cell line: 1>() ----> 1 model = lr.fit(df)
...
```

Why is this happening? Spark expects the DataFrame to have some specific formatting, and we need to indicate which ones are input features, and which one is the output feature. In particular, Spark wants all the input features in a single `Vector`-type column, which is a special type used in MLlib. By default, this column is expected to be named `'features'`, but we can give it any other name with the `featuresCol` parameter. Similarly, the `labelCol` parameter (by default `'label'`) indicates which column should be used as the output.

Before solving how to give a DataFrame the appropriate format, let's see a toy example that won't require any further processing.

Toy Example

As we said, the DataFrame must have two columns: input features and output label. The input features have to be codified using an object of class `Vector`. This `Vector` may seem unfamiliar, but behind the scenes they encapsulate numpy arrays, so they allow arithmetic operations between vectors. Here is an example:

```
from pyspark.ml.linalg import Vectors

v = Vectors.dense([1.0, 2.5, 5.0])
u = Vectors.dense([0.0, -1.5, 10.0])
u + v
```

```
DenseVector([1.0, 1.0, 15.0])
```

Let's now create a very simple example DataFrame with feature vectors and labels:

```
simple_training = spark.createDataFrame([
    (Vectors.dense([0.0, 1.1, 0.1]),  1.0),
    (Vectors.dense([2.0, 1.0, -1.0]), 0.0),
    (Vectors.dense([2.0, 1.3, 1.0]),  0.5),
    (Vectors.dense([0.0, 1.2, -0.5]), 1.5)], ["features", "label"])
```

In this DataFrame we have put four examples with three numeric input features, and the target ranges between 0 and 1.5. We could now easily fit a linear regression model as:

```
model = lr.fit(simple_training)
```

`fit()` is an action, so you will see some processing going on in the Spark UI. The type of this `model` variable is `LinearRegressionModel`, which is a Transformer, and will let us predict the output for new examples.

Above, we created an instance of `LinearRegression` and specified the hyperparameters directly. Alternatively, we could indicate the parameters when fitting the model. But to do so, we need to create a `ParamMap` object. A `ParamMap` is a set of (⟨*parameter*⟩, ⟨*value*⟩) pairs.

```
param_map = {lr.regParam: 0.1, lr.elasticNetParam: 0.55}
```

```
model = lr.fit(simple_training, param_map)
```

How do we make predictions? Let's prepare some toy test data:

```
simple_test = spark.createDataFrame([
    (Vectors.dense([-1.0, 1.5, 1.3]), 1.0),
    (Vectors.dense([3.0, 2.0, -0.1]), 0.3),
    (Vectors.dense([0.0, 2.2, -1.5]), 1.5)], ["features", "label"])
```

So, `model` is a `LinearRegressionModel`, which can be used to make predictions. How? By applying the `transform()` method giving the `test_df` DataFrame as input.

```
prediction = model.transform(simple_test)
```

`transform()` is obviously a transformation, so it is waiting for an action to trigger the prediction. When applied, it adds the column `prediction`:

```
prediction.collect()
```

```
[Row(features=DenseVector([-1.0, 1.5, 1.3]), label=1.0,
prediction=2.062193252765237),
 Row(features=DenseVector([3.0, 2.0, -0.1]), label=0.3,
prediction=1.1126615947167984),
 Row(features=DenseVector([0.0, 2.2, -1.5]), label=1.5,
prediction=2.6273449526716033)]
```

How do we get only the predictions? Using the transformations we learned with Spark SQL:

```
prediction.select('prediction').show()
```

```
+------------------+
|        prediction|
+------------------+
| 2.062193252765237|
|1.1126615947167984|
|2.6273449526716033|
+------------------+
```

Okay, it seems easy, but how do we do the same with the DataFrame we read from a CSV file? We need to transform the data into the right shape, and for that it will be useful to create a Pipeline.

Pipelines

As stated above, we need to get all the columns that are input features together. For now, our data looks like this:

```
train_df.show(2)
```

```
+----+----+----+----+-------+----+
|Ex01|Ex02|Ex03|Ex04|Project|Exam|
+----+----+----+----+-------+----+
|60.0|85.0|60.0|20.0|   70.0|33.0|
|60.0|85.0|75.0|85.0|   70.0|32.0|
+----+----+----+----+-------+----+
only showing top 2 rows
```

To transform our DataFrame into something that MLlib can process, we use the `VectorAssembler`. This is a Transformer that combines a given list of columns into a single vector column, which is what MLlib requires for the Estimators.

First, let's import the right class:

```
from pyspark.ml.feature import VectorAssembler
```

Then, we are going to create a list with the names of the input features:

```
feature_cols = train_df.columns
feature_cols.remove('Exam')
feature_cols
```

```
['Ex01', 'Ex02', 'Ex03', 'Ex04', 'Project']
```

Now, we create the assembler, indicating the input features and the name we will give to the new column (in this case `'features'`).

```
assembler = VectorAssembler(inputCols=feature_cols, outputCol="features")
```

To understand what the assembler does, let's apply it to the training data:

```
assembler.transform(train_df).show(5)
```

```
+----+----+----+-----+-------+----+--------------------+
|Ex01|Ex02|Ex03| Ex04|Project|Exam|            features|
+----+----+----+-----+-------+----+--------------------+
|60.0|85.0|60.0| 20.0|   70.0|33.0|[60.0,85.0,60.0,2...|
|60.0|85.0|75.0| 85.0|   70.0|32.0|[60.0,85.0,75.0,8...|
|65.0|90.0|90.0| 85.0|   69.0|54.0|[65.0,90.0,90.0,8...|
|65.0|95.0|65.0| 25.0|   70.0|10.0|[65.0,95.0,65.0,2...|
|70.0|85.0|65.0|100.0|   65.0|64.0|[70.0,85.0,65.0,1...|
+----+----+----+-----+-------+----+--------------------+
only showing top 5 rows
```

We could now create a linear regression model that takes as input the `features` column and as output the `Exam` column (we indicate these using the parameters `featuresCol` and `labelCol`, respectively, when creating the model). Something like this:

```
lr = LinearRegression(
    maxIter=10, regParam=0.3, featuresCol="features", labelCol="Exam"
```

```
)
lr_model = lr.fit(assembler.transform(train_df))
```

But if we now want to apply the model on a test set, we would first have to transform the test into the right format (i.e., a vector column) using the assembler before making the predictions.

```
predictions = lr_model.transform(assembler.transform(test_df))
predictions.select('prediction').show(3)
```

```
+------------------+
|        prediction|
+------------------+
|0.3716762687677644|
| 44.76477287291376|
|  77.8069476890754|
+------------------+
only showing top 3 rows
```

In this simple example we have a process composed of two stages: assembling the vector of features and then applying linear regression. But imagine a scenario like the one we described before. In addition to the assembler, we also want to transform categorical features using one-hot encoding, while normalizing numerical ones with the standard scaler. If we had to do this manually, we would need to perform several operations on the training set, first applying the one-hot encoding (calling the trans-form() method), then fitting the Estimator of the standard scaler (using the fit() method) and applying it (with the transform() method), and finally fitting the estimator of the linear regression (calling fit()). Afterward, for a test set, we would have to just apply the three Transformers (using the last two resulting from the Estimators). This is a simple process and yet it is easy for us to forget to apply some of the steps (we haven't even mentioned the assembler needed to make it simpler). This is when Pipelines come in very handy, allowing us to group all the processes sequentially to apply them transparently to the training set, but also to the validation and test sets, even in production.

Let's create a Pipeline for the assembler and the linear regression:

```
from pyspark.ml import Pipeline
pipeline = Pipeline(stages=[assembler, lr])
```

Before testing this Pipeline, let's discuss some important details:

- When putting objects in that Pipeline (i.e., assembler, lr), we need to be cautious about the name of the input and output features of those Transformers or Estimators. We need to make sure that the output will match the input of the next element of the Pipeline.
- The stages of a Pipeline should be unique. This means that the objects included in a Pipeline need to be different. If you need to include the same operation twice, for example, one-hot encoding of several columns, you would need to have two different instances of that Transformer.

Now we are ready to call the fit() method of the Pipeline (remember that it is an Estimator) using the training data as input parameter:

```
pipeline_model = pipeline.fit(train_df)
```

> By the way, if you fed a DataFrame with the wrong schema to a Pipeline, Spark would throw an error as it performs a quick runtime check before actually running a Pipeline. This is simply a type check, making sure that the DataFrame schema is appropriate for the model.

We can now apply the pipeline model to the (raw) test_df, which will assemble the vectors into a feature column and predict the outputs:

```
prediction = pipeline_model.transform(test_df)

prediction.select('prediction', 'Exam').show(5)
```

```
+------------------+----+
|        prediction|Exam|
+------------------+----+
|0.3716762687677644|32.0|
| 44.76477287291376|65.0|
|  77.8069476890754|20.0|
|60.282789381651796|57.0|
| 68.43688802640413|38.0|
+------------------+----+
only showing top 5 rows
```

When fitting the linear regression model, it should have learned some parameters that we can explore now. To do so, we need to remember that we have embedded the linear regression object lr as one of the stages of the pipeline. To access the resulting LinearRegressionModel that contains the parameters (known as coefficients in Spark), we can look at the second element of the stages list in pipeline_model:

```
pipeline_model.stages[1]
```

```
LinearRegressionModel: uid=LinearRegression_4cb14ba06ffa, numFeatures=5
```

If we now look at the Spark documentation for a LinearRegressionModel[8] we find that there are attributes for the coefficients and the intercept:

```
pipeline_model.stages[1].coefficients
```

```
DenseVector([0.4588, -0.3587, -0.3248, 0.389, 0.4693])
```

```
pipeline_model.stages[1].intercept
```

```
8.712374416651206
```

---

[8] https://spark.apache.org/docs/3.3.0/api/python/reference/api/pyspark.ml.regression.LinearRegressionModel.html

We can easily plot the coefficients information with the feature names:

```python
import matplotlib.pyplot as plt
coeff = pipeline_model.stages[1].coefficients
plt.bar(
    feature_cols, coeff, color=["darkgray", "gray", "dimgray", "lightgray"]
)
plt.axhline(y=0, color="gray", linestyle="--", linewidth=0.5);
```

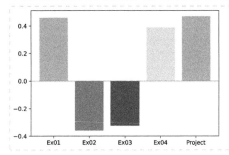

If we want to somehow interpret those coefficients, it seems that the exam mark is directly related to how well a student has performed in Exercises 1 and 4, and the project with respect to Exercises 2 and 3. We would need to study this further to work out why this is happening.

> ## Challenge #6.1
>
> We have created a Pipeline to assemble the data in the right shape and learn a linear regression model. Could you add an extra preprocessing stage to normalize the data prior to learning? Investigate how to use the StandardScaler of MLlib.

Evaluating Machine Learning Algorithms with the Evaluation Module

In machine learning, we typically use performance measures (error or accuracy metrics) to determine the success of a prediction. For our regression example, we are adopting the root mean squared error (RMSE) as one of the most common regression metrics.

MLlib offers a module for evaluating regression models. Let's import the module and create an object that allows us to evaluate regression outputs.

```python
from pyspark.ml.evaluation import RegressionEvaluator

rmse_evaluator = RegressionEvaluator(
    metricName="rmse", labelCol="Exam", predictionCol="prediction"
)
```

Here, we indicated the metric name as 'rmse' (root mean squared error), the column name of the target output, and the name of the predicted column. We now simply have to call the method evaluate on the DataFrame we obtained after transforming the test set.

```python
rmse_evaluator.evaluate(prediction)
```

```
20.963068684668492
```

This is telling us that we can predict the exam mark of a student with a certain error in the marks, which is not particularly great, but not too bad either.

Could you calculate the root mean squared error without MLlib? Let's try using Spark SQL functions:

```
mse = prediction.agg(
    sql_f.mean(
        sql_f.pow(sql_f.col("Exam") - sql_f.col("prediction"), 2)
    ).alias("mse")
)
mse.withColumn("rmse", sql_f.sqrt(sql_f.col("mse"))).show()
```

```
+------------------+------------------+
|               mse|              rmse|
+------------------+------------------+
|439.4502486781287|20.96306868466849|
+------------------+------------------+
```

Should we try other parameters or models? As we mentioned above, in machine learning it is common to choose the best hyperparameters of a model based on a validation set extracted from the training set. Spark also helps in this task, as we'll see now.

6.3.3   Hyperparameter Tuning

Spark allows us to carry out hyperparameter tuning in two ways:

- A *CrossValidator* allows splitting the training data into different "folds" and performing a cross validation. For example, with three folds, a CrossValidator generates three (training, validation) dataset pairs, each of which uses two-thirds of the data for training and one-third for validation.
- A *training/validation split* divides the training dataset into two subsets, training and validation, and determines the parameters based on the performance on the validation set.

In both cases, we use only the training data to find the best parameters, and when those have been identified with the validation set(s), the final model is trained again using the entire training data. Let's now see how they are used in Spark.

CrossValidator

To create a CrossValidator[9] we need an Estimator, a set of hyperparameters, and an evaluator. In addition, we also need to indicate the number of partitions into which the training data will be split. Let's import the appropriate classes:

```
from pyspark.ml.tuning import CrossValidator, ParamGridBuilder
```

First, we create a "grid" of hyperparameters, that is, the hyperparameters and their different values that we want to investigate. To do this, we use `ParamGridBuilder` as follows:

[9] https://spark.apache.org/docs/3.3.0/api/scala/org/apache/spark/ml/tuning/CrossValidator.html

```
paramGrid = (
    ParamGridBuilder()
    .addGrid(lr.regParam, [0.1, 0.3])
    .addGrid(lr.maxIter, [2, 5, 10, 20])
    .build()
)
```

This grid will investigate 2×4 hyperparameter combinations.

We can now create a CrossValidator that uses the Pipeline object we created before as an Estimator, the `paramGrid` we just defined, and `rmse_evaluator` to evaluate the predictions. We will use three folds for the model selection (we also set the `seed` to make it reproducible).

```
crossval = CrossValidator(
    estimator=pipeline,
    estimatorParamMaps=paramGrid,
    evaluator=rmse_evaluator,
    numFolds=3,
    seed=123456,
)
```

Once the CrossValidator is prepared, we can call the `fit()` method, since it is an Estimator.

```
cv_model = crossval.fit(train_df)
```

This should take way longer than before, shouldn't it? We have built a few models here to figure out which one is best! Note that the Estimator is eventually refitted using the best `ParamMap` found with the entire training data.

Now we use `cv_model`, which is a cross-validated pipeline model, to transform the test and make predictions.

```
prediction = cv_model.transform(test_df)
```

How well have we done now?

```
rmse_evaluator.evaluate(prediction)
```

```
20.963068684668492
```

Unfortunately, we haven't improved the results, but let's see if the hyperparameters are any different. How do we know which one was the best model configuration?

```
best_pipeline = cv_model.bestModel
```

> If you are a pure Python programmer, you may not like the Spark variable naming convention, as they use camelCase rather than snake_case for composed names (e.g., `bestModel` instead of `best_model`). This is due to the Java/Scala inheritance, and they have respected the same names to keep all APIs uniform.

If we now want to see what happened to that best pipeline in stage 1 (stage 0 of our pipeline was the assembler):

```
best_lr_model = best_pipeline.stages[1]
best_params = best_lr_model.extractParamMap()
```

If you print the content of `best_params` you will see all the hyperparameters used for the best model. Most of them were fixed and the default ones. The two hyperparameters we have investigated are `maxIter` and `regParam`. It turned out that the pair `regParam = 0.3` and `maxIter = 2` worked best. Compared to our previous "random" choice (`regParam = 0.3, maxIter = 10`), we can see how only two iterations were actually needed to fit the model. This might be telling us that due to the simplicity of the model and the limited data, the learning algorithm converges quickly.

We can also find the coefficients and intercept of the best pipeline:

```
coeff = best_lr_model.coefficients
plt.bar(
    feature_cols, coeff, color=["darkgray", "gray", "dimgray", "lightgray"]
)
plt.axhline(y=0, color="gray", linestyle="--", linewidth=0.5)
coeff
```

```
DenseVector([0.4588, -0.3587, -0.3248, 0.389, 0.4693])
```

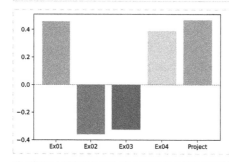

```
best_lr_model.intercept
```

```
8.712374416651206
```

If you check the learned coefficients with the previous ones, you will notice that the final model hasn't really changed.

> ## Challenge #6.2
>
> Linear regression seems to make an OK prediction, but how does it compare to other regression models? Explore MLlib and test a different machine learning algorithm and its hyperparameters.

TrainValidationSplit

A CrossValidator may easily become very expensive with large datasets. Alternatively, you can use `TrainValidationSplit`, which only evaluates each combination of parameters once. As with CrossValidator, this requires an Estimator, a set of hyperparameters, and an evaluator (we use the objects we created before, `pipeline`, `paramGrid`, and `rmse_evaluator`). In addition, we also need to indicate the training and validation split ratio (don't forget the seed if you want to make it reproducible).

```python
from pyspark.ml.tuning import TrainValidationSplit

tvs = TrainValidationSplit(
    estimator=pipeline,
    estimatorParamMaps=paramGrid,
    evaluator=rmse_evaluator,
    # 80% of the data will be used
    # for training, 20% for validation.
    trainRatio=0.8,
    seed=123456,
)

tvs_model = tvs.fit(train_df)

prediction = tvs_model.transform(test_df)

rmse_evaluator.evaluate(prediction)
```

```
20.963068684668492
```

> **Challenge #6.3**
>
> In this example we treated the prediction of the Exam mark as a regression problem, but we could also be interested in predicting the total mark that the students will get (taking the coursework and the project into consideration, before doing the Exam), for example, Fail: < 50; Pass: [50, 60); Merit: [60, 70); Distinction: > 70. To do this, you will need to use the column 'Total', where the final numerical marks are, and transform your DataFrame, adding a column with the right labels (e.g., Fail, Pass, Merit, or Distinction). You may choose any classifier available in MLlib, and any metric you consider useful to measure the success in classification.

6.4   Take-Home Message

This chapter has provided a gentle introduction to machine learning with big data. After providing some key terminology and basic background on machine learning, as well as some motivation for doing this, we focused on MLlib as a great resource for running machine learning no big datasets. Some of the take-away messages from this chapter are:

- In machine learning, we typically follow a series of stages to extract insights from data. Among others, these include data preparation and preprocessing, model selection, and evaluation.

- Pipelines are programming constructs to streamline some of the stages of the machine learning life cycle. For example, they allow us to concatenate preprocessing techniques (e.g., normalization) with a machine learning model to ensure that every example going through the model will be processed in the same manner, avoiding potential mistakes.
- Machine learning algorithms are affected by the Vs of big data, and all the stages of the machine learning life cycle may require solutions to cope with the requirements of big data, although not all problems need have all the phases affected, and these requirements may only be necessary for some of them.
- Machine learning algorithms are commonly characterized by requiring long runs, performing transformation on the data (e.g., via preprocessing) and taking multiple passes through the data to build a model. Those needs suit well the design principles of Spark and its distributed data structures.
- The science of deploying machine learning in big data lies in designing solutions that keep in mind the principles of data locality and avoid unnecessary operations.
- Spark MLlib is based on DataFrames and contains some of the most common machine learning algorithms such as decision trees, logistic regression, and support vector machines, along with a number of standard data preprocessing methods.
- MLlib distinguishes between Estimators and Transformers. A Transformer is an algorithm that will modify a DataFrame by *adding* one or more columns. An Estimator is any machine learning process or algorithm that requires parameters to be fitted based on data. It can either be a preprocessing method or a machine learning algorithm, and it therefore fits the parameters with the input DataFrame and produces a Transformer with the fitted parameters.
- Before fitting a machine learning model in MLlib the data needs to be formatted, joining together all the features as a `Vector`. MLlib provides tools to do such transformation (and many others) prior to learning a model. It also includes a module to evaluate the goodness of the predictions made by a model. All of these steps can be coupled together within a Pipeline.
- MLlib facilitates hyperparameter tuning with tools such as a CrossValidator and `TrainValidationSplit`.

In conclusion, implementing any machine learning algorithm in the context of big data may just not be possible (or reasonable) due to the difficulties in efficiently distributing the computations. MLlib provides a good number of classical algorithms with some limitations. In the next chapter we will learn more about how to design big data solutions for machine learning algorithms.

6.5   To Learn More

If you are not very familiar with machine learning, we have prepared a list of recommended reading and online courses:

> Classic machine learning books include Bishop (2006), Hastie et al. (2001), and Ng (2017).

Data preprocessing books: García et al. (2015); Luengo et al. (2020).

Online courses: "Machine Learning Specialization" by Coursera;[10] the "Machine Learning in Python with scikit-learn" MOOC.[11]

Hands-on machine learning with Python: Garreta et al. (2017); Géron (2022).

Keep up to date with the latest version of MLlib[12] for new additions. You can also look at Meng et al. (2016), a journal paper describing the details of this library.

Spark Packages[13] is a community repository of big data tools in Spark. This includes various machine learning algorithms that are not offered as part of MLlib.

Other libraries include FlinkML[14] and DaskML (Daniel, 2019).

6.6 Solutions to Challenges

Challenge #6.1

We have created a Pipeline to assemble the data in the right shape and learn a linear regression model. Could you add an extra preprocessing stage to normalize the data prior to learning? Investigate how to use the StandardScaler of MLlib.

Let's recap. We have some training and test data where we want to fit a linear regression model to predict the total marks based on the exercise and group project marks.

```
train_df.show(2)
```

```
+----+----+----+----+-------+----+
|Ex01|Ex02|Ex03|Ex04|Project|Exam|
+----+----+----+----+-------+----+
|60.0|85.0|60.0|20.0|   70.0|33.0|
|60.0|85.0|75.0|85.0|   70.0|32.0|
+----+----+----+----+-------+----+
only showing top 2 rows
```

Usually, we use the standard scaler in gradient-based machine learning models to simplify the optimization of the loss function, making all the features have the same mean (0) and standard deviation (1.0). Normalizing the data may not be particularly necessary in this simple example, as the range of all the features is between 0 and 100 marks and although the means vary, the standard deviations are not very different (you

---

[10] www.coursera.org/specializations/machine-learning-introduction
[11] https://inria.github.io/scikit-learn-mooc/
[12] https://spark.apache.org/docs/latest/
[13] https://spark-packages.org/
[14] https://nightlies.apache.org/flink/flink-docs-stable/

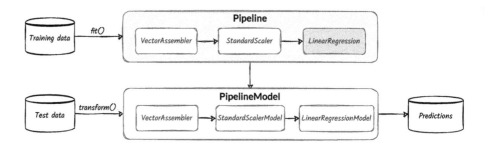

Figure 6.3 Pipelining a Transformer (`VectorAssembler`) with two Estimators, `StandardScaler` and `LinearRegression`.

could check this with the `describe()` transformation). Nevertheless, the idea is to learn how to add this step in a Pipeline.

Before creating the Pipeline, let's see how the `StandardScaler` module works in the official documentation.[15] By default, the features will be scaled to have a standard deviation of 1.0, but it won't remove the mean to make all features have a zero mean (which is the default behavior in other packages like scikit-learn). To make this happen, we should use the parameter `withMean = True`. `StandardScaler` is an Estimator, and therefore it has a `fit()` method which will calculate the mean and standard deviation of each feature in the `inputCol` column in our DataFrame. So, we need to assemble all the features first using a `VectorAssembler`, and then apply the scaler. After these stages, we can finally learn the linear regression model. Figure 6.3 depicts the Pipeline we are aiming to build up.

Let's start building our pipeline. We first need to create the different objects that will compose the stages of the pipeline. In this case, we will be telling the assembler to put the vectors in the column `'raw_features'`, since we will then use `'features'` to be the output of our new `StandardScaler`.

```
assembler = VectorAssembler(inputCols=feature_cols, outputCol="raw_features")
```

We can now create our `StandardScaler` with input features given by the assembler (`'raw_features'`) and output column `'feature'`. Let's import the `StandardScaler` first and then create the scaler:

```
from pyspark.ml.feature import StandardScaler
scaler = StandardScaler(
    inputCol=assembler.getOutputCol(), outputCol="features", withMean=True
)
```

> When concatenating multiple processes in pipelines you must ensure that the `outputCol` of one process matches the `inputCol` of the subsequent one. For this, you can also consider using the attribute of the previous process, for example `assembler.getOutputCol()`.

---

[15] https://spark.apache.org/docs/3.3.0/api/python/reference/api/pyspark.ml.feature.StandardScaler.html

Finally, we just need to create the linear regression object, put everything into the pipeline and fit it.

```
lr = LinearRegression(
    maxIter=10, regParam=0.3, labelCol="Exam", featuresCol="features"
)
pipeline = Pipeline(stages=[assembler, scaler, lr])
pipeline_model = pipeline.fit(train_df)
```

Let's transform the test set to see our new predictions.

```
prediction = pipeline_model.transform(test_df)
```

If we now have a look at the `prediction` DataFrame:

```
prediction.show(2)
```

```
+----+----+----+----+-------+----+--------------------+--------------------+-
----------------+
|Ex01|Ex02|Ex03|Ex04|Project|Exam|        raw_features|            features|
prediction|
+----+----+----+----+-------+----+--------------------+--------------------+-
----------------+
|60.0|80.0|70.0|40.0|
0.0|32.0|[60.0,80.0,70.0,4...|[-2.3543803544392...|0.371676268767537|
|80.0|80.0|65.0|60.0|
55.0|65.0|[80.0,80.0,65.0,6...|[-0.7505229950832...|44.76477287291367|
+----+----+----+----+-------+----+--------------------+--------------------+-
----------------+
only showing top 2 rows
```

We can appreciate how each preprocessing stage has added a new column. The assembler generated the `'raw_features'` column, which was used as input to the scaler. The latter added the `'features'` column, and finally `lr` produced the prediction.

Out of curiosity, let's see the root mean squeared error of this pipeline:

```
rmse_evaluator.evaluate(prediction)
```

```
20.963068684668464
```

We got the same result again. You might be thinking that the scaler didn't make any difference because all the features were already on the same scale. Funnily enough, that's not really the reason. A careful read of the documentation for the Spark linear regression model tells us that it has actually embedded the standardization process as a hyperparameter that is true by default. So, creating this pipeline isn't really providing anything new, but it shows a simple example of a pipeline.

Challenge #6.2

Linear regression seems to make an OK prediction, but how does it compare to other regression models? Explore MLlib and test a different machine learning algorithm and its hyperparameters.

You could have picked any of the regressors available in the MLlib for this. In our case, we have selected the gradient boosted tree (GBT)[16] regressor. Let's import it and create a `GBTRegressor` object. We also reinitialize the `assembler`:

```
from pyspark.ml.regression import GBTRegressor
assembler = VectorAssembler(inputCols=feature_cols, outputCol="features")
gbt = GBTRegressor(labelCol="Exam", featuresCol="features")
```

We can create a pipeline and test it with default parameters:

```
pipeline = Pipeline(stages=[assembler, gbt])
pipeline_model = pipeline.fit(train_df)


prediction = pipeline_model.transform(test_df)


rmse_evaluator.evaluate(prediction)
```

```
28.21765417483108
```

Oh, well. Looks like GBT is not making a great prediction compared to linear regression. Let's see if we can tune its hyperparameters to reduce the error.

```
paramGrid = ParamGridBuilder() \
    .addGrid(gbt.maxBins, [2,5,15]) \
    .addGrid(gbt.maxDepth, [2, 5, 10, 20]) \
.build()
```

> When creating this `paramGrid`, it is tempting to copy and paste from previous examples. In doing so, you may get in trouble if the hyperparameters added to the grid are not linked to the object that represents the classifier/regressors we want to test. Note how we use `gbt.maxBins` to refer to the hyperparameter of the `gbt` regressor we are testing on this occasion. If, by mistake, you used an existing object but the wrong one (e.g., `lr`), Spark wouldn't complain if you put this `paramGrid` within a `CrossValidator`, but of course, it wouldn't test those hyperparameters.

```
crossval = CrossValidator(
    estimator=pipeline,
    estimatorParamMaps=paramGrid,
    evaluator=rmse_evaluator,
    numFolds=3,
    seed=123456,
)


cv_model = crossval.fit(train_df)


prediction = cv_model.transform(test_df)


rmse_evaluator.evaluate(prediction)
```

```
19.78548564472623
```

---

[16] https://spark.apache.org/docs/3.3.0/api/python/reference/api/pyspark.ml.regression.GBTRegresso
r.html#pyspark.ml.regression.GBTRegressor

In this particular case, the hyperparameter tuning has been very successful, and we have reduced the error a lot compared to the original hyperparameter setting. We invite those readers familiar with machine learning to have a look at the best hyperparameters by running

```
best_gbt = cv_model.bestModel.stages[1]
best_gbt.extractParamMap()
```

and analyzing what those might mean. Nevertheless, the dataset is rather small, and it might be challenging to find precise conclusions.

> ### Challenge #6.3
>
> In this example we treated the prediction of the Exam mark as a regression problem, but we could also be interested in predicting the total mark that the students will get (taking the coursework and the project into consideration, before doing the Exam), for example, Fail: < 50; Pass: [50, 60); Merit: [60, 70); Distinction: > 70. To do this, you will need to use the column 'Total', where the final numerical marks are, and transform your DataFrame, adding a column with the right labels (e.g., Fail, Pass, Merit, or Distinction). You may choose any classifier available in MLlib, and any metric you consider useful to measure the success in classification.

As we need to recover the 'Total' column from the original dataset, we are going to reload the dataset. In this case, we remove the 'Exam' column instead of 'Total' (as well as the question columns):

```
df = spark.read.format("csv").option("header", "true").load("data/marks.csv")
df = df.select([sql_f.col(c).cast("float").alias(c) for c in df.columns])
df = df.drop('Question 1').drop('Question 2').drop('Question 3')\
       .drop('Question 4').drop('Exam')
```

We have to transform the 'Total' mark column into a degree classification (a string). We do this before partitioning the dataset into training and test partitions using Spark SQL transformations.

```
df = df.withColumn('Classification',
                   sql_f.when(df.Total < 50, 'Fail')\
                   .when(df.Total < 60, 'Pass')\
                   .when(df.Total < 70, 'Merit')\
                   .otherwise('Distinction'))
train_df, test_df = df.randomSplit([0.7, 0.3], seed=123456)


train_df.show(2)

+----+----+----+----+-------+-----+--------------+
|Ex01|Ex02|Ex03|Ex04|Project|Total|Classification|
+----+----+----+----+-------+-----+--------------+
|60.0|85.0|60.0|20.0|   70.0| 48.0|          Fail|
|60.0|85.0|75.0|85.0|   70.0| 53.0|          Pass|
+----+----+----+----+-------+-----+--------------+
only showing top 2 rows
```

If we now try to use, for example, a random forest classifier for this, we will run into a problem. Let us show you:

```
feature_cols = train_df.columns
feature_cols.remove("Classification")
assembler = VectorAssembler(inputCols=feature_cols, outputCol="features")

from pyspark.ml.classification import RandomForestClassifier
rf = RandomForestClassifier(labelCol="Classification",\
                            featuresCol="features")
pipeline = Pipeline(stages=[assembler, rf])


pipeline_model = pipeline.fit(train_df)
```

```
-----------------------------------------------------------------------
IllegalArgumentException Traceback (most recent call last)
C:\Users\MIKEL~1.GAL\AppData\Local\Temp\ipykernel_23252/2218242543.py in <mod-
ule> ----> 1 pipeline_model = pipeline.fit(train_df)
...
```

Although RandomForestClassifier, and any other classifier in Spark, is designed for classification tasks, it expects the label column to be of numeric type rather than a string. To deal with this, we need to transform that 'Classification' column, and MLlib provides tools for this. For example, StringIndexer[17] will help with this. Let's try it out first:

```
from pyspark.ml.feature import StringIndexer
labelIndexer = StringIndexer(inputCol="Classification",\
                             outputCol="ClassificationIndex")
indexing = labelIndexer.fit(train_df)
```

We used fit() because StringIndexer is an Estimator, which needs to look for the different labels existing in the input column. Once these values are known, the resulting Transformer will be adding a 'ClassificationIndex' column:

```
indexing.transform(train_df).show(2)
```

```
+----+----+----+----+-------+-----+--------------+-------------------+
|Ex01|Ex02|Ex03|Ex04|Project|Total|Classification|ClassificationIndex|
+----+----+----+----+-------+-----+--------------+-------------------+
|60.0|85.0|60.0|20.0|   70.0| 48.0|          Fail|                3.0|
|60.0|85.0|75.0|85.0|   70.0| 53.0|          Pass|                2.0|
+----+----+----+----+-------+-----+--------------+-------------------+
only showing top 2 rows
```

So, we can now create the pipeline, adding labelIndexer as a stage.

```
rf = RandomForestClassifier(labelCol="ClassificationIndex",\
                            featuresCol="features")
pipeline = Pipeline(stages=[assembler, labelIndexer, rf])
```

---

[17] https://spark.apache.org/docs/3.3.0/api/python/reference/api/pyspark.ml.feature.StringIndexer.html#py
spark.ml.feature.StringIndexer

Let's fit this pipeline with default hyperparameters for the random forest algorithm and check its performance.

```
pipeline_model = pipeline.fit(train_df)

prediction = pipeline_model.transform(test_df)
```

To evaluate the predictions made by this classifier, we need to check the tools available in the evaluation package of MLlib. In particular, we are dealing with a multi-class classification problem, as we have four different labels. Let's import the appropriate class and check the performance:

```
from pyspark.ml.evaluation import MulticlassClassificationEvaluator
acc_evaluator = MulticlassClassificationEvaluator(
    metricName="accuracy", labelCol="ClassificationIndex"
)

acc_evaluator.evaluate(prediction)
```

```
0.9545454545454546
```

That's a great result, but let's see if we can tune the hyperparameters of the random forest to go any further with a simple cross validation:

```
paramGrid = ParamGridBuilder() \
    .addGrid(rf.maxBins, [5, 10, 15]) \
    .addGrid(rf.numTrees, [5, 20, 100]) \
    .addGrid(rf.maxDepth, [2, 5, 10, 20]) \
.build()

crossval = CrossValidator(
    estimator=pipeline,
    estimatorParamMaps=paramGrid,
    evaluator=acc_evaluator,
    numFolds=3,
    seed=123456,
)

cv_model = crossval.fit(train_df)

predictions = cv_model.transform(test_df)

acc_evaluator.evaluate(prediction)
```

```
0.9545454545454546
```

Well, that didn't improve the results because they were already quite good. We could also have a look at the confusion matrix to understand a bit more about where the misclassifications are. To do this, we may have to use the RDD-based MLlib API:

```
from pyspark.mllib.evaluation import MulticlassMetrics
preds_and_labels = predictions.select(["prediction", "ClassificationIndex"])
metrics = MulticlassMetrics(preds_and_labels.rdd)
print(metrics.confusionMatrix())
```

```
DenseMatrix([[12.,   0.,   0.,   0.],
             [ 1.,   5.,   1.,   0.],
             [ 0.,   0.,   2.,   0.],
             [ 0.,   0.,   0.,   1.]])
```

We have simply shown you how to apply these techniques and how to fine-tune their hyperparameters. Looking for better models to improve these results would be more of a machine learning problem per se, and in this book we are more interested in how to distribute the computation rather than solving a particular machine learning problem.

6.7   Exercises

6.1 Briefly explain what the machine learning life cycle is. Name a few of the key stages.

6.2 Indicate whether the following statements about machine learning are true or false:
   (a) Data preprocessing consists of distributing the data evenly in a cluster of computing nodes.
   (b) Evaluation strategies are needed to perform hyperparameter tuning.
   (c) A Pipeline is an algorithm to automatically find the best machine learning algorithm for a given dataset.
   (d) Overfitting the training data may result in models that don't perform well on unseen data.

6.3 What is the difference between parameters and hyperparameters?

6.4 What are the key aspects of machine learning algorithms that need to be considered to develop big data solutions?

6.5 Why would you prefer Spark over Hadoop to perform machine learning? Briefly explain your answer.

6.6 Explain the differences between a Pipeline and a PipelineModel, and indicate whether they are Transformers and/or Estimators.

6.7 Could you create a Pipeline of only Transformers? Briefly explain your answer.

6.8 Would it make sense to concatenate a logistic regression Estimator right after a decision tree Estimator and an SVM Estimator in a Pipeline?

6.9 We have seen that when creating a CrossValidator object, we can use a Pipeline as an Estimator:
```
crossval = CrossValidator(estimator=pipeline,
                          estimatorParamMaps=paramGrid,
                          evaluator=rmse_evaluator,
                          numFolds=3,
                          seed=123456)
```
Would it be possible (and would it make sense) to create a pipeline that includes a CrossValidator object? Something like this:

```
cv = CrossValidator(estimator=lr,\
                        evaluator=evaluator,\
                        estimatorParamMaps=paramGrid)
pipeline = Pipeline(stages=[vectorAssembler, cv])
```

Briefly explain your answer.

6.10 You are using your own laptop to run the logistic regression from MLlib, and you are testing it in pseudo-distributed mode (i.e., option `local[*]`). You test the accuracy and you are happy with it; however, it takes three days to train the model. If you were to use a "real" cluster of computing nodes (e.g., 10 nodes), would you expect the accuracy to remain the same? Briefly explain your answer.

7 Machine Learning for Big Data

Learning Outcomes

[KU]	Understanding different approaches to designing machine learning solutions for big data: local versus global
[KU]	Studying how these approaches can be applied to design a big data solution for decision trees
[KU, IS, PPS]	Measuring the scalability of a big data solution
[IS, PPS]	Learning how to implement a local-based solution for decision trees in big data

The premise of big data is that having a world rich in data may enable machine learning algorithms to obtain more accurate models than ever before (and therefore provide more *value*), but classical methods fail to handle the new data space requirements. We mentioned before that the "science" of doing machine learning in the context of big data lies in how to effectively distribute the computation to exploit all the existing data. With the leveraging of distributed technologies and the appearance of the MapReduce programming paradigm and big data frameworks such as Spark, some classical machine learning algorithms are being adapted to this scenario.

In the previous chapter we saw how to use Spark MLlib, which contains multiple big data solutions for a good number of machine learning algorithms, and allows us to create pipelines of diverse methods to solve a problem. However, we have not yet discussed how these techniques were designed or whether they perform exactly the same procedure as the original (i.e., sequential) version.

7.1   Designing Machine Learning Methods for Big Data

Multiple MapReduce-like strategies have been developed to adapt traditional machine learning algorithms to the big data scenario. Most of these methods are approximations of the original algorithms, and only a few of them are exact replicas of the sequential version. The first solutions were based on Hadoop, and implemented in the Mahout library, where we find both exact replicas and approximations/variations. As a bit of a spoiler, MLlib provides solutions that try to follow the original algorithms as much as possible, but it usually sacrifices certain features.

Before making any definitions, let's focus on a simple example.

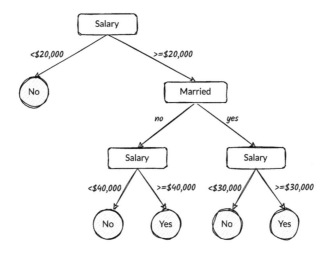

Figure 7.1 Decision tree example for loan prediction.

7.1.1 Example with Decision Trees

Without going into too much detail, decision trees[1] are a classical supervised machine learning method for classification and regression problems. The simplest way to understand how this method works is to look at its output. Figure 7.1 presents a simplistic decision tree to decide whether a bank should give a loan to a customer based on a couple of features: their civil status and salary. If a person applyied for a loan, we could use the tree to make the decision. Starting from the root node of that tree (salary), we would first consider if the person makes less than $20 000. If they do, we would follow the left branch, meaning that they wouldn't qualify for a loan. In the case that they do make at least $20 000, we'd walk down the right branch of the tree. We would check their civil status (the "Married" node), which would take us to two different scenarios. If they are married, the salary would need to be at least $30 000 for the model to grant a loan, but if they weren't, their salary would need to be at least $40 000.

The problem in machine learning is to find a way to build that tree based on some training data. In a nutshell, this is how it works. The technique partitions the data into different subsets depending on the input features. It starts off by measuring the ability of each input attribute/feature to break the data into groups of the same nature (e.g., class label), using dispersion metrics (e.g., Gini[2] or entropy[3]). The feature and value with the highest power to split the data are selected as the root node, and the data is split into two child nodes (i.e., it usually builds binary trees). This process is applied recursively until each node reaches a certain size that we don't want to split further. The final model is a tree-like structure that allows us to predict the output of unseen cases.

Some of the most relevant properties of decision trees are:

---

[1] https://en.wikipedia.org/wiki/Decision_tree_learning
[2] https://en.wikipedia.org/wiki/Gini_coefficient
[3] https://en.wikipedia.org/wiki/Entropy_(information_theory)

- they can handle both numerical and categorical data;
- they are quite interpretable; and
- they perform an implicit feature selection process which provides information about the importance of the features.

Decision trees are commonly used in ensemble methods like random forests.

To show you a more realistic example of what the output of looks like, we are going to build a decision tree with the data from the previous chapter. Instead of building a regression model to predict the exam mark of the students according to their marks in coursework and the group project, in this chapter we want to focus on their total marks. In this case, rather than predicting the numerical total mark, we will treat it as a classification problem to simply predict whether a student will get a first class mark (total mark >= 70) or not. Let's initialize Spark, read the data, and transform the DataFrame accordingly.

```python
from pyspark.sql import SparkSession
import pyspark.sql.functions as sql_f
import pandas as pd
spark = SparkSession \
    .builder \
    .master("local[*]") \
    .appName("MLbig") \
    .getOrCreate()
sc = spark.sparkContext
```

We load the same data we were using in the previous chapter. To do this in a slightly different way, we manually define the schema when loading the data.

```python
from pyspark.sql.types import *
schema = StructType(
    [
        StructField("Ex01", FloatType(), True),
        StructField("Ex02", FloatType(), True),
        StructField("Ex03", FloatType(), True),
        StructField("Ex04", FloatType(), True),
        StructField("Project", FloatType(), True),
        StructField("Question 1", FloatType(), True),
        StructField("Question 2", FloatType(), True),
        StructField("Question 3", FloatType(), True),
        StructField("Question 4", FloatType(), True),
        StructField("Exam", FloatType(), True),
        StructField("Total", FloatType(), True),
    ]
)
```

With this schema, we are going to read the data, create columns for the classification ('first' versus 'not-first') and remove those columns that won't be necessary. The columns with the marks for Questions 1 to 4 are part of the exam, but we are aiming to predict whether the students will get a first class before the exam takes place. Thus, those columns will be removed, together with the total, which we have transformed into the target class 'Classification'.

```
df = spark.read.format('csv').option("header", 'true')\
            .schema(schema).load("data/marks.csv")
df = df.withColumn('Classification', sql_f.when(df.Total<70, 'not-first')\
                                .otherwise('first'))
df = df.drop("Question 1").drop("Question 2").drop("Question 3")\
        .drop("Question 4").drop("Exam").drop("Total")

df.show(2)
```

```
+-----+----+----+----+-------+--------------+
| Ex01|Ex02|Ex03|Ex04|Project|Classification|
+-----+----+----+----+-------+--------------+
|100.0|85.0|80.0|70.0|   80.0|         first|
|100.0|85.0|80.0|90.0|   93.0|         first|
+-----+----+----+----+-------+--------------+
only showing top 2 rows
```

As the dataset is rather small, we could use the scikit-learn library as follows (transforming our Spark DataFrame into a pandas DataFrame first!). Note that to run this code you must have installed the `sklearn` package.

```
import pandas as pd
from sklearn.model_selection import train_test_split
from sklearn.tree import DecisionTreeClassifier
# Transform the Spark DataFrame into a Pandas DataFrame
results = df.toPandas()
# shape the Pandas DataFrame for scikit-learn
X = results.iloc[:, :-1]
y = results["Classification"]
# we do a random 70/30 split
X_train, X_test, y_train, y_test = train_test_split(
    X, y, test_size=0.3, random_state=1
)
# we train the model with a depth of 2
clf = DecisionTreeClassifier(random_state=0, max_depth=2)
clf.fit(X_train.values, y_train.values)
```

```
DecisionTreeClassifier(max_depth=2, random_state=0)
```

Figure 7.2 plots the tree generated with the scikit-learn library. The tree is so small (only two levels) because we intentionally used the parameter `max_depth = 2` when creating the tree. You may want to play with that hyperparameter to see if the result changes.

Bearing in mind that we have a binary classification problem, the predicted class output is given by the class with the maximum number of elements in a leaf. This is represented in scikit-learn as `value = [x,y]`, where x would be the number of samples of class 0, and y the ones from class 1 which belong to that leaf. Class 0 corresponds to First, and class 1 Not-First. Thus, we can interpret this tree as follows:

- If the Ex03 mark is less than or equal to 72.5 and Project is less than or equal to 91.0, the final classification will be Not-First.
- If the Ex03 mark is less than or equal to 72.5 and Project is greater than 91.0, the final classification will be First.

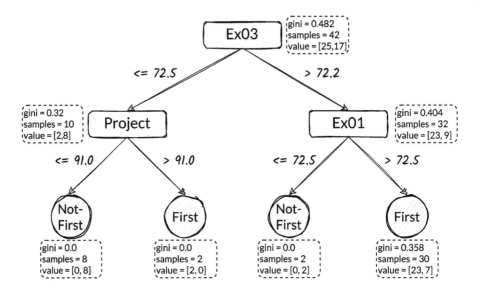

Figure 7.2 Decision tree generated with a maximum depth of 2.

- If the Ex03 mark is greater than 72.5 and the Ex01 mark is less than or equal to 72.5, the final classification will be Not-First.
- If the Ex03 mark is greater than 72.5 and the Ex01 mark is greater than 72.5, the final classification will be First.

We built that tree using the scikit-learn library, which is a library for standard machine learning algorithms without any parallelization. What would happen if we fed a very big dataset in? Well, it would either take ages to create the tree, or it might actually run out of memory while building it. Without using MLlib, why don't we try to do this with what we have learned so far about Spark? What is the easiest way to apply machine learning to big datasets? Divide and Conquer!

When we load the data with Spark, the data is distributed among the workers. Using the idea of MapReduce (divide and conquer), why don't we simply create a separate decision tree for each partition of the data (only using the data of that partition)?

Let's imagine that the data is split into three partitions (P0, P1, and P2). We train three independent decision trees, one on each worker. This would happen in parallel and with less data, which highly reduces the required runtime and memory constraints for building a model. Figure 7.3 shows how this training phase would look.

The problem then lies in how to combine all these models to make predictions. The easiest way to do this would be to use each model as an independent classifier that gives us a "vote" on the predicted output for an unseen example. Let's assume that the model trained with P0 predicts First for an unseen example, the model trained with P1 predicts Not-First, and the P2 model thinks it is a First. A majority vote from the three classifiers would suggest a prediction of First. If we were dealing with a regression

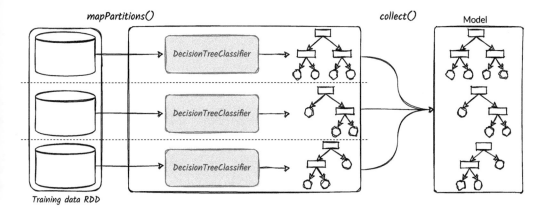

Figure 7.3 Building a decision tree with a divide-and-conquer approach.

problem, the aggregation could simply be the average of the marks predicted at each partition. In other words, we are going to create an *ensemble* of trees.

> More sophisticated aggregations exist. For example, we could take into consideration not only the predicted output but also the probability associated with that prediction, and apply a weighted average/vote.

By the way, is this way of "merging" the different models going to be general for all machine learning models? Definitely not. There are methods that don't create any model, for example, *lazy learning* methods like k-nearest neighbor, or clustering algorithms. But for most *eager learning*[4] methods that build a model, this approach would actually do the trick to use all the data in some way. Of course, there may be some caveats, as we will discuss later.

Let's begin by splitting the data into training and test partitions:

```
train_df, test_df = df.randomSplit([0.7, 0.3], seed=654321)
```

We are not going to use MLlib. Instead, we want to do this ourselves using Spark. Unfortunately, the DataFrame API is not really flexible enough to apply that divide-and-conquer approach, and in Python we don't have Spark Datasets, which would allow us to perform map-like transformations as we did with RDDs. However, if you remember from the chapter about Spark RDDs, there was a transformation called `mapPartitions()` that does exactly what we need; apply a function to an entire partition of the data.

So, while we have read the data as a DataFrame, we are going to use the underlying RDD (obviously, this is not ideal as the RDD API is not as efficient, but our focus here is on the design of a distributed big data solution). As you may remember, the DataFrame API determines the number of partitions automatically when loading the data. As we are using a very small dataset, it is likely that df has only one partition. To illustrate the suggested divide-and-conquer strategy, we are going to manually split the training data into three partitions using `repartition()`, and store it in a new variable:

---

[4] https://en.wikipedia.org/wiki/Eager_learning

```
train_rdd = train_df.rdd.repartition(3)
```

We also split the test set, so we can also parallelize the testing phase. Let's get two different partitions:

```
test_rdd  = test_df.rdd.repartition(2)
```

We will need to know the names of the columns later, so we are going to store them in a global variable.

```
column_names = df.columns
```

Building the Model in Parallel

So, the idea is to use mapPartitions(func) to build a model with each partition of the data. Let's remember how this operation works. From Table 4.7, it "applies the function func to each partition of the RDD; func receives an iterator and returns another iterator that can be of a different type."

In this case, the func function will create a decision tree model with the data in the partition, which means that we will train a tree locally in each worker. Rather than implementing our own decision tree, we will use the scikit-learn library. This function will get an iterator, which will allow us to go through all the instances/rows of a partition, returning a model for each partition. Thus, we will be transforming the data in train_rdd into a decision tree model per partition.

Let's say we are going to implement a function build_model(), doing something like this:

```
train_rdd.mapPartitions(build_model)

def build_model(partition_data_it):
    # Code to build a model from data_partition

    return [model]   # we need to return an iterator,
                     # although it may only have one element
```

partition_data_it is an iterator. Before feeding the examples to the scikit-learn decision tree, we have to create a pandas DataFrame from this iterator. This will just be a single instruction, as you can see in the following code. After that, we can simply copy the code we have to train a scikit-learn decision tree classifier.

```
def build_model(partition_data_it):
    # transform the iterator to pandas
    partition_data_df = pd.DataFrame(partition_data_it, columns=column_names)
    clf = DecisionTreeClassifier(random_state=0, max_depth=2)
    # shape the pandas DataFrame for scikit-learn
    X_train = partition_data_df.iloc[:, :-1]
    y_train = partition_data_df["Classification"]
    # fit the model
    model = clf.fit(X_train.values, y_train.values)
    return [model]
```

There are a few details to highlight on the above code:

- You might be surprised that the pandas API is capable of creating a pandas DataFrame from an iterator (a list) of RDD objects. Why does this work? Because each element of `partition_data_it` is of type Row, which extends `tuple`.
- For simplicity, we have hard-coded the name of the label column as `'Classifi-cation'`, and the column names as `partition_data_df.iloc[:,:-1]`. This is probably not a good programming practice, as this code would only work for the dataset we provided, and assumes the output column is always at the end. We leave this for the reader to improve.
- It returns a list with a single element. Why? Because for this function to work within `mapPartitions()`, we need to return an iterator.
- Note how we are using the variable `column_names` inside this function. You may remember that Spark sends out functions and global variables to the workers, and `column_names` is currently a global variable here.

Now let's train the model; this is going to be our equivalent to the `fit()` function of MLlib. As the models will be relatively lightweight, we can bring them all back to the driver with `collect()`:

```
models = train_rdd.mapPartitions(build_model).collect()
```

How many elements do we have in `models`?

```
len(models)
```

```
3
```

As we had three partitions in the training, we have created an independent tree for each of them. Changing the number of partitions would also change the number of classifiers learned. Do you anticipate any issues with this? What do you think would happen if we used a very high number of partitions?

Testing the Model in Parallel

We have the test data as an RDD in `test_rdd` and we want to classify all its examples in parallel. As we have three models, we will need to predict the output of each example for all three models, and then compute the majority vote to get the final prediction. We will break this into two phases. First, for each test instance, we predict its output with all the models in `models`. Later, we will have to compute the majority vote of the predictions.

Let's begin with the prediction phase. We define a function `predict()` that will take an instance of the test set and predict its output with each of the models, generating a list of predictions:

```
def predict(instance):
    return [m.predict([instance[:-1]])[0] for m in models]
```

For simplicity, we pass the instance to the `predict()` function of scikit-learn as a list with a single example, so we then take the prediction of the first one (`[0]`).

You may remember that `models` is a variable that lives in the driver program. In this function, we need the models to be available to the executors as we are distributing the testing phase. If the size of the variable `models` was too large, we would suggest broadcasting the models! (And we expect the readers to do so.) In our case, however, it is a very small list of models, we will pass it as a global variable to the executors.

Let's see if it works:

```
test_rdd.map(predict).take(3)
```

```
[['not-first', 'not-first', 'not-first'],
 ['first', 'not-first', 'not-first'],
 ['first', 'first', 'not-first']]
```

To aggregate the predictions and compute the majority class, we could create a dictionary and count how many times we have a Not-First and how many times we have a First for a given list of predictions. Lastly, we could get the key of the class with the maximum number of votes:

```
def agg_predictions(preds):
    predictions = { "first": 0, "not-first" : 0 }

    for elem in preds:
        predictions[elem]+= 1

    return max(predictions, key=predictions.get)
```

```
test_rdd.map(predict).map(agg_predictions).take(5)
```

```
['not-first', 'not-first', 'first', 'not-first', 'first']
```

We could also have used the `multimode()` function from the statistics library in Python to do this even more simply:

```
from statistics import multimode
test_rdd.map(predict).map(lambda l: multimode(l)[0]).take(5)
```

```
['not-first', 'not-first', 'first', 'not-first', 'first']
```

Of course, we could have done both the prediction and aggregation in one go. Having said that, we would recommend keeping two separate functions, so that the code is more reusable. For example, you may want to test different aggregation mechanisms, or reuse the `predict()` function for regression problems.

We can use these functions to make the output more similar to how MLlib works. We create a new function `transform()` that will use the prediction and aggregation functions to transform the input RDD (of Rows), adding a new column with the prediction.

```
def transform(instance):
    return Row(**instance.asDict(),\
            raw_prediction=agg_predictions(predict(instance)))
```

You may have noticed that we are creating a new Row object with the content of the instance, and an additional pair `'raw_prediction'` with the aggregated prediction. We need to do this because Rows are also immutables. Let's test it:

```
prediction = test_rdd.map(transform).toDF()
```

```
prediction.show(2)
```

```
+----+----+----+-----+-------+--------------+--------------+
|Ex01|Ex02|Ex03| Ex04|Project|Classification|raw_prediction|
+----+----+----+-----+-------+--------------+--------------+
|60.0|85.0|60.0| 20.0|   70.0|     not-first|     not-first|
|70.0|85.0|65.0|100.0|   65.0|     not-first|     not-first|
+----+----+----+-----+-------+--------------+--------------+
only showing top 2 rows
```

If we want to evaluate the classification performance of this divide-and-conquer solution, we may use the MLlib `MulticlassClassificationEvaluator` module to measure the accuracy. However, MLlib does not accept predictions as strings (i.e., `'first'` versus `'not-first'`), but it requires a double. We can easily modify our prediction DataFrame as follows:

```
prediction_num = prediction.select(
    (prediction["Classification"] == "first").cast("double").alias("label"),
    (prediction["raw_prediction"] == "first").cast("double").alias("pred"),
)
```

```
from pyspark.ml.evaluation import MulticlassClassificationEvaluator
acc_evaluator = MulticlassClassificationEvaluator(
    metricName="accuracy", labelCol="label", predictionCol="pred"
)
```

```
acc_evaluator.evaluate(prediction_num)
```

```
0.8571428571428571
```

With the current 70/30 data split and without looking at the hyperparameters of the trees, the model seems to distinguish quite accurately between First and Not-First students in the test phase.

> ## Challenge #7.1
>
> We have used map to classify the instances in the test set. You are now asked to reimplement the testing phase using `mapPartitions()` instead of map. Would you expect it to be faster? Why?

We have completed the first implementation of a big data solution, splitting the original data into chunks and applying locally independent models. This is what we could call a *local approach*, which is obviously an approximation of the original decision tree. This doesn't "see" the data as a whole but in different chunks. In the early versions of Apache Mahout (using Hadoop), a similar approach to parallelizing decision trees was implemented.

How does this differ from using the sequential implementation? Our approximation should be worse, right? Let us use scikit-learn on the same training and test data.

```
train_pd = train_df.toPandas()
test_pd = test_df.toPandas()
```

```
from sklearn.tree import DecisionTreeClassifier
clf = DecisionTreeClassifier(random_state=0, max_depth=2)
X_train = train_pd.iloc[:, :-1]
y_train = train_pd["Classification"]
clf.fit(X_train, y_train)
```

```
DecisionTreeClassifier(max_depth=2, random_state=0)
```

```
from sklearn.metrics import accuracy_score
X_test = test_pd.iloc[:, :-1]
y_pred = clf.predict(X_test)
y_test = test_pd['Classification']
accuracy_score(y_test, y_pred)
```

```
0.8571428571428571
```

Oh, this is fun! We have used a *local* model, which is obviously not seeing all the data at once, but we have got the exact same result! Sometimes, you could be surprised and get a better result. How is this possible? A higher result may be due to what we call the "ensemble effect." Ensemble learning[5] is a well-known approach in machine learning to improve the accuracy of single models by combining several variations of the same model. The different models in the ensemble are supposed to be diverse, which helps in correcting their mistakes. Consequently, one usually expects the ensemble to outperform all of its counterparts. In our case, we have three partitions, and therefore, "weak" classifiers that agree on a final result. Although each model may be worse than the single model trained with scikit-learn, their combination has led to the same final accuracy. It is not uncommon to beat that single-model performance if the models are appropriately trained. However, in our case this will just depend on the number of partitions we use. Here, we have exploited the concept of ensembles to reduce the error and use all the data in a straightforward way with little effort, and it is probably very quick to build the model.

It is somehow remarkable how easy this was; we didn't even need to understand much about the underlying model. We could replace decision trees with any other regression or classification algorithm from the scikit-learn library. So, should we always develop this kind of local approach? As we said before, the merging phase may become complicated, or even infeasible, for methods that don't build a model. But that is not the only reason why local approaches may not always be the best choice. To elaborate more on this, we would like to come back to one of the questions we asked when building the model: What will happen if we increase the number of partitions?

[5] https://en.wikipedia.org/wiki/Ensemble_learning

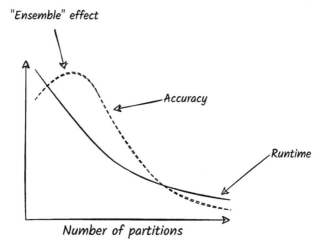

Figure 7.4 Hypothetical changes in performance when the number of partitions increases. The runtime of the building phase will tend to reduce, but it will plateau at some point. The accuracy will decrease as the number of partitions becomes bigger, but we may observe the ensemble effect with the right number of partitions. The real shape of those lines will depend on the dataset and the machine learning method we are parallelizing.

Figure 7.4 presents the expected performance change when the number of partitions increases. Let's discuss this in more detail.

- The building phase will probably be faster, because we have less data in each data partition, and we can parallelize the process even further.
- The final performance (i.e., the classification/error rate) will depend on the number of partitions we make.
  - If we split the data into a few partitions, we may observe the ensemble effect improving the performance of a single model.
  - However, if we split the data into too many partitions, we may end up with insufficient data to train any significant model!
- The test phase will become slower, as we would end up with a higher number of models that will have to make predictions, and we will have to aggregate them.

What is the alternative to this local model? The alternative would be to create a single *global model* using all the available data at once. In other words, try to obtain the same model as would be obtained if the method could be executed in a single node. What does this imply? It means that we need to understand how the method works and parallelize its operations, rather than distributing the execution of the whole method on pieces of the data.

As we mentioned before, MLlib aims to provide solutions that follow the original algorithms as far as possible (sometimes sacrificing some features of the algorithm), and this means implementing global methods to exploit all the data available as a whole, rather than in chunks. With Spark, we are not limited to a single MapReduce stage, so it is a suitable platform to attempt global models in which we may need to iterate through the data multiple times.

Global Decision Trees: The MLlib Implementation

MLlib aims to distribute the internal mechanisms of a decision tree, providing a global-based solution. Databricks[6] provided a great presentation describing the details of how Spark parallelizes decision trees. Although that's how it was implemented using RDDs, the underlying ideas are the same.

> If you look at the source code,[7] you will see that a decision tree is implemented as a random forest[8] of a single tree, using all the features.

Our goal in this section is not to discuss all the details of how this specific solution is implemented, but for you to get an idea of how the processing has been distributed, so that you can see how different this is from the local-based approach. We will show you our own examples of global-based big data solutions in later chapters.

As described previously, a decision tree searches for the best feature/attribute and cut-point value that allow us to split the data into two groups that are more similar among themselves with respect to the target output; this process is repeated recursively to construct the tree. In short, implementing a decision tree as a global model for big data may raise two main issues:

- Recursion may result in an excessive number of jobs. In traditional implementations of decision trees, recursion is commonly used to build the tree nodes, deciding how to split a tree node further, and this may result in up to 2^D splits that must be computed (D being the maximum depth of the tree). Tree nodes represent subsets of the data that share some commonalities (e.g., the Married node in Figure 7.1 involves all the training data with a salary greater than or equal to \$20 000), and the amount of data considered at each tree node will be smaller as we split, that is, as we go deeper in the tree (e.g., the Married node is split into yes/no subsets).

  If we were to implement the splitting recursively in Spark, we would be launching entire jobs to perform fewer and fewer calculations as we progress in the recursion, and that would yield very low CPU use and performance. Even though caching helps to iterate through big datasets, there are some costs associated with launching Spark jobs. The idea of implementing a high-performance distributed solution on big data is to reduce the number of jobs by performing all possible computations in each one. To solve this, the decision tree is built on a *level-by-level* basis. This means that all nodes of the same level are learned simultaneously, yielding a maximum of D jobs and, consequently, D iterations through the data.

- Dealing with continuous attributes may be problematic. In a categorical feature, for example color, which takes values, green, red, or blue, we can measure the dispersion of the target output when the input feature is red, green, and blue and determine which one is best to split the data. However, in a numerical/continuous attribute, this is slightly more difficult because if the values of a feature are in the range [0, 10],

[6] https://speakerdeck.com/jkbradley/mllib-decision-trees-at-sf-scala-baml-meetup
[7] https://github.com/apache/spark/blob/master/mllib/src/main/scala/org/apache/spark/ml/regression/DecisionTreeRegressor.scala
[8] https://github.com/apache/spark/blob/master/mllib/src/main/scala/org/apache/spark/ml/tree/impl/RandomForest.scala

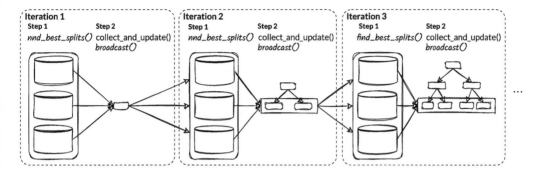

Figure 7.5 An overview of how global-based decision trees are implemented in Spark. The best splits are calculated iteratively for each level of the tree.

there are infinite cut-points we could test there. In most sequential implementations of decision trees, all the values existing in the training data for a given continuous attribute would be sorted and every middle point between two values would be considered a cut-point. This may not pose a challenge for small datasets, but for datasets with millions of instances it would soon become intractable.

A well-known solution to reduce the number of cut-points considered in numerical attributes is to discretize them. This process is usually called "binning," and only some points of the continuous interval are considered (e.g., using the quantiles, or uniformly selected in the interval). Using the example of a continuous attribute in the range [0, 10], we could uniformly discretize this attribute into 12 bins, and only consider the cut-points at $0, 1, 2, \ldots, 9$, and 10. Using this with big data will be key to reducing the number of computations.

With these issues in mind, we can focus on how to implement decision trees in parallel with Spark. Note that the tree structure is actually not expected to be a massive data structure, as it contains nodes with information about which attributes are more important, and the values that are used to virtually "split" the data. Thus, in the Spark implementation of decision trees, the model is a variable that lives in the driver node, and it is constructed iteratively from the information/statistics provided by the executors. To do this, the current model will have to be shared/distributed with all executors at each iteration. This is carried out in two main steps over a number of iterations as shown in Figure 7.5. We assume that we have the training data as either a DataFrame or an RDD, distributed and cached in the main memory of multiple executors, so that each executors has access to a fraction of the data.

Here is a brief description of the two main steps that are performed in each iteration:

Step 1: Find the best splits of a tree node in parallel. When considering splitting a node of the tree (initially the root node), we need to compute the best cut-points using impurity metrics like Gini, or other dispersion metrics, for each feature in the training data. This process involves the computation of some statistics for each attribute, which can easily be done in parallel. Computing that impurity may be similar to our Word Count, as we typically count the number of examples of a given class with a particular value for the feature under consideration. Thus, each executor only needs to make one pass over its subset of examples, collecting (partial) statistics about the splitting (i.e., the counting). The statistics from each executor are aggregated with a `reduceByKey()` that chooses the *global* best ($\langle feature \rangle$, $\langle split \rangle$) pair, or chooses to stop splitting if the stopping criteria are met.

> If you are wondering why `reduceByKey()`, and what the key is, this corresponds to the node of the tree that is being processed. Initially it is only the root node, so it will be only one executor. In the following iterations of the algorithm, multiple nodes (on the same level) are dealt with simultaneously, and the statistics of each tree node are aggregated in a single executor.

Step 2: Collect statistics, update, and broadcast the current model to all executors. The driver program collects the decisions made, that is, the feature and split for each node in the current iteration, and updates the model. In the first iteration, a single decision (one feature and split) corresponding to the root node is collected, whereas in subsequent iterations, various decisions, one per tree node at the current level, are collected to update the model. To further construct the model, all the executors need to know the current shape of the tree. Thus, the current model is broadcast to all executors before computing the next level of the tree.

These two steps are applied iteratively on a level-by-level basis until a given depth of the tree is reached, which is the maximum number of levels that are going to be considered to build the model. Being able to do the processing of all the nodes of a level at once would theoretically mean that the running time scales linearly with dataset size. Nevertheless, it does not scale linearly with the depth of the tree. If you run and analyze the MLlib decision tree you will notice that every iteration becomes slower; this is due to the number of transformations and calculations required to aggregate the statistics for each tree node, which increases the network traffic.

While the statistics are computed globally, and this is very similar to the original implementation of the decision tree in sequential mode, there are a few things that are different:

- Binning for continuous attributes is always required and the maximum number of bins would be limited.
- The maximum depth of the tree (i.e., the number of levels/iterations) is capped to a certain level to limit the runtime required to construct the tree. Also, as mentioned, the runtime at each level becomes slower.
- While having a maximum depth might be relatively problematic, the main issue we might have with decision trees is that they may overfit the training data if they build very deep trees. We usually use pruning techniques to reduce overfitting, but this has not been included in MLlib.

On a final reflection, the key question is: Is this global implementation better than the local model we did before?

Table 7.1 Local versus global: Summary of advantages and disadvantages.

Local models	Global models
Key idea	
Divide and conquer	**Use the whole dataset**
Generate multiple models	Single model
Advantages	
✓ Simplicity	✓ Algorithm behavior closer to sequential version
✓ Existing (eager) algorithms can be applied on each partition	✓ Performance not affected by number of partitions / degree of parallelism
Disadvantages	
✕ Interrelations among different partitions might be ignored	✕ Must inherently support distributed computations
✕ Performance affected by number of partitions / degree of parallelism	✕ Hard to implement

7.1.2   Definitions: Global versus Local

In the examples above, we have seen that when designing machine learning algorithms for big datasets there are two main approaches that can be followed.

- Local approaches exploit the fact that the data is distributed into partitions, applying the original algorithm locally at each chunk of the data. Then, the results from each individual partition are (smartly) combined. Obviously, these models are partial because they are trained only considering part of the data and without interacting with the rest.
- Global models aim to replicate the behavior of the sequential version by looking at the data as a whole (and not as a combination of smaller parts). This means that we need to understand how the original machine learning method works, and what the bottlenecks to distributing its processing might be. All the machine learning algorithms developed in Spark's MLlib library are global models. While it is sometimes possible to replicate the exact same behavior of the original algorithm, we typically find approximations of the original algorithms or distributed versions with limited features.

Let's compare these two approaches. Table 7.1 summarizes the key differences. The advantages of local models over global models are:

- Local models are typically faster in the training phase, as various machine learning models (one per partition) are built in parallel with subsets of the data.
- Local models are conceptually very simple to understand, and we could "virtually" design any machine learning model in that way, while global models require careful design. The only aspect that needs to be designed carefully in local models is the aggregation phase, which might not be suitable for every machine learning technique.

For example, although possible, we don't see a nice way of doing k-means with a local model.

- If we found a good number of partitions for a dataset, it might benefit from the ensemble effect, but determining the best number of partitions for a dataset requires experimental validation. An excessive number of partitions may end up dramatically decreasing the performance.

The main advantages of global models over local models are:

- The behavior of a global solution for an existing machine learning algorithm should be closer to the sequential version, although it may not have the same exact features (e.g., lack of pruning for the global decision tree in Spark).
- In global models, all the data is used as a whole, so that we would expect them to be more robust and to yield greater accuracy. However, this is not always the case in practice.
- The classification/regression performance of global models is independent of the number of partitions. If we have more cores, we can split the data further, and we will get the exact same result, but faster. However, in local models, the final performance, error/accuracy, and runtime depend on the number of partitions. If we increase the number of partitions, we might reduce the runtime, but we might also decrease the accuracy.
- Although global models do not inherently benefit from the ensemble effect by design, we could still implement global ensemble models that are not limited to building models with data from a single partition.
- The test phase of a global model would be really quick, as we only have one model. However, in a local design, if we have too many models this might become very slow in the test phase.

At this point, you might be wondering: Is there any difference between local and global models for designing big data solutions? Well, it is not all black and white! We've said that the key difference lies in the idea that global approaches aim to parallelize all the operations of the original algorithm. But there might be occasions in which some sort of hybrid approach could make sense, for example, an attempt to make a global solution, but with some local features. There are many techniques that are composed of multiple steps (sometimes entire algorithms), and those might be approached as hybrid solutions in which some components are fully parallelized and others are devised as local-based solutions.

Challenge #7.2

You are asked to compare the performance of the local decision tree we implemented above against the decision tree available in MLlib. What would happen to the performance if you varied the number of partitions of the training data?

7.2   Scalability Measures: Is My Algorithm Scalable?

We have just learned two key approaches to designing a big data solution for machine learning. However, how can we say if the solution we came up with is scalable? That is, we want to ensure that the solution would be capable of handling an arbitrarily large dataset (given sufficient computational resources) without incurring much additional overhead. This is determined by the way we parallelize things. For example, if we forgot to cache a DataFrame, or we used a transformation that generates way too much traffic across the network, our solution may not scale up. To demonstrate the performance of the solution, we should test it empirically in different scenarios with different data sizes and different resource availability. In this section we present some classical scalability metrics which may be used to do this, and investigate the scalability of the previous local model for decision trees.

The performance measurement of distributed algorithms is well studied and many different metrics exist. Here we present three classical ones which we consider are more appropriate for large-scale processing. To compute them, two main factors are taken into consideration: computational power (e.g., number of cores available) and the size of the data we are dealing with.

7.2.1   Speed-Up

The *speed-up* aims to answer the question: How much faster can the same data be processed with n cores instead of one core?. This could be calculated as

$$\text{Speed-up}(n) = \frac{\text{runtime in 1 core}}{\text{runtime in } n \text{ cores}}.$$

The input data remains the same independent of the number of cores used. To characterize the speed-up of our solution, we should vary n from 1 to the largest number of cores we could make use of. Ideally, the speed-up is linear (i.e., Speed-up$(n) = n$), so that, if we have five cores, we should get the results five times faster. However, in practice that wouldn't be the case as we can't have an arbitrary number of cores in a single computer and we are testing horizontal scalability, so network and synchronization overheads will slow down the process.

Depending on the size of the dataset, it may turn out too slow (or even impossible, e.g., due to memory issues) to run a sequential version (one core) of the algorithm. When that happens, we may consider two different options. Typically, we would use a larger number of cores (e.g., 10) as a baseline, and n should grow from that base (e.g., 10, 20, 40, 80, etc.). Thus, if we were to use b cores as our baseline, the formula would be

$$\text{Speed-up}(n) = \frac{\text{runtime in } b \text{ cores}}{\text{runtime in } b \cdot n \text{ cores}}.$$

If we did not have enough resources to increase the base number of cores, we could alternatively calculate the speed-up using a subset of the original data that allows us to run the sequential version of the algorithm. Note, however, that the size of the data we process should be large enough to ensure that the overhead added by the framework we are using (e.g., Spark) doesn't limit our scalability study. For this reason, the analysis will be more robust if we compute the speed-up for varying data sizes.

7.2.2   Size-Up

The *size-up* focuses on how an algorithm is capable of handling larger amounts of data: How much time does it take to process a dataset n times larger? This could be computed as

$$\text{Size-up}(n) = \frac{\text{runtime to process } n \cdot data}{\text{runtime to process } data}.$$

In this case, the number of cores is kept fixed, as we only want to measure the impact of the size of the data (but we could compute the size-up with different core configurations for more robust results). To do this analysis, we can create subsets of the original training data, for example, 10%, 20%, 30%, up to 100%. We could take 10% as the lowest expected runtime, and then we investigate how much this time increases for larger subsets. Similarly to speed-up, in an ideal world the size-up achieved should be linear (i.e., Size-up($data, n$) = n). As before, few algorithms are linear with respect to the data size.

> We should bear in mind that bigger datasets may require more resources, for example more RAM, and resource availability shouldn't limit the correct calculation of this metric. This means that to measure the size-up, we should keep the cluster configuration fixed, but we should make sure that the largest execution ($n \cdot data$) doesn't lose performance because of insufficient RAM. As before, we should also ensure that we work with enough data (even for the 10% subset) to obtain meaningful conclusions.

7.2.3   Scale-Up

The *scale-up* measures the ability of a system to run an n-times larger dataset on an n-times larger system. It is calculated as

$$\text{Scale-up}(n) = \frac{\text{runtime to process } data \text{ in 1 core}}{\text{runtime to process } n \cdot data \text{ in } n \cdot \text{cores}}.$$

Therefore, we compare the sequential version against running it with different settings, in which both the number of cores and the data size are increased proportionally. That is, if we duplicate the size of the data, we double the number of cores. This could be 10% of the data with one core, 20% on teo cores, and so on. The perfect scale-up would be 1 (Scale-up($data, n$) = 1). Once again, few algorithms achieve a scale-up of 1 as we need to consider the slowdown produced by network communication.

As before, it may not be possible to be run the sequential version with one core and 10% of the data. In that case, a baseline that is doable may be set (e.g., eight cores in

Table 7.2 Hypothetical ideal runtime of a linearly scalable algorithm for varying dataset size and number of cores. We take 8 cores as a baseline, which are then increased up to 80 cores (i.e., 10 times more).

Dataset size	8 cores	16 cores	32 cores	64 cores	80 cores
10%	10	5	2.5	1.25	1
20%	20	10	5	2.5	2
40%	40	20	10	5	4
80%	80	40	20	10	8
100%	100	50	25	12.5	10

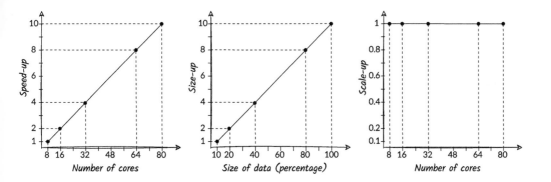

Figure 7.6 Ideal speed-up, size-up, and scale-up plots according to the runtimes in Table 7.2.

10% of the data). Then, both the number of cores and the size of the data are multiplied by the same factor (e.g., 16 cores and 20% of the data, 24 cores and 30%, and so on).

To get a better idea of these measures, we provide some hypothetical runtime results that could be obtained by a linearly scalable algorithm for varying numbers of cores and dataset sizes (Table 7.2). With these runtimes, you can use the previous formulas to compute the speed-up, size-up, and scale-up measures, which are displayed in Figure 7.6. You can now play with the numbers in this table to better understand how they would affect the corresponding measures.

In the next section we will put this into practice by computing these metrics on the local-based solution we proposed before.

7.2.4 A Test on Decision Trees

To do this kind of analysis, we need to modify the number of cores and the size of a dataset. Rather than using a real cluster, we are going to be using a single machine, so you can replicate this analysis at home. However, this means that the results are over-optimistic, as we won't be taking into consideration network costs. Running this kind of analysis on a Jupyter Notebook may not be straightforward, as we have already initialized a SparkSession to use all the cores available on our computer.

Creating a Standalone PySpark Program

We are going to use this opportunity to show you how to create standalone pyspark programs outside Jupyter Notebooks. While Jupyter Notebooks are really good for prototyping and displaying results, using standalone programs is possibly the best way to design new machine learning algorithms and test them. To do this, we simply have to create a new python file (extension .py) which you can edit in your favorite Python IDE. This should contain a `main()` function that will take a list `argv` as a parameter, and a way to invoke that function when running the program in standalone mode:

```python
def main(argv):
    # Main body of the program

if __name__ == "__main__":
    main(sys.argv[1:])
```

If you were to put this code in a file called `train.py`, you could run it in a terminal (Powershell on Windows) like this:

```
python train.py
```

The program won't do anything as we haven't added any code yet.

What is this `argv` list? And why did we do slicing `sys.argv[1:]`? We have run the previous command without any parameters, but as we are going to change the number of cores and data size, we will need two extra parameters. If we run the program like this to use four cores and 100% of the data . . .

```
python train.py 4 100
```

. . . `argv` would contain a `'4'` and `'100'` (as strings!). We do the slicing in `sys.argv` to remove the name of the file (`'train.py'`).

So, as these parameters are read as strings, the first thing we need to do is to coerce them to their right data type. We should do this within the `main()` function:

```python
def main(argv):
    cores = int(argv[0])
    percentage = int(argv[1])
    ...
```

We can then initialize the `SparkSession` according to the number of cores. We may need to increase the amount of memory given to a Spark executor depending on the amount of data used.

```python
from pyspark.sql import SparkSession
import pyspark.sql.functions as sql_f

spark = (
    SparkSession.builder.master(f"local[{cores}]")
    .appName(f"Local DT with {cores} partitions")
    .config("spark.driver.memory", "16g")
    .config("spark.executor.memory", "16g")
    .getOrCreate()
)

sc = spark.sparkContext
```

We are now ready to load the data. Instead of using the dataset we used before, which was rather small, we have chosen a larger one from the UCI Machine Learning repository. In particular, we have selected the SUSY[9] dataset, which is a classification dataset that aims to distinguish between background or signal in high-energy physics experiments. This dataset contains 18 attributes, including kinematic properties measured by the particle detectors in the particle accelerator and features derived from them, all of them numeric. The first column of the data denotes whether the sample was considered signal (1) or background (0).

We have downloaded the data and named the file `susy-100.csv` to indicate that this is the full dataset (100%).

> If we attempt to measure the scalability of an algorithm with a very small dataset, the overhead caused by launching Spark jobs may prevent us from analyzing correctly its scalability!

So, we can now read the dataset as a DataFrame, renaming the first column as `'output'` and coercing all columns to numerical values (floats).

```
df = (spark.read.format("csv").option("header", "false")
    .load(f"data/susy-{percentage}.csv")
)
df = df.withColumnRenamed("_c0", "output")
df = df.select([sql_f.col(c).cast("float").alias(c) for c in df.columns])
```

We have two parallel implementations, one for building a model and one for testing a model. In this analysis, we are only going to study the scalability of the building phase, as it should (normally) be the most time-consuming one. Thus, we are not going to split the data into training and test sets, and we will simply use all the data to train. Then, we use `repartition()` to ensure we have the same number of partitions and cores:

```
data_rdd = df.rdd.repartition(cores).cache()
```

Note that we have cached our data after the repartitioning. As we will see later, we may perform multiple actions on the data, so we want the split and repartitioning to be done only once.

You may remember that the function to build a model needs to have access to the column names, so we add the following three lines of code to the main function:

```
global column_names
column_names = df.columns

models = train_rdd.mapPartitions(build_model).collect()
```

You may have noticed that we said `global column_names`, which is something we didn't need to do in the Notebook. This is because we are working within the `main()` function, and we need to explicitly tell Python we are referring to the global variable, so that this is sent to the executors. Additionally, the model-building function makes use of the scikit-learn `DecisionTreeClassifier` and pandas DataFrames. Those libraries,

---

[9] https://archive.ics.uci.edu/ml/datasets/SUSY

that may be used globally by the workers and the driver, should be imported at the very beginning of the Python file.

```
import pandas as pd
from sklearn.tree import DecisionTreeClassifier
```

Last, but not least, we should stop the `SparkSession`. This is good practice, although if you forget to include this the `SparkSession` will still stop when the Python script ends.

```
    spark.stop()
```

Of course, the function `build_model()` needs to be added to this file, outside the `main()` function. We have made two slight modifications to this function. On the one hand, the `max_depth` of the tree has not been limited to 2, but we have allowed scikit-learn to grow a tree as big as necessary according to the complexity of the dataset (note that this will affect our scalability measures). On the other hand, this particular dataset has the class label in the first column rather than the last one, so we have to select the columns accordingly when creating `X_train`:

```
    clf = DecisionTreeClassifier(random_state=0, max_depth=None)
    X_train = partition.iloc[:,1:]
```

The entire script is available in the supplementary material at `07-MLbig/code/scalability-localDT.py`. By the way, we don't have to go to a terminal to run this, as we can run commands on a Jupyter Notebook using the exclamation mark (!) prior to the instruction, like this:

```
!python code/scalability-localDT.py 4 100
```

Measuring Runtime

We are now *almost* ready to analyze the scalability of this model, but there are a few things we need to bear in mind for measuring the runtime and the scalability of the implementation. If we were to measure the runtime like this . . .

```
%time !python code/scalability-localDT.py 4 100
```

. . . the wall time provided would take into consideration the time to start a `SparkSession` and read the dataset, which is common for all the experiments we need to execute to compute the different metrics. In this example, we may see very few differences in the total runtime, as most of the time goes on starting the jobs, reading the data, and repartitioning it accordingly.

Thus, to establish a fair comparison, we should measure the runtime *within* the program. However, we have a little bit of an issue with the lazy evaluation of Spark. The splitting of the data and repartitioning, as well as the caching, won't take place until an action is triggered, which adds time to the execution. As a workaround to run a fairer scalability analysis we have added a line to `count()` the number of elements in the dataset after the repartition and caching. After that point we start the timer, run the `mapPartitions()` function together with a `collect()`, and observe the runtime needed to build the method.

In addition to that, we would also like to investigate the overhead caused by Spark, that is, the time not spent in building the tree. To do so, we should measure how long it really takes to build the decision tree and compare it with the total runtime taken to run the whole job. So, we slightly modify the `build_model` function to measure exactly the runtime needed to build the decision tree in each worker. Instead of returning the model, this version of the function returns that runtime together with the model. This means that when we do the `collect()` of the `mapPartitions()`, we get a runtime for each partition of the data. We then simply average these and take this as a representative runtime for building a decision tree in a worker without accounting for Spark overhead.

At the end of the program we write all of that information to a file, whose name is given as an input parameter of the Python script. This file will be in CSV format, and each line will contain the result of an execution as: `cores`, `pct` (percentage), `runtime`, `runtime_no_overhead`.

> *Caveat:* This is the result of one *single* execution with a given configuration. As we are running this on top of an operating system that may be running other processes, the results may vary (slightly) from one execution to another, so we would recommend running this multiple times and taking the average time in order to obtain representative metrics.

Starting Hypotheses

Before we actually run the experiments, what should we expect to happen with the metrics we introduced above? The first thing we should think about is the complexity of the machine learning model we are building locally. The decision tree is $O(n \cdot \log n \cdot d)$, where n is the number of instances and d is the number of features. Thus, the number of instances matters, and its runtime can't be expected to be linear. For example, if we say that for 1000 instances the decision tree takes 100 seconds, for 2000 instances (and the same number of features) we can't expect it to be 200 seconds, but more.

With this in mind, and taking into account that we are training local decision tree models in each partition, we may expect the following behaviors for the three metrics:

- **Speed-up**: We should probably be able to reach a superlinear speed-up (better than linear) as we are running this on a single computer without network communication overhead. Also, the complexity of the decision tree would mean that with more cores we reduce the number of instances in each partition, and therefore training each decision tree would become faster, reducing the total runtime.
- **Size-up**: As we fix the number of partitions, the runtime required to process larger partitions will increase according to the number of instances. The nonlinear complexity of the decision tree will probably prevent us from obtaining an ideal linear size-up.
- **Scale-up**: Changing both the number of cores and the dataset size proportionally would compensate for the increase in the dataset size with the number of cores, so that we will still have the same amount of data in each partition. Assuming negligible communication overhead as we are running this in a single computer, we may achieve close to linear behavior.

Let's see what happens in reality!

> ## Challenge #7.3
>
> The Python script is designed to analyze the scalability and runtime required when varying the number of cores and the size of the data. Could you now analyze the difference in terms of classification accuracy as we increase the number of partitions? You are asked create a new Python script for this and use the SUSY dataset.

Speed-Up

Let's investigate the runtime with different numbers of cores:

```
num_cores = [1, 2, 4, 8, 12]
```

We went for a range of 1 to 12, and the computer we are using to run this has a total of 16 cores. To account for potential variability of runtime across executions, we are going to run each configuration 10 times, recording the runtime:

```
for i in range(10):
    for j in num_cores:
        !python code/scalability-localDT.py {j} 100 speedup.csv
```

We can read the CSV file with the results of this analysis, and compute the average runtime for the 10 runs with each number of cores:

```
results = pd.read_csv('speedup.csv', names=['cores', 'pct',
                      'runtime', 'runtime_no_overhead'])
avg_results = results.groupby('cores').mean()
avg_results['overhead'] = avg_results['runtime'] \
    - avg_results['runtime_no_overhead']
avg_results
```

	pct	runtime	runtime_no_overhead	overhead
cores				
1	100.0	275.955786	275.549436	0.406350
2	100.0	125.233562	124.242992	0.990570
4	100.0	60.596741	59.865748	0.730993
8	100.0	31.586154	30.666868	0.919285
12	100.0	22.409688	21.656439	0.753249

> In this case the overhead is rather small, but this can vary quite a bit depending on the PC and its configuration. This particular experiment was run on an AMD Ryzen 9 5950X 16 × 3.4 GHz using the Linux Fedora 35 operating system.

Using these statistics we can compute the speed-up values for the total runtime, and the runtime without overhead:

```
def speed_up(results, runtime_col):
    return results[runtime_col].iloc[0] / results[runtime_col]


avg_results['speed-up'] = speed_up(avg_results, 'runtime')
avg_results['speed-up_no_overhead'] = speed_up(avg_results,
        'runtime_no_overhead')
```

```
avg_results[['runtime', 'runtime_no_overhead', 'speed-up',
             'speed-up_no_overhead']]
```

cores	runtime	runtime_no_overhead	speed-up	speed-up_no_overhead
1	275.955786	275.549436	1.000000	1.000000
2	125.233562	124.242992	2.203529	2.217827
4	60.596741	59.865748	4.553971	4.602789
8	31.586154	30.666868	8.736606	8.985249
12	22.409688	21.656439	12.314129	12.723672

We can visualize this together with a linear speed-up. We create a helper function for this that we will be reusing for all the measures.

```
from matplotlib import pyplot as plt
def plot_scalability_measure(name, stats, xlabel, x_vals, linear_vals):
    # Create the plot
    fig, ax = plt.subplots(1, 2, figsize=(9, 4))
    fig.suptitle(
        f"{name.capitalize()} of a Local-based model with Decision Trees"
    )
    # Plot the measure with and without overhead
    ax[0].plot(x_vals, stats[name], "k", label=f"Real {name}")
    ax[1].plot(x_vals, stats[f"{name}_no_overhead"], "k",
               label=f"{name} without overhead")
    # Plot the linear values for the measure
    for i in [0, 1]:
        ax[i].plot(x_vals, linear_vals, "--", color="gray",
            label=f"Linear {name}", linewidth=1)
        ax[i].set(xlabel=xlabel, ylabel=name.capitalize())
        if name == "scale-up":
            ax[i].set_ylim([0, 1.1])
        ax[i].legend()

plot_scalability_measure('speed-up', avg_results, 'Number of cores',
                         num_cores, num_cores)
```

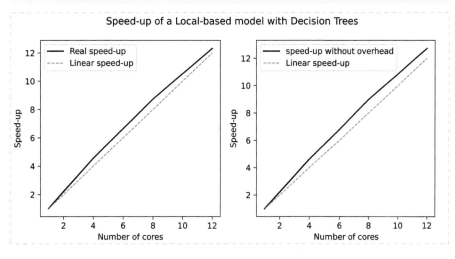

Looking at the results, it seems that from 1 core to 2 cores we are indeed more than twice as fast (from 275 s to 124 s, a speed-up of more than 2). However, this progression slows down at 8 and 12 cores, where the improvement is not so great (we still get speed-ups over linear, but compared with the runtimes for 4 cores we are not twice as fast as with 8 cores). We could think that this is due to the decision tree having a lower complexity than expected, but we ran some tests with the scikit-learn implementation computing its size-up, and it works as expected (see later size-ups without overhead). Therefore, it is more likely that it is because the computer cannot reach its full potential, either because Spark doesn't exploit it or because there are other processes competing for resources.

> To perform a rigorous scalability analysis we should ensure that the computer(s) in which we run the experiments have enough computing power available for the planned experiments.

If we now look at the speed-up in the plots, we can corroborate that the real speed-up is not quite what we assumed before. However, the speed-up without overhead seems to be closer to the superlinear speed-up we were expecting. Even so, we would have expected the gap to the linear speed-up to be bigger. As explained before, there are multiple factors that could prevent us from reaching a better speed-up:

- We are running this in pseudo-distributed mode on top of an operating system that is running other processes. This might be influencing the ability to exploit all the cores available.
- The overhead caused by Spark becomes larger in proportion to the total runtime with a higher number of cores, limiting the speed-up values.

Size-Up

To do this, we first need to create different datasets with different sizes. For the sake of simplicity, we are going to do this with pandas:

```
sizes = [10, 20, 40, 80, 100]

full = pd.read_csv('data/susy-100.csv')
for fraction in sizes[:-1]:
    full.sample(frac=fraction/100)\
        .to_csv(f"data/susy-{fraction}.csv",index=False)
```

We can now record the runtime using the different versions of the dataset. We have selected eight cores for this experiment, which will be kept fixed for each data size:

```
for i in range(10):
    for fraction in sizes:
        !python code/scalability-localDT.py 8 {fraction} sizeup.csv
```

As before, we will read the generated CSV file and compute the average for the 10 runs for the analysis:

```
results = pd.read_csv('sizeup.csv', names=['cores', 'pct',
                      'runtime', 'runtime_no_overhead'])
avg_results = results.groupby('pct').mean()
```

```
avg_results['overhead'] = avg_results['runtime'] \
    - avg_results['runtime_no_overhead']
```

We can use this data to compute the size-up values for both the total runtime and the total runtime without overhead:

```
def size_up(results, runtime_col):
    return results[runtime_col] / results[runtime_col].iloc[0]

avg_results['size-up'] = size_up(avg_results, 'runtime')
avg_results['size-up_no_overhead'] = size_up(avg_results,
        'runtime_no_overhead')
avg_results[['runtime', 'runtime_no_overhead', 'size-up',
        'size-up_no_overhead']]
```

	runtime	runtime_no_overhead	size-up	size-up_no_overhead
pct				
10	2.612993	2.092479	1.000000	1.000000
20	5.331032	4.745066	2.040202	2.267676
40	11.312207	10.742516	4.329215	5.133870
80	24.880583	24.170563	9.521872	11.551160
100	31.997075	31.073377	12.245374	14.850029

We may get a better view by plotting this with the linear size-up, which is 2, 4, 6, 8, and 10 times higher than the smallest dataset (the 10%):

```
linear_sizeup = [1, 2, 4, 8, 10]
plot_scalability_measure('size-up', avg_results, 'Size of data (%)',
                sizes, linear_sizeup)
```

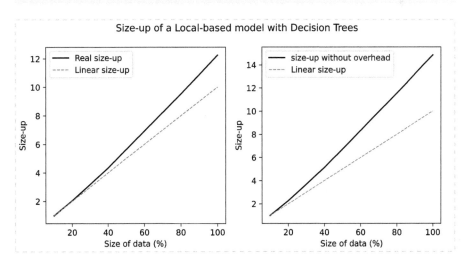

Size-up of a Local-based model with Decision Trees

As we encountered before with the speed-up, we did not get the result we thought we would. The size-up is worse than the linear one, which was expected from the complexity of the decision tree. However, the size-up for the total runtime is better than we initially expected. We can observe that the runtime increases linearly for

20% and 40% (2 and 4.3, respectively), but not so much for 80% and 100% (9.5 and 12.24, respectively). The results without overhead are quite different, showing that the decision tree doesn't scale linearly even for 20% of the data (speed-up of 2.27). Why is it different? We should take a look at the overheads. They seem to be very similar for all data percentages. For 10% we have almost the same overhead as for 20% and 40%, so it is not growing linearly with the size of the data. This means that the Spark overhead is very high for 10% of the dataset in proportion to the runtime compared to the overhead proportion in larger datasets, which is altering the results we observe. Let's show this overhead in terms of percentage with respect to the runtime:

```
avg_results["overhead"] / avg_results["runtime"] * 100
```

```
pct
10      19.920208
20      10.991612
40       5.036073
80       2.853710
100      2.886821
dtype: float64
```

The percentage of overhead is almost 20% of the runtime in the baseline! As we can see, this diminishes with larger amounts of data. Therefore, if we are looking for more accurate estimations, we had better use a larger dataset as a baseline.

> The baseline used for the computation of scalability metrics can have a great influence on the results obtained, so it should be carefully selected depending on the problem at hand.

Scale-Up

Now we are going to align the number of cores and sizes we test, so that, we run one core with the smallest dataset (10%), two cores with 20, and so on.

```
num_cores = [1, 2, 4, 8, 10]
sizes = [10, 20, 40, 80, 100]

for i in range(10):
    for j in range(len(num_cores)):
        !python code/scalability-localDT.py {num_cores[j]} \
                            {sizes[j]} scaleup.csv
```

We compute the scale-up with respect to the runtime required with one core and 10% of the data:

```
results = pd.read_csv("scaleup.csv",
    names=["cores", "pct", "runtime", "runtime_no_overhead"],
)
avg_results = results.groupby(["cores", "pct"]).mean()
avg_results["overhead"] = (
    avg_results["runtime"] - avg_results["runtime_no_overhead"]
)
```

```
def scale_up(results, runtime_col):
    return results[runtime_col].iloc[0] / results[runtime_col]

avg_results['scale-up'] = scale_up(avg_results, 'runtime')
avg_results['scale-up_no_overhead'] = scale_up(avg_results,
                                          'runtime_no_overhead')
avg_results[['runtime', 'runtime_no_overhead', 'scale-up',
             'scale-up_no_overhead']]
```

		runtime	runtime_no_overhead	scale-up	scale-up_no_overhead
cores	pct				
1	10	20.411578	20.004176	1.000000	1.000000
2	20	20.504888	20.026253	0.995449	0.998898
4	40	21.840869	21.086643	0.934559	0.948666
8	80	24.491947	23.789118	0.833400	0.840896
10	100	26.250733	25.222097	0.777562	0.793121

In a perfect world, the scale up would always be 1.

```
ideal_scaleup = [1] * 5
plot_scalability_measure('scale-up', avg_results, 'Number of cores',
                          num_cores, ideal_scaleup)
```

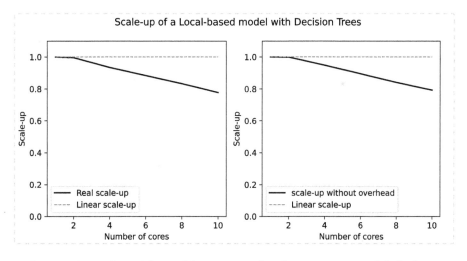

Once again, we haven't been able to get exactly what we conjectured. In both cases, with and without overhead, we observe similar patterns, with the scale-up starting close to 1 but dropping to 0.8 with 100% and 10 cores. Recall that we were expecting to scale linearly (we had an additional core for each additional partition of data that we were processing), so where does this unexpected difference come from? We already discarded the overhead of Spark, but we should keep in mind that Spark is being run on top of an operating system running other processes that fight for computing resources. Either Spark is not able to exploit the full potential of the computer or there are other processes competing for resources, which prevent Spark from achieving a linear scale-up.

Wrap-Up on Scalability Measures

In conclusion, these metrics are very useful to check whether our design is really scalable. However, there are some caveats to demonstrating the scalability of a given design when running it in a real environment:

- It is important to correctly measure the runtime inside the code to avoid issues with lazy operations in Spark. In our tests, we did a bit of a trick using `count()` to ensure we were only measuring the runtime needed to build the model.
- Despite removing the impact of some of the operations that are common for all the experiments, for example, initializing the `SparkSession`, reading the data, and using the trick above, there is an intrinsic overhead to running Spark jobs. The more jobs we run, the higher the overhead. We need to ensure that if we are going to parallelize using many cores, the reduction in runtime is worthwhile with respect to the overhead costs.
- If we were to run this on a cluster, which would be the most usual scenario for real big data, the influence of the network should be investigated. That will expose whether we are sending a lot of data across nodes, which we should avoid as much as possible.

> ### Challenge #7.4
>
> You are asked to compare the scalability of the local-based model with the MLlib decision tree.

7.3   Take-Home Message

Instead of using the MLlib library, this chapter has been devoted to designing our own solutions to run machine learning algorithms in the context of big data. In the first part of the chapter we introduced two different alternatives to this, which we called local and global approaches. Local-based solutions simply apply existing sequential machine learning implementations to different partitions of a big dataset, finding ways to then aggregate what is learned in each separate block of the data. However, a global-based design aims to mimic the behavior of the original machine learning algorithm, parallelizing the operations of the method that are limited by the size of the data. To showcase how these two strategies work, we have focused on the classical decision tree algorithm, revising its basic functioning and some of the details that need to be modified if we want to deal with large datasets.

When comparing local and global strategies, we would like you to remember the following ideas:

- Local models are simple to understand and implement. Many machine learning methods (especially eager methods) could easily be used within this framework without knowing anything about the underlying model. The key lies in how to aggregate the models that are created from each partition. To do so, we typically use ensemble-like strategies, such as a majority vote.

- In terms of results, the performance of local models depends on the number of partitions. The more partitions, the faster the building phase, but it may decrease the classification/regression performance. Having said that, given the right number of partitions, we may benefit from the ensemble effect.
- Global models are more difficult to implement and require us to know much more about the machine learning method we want to parallelize.
- We haven't yet seen our own implementation of a global model (we will, in the next chapter), but we have discussed in depth the solution adopted in MLlib to parallelize the decision tree. For example, we have seen how an iterative version of the method makes more sense for big data to reduce the number of jobs that are required. To do this, parallelization is introduced on a level-by-level basis.
- Global models may come with certain limitations. On many occasions they will be approximations of the original method. For example, the MLlib decision tree requires binning to reduce the number of computations, and the depth of the tree is capped to a certain level as each level becomes slower.
- Although Spark allows us to repeatedly use data by caching it, running many jobs will have a cost that must be considered when designing a global-based solution.

In summary, it is difficult to say which option is better; it depends on the problem. Testing a local-based solution will usually be straightforward. A global-based one is more difficult unless pre-existing solutions like the ones available in MLlib are used.

In the second part of the chapter we learned how to measure the scalability. In particular, we introduced speed-up, size-up, and scale-up as three different metrics that help us understand how good our parallel solution is.

- The speed-up tells us how much faster an implementation will be if we use a larger number of cores with the same dataset. Size-up measures how much slower an implementation gets if we increase the size of the data. Finally, the scale-up tests whether an implementation takes the same time when both the size of the dataset and the number of cores are increased proportionally.
- A good parallel design would ideally obtain the best values for these metrics (e.g., linear behavior). However, for big data we need to bear in mind that the metrics are affected by the complexity of the algorithm we are parallelizing, the potential costs of network communication, and the number of jobs that need to be executed.
- When calculating scalability metrics, theory and reality may differ quite a bit due to the complexity of the underlying distributed system which sits on top of an operating system.
- To ensure that the metrics are correctly computed:
  - we need to carefully measure the runtime (avoiding issues with lazy operations in Spark);
  - we should set a significant baseline with an appropriate dataset size, so that the Spark overhead is not the dominant factor in the calculations;

- we must verify that the computer resources are sufficient for the planned experiments;
- we should repeat the experiments multiple times and compute the average runtime.

7.4   To Learn More

To the best of our knowledge, there are no sources that discuss in detail the different approaches to designing big data solutions for machine learning. Nevertheless, there are some research papers in which these methods may have been used or discussed briefly:

> See Ramírez-Gallego et al. (2018) for a tutorial on big data design. Note that their definition of global and local are not exactly the same, as we do not consider global approaches to be exact (as they may be limited), and local models are referred to as approximations.

> If you want to learn more about the global-based implementation of decision trees, we recommend you look at the Spark documentation[10] to learn more about global-based solutions for decision trees.

> See Panda et al. (2009) (PLANET) and Abuzaid et al. (2016) (YGGDRASIL) for research papers related to the MLlib implementation of decision trees.

> You may be wondering if the global-based solution for decision trees in MLlib is the only existing one. There are some research papers that have aimed to improve on this implementation, and in particular the use of decision trees within random forests, or used it to develop better-performing solutions: Lulli et al. (2017); Chen et al. (2017); Juez-Gil et al. (2021); Segatori et al. (2018).

> A classical reference introducing speed-up and scale-up: DeWitt and Gray (1992).

> Another classic that goes more deeply into scalability metrics in distributed systems: Jogalekar and Woodside (2000).

> Hai et al. (2017) investigates the performance of MLlib. This paper evaluates random forest and naïve Bayes implementations using the same metrics we introduced in this book.

7.5   Solutions to Challenges

> ### Challenge #7.1
>
> We have used map to classify the instances in the test set. You are now asked to reimplement the testing phase using mapPartitions() instead of map. Would you expect it to be faster? Why?

---

[10] https://spark.apache.org/docs/3.3.0/ml-classification-regression.html#decision-tree-classifier

Assuming that we have built the local model previously, and the variable `models` contains a list of decision trees from the scikit-learn library, we need to define a `predict_set()` function that is compatible with `mapPartitions`. This means that instead of taking one single instance as an argument of the function, it will process a set of instances. Therefore, we could simply iterate over all the instances of the set and make a prediction with each one of the models, generating a double list of predictions (with a prediction for each instance and model):

```
def predict_set(instances):
    return [[m.predict([instance[:-1]])[0] for m in models]\
            for instance in instances]
```

If we test it by taking the first element of that RDD . . .

```
test_rdd.mapPartitions(predict_set).take(1)
```

```
[['not-first', 'not-first', 'not-first']]
```

. . . we can now perform the aggregation using the same `agg_predictions` function from before.

```
test_rdd.mapPartitions(predict_set).map(agg_predictions).take(4)
```

```
['not-first', 'not-first', 'first', 'not-first']
```

Shall we compare it against the time needed to use map instead?

```
%time test_rdd.mapPartitions(predict_set).map(agg_predictions).collect()[:5]
```

```
CPU times: user 5.86 ms, sys: 3.52 ms, total: 9.37 ms
Wall time: 54.2 ms
```

```
['not-first', 'not-first', 'first', 'not-first', 'first']
```

```
%time test_rdd.map(predict).map(agg_predictions).collect()[:5]
```

```
CPU times: user 5.54 ms, sys: 3.61 ms, total: 9.15 ms
Wall time: 52 ms
```

```
['not-first', 'not-first', 'first', 'not-first', 'first']
```

One may have thought that using `mapPartitions()` would be faster than using `map()`. In Chapter 4 we saw an example to compute the average of a list of numbers, which showed that precomputing things in each partition would save time. In that case, `mapPartitions()` was reducing the amount of data sent across to workers (from the map to the reduce phase). However, in this case we are not reducing the amount of data sent across the network as we are just transforming each test instance into their prediction with two narrow transformations. So, in the end, we are doing almost the same and we won't get much benefit from using `mapPartitions()` in this case.

> ## Challenge #7.2
>
> You are asked to compare the performance of the local decision tree we imple-
> mented above against the decision tree available in MLlib. What would happen
> to the performance if you varied the number of partitions of the training data?

We managed to obtain an accuracy of around 0.8571 with the local model. Using the
same data, we are going to create a pipeline to build a decision tree from MLlib.

```
from pyspark.ml.feature import VectorAssembler
feature_cols = train_df.columns
feature_cols.remove('Classification')
feature_cols
```

```
['Ex01', 'Ex02', 'Ex03', 'Ex04', 'Project']
```

```
assembler = VectorAssembler(inputCols=feature_cols, outputCol="features")
```

As MLlib doesn't seem to like strings as output features, we have to transform it using
`StringIndexer`.

```
from pyspark.ml.feature import StringIndexer
labelIndexer = StringIndexer(inputCol='Classification',
                             outputCol='ClassificationIndex')
# This import is to avoid overriding DecisionTreeClassifier from sklearn
import pyspark.ml.classification as spark_ml
dt = spark_ml.DecisionTreeClassifier(labelCol='ClassificationIndex',
        featuresCol='features')
```

We are now ready to build and fit the pipeline:

```
from pyspark.ml import Pipeline
pipeline = Pipeline(stages=[assembler, labelIndexer, dt])
pipeline_model = pipeline.fit(train_df)
```

We transform the test and evaluate it using the multiclass classification evaluator:

```
prediction = pipeline_model.transform(test_df)
```

```
prediction.select('ClassificationIndex','prediction').show(4)
```

```
+-------------------+----------+
|ClassificationIndex|prediction|
+-------------------+----------+
|                1.0|       1.0|
|                1.0|       1.0|
|                0.0|       0.0|
|                1.0|       1.0|
+-------------------+----------+
only showing top 4 rows
```

```
acc_evaluator = MulticlassClassificationEvaluator(
    metricName="accuracy",
    labelCol="ClassificationIndex",
```

```
        predictionCol="prediction",
)
```

```
acc_evaluator.evaluate(prediction)
```

```
0.9285714285714286
```

In this case, the global model implemented in MLlib has obtained a better result than the local model. But, why is that happening? Is this only due to the comparison of global versus local? Well, not quite; there may be various reasons why the results differ. If you remember from before, we actually ran the scikit-learn decision tree on all the data (which would be the equivalent of a global model), and the result was exactly the same, 0.8571. So, why is the global version of MLlib performing better in this case? For starters, the hyperparameters may have been set differently. For example, the maximum depth was set to 2 when running the scikit-learn library, but we have used the default value for MLlib (which is 5). In addition, there might also be some subtle differences between the implementations in scikit-learn and MLlib, which may change the results.

Let's move on to study what would happen if we changed the number of partitions for the global model. We will do a quick experiment, varying the number of partitions:

```
partitions = [2, 4, 8, 16]
for i in partitions:
    train_df_repartition = train_df.repartition(i).cache()
    # Global model
    pipeline_model = pipeline.fit(train_df_repartition)
    prediction = pipeline_model.transform(test_df)
    print(
        f"Accuracy of the global model with "
        f"{i} partitions: {acc_evaluator.evaluate(prediction)}"
    )
```

```
Accuracy of the global model with 2 partitions: 0.9285714285714286
Accuracy of the global model with 4 partitions: 0.9285714285714286
Accuracy of the global model with 8 partitions: 0.9285714285714286
Accuracy of the global model with 16 partitions: 0.9285714285714286
```

As you probably expected, with a global approach the result is always the same, independent of the number of partitions. But, what will happen with the local model? Can we do the same analysis?

```
for i in partitions:
    # Local model
    train_rdd = train_df.rdd.repartition(i).cache()
    models = train_rdd.mapPartitions(build_model).collect()
    prediction_local = test_rdd.map(transform).toDF()
    prediction_num = prediction_local.select(
        (prediction_local["Classification"] == "first")
        .cast("double").alias("ClassificationIndex"),
        (prediction_local["raw_prediction"] == "first")
        .cast("double").alias("prediction"),
    )
```

```
print(
    f"Accuracy of the local model with "
    f"{i} partitions: {acc_evaluator.evaluate(prediction_num)}"
)
```

```
Accuracy of the local model with 2 partitions: 0.8571428571428571
Accuracy of the local model with 4 partitions: 0.8571428571428571
```

```
---------------------------------------------------------------------

Py4JJavaError Traceback (most recent call last)
~\AppData\Local\Temp\ipykernel_12124\1266068800.py in <module> 3
train_rdd = train_df .rdd.repartition(i).cache() 4 ----> 5 models =
train_rdd.mapPartitions(build_model) .collect() 6 prediction_local = test_rdd
.map(transform).toDF() 7 prediction_num = prediction_local.select(
...
```

It turns out that the toy dataset we are using in this chapter is so small that whenever we go beyond four partitions there may be empty partitions, causing an error when building the model. We can easily verify that this is the problem:

```
train_rdd.mapPartitions(lambda p: [len(list(p))]).collect()
```

```
[10, 10, 7, 0, 0, 0, 10, 10]
```

We can see how the partitioning is not uniform, which causes our `build_model` function to fail. Of course, we could have prevented this in our function to make it work, but we couldn't expect a partition to be empty for big data!

> ## Challenge #7.3
>
> The Python script is designed to analyze the scalability and runtime required when varying the number of cores and the size of the data. Could you now analyze the difference in terms of classification accuracy as we increase the number of partitions? You are asked create a new Python script for this and use the SUSY dataset.

As we are not interested in measuring the runtime, we could either do this with a standalone program or directly in the Notebook. Actually, in the previous challenge, we already did this in the Notebook using that small dataset. The goal of this challenge was for you to try to familiarize yourself with creating standalone programs and see the impact of changing the number of partitions in a real-world dataset. The entire script with our solution is available in the supplementary material at `07-MLbig/code/performance-localDT.py`.

What are the key changes needed in the Python script to do this?

- For starters, we are going to measure the classification performance, so we need to include the functions to make predictions and aggregate them (i.e., `predict`, `agg_predictions`, and `transform`). Note that we hard-coded the `agg_predictions` function to work with the classes 'first' vs. 'not-first', and that needs to be changed. We also hard-coded the position of the label in `predict`, so we mustn't forget to change this according to the dataset. Finally, we need to add some imports as well (e.g., from pyspark.sql import Row).

- We need to add the code to split the data into training and test. The repartitioning is only needed for train_rdd, as we know that for the test phase the result wouldn't change if we split the test further (it would only accelerate the processing).
- We should get rid of all the tricks we made to measure the runtime effectively. For example, there was an extra count() which is not needed any more, and the build_model function was not returning the model only, but also the runtime.
- We need to write out the accuracy obtained in the output file.

Once those changes are made, we can now run the script as we did before. As we are not measuring the runtime, we could increase the number of partitions to a number higher than the number of cores available.

```
num_cores = [1, 2, 4, 8, 12, 24, 48, 128]
```

```
for i in num_cores:
    !python code/performance-localDT.py {i} 100 acc_local.csv
```

You may have noticed that we are not running this multiple times, because in this case we are not measuring the runtime, and the algorithm is deterministic. Let's read the results and plot the accuracy obtained with different numbers of cores:

```
results = pd.read_csv('acc_local.csv', names=['cores', 'pct',
                     'accuracy'])
```

```
plt.figure(figsize=(5, 4))
plt.plot(results['cores'], results['accuracy'], 'k',
        label='Local Decision Tree Accuracy')
plt.xlabel('Number of cores')
plt.ylabel('Accuracy (%)')
plt.legend();
```

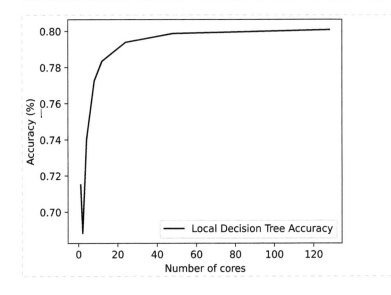

Perhaps this comes as a surprise. Apart from the small drop when moving from one to two partitions, the accuracy is not only not reducing as the number of cores increases, it is actually increasing. In this particular dataset, we haven't yet reached a sufficient number of partitions to see that drop, and what we observe in this plot is all from the ensemble effect. We couldn't go further than 128 partitions due to memory limitations.

How does this compare with the accuracy of the MLlib decision tree? We have created a new script, which is available in the supplementary material at 07-MLbig/code/performance-globalDT.py. It is important to note that a straight comparison may not be completely fair as the implementation of the tree is not exactly the same. We have set the maximum depth of the tree to 30, as this would be the closest to growing the tree "fully" with the scikit-learn library. We run it with 12 cores, as it should be faster, and return the same result:

```
!python code/performance-globalDT.py 12 100
```

This is very interesting! The accuracy (0.7263) is way lower than most of the ones we got with the local model. Actually, it is only slightly higher than the one we found with one single partition. This shows how the ensemble effect can be very beneficial in some cases, and the SUSY dataset is an example of that.

> **Challenge #7.4**
>
> You are asked to compare the scalability of the local-based model with the MLlib decision tree.

We have to create a similar script, in which we now use the MLlib decision tree. The entire script with our solution is available in the supplementary material at 07-MLbig/code/scalability-globalDT.py. Once again, we need to bear in mind to do a count() and cache the DataFrame before starting the timer. In addition, to focus only on the time of building the model, we should probably disregard the operations to create the assembled vector and transform the class label with StringIndexer. However, that would imply doing this without pipelines, and its cost is expected to be negligible. So, in our solution, we consider all operations to create a training pipeline as part of the execution. Once the model is fitted, we can stop the timer.

> Note that, on this occasion, we are not able to measure the Spark overhead in the same manner we did for the local model.

Once again, to make a strict comparison with the local-based model, we should probably grow the trees to the maximum depth allowed by MLlib (i.e., 30), as the local model is growing the trees as much as it can. However, as we explained before, the deeper we go, the slower the MLlin decision tree would become. Thus, for this experiment we show the results with maxDepth = 10.

To avoid repeating the code to compute the scalability metrics and create the plots, we are going to simply present the results we have obtained. Nevertheless, the code necessary to run everything and get the plots is available at 07-MLbig/code/plot-scalability-global.py. Figure 7.7 plots all the scalability metrics for this experiment.

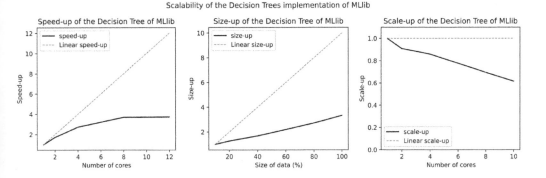

Figure 7.7 Scalability metrics for the MLlib decision tree algorithms (maxDepth = 10).

```
!python code/plot-scalability-global.py 10
```

As we probably expected, the scalability of the local model is much better than the global counterpart. If we look at the speed-up, for example, we can observe how increasing the number of cores after eight doesn't seem to make much difference. This is probably due to the overhead created by Spark. Note that if we were to use maxDepth = 30, we would observe even worse results. Having said that, a larger experiment on a cluster of computing nodes might show different results. Looking at these results and those from the previous challenge, one may think that local-based models are better, as they scale up better and the accuracy is higher. However, this might not always be true, depending on the dataset we have at hand.

7.6 Exercises

7.1 Indicate whether the following statements about local approach solutions are true or false:
   (a) The results obtained depend on the degree of parallelization (e.g., number of partitions).
   (b) The test phase may become very slow if we split the training dataset into a large number of partitions.
   (c) It generates a single model at the end of the building phase.
   (d) It does not benefit from the ensemble effect as global models do.

7.2 Can we always design a local-based solution for any existing machine learning algorithm? Explain your answer using one or more examples.

7.3 Indicate whether the following statements about global approach solutions are true or false:
   (a) Global approaches usually create a single model.
   (b) The test phase does not happen in parallel.

(c) The number of partitions does not affect the accuracy/error performance, but it does change the required runtime.

(d) The behavior of the method is closer to the sequential version, but it may come with limited features.

7.4 We ran the MLlib decision tree on a relatively small dataset, and we got quite a different result from what we got using the scikit-learn library. Briefly explain why this might be happening.

7.5 The premise of big data is that using more data will provide better models. With that in mind, which kind of approach, local or global, would you expect to obtain the best results? Explain why, and provide an example in which having more data may not be useful.

7.6 Explain why the global-based implementation of decision trees in Spark is iterative instead of recursive?

7.7 You are using your own laptop to run the MLlib logistic regression, and you are testing it in pseudo-distributed mode (i.e., option `local[*]`). You test the accuracy and you are happy with it; however, it takes three days to train the model. If you were to use a "real" cluster of computing nodes (e.g., 10 nodes), would you expect the accuracy to remain the same?

7.8 After the previous experiment, we decide to implement our own local-based solution for logistic regression. Briefly explain how the training and test phases would be designed.

7.9 Using the same data as we did in Exercise 7.7, you run it on your own laptop in pseudo-distributed mode (i.e., option `local[*]`). Would you expect it to take around three days to train a model again? When testing it in the "real" cluster, would you expect the accuracy to remain the same? Briefly explain your answers.

7.10 Imagine an unbalanced classification problem in which there are about 1000 positive instances (minority class), and two million negative instances (majority class). Could we apply a local approach to tackle this problem? If yes, briefly explain how you would do it. Otherwise, indicate why it wouldn't be suitable.

7.11 Rather than using the scikit-learn library, we want to build a local model using MLlib. We have managed to produce the following code for linear regression:

```
rdd = sc.textFile("mlbig-dataset.csv")

def build_model(instances):
    from pyspark.ml.regression import LinearRegression
    # transform the iterator to pandas
    partition_data_df = pd.DataFrame(partition_data_it,\
                                 columns = column_names)

    df = spark.createDataFrame(partition_data_df)
    lr.fit(df)
    ...

rdd.mapPartitions(build_model)
```

However, this doesn't seem to work. Explain why, and, if you can, find a solution for it.

7.12 We want to build a local model that performs the testing phase directly. Later we will have to aggregate the results after `mapPartitions`, but for now we have managed to produce the following code:

```
# We read a file in CSV format as a DataFrame
df = spark.read.csv("data.csv")
train,test = df.randomSplit([0.8,0.2]) # split into training and test
# we define a function that receives two arguments,
# a partition of the training data and the test.
def my_ml_method(partition,test):
    # this method uses the sklearn library to fit
    # a model and aims to predict the test
# we use this function within `mapPartitions`
train.rdd.mapPartitions(lambda partition : my_ml_method(partition, test))
```

However, this doesn't seem to work. Explain why, and provide a solution for it. Note that the output of the `randomSplit` function is two Spark DataFrames, `train` and `test`.

7.13 Indicate whether the following statements about scalability measures are true or false:

(a) The complexity of an algorithm is an important factor when analyzing the scalability of a distributed solution.

(b) If we analyze the scalability of a solution in pseudo-distributed mode, we may get a pessimistic assessment of the solution.

(c) To compute these metrics we don't have to use big datasets, we could do it with small ones.

(d) We always need to be able to run a sequential version of the algorithm (i.e., using one core) to establish a significant baseline.

7.14 The scalability of a big data solution in a real environment may be affected by various factors. Briefly describe the main caveats we need to bear in mind to correctly measure the scalability.

7.15 We have implemented our own global solution for the decision tree algorithm. We have tested it in a real cluster with a dataset of 10 million instances, and we have obtained the following results.

Dataset size	1 core	2 cores	4 cores	8 cores
10%	25	15	10	6
20%	55	32	22	13
40%	140	72	44	26
80%	250	130	90	54
100%	325	170	120	65

You are asked to calculate the speed-up, size-up, and scale-up, and discuss whether the results are as expected or not.

8 Implementing Classical Methods: k-Means and Linear Regression

---

Learning Outcomes

[KU IS]   Delving into the design of global approaches

[IS, PPS]   Learning how to implement traditional machine learning algorithms in big data with a global approach

We have learned two distinct approaches to designing machine learning solutions for big data: local and global approaches. The former is a simple divide-and-conquer strategy which allows us to quickly exploit existing sequential machine learning implementations, using them in different partitions of the data. The latter requires us to know the nitty-gritty detail of a particular technique to parallelize its operations.

In the previous chapter we focused on decision trees as a classical technique for classification. In this chapter, we want to cover clustering and regression, looking at two traditional machine learning methods: k-means and linear regression, respectively. We are going to briefly discuss how to implement these methods in a non-distributed manner first, and then carefully analyze the bottlenecks of these methods when manipulating big data. This will allow us to design global-based solutions based on the Spark DataFrame API. Our main focus will be on the principles for designing solutions effectively. Nevertheless, some of the challenges in this chapter will ask you to investigate particular tools from Spark to speed up the processing even further.

> If you need it, you could refresh your knowledge or learn about linear regression and k-means with Andrew Ng's notes (Ng, 2012), and also with any of the machine learning references given in Section 8.4.

8.1 Clustering: k-Means

k-means is an unsupervised learning algorithm that aims to discover natural structures and patterns within the data by clustering the data according to their similarity. Clustering the data allows us to better describe and understand it, and it has proven very important for making decisions in plenty of real-world applications.

Without discussing its cost/distortion function or convergence properties, we will give you a high-level intuitive description of k-means. Assuming that we have a dataset with a number of instances/examples for which we know a number of attributes (e.g., we could have data for a number of patients, the instances; the information we have are the attributes), the goal of *k*-means is to cluster those instances by similarity. In essence, the *k*-means algorithm works as follows.

- It starts off by randomly initializing the number of clusters *k* that you expect to find in the dataset. What does it mean? Well, we simply take *k* random instances from the data, which we will call cluster "centroids." This *k* becomes a hyperparameter of the *k*-means algorithm. There are more advanced methods that aim to automatically find the most suitable number of clusters.
- Then, we need to assign each instance of the dataset to the nearest centroid. How do we do that? We need to compute the distance (e.g., Euclidean distance) between the centroids and all the instances of the dataset, and we assign each instance to (or label each instance with) the nearest (shortest distance) centroid. This will be quite a time-consuming operation if we have a big dataset!
- The next step is to recompute the centroids of the clusters. We have temporarily assigned some instances of the dataset to a centroid (initially picked up at random); we can now "refine" those centroids if we compute the mean value of all the instances that belong to a cluster.

However, that is not the end of the algorithm. We need to repeat the last two steps for a number of iterations until the centroids "stabilize," meaning that they don't move (or at least not much) from one iteration to the next. When that happens, we say that the algorithm has converged to finding the centroids. Here is some brief pseudocode:

```
1. Initialize k cluster centers
2. Repeat until convergence:
    2.1 Assign each data point to the cluster
        with the closest center.
    2.2 Assign each cluster center to be the mean
        of its cluster's data points.
```

As an example of the use of *k*-means, we are going to use the same data we had in the previous chapter with student marks. Instead of distinguishing between predefined classes, First vs. Not-First, the goal of the clustering is to find different sets of students who perform similarly in the different exercises and project. Let's start our Spark session, and read the data:

```
from pyspark.sql import SparkSession
import pyspark.sql.functions as sql_f
spark = SparkSession \
    .builder \
    .master("local[*]") \
    .appName("MLexamples") \
    .getOrCreate()
sc = spark.sparkContext

from pyspark.sql.types import *
schema = StructType(
    [
        StructField("Ex01", FloatType(), True),
        StructField("Ex02", FloatType(), True),
        StructField("Ex03", FloatType(), True),
```

```
        StructField("Ex04", FloatType(), True),
        StructField("Project", FloatType(), True),
        StructField("Question 1", FloatType(), True),
        StructField("Question 2", FloatType(), True),
        StructField("Question 3", FloatType(), True),
        StructField("Question 4", FloatType(), True),
        StructField("Exam", FloatType(), True),
        StructField("Total", FloatType(), True),
    ]
)

df = spark.read.format('csv').option("header", 'true')\
            .schema(schema).load("data/marks.csv")
df = df.drop('Question 1').drop('Question 2').drop('Question 3')\
        .drop('Question 4').drop('Exam').drop('Total')
```

Let's have a look at the shape of our DataFrame and some of the data points:

```
df.printSchema()
```

```
root
 |-- Ex01: float (nullable = true)
 |-- Ex02: float (nullable = true)
 |-- Ex03: float (nullable = true)
 |-- Ex04: float (nullable = true)
 |-- Project: float (nullable = true)
```

```
df.show(4)
```

```
+-----+-----+-----+----+-------+
| Ex01| Ex02| Ex03|Ex04|Project|
+-----+-----+-----+----+-------+
|100.0| 85.0| 80.0|70.0|   80.0|
|100.0| 85.0| 80.0|90.0|   93.0|
|100.0|100.0| 85.0|30.0|   70.0|
| 95.0| 95.0|100.0|55.0|   87.0|
+-----+-----+-----+----+-------+
only showing top 4 rows
```

In the *k*-means algorithm, the Euclidean distance is used to calculate the similarity between examples (other distance metrics could be used). For this reason, it is usual to normalize the dataset so that when we calculate the distances between examples there are no features that may be contributing more than others to the result due to their magnitude. Although in our dataset all of our features are in the $[0, 100]$ range, it is a good practice for clustering, and we will use a min–max normalization. To do so, we could use the `MinMaxScaler` of MLlib. We need to create the vector assembler first:

```
feature_cols = df.columns
```

```
from pyspark.ml.feature import VectorAssembler
assembler = VectorAssembler(inputCols=feature_cols, outputCol="features")
df = assembler.transform(df)
```

After creating the column with the features, we can get rid of the rest of the columns.

```
df = df.drop('Ex01').drop('Ex02').drop('Ex03').drop('Ex04').drop('Project')
```

Finally, we apply the MLlib `MinMaxScaler` to the `features` column, creating a new column, `scaled_features`:

```
from pyspark.ml.feature import MinMaxScaler
scaler = MinMaxScaler(inputCol="features", outputCol="scaled_features")
scaler_model = scaler.fit(df)

df = scaler_model.transform(df)

df.show(3, truncate=False)
```

```
+----------------------------+-------------------------------------------
------+
|features                    |scaled_features
|
+----------------------------+-------------------------------------------
------+
|[100.0,85.0,80.0,70.0,80.0]
|[1.0,0.625,0.6363636363636364,0.7000000000000001,0.8]|
|[100.0,85.0,80.0,90.0,93.0] |[1.0,0.625,0.6363636363636364,0.9,0.93]    |
|
|[100.0,100.0,85.0,30.0,70.0]|[1.0,1.0,0.7272727272727273,0.3,0.7000000000000
001]  |
+----------------------------+-------------------------------------------
------+
only showing top 3 rows
```

As we now want to work with the normalized features, we could select only that column and rename it as `features`:

```
df = df.select(df['scaled_features'].alias('features'))

df.show(3, truncate=False)
```

```
+------------------------------------------------------+
|features                                              |
+------------------------------------------------------+
|[1.0,0.625,0.6363636363636364,0.7000000000000001,0.8]|
|[1.0,0.625,0.6363636363636364,0.9,0.93]               |
|[1.0,1.0,0.7272727272727273,0.3,0.7000000000000001]   |
+------------------------------------------------------+
only showing top 3 rows
```

We are now ready to implement the *k*-means algorithm. This technique is so simple that rather than using the scikit-learn library, we are going to code it ourselves in Python, before considering how to parallelize it with Spark.

8.1.1   Non-distributed Implementation

To implement *k*-means with Python, we use the numpy library to manipulate our data. We can collect the previous DataFrame to the driver and convert it into a numpy array:

```
import numpy as np
raw_data = df.collect()
# without squeeze we get a 3-dimensional array
```

```
data = np.array(raw_data).squeeze()
data[:3]
```

```
array([[1.      , 0.625   , 0.63636364, 0.7 , 0.8  ],
       [1.      , 0.625   , 0.63636364, 0.9 , 0.93 ],
       [1.      , 1.      , 0.72727273, 0.3 , 0.7  ]])
```

> We have used the function squeeze() to avoid getting too many nested arrays/lists. When collecting from the DataFrame we get a list of Rows, each of which has a DenseVector inside. Coercing it to np.array() would create an array of double lists, which are removed with this function.

Now that we have the data ready, we define our *k*-means function. But first, we implement a function to calculate the Euclidean distance, which will be used throughout the rest of this section. For simplicity, we have decided to keep the square root as part of the Euclidean distance calculation, but it wouldn't really be necessary for *k*-means as finding the nearest centroid wouldn't be affected by using the squared distance.

```
def dist(a, b, axis=1):
    return np.sqrt(np.sum((a - b)**2, axis=axis))
```

You may have noticed that we have included an extra parameter axis, which allows us to: (i) compute the total distance between two matrices/arrays (when axis is set to None); (ii) calculate the distances between each row of a matrix and an array (axis = 1), which is the default behavior we need.

```
def kmeans(X, k, threshold=0.001, seed=12345):
    # Fix the random seed
    np.random.seed(seed)
    # Randomly choose k examples from the training data
    centroids = X[np.random.permutation(X.shape[0])[:k], :]
    converged = False
    while not converged:
        # Step 1: Assign each example to its nearest center
        distances = np.zeros((X.shape[0], centroids.shape[0]))
        for i in range(centroids.shape[0]):
            distances[:, i] = dist(X, centroids[i])
        # Store the cluster index of the nearest cluster for each instance
        nearest_c = np.argmin(distances, axis=1)
        # Step 2: Create new centroids
        new_centroids = np.zeros((centroids.shape[0], centroids.shape[1]))
        for i in range(centroids.shape[0]):
            new_centroids[i, :] = np.mean(X[nearest_c == i, :], axis=0)
        # Step 3: Check if we have converged
        # Compute difference between new centroids and previous ones
        diff = dist(new_centroids, centroids, axis=None)
        if diff < threshold:
            converged = True
        else:
            centroids = new_centroids
    return centroids, nearest_c
```

We first initialize the centroids as random rows of data. Then, we start a loop to optimize their position. In the loop, Step 1 consists of assigning each example to its nearest centroid. To do this, we compute the Euclidean distance between all elements of the data and each centroid. Note how that generates a distance matrix, and how we use it to compute the nearest centroid as the `argmin` of that matrix. After that, Step 2 calculates the new centroids as the mean value of those examples that have been assigned to the same cluster index. Lastly, to determine whether the algorithm has converged (Step 3), we have simply calculated the difference between the current centroids and the new ones. If they haven't changed much (less than a given threshold), the algorithm will stop; otherwise, it will continue reassigning examples to their nearest centroid.

We fix the number of clusters to find to $k = 2$.

```
k = 2
centroids, nearest_c = kmeans(data, k)

centroids
```

```
array([[0.525     , 0.45      , 0.5       , 0.6225    , 0.679     ],
       [0.90853659, 0.75304878, 0.74944568, 0.79268293, 0.80853659]])
```

Although we have a five-dimensional problem, we could try to plot the result of the clustering using only two of its features. For example, if we take `'Ex02'` and `'Project'` and we plot the data together with the resulting centroids, we could get something like this:

```
import matplotlib.pyplot as plt
plt.figure(figsize=(5, 4))
plt.scatter(data[nearest_c==0, 1], data[nearest_c==0, 4],
            c='lightgray', marker='o', s=100, label='Cluster 1')
plt.scatter(data[nearest_c==1, 1], data[nearest_c==1, 4],
            c='dimgray', marker='+', s=100, label='Cluster 2')
plt.scatter(centroids[0, 1], centroids[0, 4], marker='o',
            c='k', s=400, label='Cluster 1 centroid')
plt.scatter(centroids[1, 1], centroids[1, 4], marker='x',
            c='k', s=400, label='Cluster 2 centroid')
plt.legend(loc='lower right', markerscale=0.5); plt.show()
```

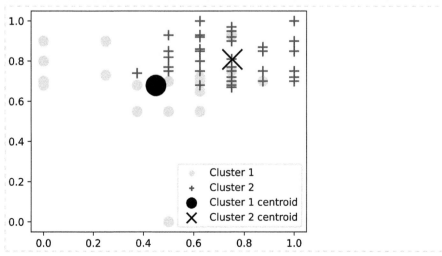

This simple implementation works just fine. But, what will be the problem if we have a big dataset? What is the main bottleneck of the k-means algorithm? Intuitively, the primary limitation we may encounter seems to be on the number of distance computations we need to perform at each iteration of the loop. Additionally, recomputing the centroids would also require parallelization, as this entails calculating the average of many samples (which would be very similar to what we learned in Chapter 4 to compute the average of a list of elements!). How do we distribute k-means with Spark?

8.1.2   Distributed Implementation

k-means is a relatively efficient algorithm. If we pay attention to its complexity, we can see that it is $O(n \cdot d \cdot k \cdot i)$, where n is the number of instances, d the number of features, k the number of neighbors, and i the number of iterations. The method is bound to compute the Euclidean distance of the k centroids against the entire dataset to assign each example of the training data to its nearest center, and this may become its Achilles heel. In this section we are going to design a parallel solution that aims to enable k-means to tackle datasets of a large number of instances n, which in most practical examples will be the largest factor increasing the runtime needed to apply k-means.

> One may argue that in some scenarios the number of features may also be big. However, that would not only mean that the computation would be slower, but also that the distance calculation will be affected by the curse of dimensionality, and other strategies should be considered.

Keeping that in mind, let's think carefully about how we could implement k-means in parallel. If we have a dataset $X = (x^{(1)}, \ldots, x^{(m)})$, the number of instances m is meant to be big. We will simply distribute its m examples across a number of machines reading it as a Spark DataFrame. In fact, we have already done so. The main issue lies in determining the nearest centroid for each of the elements of that DataFrame (step 1). Luckily, this can be done in parallel as long as we have the centroids available to perform this computation. The set of centroids, $C = (c^{(1)}, \ldots, c^{(k)})$, is going to be composed of a very small number of instances k that is easily manageable in memory, so we can afford to have them in the driver and broadcast them (every time we update them) to the workers to calculate the nearest centroid to each element of the DataFrame in parallel.

Once we have determined the nearest centroid to each instance of the training data, step 2 will have to group together those instances with the same cluster index and compute its mean value. We have already seen various ways to perform aggregations with DataFrames.

The main loop will repeat steps 1 and 2, meaning that we have to repeatedly access the data to recompute the centroids. Thus, we will have to cache our DataFrame. Figure 8.1 presents an overview of this distributed solution, in which we can see how in the first step we give every instance of the data a nearest centroid (represented by the cluster index), and those instances that belong to the same cluster are aggregated

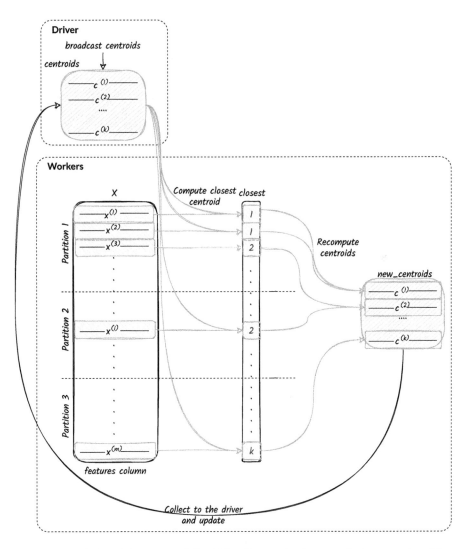

Figure 8.1 Workflow of *k*-means with Spark DataFrames. In this example, instances 1 and 2 are assigned to cluster 1, instance *i* to cluster 2, and the last instance to cluster k.

to create the new centroids (which must be collected back to the driver and broadcast to all workers in the next iteration).

Would the result obtained with this design change if we vary the number of partitions of the DataFrame? Of course not, this is a global design. Indeed, this would be an exact replica of the original algorithm, and the number of partitions/workers we use will not influence the final result, so here we have a very simple and intuitive global solution! Unfortunately, this won't be so easy for any machine learning method, but this is a great example of simplicity and high performance.

Let's implement it. The first thing we do not want to forget is to cache the training data because we are going to iterate through it multiple times.

```
df = df.cache()
```

Then, what we need to do is to randomly choose k initial centroids from the DataFrame with the data. As we said before, the centroids are a very limited number of instances, so it is fine to keep it in the main memory, but we will actually need them available in all workers. Thus, we should bring those centroids to the driver node, and we will later broadcast them to the workers.

To do so, we can use a transformation called `sample` on the DataFrame. That function allows us to obtain a random fraction of the dataset. The fraction should be in the range $[0.0, 1.0]$. Unfortunately, it is not guaranteed that this function will provide exactly the fraction specified of the total count of the given DataFrame. That's not a big problem as we can use the function `limit()` to obtain exactly k elements, but we need to ensure that the fraction is sufficiently big to obtain at least k elements. For this example, we are going to select a fraction of 5% of the data (which in our dataset is around three or four instances), and limit it to two:

```
centroids = df.sample(fraction=0.05, seed=123456).limit(2).collect()

centroids
```

```
[Row(features=DenseVector([0.125, 0.875, 0.3636, 0.25, 0.7])),
 Row(features=DenseVector([0.625, 0.25, 0.4545, 0.0, 0.73]))]
```

Currently, `centroids` is a list of Rows. As we used MLlib before to normalize the data, each element of the column `'features'` is of type `DenseVector`. As we are going to compute distances between these and each `DenseVector` within the feature columns, we need to transform this into "proper" arrays, which we can do again using `np.array` and the `squeeze()` function.

```
centroids = np.array(centroids).squeeze()

centroids
```

```
array([[0.125    , 0.875    , 0.36363636, 0.25    , 0.7    ],
       [0.625    , 0.25    , 0.45454545, 0.    , 0.73    ]])
```

In this particular example, `centroids` is tiny and could be used as a global variable. Nevertheless, assuming it could become a bit larger, we will broadcast it to all workers:

```
centroids_bc = sc.broadcast(centroids)
```

Now that we have the centroids accessible from everywhere, the next step is to assign all the elements of `df` to their closest centroid. Unfortunately, there isn't a Spark function that would do that job easily. Thus, we define a UDF, `closest_centroid`, which transforms a given instance into the index of its nearest centroid. In the sequential implementation we created a distance matrix containing the distances between all the data and the centroids. For this distributed version, we simply apply this operation one by one. For a given instance of the DataFrame, we just compute its distance to all the centroids and return the index of the closest one.

```
closest_centroid = sql_f.udf(
    lambda x: int(np.argmin(dist(centroids_bc.value, x)))
)
```

We can apply that UDF to df to add a new column with the index:

```
df_closest = df.withColumn('closest', closest_centroid('features'))
df_closest.show(4)
```

```
+--------------------+-------+
|            features|closest|
+--------------------+-------+
|[1.0,0.625,0.6363...|      1|
|[1.0,0.625,0.6363...|      1|
|[1.0,1.0,0.727272...|      1|
|[0.875,0.875,1.0,...|      1|
+--------------------+-------+
only showing top 4 rows
```

The last thing to do is to recalculate the positions of the centroids based on the column closest. We have to aggregate all of those DenseVectors with the same nearest neighbor. To do this very easily, we can use another feature from Spark MLlib called Summarizer.[1] This tool allows one to compute aggregations (such as the mean, minimum, maximum, etc.) over MLlib Vector columns.

```
from pyspark.ml.stat import Summarizer
new_centroids_df = df_closest.groupBy("closest").agg(
    Summarizer.mean(sql_f.col("features"))
)
```

> Note that groupBy in conjunction with Summarizer form a wide transformation, and provoke some network traffic. However, due to the nature of the aggregation, partial aggregations can be made at each worker before sending info across the network (do you remember combiners?), so they are very efficient.

Let's have a look at the new centroids:

```
new_centroids_df.show(truncate=False)
```

```
+-------+----------------------------------------------------------
--------------------------+
|closest|mean(features)
|
+-------+----------------------------------------------------------
--------------------------+
|0      |[0.6422413793103448,0.7887931034482758,0.664576802507837,0.782758620
6896552,0.7437931034482759]|
|1      |[0.91015625,0.5312499999999999,0.6704545454545453,0.6953124999999998
,0.78625]                  |
+-------+----------------------------------------------------------
--------------------------+
```

From that DataFrame we are only interested in the new centroids (column mean(features)), which have to be collected to the driver. Once again, collect() gives us a list of Rows, and we convert it into numpy arrays.

---

[1] https://spark.apache.org/docs/3.1.1/api/python/reference/api/pyspark.ml.stat.Summarizer.html

```
centroids = np.array(
    new_centroids_df.select("mean(features)").collect()
).squeeze()

centroids
```

```
array([[0.64224138, 0.7887931 , 0.6645768 , 0.78275862, 0.7437931 ],
       [0.91015625, 0.53125   , 0.67045455, 0.6953125 , 0.78625   ]])
```

> You may have noticed that we are using `collect()` quite a lot in this parallel implementation. We have mentioned before that this is usually not a good idea, and that it should only be used when we are sure that the amount of data brought to the driver is very small. This is an exception, as the number of clusters would normally be very small.

And that's all! We have all the elements of this puzzle. We can now put this into a loop and keep updating the centroids until we converge. Let's create a function just like the one before, but that takes a Spark DataFrame with a `'features'` column as a DenseVector:

```
def distributed_kmeans(df, k, fraction, threshold=0.001, seed=12345):
    # Fix the random seed
    np.random.seed(seed)
    # Randomly choose k examples from the training data
    centroids = df.sample(fraction=fraction, seed=seed).limit(k).collect()
    # Convert them into np arrays:
    centroids = np.array(centroids).squeeze()
    converged = False
    while not converged:

        # Broadcast the current centroids
        centroids_bc = sc.broadcast(centroids)

        #  Step 1: Assign each example to its nearest center
        closest_centroid = sql_f.udf(
            lambda x: int(np.argmin(dist(centroids_bc.value, x)))
        )
        df_closest = df.withColumn("closest", closest_centroid("features"))
        # Step 2: Create new centroids
        new_centroids_df = df_closest.groupBy("closest").agg(
            Summarizer.mean(sql_f.col("features"))
        )
        # Collect the aggregated centroids
        # and convert it to np arrays
        new_centroids = np.array(
            new_centroids_df.select("mean(features)").collect()
        ).squeeze()
        # Step 3: Check if we have converged
        # Compute difference between new centroids
        # and previous ones
        diff = dist(new_centroids, centroids, axis=None)
        if diff < threshold:
            converged = True
        else:
```

```
                centroids = new_centroids
        return centroids, df_closest

centroids, c = distributed_kmeans(df, k, fraction=0.05)
```

> Note that due to the way the function `sample` works with DataFrames, we would need some prior knowledge about the size of the dataset to determine an appropriate fraction of the data that needs to be sampled to ensure we get k elements. We could compute this in advance, by calculating the total number of elements in `df`.

Let's have a look at the centroids we have found:

```
centroids
```

```
array([[0.91032609, 0.69293478, 0.73715415, 0.77717391, 0.79913043],
       [0.39166667, 0.53333333, 0.45454545, 0.61333333, 0.66466667]])
```

Oh, these are not the same centroids! Why? Didn't we say that we are implementing an exact replica of the original k-means algorithm? Yes, we are, but although we are using the same seeds, the ways we obtain the initial centroids are not quite the same, so the starting point for k-means is not the same. If we found a way to ensure that the initial centroids were the same, the final centroids would always be identical.

> **Challenge #8.1**
>
> k-means is one of the most straightforward applications of MapReduce. Thus, we would like you to think about how to implement it in terms of key–value pairs, code a global-based solution using the Spark RDDs API instead of DataFrames, and compare their efficiency.

8.2   Linear Regression

The global version of k-means was easy enough and did not pose too many challenges, apart from distributing the distance calculations and recomputing the new centroids. We now want to design a global-based solution for linear regression, which will require some more considerations to implement effectively for big data.

Linear regression is one of the simplest and most classical machine learning algorithms. However, with the appropriate feature engineering (e.g., with polynomial features, which are available in MLlib) more complex nonlinear models can also be built.

The basic assumption of linear regression is that the target (output feature) can be modeled as a linear combination of the input features. We can represent this model as a function $h_\theta(x)$, usually called the hypothesis:

$$h_\theta(x) = \theta_0 x_0 + \theta_1 x_1 + \theta_2 x_2 + \theta_3 x_3 + \cdots + \theta_n x_n,$$

where n is the number of input features, $x = (x_0, \ldots, x_n)$ the input example, and $\theta = (\theta_0, \ldots, \theta_n)$ the parameters of the model, also known as weights or coefficients. Note that we use a dummy feature x_0, which always takes the value 1. This is done just to simplify working with matrix notation, which is also very common in this case. If we define x and θ as column vectors, we can rewrite $h_\theta(x)$ as

$$h_\theta(x) = \theta^T x,$$

where θ^T is the transpose of θ.

Hence, the machine learning problem here is how to learn the θ parameters that best fit the training data. However, this is still too abstract for a machine to learn, so we need a way to define how well a model fits our data. This is, in fact, the cost function, which usually aggregates the loss obtained for each example $(x^{(i)}, y^{(i)})$, where $x^{(i)}$ represents the input features of the example and $y^{(i)}$ its corresponding label (target). In the previous chapter, we used the root mean squared error (RMSE) as an evaluator in MLlib. In linear regression, the MSE (without the root) is used as the cost function:

$$J(\theta) = \frac{1}{2m} \sum_{i=1}^{m} (h_\theta(x^{(i)}) - y^{(i)})^2,$$

where $J(\theta)$ is the cost function for a given set of parameters θ, and m is the total number of examples in our dataset. Therefore, in linear regression we measure the error as the squared difference between the prediction and the actual output for each example.

Using the squared difference instead of, for example, the absolute difference not only facilitates the optimization of the cost function, but also causes larger errors to contribute more to the cost. You may also have noticed that this formula is not exactly the MSE, but half of it, due to the 2 we have introduced in the denominator. This just changes the magnitude of the error but not the shape of the cost function, so the optimal parameters won't change, while it will simplify the derivatives we need to compute.

Once the cost function has been defined, the learning problem is to find the θ parameters that minimize the cost function:

$$\min_\theta J(\theta).$$

To find these parameters, we will explore two options: the closed-form solution and the gradient descent algorithm. We will study whether it is possible to implement global models for them in Spark. In this case, we will look for exact global replicas of the original non-distributed algorithms.

8.2.1   Closed-Form Solution

Something very interesting about the MSE cost function in the linear regression model is that it is continuous, differentiable, and convex, and we therefore have a single global minimum, which makes the problem relatively easy to optimize. Actually, we can simply find a direct solution to the problem by deriving the cost function with respect to each parameter and setting it equal to 0 (Ng, 2012). If we follow this process, we arrive at this equality:

$$(X^T X)\theta = X^T y,$$

where X is a matrix storing all the examples (one per row, i.e., $m \times (n + 1)$) and y is a column vector with all the target values. From now on, we will be using $d = n + 1$ for simplicity, so that X is an $m \times d$ matrix. From the previous equation, we can therefore derive θ as follows:

$$\theta = (X^T X)^{-1} X^T y.$$

This is known as the closed-form or direct solution, which can be easily implemented in Python. Let's see an example before going with Spark.

Non-distributed Implementation

To illustrate this section, we start by creating a synthetic dataset consisting of predicting house prices from their size in square meters.

```python
import matplotlib.pyplot as plt
import numpy as np
import pandas as pd
def gen_house_prices(n, seed):
    np.random.seed(seed)  # For reproducibility
    # Random sample generation (x, y) - (size, price)
    X = np.random.randint(60, 200, n).reshape(-1, 1)   # size
    # price in €
    y = 10 + X * 2.5 + np.random.randint(-60, 60, n).reshape(-1, 1)
    # We add the dummy feature of ones as the first column
    X = np.hstack((np.ones((X.shape[0], 1)), X))
    return X, y
X, y = gen_house_prices(10, seed=123456)
```

Let's plot our dataset.

```python
def plot_data(X, y, labelx, labely):
    fig, ax = plt.subplots(figsize=(5, 4))
    # Column 0 is the dummy feature, so we plot column 1
    ax.plot(X[:, 1], y, '+', markersize=8, color='dimgray')
    ax.set_xlabel(labelx)
    ax.set_ylabel(labely)
    return ax
plot_data(X, y, 'Size ($m^2$)', 'Price (k€)');
```

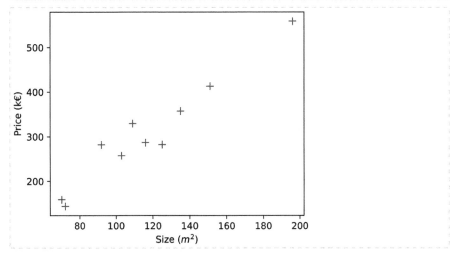

We are now looking for the best set of θ for this dataset. The closed-form solution could be implemented as follows:

```
def closed_form_solution(X, y):
    thetas = np.linalg.pinv(X.T.dot(X)).dot(X.T).dot(y)
    return thetas
```

If you are not familiar with numpy, `X.T` refers to the transpose of the matrix `X`, the `dot` method implements matrix multiplication, and the function `pinv` from `np.linalg` allows us to compute the pseudo-inverse of a matrix. Let's now use this function to learn the parameters.

```
thetas = closed_form_solution(X, y)
thetas
```

```
array([[-52.39524522],
       [  3.07566506]])
```

Can we check if they make sense? Let's plot our model on top of the previous plot of the dataset. To do so, we create a function that needs the `thetas`, the object where we are plotting (`ax`), and `xlim`, which refers to the range in which we will be plotting our model.

```
def plot_linear_regression(thetas, ax, xlim):
    # Create a set of points (examples) in xlim rang
    X = np.linspace(*xlim).reshape(-1, 1)
    # Add the dummy variable as the first column
    X = np.hstack((np.ones((X.size, 1)), X))
    # Compute the linear regression
    y = X.dot(thetas)
    # Plot the model
    ax.plot(X[:, 1], y, linewidth=2, color='black')
    # Add some annotations
    ax.annotate(r'$h_\theta(x)={:.2f} + {:.2f}x$'\
                .format(thetas[0, 0], thetas[1, 0]),
                (np.min(X[:, 1]), np.max(y)), fontsize=11)
```

```
ax = plot_data(X, y, 'Size ($m^2$)', 'Price (k€)')
plot_linear_regression(thetas, ax=ax, xlim=(60, 200))
```

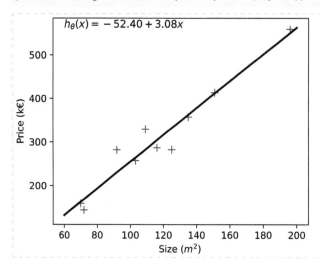

It seems like our one-line implementation of the closed-form solution is working fine. Do you see any problem with this solution? It is well known that closed-form solutions may encounter problems when $(X^T X)$ is not invertible, which can be due to the existence of redundant features (e.g., having square meters and square feet, simultaneously) or because there are more examples than features, which causes the solution not to be unique. Of course, we could do something to solve this, like eliminating variables or using regularization. Nevertheless, in this book we are more interested in the problems related to the volume. So, do you envision any problem if we were to implement this with Spark?

Distributed Implementation

Let's try to answer this question (if at all possible). To do so, we need to compute the following equation in Spark:

$$\theta = (X^T X)^{-1} X^T y.$$

We need to give it some thought. Let's revise the steps required to yield θ following Figure 8.2. X is an $m \times d$ matrix and y is of size $m \times 1$. Consequently, X^T will be of size $d \times m$. This means that $X^T X$ will result in a $d \times d$ matrix (Step 1), whose inverse will maintain the shape (Step 2). Then, this inverse matrix is multiplied by X^T to give a $d \times m$ matrix (Step 3), whose product with y will finally lead to a $d \times 1$ matrix (column vector) with the learned θ parameters (Step 4). Why should we pay attention to this? Because the sizes of m and d matter for big data.

When m becomes too big to work with a single machine, it may be evident that we will be using either an RDD or a DataFrame to store X, distributing the examples across workers. With enough resources, this won't be a problem, since the need for resources scales linearly with the number of examples (X^T will also be distributed by examples; as with a large m, we cannot assume that a feature will fit into a single node). But, how can we compute $X^T X$ with this distribution scheme?

Calculation of the product of two matrices usually requires combining all the rows of the first matrix with all the columns of the second. You should get a paper and pencil and check this, taking Figure 8.3 as a basis. To calculate the product, we would need to have access to all the values of the examples for a feature and combine this with all the values for the rest of the features, but we have distributed the data by examples, not by features! Should we change this? As we have just mentioned, that wouldn't be a good idea, so we may not be able to get the closed-form solution with Spark; or may we?

This is an example of how big data forces us to think differently to address a problem. Fortunately for us, there are other ways of performing matrix multiplication,[2] although they are not so well known. One is computing the multiplication as the sum of outer products. This means that we can do the matrix multiplication between each column of the first matrix ($d \times 1$ in our case) and the corresponding row of the second matrix ($1 \times d$ in our case), that is, the outer product, and sum all the resulting $d \times d$ matrices to finally get the product matrix of the same dimension. Let's illustrate this first with two random matrices:

[2] Additional information: http://mlwiki.org/index.php/Matrix-Matrix_Multiplication.

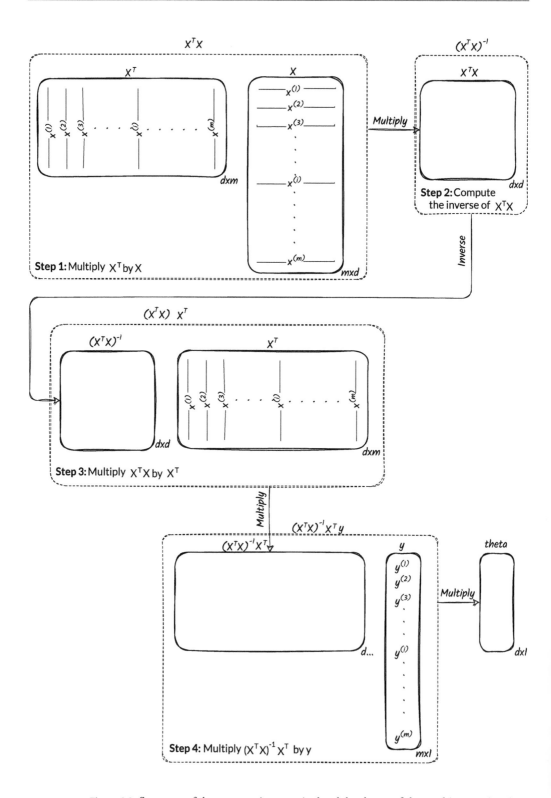

Figure 8.2 Summary of the computations required and the shapes of the resulting matrices in the closed-form solution.

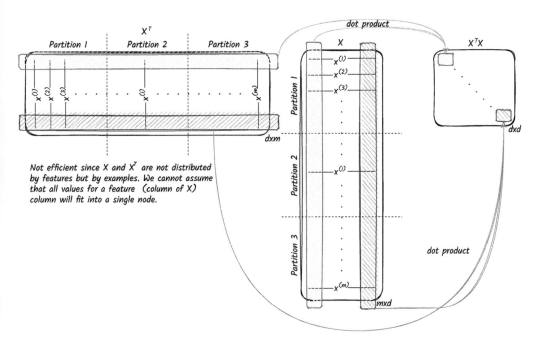

Figure 8.3 Traditional way of computing the multiplication between X^T and X, with X and X^T being distributed by examples (rows and columns, respectively) in three different partitions.

$$A = \begin{pmatrix} 1 & 2 & -1 \\ 3 & 4 & 1 \end{pmatrix}, \qquad B = \begin{pmatrix} -1 & -3 \\ 4 & 5 \\ 2 & -1 \end{pmatrix}.$$

If we perform traditional matrix multiplication with the dot products of each row of A with each row of B, we would get

$$AB = \begin{pmatrix} 5 & 8 \\ 15 & 10 \end{pmatrix}.$$

But we could get the same result by summing the outer products of each column of A and the corresponding column of B:

$$AB = \begin{pmatrix} -1 & -3 \\ -3 & -9 \end{pmatrix} + \begin{pmatrix} 8 & 10 \\ 16 & 20 \end{pmatrix} + \begin{pmatrix} -2 & 1 \\ 2 & -1 \end{pmatrix} = \begin{pmatrix} 5 & 8 \\ 15 & 10 \end{pmatrix}.$$

Note that the first matrix is obtained by matrix multiplication of the first column of A and the first row of B, the second matrix is obtained by multiplying the second column of A with the second row of B, and so on.

Can we then apply this strategy to our problem efficiently? If we have to take a column from X^T and the corresponding row from X, you could check that, luckily, we will be taking the same example $x^{(i)}$ twice and computing the outer product with itself! This is great for our data distribution strategy, since we just need to compute the outer

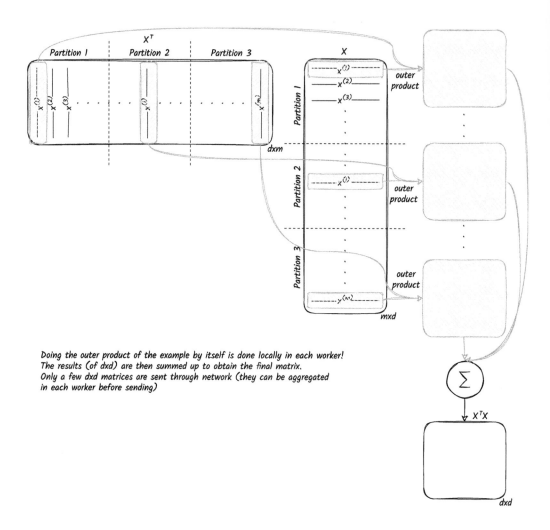

Doing the outer product of the example by itself is done locally in each worker!
The results (of dxd) are then summed up to obtain the final matrix.
Only a few dxd matrices are sent through network (they can be aggregated
in each worker before sending)

Figure 8.4 A schema of how to compute $X^{\mathrm{T}}X$ as the sum of outer products, which can be done efficiently with the dataset distributed by examples.

product for each example with itself and then sum all the outer products. This will be enough for computing the multiplication (Figure 8.4 depicts this idea).

Therefore, when implementing this, we will not have two copies of X distributed as X and X^{T}, but we will work with a single copy of X distributed by rows that we will use to compute the product of each example with itself. Figure 8.5 illustrates this simplification. Of course, all of these computations will be happening on the workers.

> The problem with this multiplication is that the output of each outer product and the aggregated matrix is of size $d \times d$. Storing $d \times d$ matrices could become a problem with large d values. So here is one of the limitations of the closed-form solution for big data.

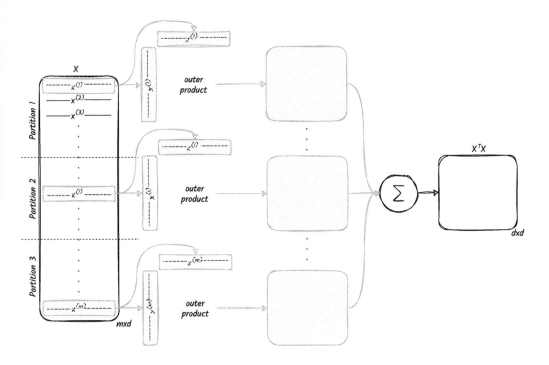

Figure 8.5 A schema of how the computation of $X^T X$ can be distributed with a single copy of X distributed by examples (rows). (Simplification of Figure 8.4).

Let's implement this in Spark following a global approach. Although programming this with RDDs may result in a more intuitive solution, in this case we'll consider DataFrames to get used to them and to try to benefit from their higher performance. Unfortunately, we will need to use some UDFs. Of course, if we were looking for a high-performance solution, we should move to Scala where we could take advantage of Datasets.

> In what follows, you will find some implementation tricks that are more related to Spark than to general concepts of machine learning for big data. Thus, changing the framework you work with implies bigger changes, but the general idea will remain the same.

We are going to create a DataFrame in which we have a column with our input features (of `DenseVector` type) and another column with the target output. Using the `Vector` type of Spark MLlib for the features will allow us to perform vectorized operations inside the UDFs.

```
from pyspark.ml.linalg import Vectors
```

```
pandas_df = pd.DataFrame(np.hstack((X, y)),\
                    columns=['dummy', r'$m^2$', 'Price (k€)'])
df = spark.createDataFrame(pandas_df)
```

We need to assemble the dummy feature with the square meters to form the `'features'` column, and then drop the unnecessary columns. Since we will be reusing the DataFrame multiple times, we should also not forget to cache it.

```
assembler = VectorAssembler(inputCols=['dummy', '$m^2$'],\
                            outputCol='features')
df = assembler.transform(df)
df = df.drop('$m^2$').drop('dummy')\
       .withColumnRenamed('Price (k€)', 'label').cache()
df.show(4)
```

```
+-----+-----------+
|label|   features|
+-----+-----------+
|282.5|[1.0,125.0]|
|329.5|[1.0,109.0]|
|287.0|[1.0,116.0]|
|257.5|[1.0,103.0]|
+-----+-----------+
only showing top 4 rows
```

We now need to focus on the `'features'` column and perform, for each example, the outer product with itself (recall the schema from Figure 8.5). Our features are of `Vector` type from Spark, so we should check how we can compute the outer product of a `Vector` with itself before creating a UDF.

```
v = Vectors.dense([1, 2, 3])
np.outer(v, v)
```

```
array([[1., 2., 3.],
       [2., 4., 6.],
       [3., 6., 9.]])
```

We have simply made use of the `outer` function provided by numpy that computes the outer product. That was easy, but the output is a numpy array, not a `Vector`, nor a `Matrix`. In fact, there is a `Matrix` type in Spark MLlib, which we could be tempted to use. We won't be doing that, however, because we wouldn't be able to sum matrices as this is not yet implemented in Spark, but it is possible with the `Vector` type. Hence, we will represent our matrix in a vector using a row-major format, which means that the rows of the matrix are concatenated one after the other in a single vector (in column order; columns are concatenated). Of course, we will be able to restore the original shape afterward as we already know the dimension that the matrix will have.

Let's now put everything into a UDF, so that we can apply this to our DataFrame.

```
from pyspark.ml.linalg import VectorUDT
@sql_f.udf(returnType=VectorUDT())
def outer_product(v):
    return Vectors.dense(np.outer(v, v).ravel())
```

You may have noticed a few details in this UDF. First, we used what is called a decorator in Python (`@sql_udf`). This helps us to create more concise and comprehensible code, where we tell Python to wrap the immediately next function into a Spark SQL UDF.

Second, we used `VectorUDT` as the return type of the UDF, which we need to import from the MLlib. This is required to make the output compatible with DataFrames (we cannot directly encode numpy vectors). This is why we create a `DenseVector` before returning our matrix as a `vector`. Finally, the `ravel()` method from numpy allows us to do exactly that, to flatten the matrix into a vector concatenating all rows.

We can now apply this to our DataFrame, getting a new DataFrame with the outer products.

```
outer_product_df = df.select(outer_product(sql_f.col('features')))\
                      .alias('outer_product'))
outer_product_df.show(4, truncate=False)
```

```
+------------------------+
|outer_product           |
+------------------------+
|[1.0,125.0,125.0,15625.0]|
|[1.0,109.0,109.0,11881.0]|
|[1.0,116.0,116.0,13456.0]|
|[1.0,103.0,103.0,10609.0]|
+------------------------+
only showing top 4 rows
```

Remember that they are matrices, even though we are storing them as vectors. This enables us to once again use an MLlib `Summarizer` to compute aggregations over those vectors. For example, we can sum all the outer products, which will finally give us the result for $X^T X$.

```
xtx_df = outer_product_df.agg(Summarizer.\
                          sum(outer_product_df['outer_product']))
```

Of course, this is still a DataFrame, although we already know that it contains a single $d \times d$ matrix stored as a vector. As you may remember, to be able to compute the closed-form solution we assumed that d is small enough to fit into a single node, so we will be collecting it to the driver (using `first()`):

```
xtx = xtx_df.first()[0] # get the resulting vector
xtx
```

```
DenseVector([10.0, 1169.0, 1169.0, 149561.0])
```

To recover the shape of the matrix we just need to do a reshape, as we can work with the `Vector` type of Spark as with numpy.

```
xtx = xtx.reshape(2, 2)
xtx
```

```
array([[1.00000e+01, 1.16900e+03],
       [1.16900e+03, 1.49561e+05]])
```

We have reshaped the vector to a 2×2 matrix. It would be better software practice to derive the shape of the matrix, but we leave this for the reader. Following our assumptions, even if we were dealing with a huge dataset, as long as the number of features was kept low, the resulting matrix would be sufficiently small that we could compute its inverse locally in the driver node with numpy. Then, we can continue with the rest of the steps, distributing the resulting matrix to the workers and computing the remaining multiplications in parallel, leaving the computation to the workers.

> We previously mentioned that with a large d, we could have problems with the storage of the matrix resulting from $X^T X$. Nevertheless, the problems would probably arise earlier in the computation of the inverse matrix, whose complexity increases cubically with d.

```
xtx_inv = np.linalg.pinv(xtx)
xtx_inv
```

```
array([[ 1.15894738e+00, -9.05857465e-03],
       [-9.05857465e-03,  7.74899457e-05]])
```

Again, we made use of the numpy `linalg.pinv()` function to compute the pseudo-inverse of the matrix (with the pseudo-inverse, we ensure getting something like an inverse matrix even if it doesn't exist).

The next step is to multiply this matrix by X^T, which you will remember is still distributed by columns (since X is distributed by rows). Recalling the dimensions, our inverse matrix is $d \times d$ (with $d = 2$) and X^T is $d \times m$. Hence, their multiplication will yield a $d \times m$ ($2 \times m$) matrix. Since we know that our inverse matrix is small enough to fit into a single machine, we can broadcast it to all the workers and compute the product between it and each example, which is exactly what we are looking for. Figure 8.6 summarizes this step. Note that each column of the resulting matrix is obtained by multiplying the inverse matrix by each column of X^T, which is the same as multiplying by each example! That's why we can still compute it in parallel, on the workers, for all the examples. We suggest you check this with pen and paper.

Let's now implement this in Spark. We first broadcast our inverse matrix and then create a UDF to do the job.

```
xtx_inv_bc = spark.sparkContext.broadcast(xtx_inv)
```

```
@sql_f.udf(returnType=VectorUDT())
def multiply_bc_matrix(v):
    return Vectors.dense(xtx_inv_bc.value.dot(v.reshape(-1, 1)))
```

In our UDF we will have our inverse matrix available, so we just need to do the matrix product with the corresponding feature vector v (we need to explicitly reshape the vector to a column vector, so that the dimensions for the product match properly). This is then performed for every example in our dataset.

```
product_df = df.select(multiply_bc_matrix('features')\
                    .alias('product'), 'label')
product_df.show(4, truncate=False)
```

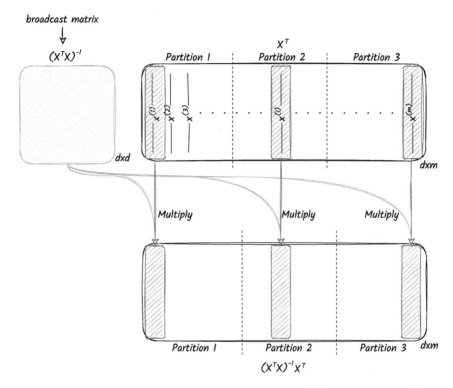

Figure 8.6 A schema of how to do the multiplication of $(X^T X)^{-1}$ by X^T, considering X^T is distributed by columns (examples).

```
+----------------------------------------------+-----+
|product                                       |label|
+----------------------------------------------+-----+
|[0.026625545335524414,6.276685600040913E-4]   |282.5|
|[0.17156273973457725,-6.121705708688821E-4]   |329.5|
|[0.10815271718499164,-6.974095111195698E-5]   |287.0|
|[0.225914187634222,-0.0010771102449462482]    |257.5|
+----------------------------------------------+-----+
only showing top 4 rows
```

We may be expecting a $2 \times m$ matrix, but since we have our data parallelized by examples, that is, the m examples are distributed in parallel, it seems like we've got an $m \times 2$ matrix. It really depends on how you look at it. You may prefer to think that we have a matrix distributed by columns (as we did with X^T).

The last product we have to develop is by y, that is, the 'label' column of our DataFrame. Again, if you check this (see Figure 8.7), you will notice that we just need to multiply each column of our matrix, that is, each row of the 'product' column in our DataFrame, with the corresponding target value (the 'label' column). This is an elementwise operation that will require an aggregation afterward.

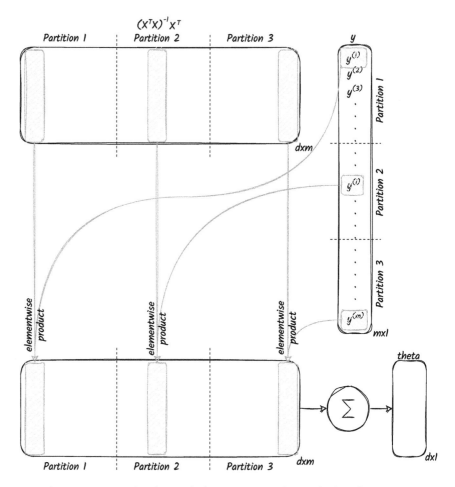

Note that Partitions are shared across both matrices since they are both in the same DataFrame with column names 'product' and 'label', respectively.

Figure 8.7 A schema of how to do the multiplication of $(X^{\mathrm{T}}X)^{-1}X^{\mathrm{T}}$ by y, considering y is distributed by rows.

```
@sql_f.udf(returnType=VectorUDT())
def multiply(x, y):
    return x * y


thetas_partial_df = product_df.select(multiply('product', 'label')\
                                    .alias('theta_partial'))
thetas_partial_df.show(truncate=False)


+--------------------------------------+
|theta_partial                         |
+--------------------------------------+
|[7.521716557285647,0.17731636820115582] |
|[56.52992274254321,-0.20171020310129664]|
```

```
|[31.0398298320926,-0.020015652969131652]|
|[58.172903315812164,-0.2773558880736589]|
|[-86.37907306527426,1.09263535556265]   |
|[91.80749947696698,-0.5441189005728394] |
|[-344.64208943894243,3.4263651791183767]|
|[83.4506970220807,-0.5778502739271091]  |
|[72.96912025666371,-0.5010189927858192] |
|[-22.865771916088455,0.5014180660058922]|
+----------------------------------------+
```

Well, we haven't really finished the product by y, whose result should be $d \times 1$. The final step is to aggregate all those rows into a single one by summing all the vectors. Let's use a Summarizer again:

```
thetas_df = thetas_partial_df.groupBy().agg(
    Summarizer.sum(thetas_partial_df["theta_partial"])
)
```

This will still be a DataFrame. In fact, we haven't performed the last transformation since we didn't apply any action yet. Since we already know that the result will be our θ parameters, we can trigger the execution and carry the results to the driver using first():

```
thetas = thetas_df.first()[0]
thetas
```

```
DenseVector([-52.3952, 3.0757])
```

Is it the same result as with numpy? Go back and check ... Yes! Exactly the same as we got with numpy, but now implemented for huge datasets.

> **Challenge #8.2**
>
> We have implemented our own linear regression algorithm in pyspark, but how does this solution compare with the MLlib solution? Does it achieve the same result? If not, could you explain why?

8.2.2   Gradient Descent

We did a good job implementing the closed-form solution for big data, but we will still have problems for larger values of d. When d becomes larger, we need to seek other methods for finding the parameters for the linear regression, since the computation of the inverse matrix will become intractable. So, our second option is the well-known gradient descent algorithm, the most widely used optimization method for machine learning. Let's recall how it works.

Conceptually, gradient descent is a very simple optimization algorithm. We start with random values of the parameters we are looking to optimize (θ in this case), stand at that position, see the direction in which the cost function reduces the most, and take a step in that direction (meaning that we modify the values we are optimizing). In fact, that direction is the opposite to that indicated by the gradient of the cost function at that point – hence the name of this strategy. Schematically, the algorithm would look like this:

1. Assign random values to $\theta = \{\theta_0, \ldots, \theta_n\}$.
2. Repeat until convergence (a given number of iterations or $|J(\theta_{it}) - J(\theta_{it-1})| <$ threshold)):

$$\theta_j = \theta_j - \alpha \frac{\partial J(\theta)}{\partial \theta_j} \qquad \text{for } j = 0, \ldots, n.$$

Note that all the θ_j should be updated simultaneously.

We have a hyperparameter α that controls the magnitude of the step we take. This is known as the learning rate, and is key for the gradient descent to work properly. It is well known that if we used an excessively large learning rate, we would end up diverging, not finding the minimum of the function. Otherwise, using a very low learning rate would result in slow convergence. The advantage with linear regression with respect to other machine learning models also using gradient descent, like neural networks, is that with the appropriate learning rate convergence is ensured, since the cost function with the linear regression model is convex, meaning that we have a single minimum, which is the global minimum. Anyway, there could also be convergence problems in this case due to variability among feature ranges and scales, since the same learning rate is generally used for all the features. In this case, it is highly recommended to standardize the features before going through gradient descent (you may recall from a challenge in the previous chapter that Spark ensures this for linear regression, even if you haven't explicitly done it).

The other key element of the gradient update formula is the gradient $(\partial J(\theta)/\partial \theta_j)$, which tells us the direction in which the function increases most quickly. Note that the update rule goes in the opposite direction of the gradient ($-$ is used), since we are minimizing it.

To apply gradient descent, we just need to compute the gradient of our cost function, which we have already defined, by differentiating the cost function with respect to each parameter. If you do this, you will reach

$$\frac{\partial J(\theta)}{\partial \theta_j} = \frac{1}{m} \sum_{i=1}^{m} (h_\theta(x^{(i)}) - y^{(i)}) \cdot x_j^{(i)} \qquad \text{for } j = 0, \ldots, n,$$

and hence the update rule will be defined as

$$\theta_j = \theta_j - \alpha \frac{1}{m} \sum_{i=1}^{m} (h_\theta(x^{(i)}) - y^{(i)}) \cdot x_j^{(i)} \qquad \text{for } j = 0, \ldots, n.$$

Therefore, the gradients are just the average of the gradients of each example i, which is computed as $(h_\theta(x^{(i)}) - y^{(i)}) \cdot x_j^{(i)}$ (this may give you a hint that this job could be done in parallel). If you have already worked with frameworks like PyTorch or Tensorflow, you will know that you wouldn't need to compute the gradients manually, since they feature auto-gradient mechanisms to compute those for any differentiable function. Nevertheless, in this case it is a good way to practise how we can distribute the computation.

Non-distributed Implementation

As with the closed-form solution, let's start implementing this with numpy before trying to distribute it with Spark. We continue with our house price example. The first thing we do is to standardize the square meters feature with the mean and the standard deviation so that we will find the minimum more easily.

```
x = X[:, 1].reshape(-1, 1)
x_norm = (x - x.mean()) / x.std()
x_norm[:3]
```

```
array([[ 0.22547983],
       [-0.21991243],
       [-0.02505331]])
```

We can now add the dummy variable (which is not standardized).

```
X_norm = np.hstack((np.ones(x_norm.shape), x_norm))
X_norm[:3]
```

```
array([[ 1.        ,  0.22547983],
       [ 1.        , -0.21991243],
       [ 1.        , -0.02505331]])
```

Note that we will then need to either transform the input features before feeding the model or apply a transformation to the θ parameters, so that we can work with the original feature space. We will solve this later.

Let's implement the gradient descent. In the for loop, we will also be computing the cost using the mean squared error from the scikit-learn library to track how it evolves along iterations.

```
from sklearn.metrics import mean_squared_error
def grad_descent_linreg(X, y, alpha=0.01, num_iters=1500):
    cost_history = np.zeros(num_iters)

    # We add the dummy feature to X
    X = np.hstack((np.ones((X.shape[0], 1)), X))

    # Initialize thetas to zeros (they could be random)
    thetas = np.zeros((X.shape[1], 1))

    # Do gradient descent
    for i in np.arange(num_iters):
        # Compute gradients and update
        h = X.dot(thetas) # model output
        # gradients
```

```
    grad = np.mean(X * (h - y), axis=0).reshape(-1, 1)
    thetas = thetas - alpha * grad # update rule

    # Keep track of the error
    # We could reuse h to be more efficient,
    # but prioritized readability
    h = X.dot(thetas) # model output
    cost_history[i] = mean_squared_error(y, h)
    print(f'Gradients = {grad.round(2).ravel().tolist()},\t'
          f'Thetas = {thetas.round(2).ravel().tolist()}\t'
          f'Cost = {cost_history[i]:.2f}')

  return thetas, cost_history
```

You will have noticed that we just needed two instructions to compute the gradients:

```
h = X.dot(thetas) # model output
grad = np.mean(X * (h - y), axis=0).reshape(-1, 1) # gradients
```

First, we computed $h_\theta(x^{(i)})$ for every example i simultaneously using numpy, and then we did the same with the gradients, computing them for all examples with X * (h - y), and then averaged them.

Let's test the learning algorithm. You can try different values for the learning rate and the number of iterations, although we already know that the following values work properly.

```
thetas, cost_history = grad_descent_linreg(x_norm, y, 0.5, 10)
thetas
print(f'Thetas: {thetas.ravel().round(2)}')
print(f'Last cost: {cost_history[-1].round(2)}')
```

```
Gradients = [-307.15, -110.49], Thetas = [153.57, 55.24]  Cost = 27474.63
Gradients = [-153.58, -55.24],  Thetas = [230.36, 82.87]  Cost = 7496.73
Gradients = [-76.79, -27.62],   Thetas = [268.76, 96.68]  Cost = 2502.26
Gradients = [-38.39, -13.81],   Thetas = [287.95, 103.58] Cost = 1253.64
Gradients = [-19.2, -6.91],     Thetas = [297.55, 107.04] Cost = 941.49
Gradients = [-9.6, -3.45],      Thetas = [302.35, 108.76] Cost = 863.45
Gradients = [-4.8, -1.73],      Thetas = [304.75, 109.63] Cost = 843.94
Gradients = [-2.4, -0.86],      Thetas = [305.95, 110.06] Cost = 839.06
Gradients = [-1.2, -0.43],      Thetas = [306.55, 110.27] Cost = 837.84
Gradients = [-0.6, -0.22],      Thetas = [306.85, 110.38] Cost = 837.54
Thetas: [306.85 110.38]
Last cost: 837.54
```

We can check the learning curve to see that it has converged.

```
plt.figure(figsize=(5, 4))
plt.plot(np.arange(1, 11), cost_history, color='black')
plt.ylabel('Cost'); plt.xlabel('Iterations');
```

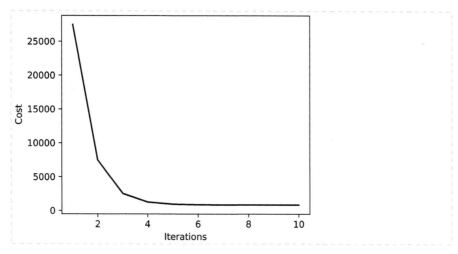

We can now see if there is any difference with the model found with the closed-form solution.

```
thetas
```

```
array([[306.85004883],
       [110.3804188 ]])
```

These parameters have nothing to do with the previous ones! What happened? You may remember that we standardized the input features, so our parameters are now working at a different scale, and are no longer comparable. We could plot the model to check this, but we would need to normalize the input data to destandardize our parameters. We opt for the second option, implementing a function to do so:

$$
\theta_j =
\begin{cases}
\theta'_0 - \displaystyle\sum_{i=1}^{n} \theta'_i \frac{\mu_{X_i}}{\sigma_{X_i}}, & j = 0, \\[2ex]
\dfrac{1}{\sigma_{X_j}} \theta'_j, & j > 0.
\end{cases}
$$

Following this formula, the standardized θ_0 can be destandardized as:

```
thetas[0] - thetas[1] * x.mean() / x.std()
```

```
array([-52.34407799])
```

And θ_1 would be:

```
thetas[1] / x.std()
```

```
array([3.07266148])
```

Let's put this in a more general function that we can reuse later.

```
def destandardize_thetas(thetas, mean, std):
    thetas_destand = np.zeros(thetas.shape)
    thetas_destand[0, 0] = thetas[0, 0] - np.sum(
        thetas[1:, :] * mean.reshape(-1, 1) / std.reshape(-1, 1)
```

```
    )
    thetas_destand[1:, 0] = thetas[1:, :] / std.reshape(-1, 1)
    return thetas_destand

thetas_destand = destandardize_thetas(thetas, x.mean(), x.std())
thetas_destand
```

```
array([[-52.34407799],
       [  3.07266148]])
```

Do you remember the values of the parameters when we used the closed-form solution? Go and look back. You will notice slight differences from the second decimal number. So we were close! Of course, gradient descent doesn't provide an exact solution, so we are happy with this. If we plotted this model, we would hardly notice a difference.

Distributed Implementation

Let's now focus on "translating" this implementation to a global solution in Spark. We continue using DataFrames and, to start with, we distribute our data (for simplicity we will distribute the normalized data). We just need to follow the same steps as before.

```
pandas_df = pd.DataFrame(np.hstack((X_norm, y)),\
                         columns=['dummy', r'$m^2$_norm', 'Price (k€)'])
df = spark.createDataFrame(pandas_df)
# Assemble the dummy column and the normalized square meters
assembler = VectorAssembler(inputCols=['dummy', '$m^2$_norm'],\
                            outputCol='features')
df = assembler.transform(df)
# Remove unnecessary columns and ensure that is cached
df = df.drop('$m^2$_norm').drop('dummy')\
       .withColumnRenamed('Price (k€)', 'label').cache()
df.show(4, truncate=False)
```

```
+-----+------------------------+
|label|features                |
+-----+------------------------+
|282.5|[1.0,0.2254798291651637]|
|329.5|[1.0,-0.21991242597590072]|
|287.0|[1.0,-0.025053314351685032]|
|257.5|[1.0,-0.3869345216537999]|
+-----+------------------------+
only showing top 4 rows
```

We will build our solution step by step, aiming to parallelize the most time-consuming operations, that is, the computation of the gradients. The gradient equation tells us that we compute the gradient for each example i as $(h_\theta(x^{(i)}) - y^{(i)}) \cdot x^{(i)}$ (where $\cdot$ is an element-wise product, resulting in a vector of gradients), and then we average them. This is great because we have the dataset distributed by examples. This means that we can easily use each example to compute their corresponding gradients and then aggregate all of them. We will be able to do this in parallel for each example as both $x^{(i)}$ and $y^{(i)}$ are a Row of our DataFrame. Figure 8.8 illustrates this idea.

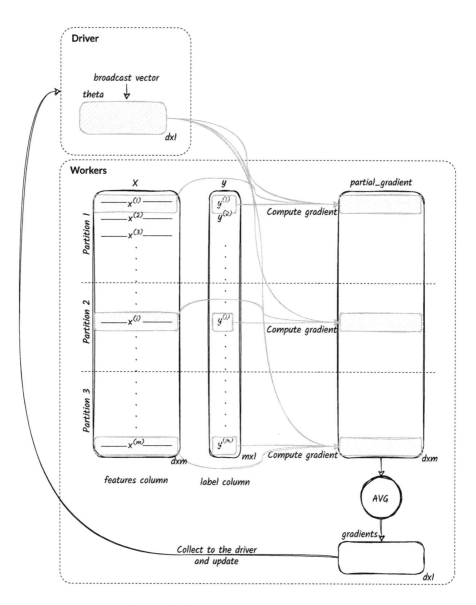

Figure 8.8 A schema of how to distribute the computation of the gradients.

As you may have noticed, to compute the gradients we need access to the θ parameters of the model, which will be shared by all workers. To do this efficiently, we start by initializing them in the driver node and broadcasting them.

```
thetas = np.zeros((2)) # In this case we use a row vector
thetas_bc = sc.broadcast(thetas)
```

We are now ready to create a UDF to compute the gradients of a single example. It will return a VectorUDT() type, meaning that we calculate the gradients with respect to all features simultaneously.

```
@sql_f.udf(returnType=VectorUDT())
def gradient(x, y):
    h = (x * thetas_bc.value).sum()
    return (h - y) * x
```

Let's check if this works:

```
grads_df = df.select(gradient('features', 'label').alias('grad'))
grads_df.show(4, truncate=False)
```

```
+--------------------------+
|grad                      |
+--------------------------+
|[-282.5,-63.69805173915875]|
|[-329.5,72.46114435905929] |
|[-287.0,7.190301218933604] |
|[-257.5,99.63563932585348] |
+--------------------------+
only showing top 4 rows
```

You can manually check that the gradients look fine. Since we have gradients of `Vector` type from Spark MLlib, we can use a `Summarizer` to compute the average gradients over the whole dataset. This will result in a single-row DataFrame that we can bring into the driver.

```
avg_grads_df = grads_df.agg(Summarizer.mean(grads_df['grad']))
avg_grads = avg_grads_df.first()[0]
avg_grads
```

```
DenseVector([-307.15, -110.4883])
```

Well, we are almost done with the implementation. We just need to apply the update rule, which will obviously be applied in the driver, where we have our parameters, and we have got our gradients.

> In gradient descent, even if we have a large d, we wouldn't expect problems storing the parameters and the gradients, since they are still one-dimensional vectors whose resource needs scale linearly with d.

```
alpha = 0.5
thetas = thetas - alpha * avg_grads
thetas
```

```
array([[153.575    , 55.24415877]])
```

We can put all this in a loop and have it sorted. However, as before, we would also like to keep track of how we reduce the cost at each iteration, so we need to compute this using Spark. In this case, instead of the mean squared error from the scikit-learn library, we use `Evaluator` from MLlib.

```
from pyspark.ml.evaluation import RegressionEvaluator
mse_evaluator = RegressionEvaluator(metricName="mse",\
                                    labelCol="label", \
                                    predictionCol="pred")
```

We are going to make the predictions for each example using a UDF:

```python
from pyspark.sql.types import DoubleType
thetas_bc = sc.broadcast(thetas) # broadcast the new thetas
@sql_f.udf(returnType=DoubleType())
def pred(x):
    h = (x * thetas_bc.value).sum()
    return float(h)
```

We can now use this function to make predictions in the training set, and compute the mean squared error with the evaluator.

```python
preds_labels_df = df.select(pred('features').alias('pred'), 'label')
mse_evaluator.evaluate(preds_labels_df)
```

```
27474.631889098346
```

Putting everything together:

```python
# Hyperparameters
iterations = 10
alpha = 0.5
# Initialization
thetas = np.zeros(2)
errors = np.zeros(iterations)
# df is cached!! Don't forget to do so
thetas_bc = sc.broadcast(thetas)
for i in range(iterations):
    # Gradients computation
    gradient = sql_f.udf(
        lambda x, y: ((x * thetas_bc.value).sum() - y) * x, VectorUDT()
    )
    grads_df = df.select(gradient("features", "label").alias("grad"))
    avg_grads_df = grads_df.agg(Summarizer.mean(grads_df["grad"]))
    avg_grads = avg_grads_df.first()[0]
    # Update rule
    thetas = thetas - alpha * avg_grads
    thetas_bc = sc.broadcast(thetas)  # broadcast the new thetas
    # Error in current iteration
    pred = sql_f.udf(
        lambda x: float((x * thetas_bc.value).sum()), DoubleType()
    )
    preds_labels_df = df.select(pred("features").alias("pred"), "label")
    cost_history[i] = mse_evaluator.evaluate(preds_labels_df)
    print(
        f"Gradients: {avg_grads.round(2)}\t"
        f"Thetas: {thetas.round(2)}\t"
        f"Cost: {cost_history[i]:.2f}"
    )
```

```
Gradients: [-307.15 -110.49]    Thetas: [153.57  55.24] Cost: 27474.63
Gradients: [-153.58  -55.24]    Thetas: [230.36  82.87] Cost: 7496.73
Gradients: [-76.79 -27.62]      Thetas: [268.76  96.68] Cost: 2502.26
Gradients: [-38.39 -13.81]      Thetas: [287.95 103.58] Cost: 1253.64
Gradients: [-19.2   -6.91]      Thetas: [297.55 107.04] Cost: 941.49
Gradients: [-9.6  -3.45]        Thetas: [302.35 108.76] Cost: 863.45
Gradients: [-4.8  -1.73]        Thetas: [304.75 109.63] Cost: 843.94
```

```
Gradients: [-2.4  -0.86]        Thetas: [305.95 110.06] Cost: 839.06
Gradients: [-1.2  -0.43]        Thetas: [306.55 110.27] Cost: 837.84
Gradients: [-0.6  -0.22]        Thetas: [306.85 110.38] Cost: 837.54
```

You should be aware of the following three aspects:

- Caching the DataFrame is vital here, since we are iterating through its data multiple times, so we won't be properly exploiting Spark's capabilities if we forget to do so.
- You may have noticed that we are broadcasting thetas and defining the UDFs at each iteration. This is required as we are changing the values of thetas on every pass through the loop. Whenever there are changes in a variable we need to broadcast and define the function using it again, so that Spark effectively broadcasts and uses the new value. We could have done this differently, adding additional parameters to the gradient function, but we prefer to maintain it as it is more readable in this case.
- Although we are not focused on performance, you may be aware of the additional time required for computing the cost in each iteration, which almost doubled the training time. This is obviously not necessary, but we could also perform other implementations reusing part of the error computation for computing the gradients. Again, we prioritized simplicity. Apart from this, there is also an overhead for using the distributed computation of Spark. For such a small dataset, the proportion of time taken by this overhead will far exceed the time required for the computation itself, hence not showing any advantage over the non-distributed implementation. Of course, this will change when the size of the dataset is large enough to make the overhead negligible with respect to the computation time required by the job.

Well, let's now check whether the results remain the same. Take a look at the learning curve:

```
plt.figure(figsize=(5, 4))
plt.plot(np.arange(1, 11), cost_history, color='black')
plt.ylabel('Cost'); plt.xlabel('Iterations');
```

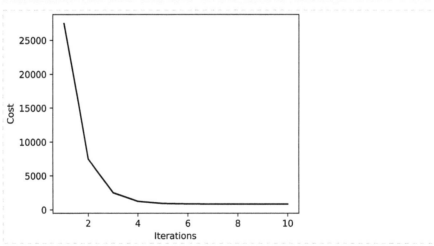

It seems like it has converged. If you checked the outputs with those of numpy, you wouldn't see any difference, apart from the time taken to perform each iteration.

We can now look at the destandardized parameters:

```
thetas_destand = destandardize_thetas(thetas.reshape(-1, 1),\
                                       x.mean(), x.std())
thetas_destand
```

```
array([[-52.34407799],
       [  3.07266148]])
```

Exactly the same as with numpy! That's great. We have an exact global solution for gradient descent, as we had for the closed-form solution.

Challenge #8.3

As we have already noted, computing the predictions of our model to measure the error is taking a long time. If we are going to repeat this for a number of iterations, our solution would take ages. There are some implementation tricks you could make use of in Spark to further accelerate this, using MLlib functions such as ElementwiseProduct[3] and vector_to_array[4] combined with Spark SQL ones (see aggregate[5]). With big data, this implementation detail could really make a difference. We challenge you to further investigate these methods and implement an optimized solution avoiding the use of UDFs. *Hint:* You can start with ElementwiseProduct and then move the output Vector to an array before using aggregate from Spark SQL.

Challenge #8.4

We did well with the linear regression. Could you modify the global linear regression algorithm we developed to learn a logistic regression model for classification? You will only have to consider two changes:

- the logistic regression model is the linear regression model passed through the sigmoid function ($g(z) = 1/(1 + e^{-z})$);
- the cost function is the binary cross entropy:

$$J(\theta) = -\frac{1}{m} \sum_{i=1}^{m} y^{(i)} \log(h_\theta(x^{(i)})) + (1 - y^{(i)}) \log(1 - h_\theta(x^{(i)})).$$

Despite these changes, the gradient update rule is exactly the same (except for the change in the model).

---

[3] https://spark.apache.org/docs/3.3.0/api/python/reference/api/pyspark.ml.feature.ElementwiseProduct.html#pyspark.ml.feature.ElementwiseProduct

[4] https://spark.apache.org/docs/3.3.0/api/python/reference/api/pyspark.ml.functions.vector_to_array.html#pyspark.ml.functions.vector_to_array

[5] https://spark.apache.org/docs/3.3.0/api/python/reference/pyspark.sql/api/pyspark.sql.functions.aggregate.html#pyspark.sql.functions.aggregate

8.3   Take-Home Message

This chapter has delved into the implementation of two classical machine learning algorithms, k-means, and linear regression, in the context of large-scale data analytics, and in particular when the number of examples available is very big. For both of these algorithms we have designed solutions that follow a global strategy. Compared to the local approach we implemented in the previous chapter, we have quickly realized that this has required us to know all the steps associated with an algorithm. We have had to think very carefully about each one of the operations that we had to carry out, finding the main bottleneck(s) in dealing with a large number of examples.

We even briefly analyzed the complexity of the algorithms to determine the most costly operations in terms of both computation and memory requirements, and to prioritize what needs parallelization. When designing a global-based solution, we recommend you draw the workflow/dataflow, which allows you to identify the best strategy to parallelize your application. We suggest keeping in mind the following general principles for good design:

- Aim to design a solution that will scale linearly. This should include both computations and the use of memory, so that, if we were to apply the scalability metrics we studied in the previous chapter, we would ideally get close to such linear behavior.
- Perform as many computations as possible in parallel, but do not overdo it. Remember that Spark (and any big data framework) comes with an overhead, which may become the dominant runtime if the data is small.
- *Cache your data if you are reusing it*. We can't emphasize this enough. It is easy to forget or cache the wrong object.
- Watch the use of actions such as `collect()`, which would move a lot of data. Try not to do it at all, but if you really need to, consider how much data will be brought back to the driver (and the memory limitations it may have).
- Minimize network communication. Make sure you understand the complexity of the operations you are using (e.g., wide versus narrow transformations).

To respect those principles, you may ask yourself questions like this:

- Do we have to repeat an operation multiple times? Cache the data involved.
- Can we maximize the number of operations we do in one go? This would reduce the number of Spark jobs, and maximize CPU usage.
- Do we need to keep anything in the driver or in all workers? That's fine, but we need to make sure it won't grow too much.
- Will the data grow too much after a transformation you need to carry out? Pay attention to the size of your data and the effect of each operation.
- Do these operations need data from other partitions? Can you think of a different way of doing this? We need to minimize data movement across the network as much as possible; once again, the principle of data locality is key.

After drafting a potential workflow solution, we advise doing a first implementation that is not excessively complicated. Use the simplest operations you can find. After analyzing its behavior, you may want to look at the particularities of the data engine (Spark in our case). We have seen how relevant this might become in terms of runtime reduction. For example, RDDs versus DataFrames, or the use of UDFs versus some predefined operations in Spark such as `ElementwiseProduct`.

If we focus on the two algorithms used in this chapter, the key messages to remember are:

- The complexity of the k-means algorithm is relatively low, but an increasing number of instances may prevent us from using large collections of data. The key limiting factor is the number of distance computations we need to perform at each iteration, together with the recalculation of the centroids. Its parallelization in a MapReduce-like fashion is quite straightforward: (i) the centroids are maintained in the driver and broadcast to workers at each iteration; (ii) we find the nearest centroid to each example of the training data (with a `map` function using RDDs, or using a UDF with DataFrames); (iii) we aggregate those that have been allocated to the same cluster (`reduceByKey` with RDDs, or a `Summarizer` with DataFrames). Steps (ii) and (iii) are repeated until convergence. Looking back at the questions and principles described above:
  - The only information we keep in the driver and all workers is the centroids, which is meant to be a very small data structure. That's the only time we use `collect()` in the solution.
  - The algorithm repeatedly computes distances between the centroids and the data, so the latter is cached from the beginning.
  - There is a need to send some information across the network. We have a wide transformation (a `groupBy` to aggregate those examples that belong to the same cluster), but as this is implemented with Spark operations, it is highly optimized (e.g., uses combiners).
- For linear regression, we discussed two different implementations: closed form and gradient descent. The former gives us an exact solution, while the latter is an approximation. A few notes about these two implementations:
  - We had some challenges implementing the closed-form solution. For example, we had to think differently about how to do matrix multiplication. We opted for the sum of outer products as an alternative, which means we have to compute the outer product for each example with itself, and then sum all the outer products. This is great because we reduce network traffic and the memory implications of doing traditional matrix multiplication.
  - We haven't parallelized all the operations of the closed-form solution. For instance, it wouldn't help to compute the inverse of the matrix in parallel, so we have done it in the driver as the amount of data is relatively small. Nevertheless, this is also its weakest point, because it won't scale up well when the dimensionality of the problem is very high, since the computation of the inverse matrix would be hard even with matrices that fit well in main memory. Unfortunately, this is not something we can really help with a distributed solution, and it is the main motivation for alternatives like gradient descent.

– Gradient descent iteratively searches for the optimal values of the parameters. The most time-consuming operation is the computation of the gradients for each example of the training data, which happens at every iteration, and later aggregated. Thus, this design is somehow similar to the one we discussed for k-means. Once more, caching the dataset becomes essential, whereas the parameters themselves are small enough to keep moving from the driver to the workers in each iteration.

8.4   To Learn More

For both k-means and linear regression, we suggest taking a look at the Spark documentation to understand the global implementations from MLlib for k-means[6] and linear regression.[7] You may want to look at the code for linear regression[8] and k-means.[9] Although it is in Scala, it may be worth taking a look at these global implementations and observing differences with respect to the ones presented in this book.

More generally, we also encourage you to investigate the clustering and regression methods available in Spark. For clustering,[10] apart from k-means we also find global-based implementations for other clustering algorithms such as Gaussian mixture models, or bisecting k-means for hierarchical clustering. For regression,[11] algorithms like generalized linear regression, more on decision trees, or isotonic regression may be worth looking at.

If you are looking for Spark-based implementations beyond those available in MLlib, check out Spark packages.[12] You may also find some implementations which are not available on Spark by default but are based on it. For example, you may find an implementation for generalized k-means.

In the literature, you may find some research papers describing global-based solutions for some other classical machine learning algorithms. Maillo et al. (2017) introduces a global-based solution to classify large sets of data using the k-nearest neighbor algorithm, using Spark DataFrames. Akram and Alamgir (2022) presents a Spark-based implementation for a fuzzy version of the k-means algorithm.

---

[6] https://spark.apache.org/docs/3.3.0/mllib-clustering.html#k-means
[7] https://spark.apache.org/docs/3.3.0/ml-classification-regression.html#linear-regression
[8] https://github.com/apache/spark/blob/master/mllib/src/main/scala/org/apache/spark/ml/regression/LinearRegression.scala
[9] https://github.com/apache/spark/blob/master/mllib/src/main/scala/org/apache/spark/ml/clustering/KMeans.scala
[10] https://spark.apache.org/docs/latest/mllib-clustering.html
[11] https://spark.apache.org/docs/latest/ml-classification-regression.html
[12] https://spark-packages.org/?q=tags%3A%22Machine%20Learning%22

8.5 Solutions to Challenges

> ### Challenge #8.1
>
> k-means is one of the most straightforward applications of MapReduce. Thus, we would like you to think about how to implement it in terms of key–value pairs, code a global-based solution using the Spark RDDs API instead of DataFrames, and compare their efficiency.

In the solution presented above, we used DataFrames to implement a distributed solution for k-means. As we discussed in Chapter 5, using DataFrames should normally be the preferred choice for Python implementations, as they perform faster than RDDs. Nevertheless, the k-means algorithm is one of the clearest applications of MapReduce, and that's why we are asking you to go back to what we learned in Chapter 2 and start thinking about how to distribute the processing of k-means in terms of key–value pairs. If you were to be implementing this with Spark Datasets, this could probably be a great choice. Actually, under the hood, DataFrames do apply MapReduce-like operations anyway.

Generally speaking, we could think of the UDF we built before as a map-like function, which transforms instances into cluster indexes. The `Summarizer` aggregates those with the same cluster index, which fits well with the idea of `reduceByKey`. Let's detail how the MapReduce phases would work. Figure 8.9 shows a MapReduce-like solution for one iteration of the k-means algorithm.

- Assuming that we have access to the current centroids from every single worker node, the map phase would assign each example to the closest centroid. So, the input of the map phase could be every single instance of the dataset as (k_1, v_1), where k_1 is not relevant, and v_1 is the instance. The output of that map phase could be (k_2, v_2) pairs in which k_2 is the index of its nearest cluster, and the value remains the same.
- The shuffle phase will put together all the examples that belong to the same cluster, defined by k_2. The reduce phase could now recompute a new centroid for the cluster, and the output $\langle k_3, v_3 \rangle$ will be the new centroids. As this is computing an average value, we may need to find a way to count the number of elements in each cluster, which will later be used to divide the resulting aggregated value.

This, however, is just one iteration of the entire algorithm. We need to run that MapReduce process multiple times until the centroids are similar to the previous iteration, or a maximum number of iterations has been reached.

> This was actually the solution proposed by Esteves et al. (2011) using Apache Mahout. But, this wasn't particularly fast. Why? Well, because Mahout used Apache Hadoop, and here we are performing multiple iterations through the dataset, which incurs lots of computational costs to reload the data.

Let's do this. First of all, we are going to use the underlying RDD of the DataFrame we already normalized, caching it:

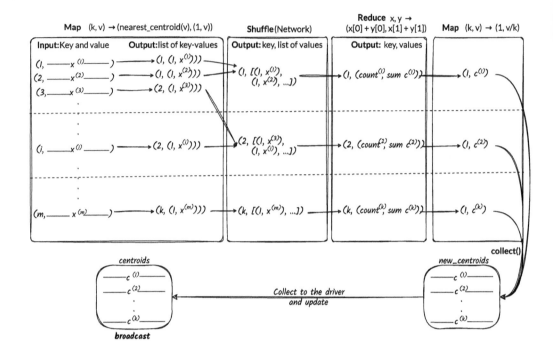

Figure 8.9 MapReduce workflow for distributed *k*-means. In this example, instances 1 and 2 are assigned to cluster 1, instance *i* to cluster 2, and the last instance to cluster 3. We have added an additional map phase at the end to compute the centroid, dividing the aggregated centroid by the number of elements in each cluster.

```
data_rdd = df.rdd.map(lambda row: row["features"]).cache()
```

Similar to the problem we had before when collecting the DataFrame to the driver, each element of the underlying RDD is of Row type, but now we only need the DenseVector that represents the example. Therefore, we have used map to take the vector inside the Row.

We keep the same idea of maintaining the centroids in the driver, and broadcasting them to the workers at every iteration. Thus, we can start by randomly sampling that RDD. With RDDs we can use the takeSample[13] function, for which we need to indicate if we want to use replacement (not in this case), the number of samples, and a random seed.

```
centroids = data_rdd.takeSample(False, k, 123456)
centroids
```

```
[DenseVector([0.75, 0.625, 0.6364, 0.6, 0.55]),
 DenseVector([0.5, 0.5, 0.3636, 0.6, 0.55])]
```

---

[13] https://spark.apache.org/docs/3.3.0/api/python/reference/api/pyspark.RDD.takeSample.htm

As before, before broadcasting them, let's convert them into numpy arrays:

```
centroids = np.array(centroids)
centroids_bc = sc.broadcast(centroids)
```

The map function will now calculate, for each element of that RDD, its closest centroid. We can define a function `nearest_centroid` that takes a single instance and returns the index of the nearest centroid. This is very similar to the UDF function `closest_centroid` we used with DataFrames.

```
def nearest_centroid(vect):
    return np.argmin(dist(centroids_bc.value, vect))
```

Let's see if that works, using it within the map function and collecting the indexes of the first 10 instances:

```
data_rdd.map(lambda vect: nearest_centroid(vect)).take(10)
```

```
[0, 0, 0, 0, 1, 0, 0, 0, 0, 0]
```

That seems to be working. But that is not yet what we said the map phase should do. For each element of `data_rdd`, the map phase should return (nearest centroid, example) pairs, using the function above. Possibly something like this:

```
closest = rdd.map(lambda p: (nearest_centroid(p), p))
```

After that, we need to put together those elements of the data that belong to the same cluster, and we need to compute the centroid. Computing the centroid is like an average, it is not a commutative or associate operation! We need to count the elements that fall within that cluster. So, we are going to modify the previous map to return a 1 together with the current example.

```
closest = data_rdd.map(lambda p: (nearest_centroid(p), (1, p)))
```

Now, `reduceByKey` should aggregate both the elements of each example in that cluster and the total of elements. As we are using DenseVectors, we can simply do x+y to add two arrays, but we need to do so for each element of the tuple (one for the count, one for the aggregation).

```
new_centroids_rdd = closest.reduceByKey(lambda x, y: (x[0]+y[0],\
                                                      x[1]+y[1]))
```

Finally, we can compute the centroid, dividing the aggregated values by the count:

```
new_centroids = new_centroids_rdd.map(lambda x:  x[1][1]\
                                    /x[1][0]).collect()
np.array(new_centroids)
```

```
array([[0.90104167, 0.68489583, 0.73106061, 0.76979167, 0.79229167],
       [0.34615385, 0.53846154, 0.43356643, 0.61538462, 0.66923077]])
```

And now we are ready to put everything into a new function:

```
def distributed_kmeans_rdd(rdd, k, threshold=0.001, seed=12345):
    # Fix the random seed
    np.random.seed(seed)
    # Randomly choose k examples from the training data
    centroids = data_rdd.takeSample(False, k, seed)
    # Convert them into np arrays:
    centroids = np.array(centroids)
    converged = False
    while not converged:
        # Broadcast the current centroids
        centroids_bc = sc.broadcast(centroids)
        #  Step 1: Assign each example to its nearest center
        closest = data_rdd.map(lambda p: (nearest_centroid(p), (1, p)))
        # Step 2: Create new centroids
        new_centroids_rdd = closest.reduceByKey(
            lambda x, y: (x[0] + y[0], x[1] + y[1]))
        # Collect the aggregated centroids and convert it to np arrays
        new_centroids = new_centroids_rdd.map(
            lambda x: x[1][1] / x[1][0]).collect()
        new_centroids = np.array(new_centroids)
        # Step 3: Check if we have converged
        #  Compute difference between new centroids and previous ones
        diff = dist(new_centroids, centroids, axis=None)
        if diff < threshold:
            converged = True
        else:
            centroids = new_centroids
    return centroids, closest
```

And voilà! We are finished! Let's test it again, and compare its efficiency against the DataFrame version:

```
%time centroids, c = distributed_kmeans_rdd(data_rdd,k)
```

```
CPU times: user 13.5 ms, sys: 2.78 ms, total: 16.2 ms
Wall time: 346 ms
```

```
%time centroids, c = distributed_kmeans(df, k, fraction=0.05)
```

```
CPU times: user 29.9 ms, sys: 8.09 ms, total: 38 ms
Wall time: 751 ms
```

With this small dataset, it looks like the RDD version is simpler and faster than the DataFrame version. We need to remember that we have used UDFs for our DataFrame version, and it is therefore not exploiting all the optimizations from Spark. Nevertheless, we should investigate what happens with very large datasets. Having said this, a version of the solution of this challenge implemented in Scala and the Datasets API of Spark would probably be very effective.

Challenge #8.2

We have implemented our own linear regression algorithm in pyspark, but how does this solution compare with the MLlib solution? Does it achieve the same result? If not, could you explain why?

Let's import `LinearRegression` from Spark.

```
from pyspark.ml.regression import LinearRegression
```

You may remember from the previous chapter that we just need to provide the features and label columns to `LinearRegression` to create our Estimator.

```
lr = LinearRegression(featuresCol='features', labelCol='label')
```

We can now fit our Estimator to get our linear regression model as a Transformer.

```
lr_model = lr.fit(df)
```

Let's test it by computing the outputs for the training data.

```
prediction = lr_model.transform(df)
prediction.show(4)
```

```
+-----+-----------+------------------+
|label|   features|        prediction|
+-----+-----------+------------------+
|282.5|[1.0,125.0]|332.06288696541617|
|329.5|[1.0,109.0]| 282.8522460460755|
|287.0|[1.0,116.0]|304.38190144828707|
|257.5|[1.0,103.0]|264.39825570132274|
+-----+-----------+------------------+
only showing top 4 rows
```

But are these the same as those obtained with our solution? We can take a look at the learned parameters to answer this question:

```
lr_model.intercept, lr_model.coefficients
```

```
(-52.395245216932956, DenseVector([0.0, 3.0757]))
```

Is there anything you weren't expecting? The intercept value is the same as our θ_0 parameters (except for rounding errors), but we are getting two coefficients! One is 0.0 and the other is the same value as our θ_1 (again, except for the rounding errors coming from the different implementations). What happened here? The 0.0 corresponds to the dummy variable. In fact, we should have told Spark not to learn the intercept (with `fitIntercept = False`), as we were providing the dummy variable in the `'features'` column. However, even with this change, Spark wouldn't do this very differently, as it internally standardizes every input feature (even if the `standardize` parameter is set to `False`). Consequently, our dummy feature is canceled, always getting 0.0 as its coefficient.

Overall, we have obtained the same result. Spark implements the same closed-form solution for problems with less than 4096 input features (unless otherwise specified), whereas the L-BFGS algorithm (a variant of gradient descent) is used for a higher number of features. The learned parameters do not exactly match due to rounding errors, among other things, because of the standardization applied by Spark, whether we indicate it or not.

> **Challenge #8.3**
>
> As we have already noted, computing the predictions of our model to measure the error is taking a long time. If we are going to repeat this for a number of iterations, our solution would take ages. There are some implementation tricks you could make use of in Spark to further accelerate this, using MLlib functions such as `ElementwiseProduct`[14] and `vector_to_array`[15] combined with Spark SQL ones (see `aggregate`[16]). With big data, this implementation detail could really make a difference. We challenge you to further investigate these methods and implement an optimized solution avoiding the use of UDFs. *Hint:* You can start with `ElementwiseProduct` and then move the output `Vector` to an array before using `aggregate` from Spark SQL.

Let's take the opportunity to do the computation of the cost a little faster with more advanced methods offered by Spark. On the one hand, we can make use of `Element-wiseProduct` from MLlib, which calculates the element-by-element product of each example of the dataset with a scaling vector. If we use our θs as the scaling vector, we will have half of the prediction done. We will only have to add the elements of each resulting vector. To do this, we can use the `aggregate()` SQL function that allows us to work with arrays and, for example, to sum their elements. However, SQL functions work with arrays, not `Vector`-type columns, so we need to convert our `Vector` to an array using the corresponding function from MLlib (`vector_to_array()`).

```
from pyspark.ml.feature import ElementwiseProduct
from pyspark.ml.functions import vector_to_array
```

```
%%time
elementwise_product = ElementwiseProduct(inputCol='features',
        outputCol='pred_vec', scalingVec=Vectors.dense(thetas))
preds_label_df = elementwise_product.transform(df)
preds_label_df = preds_label_df.withColumn('pred',
        sql_f.aggregate(vector_to_array('pred_vec'), sql_f.lit(0.0),
        lambda acc, x: acc + x))
mse_evaluator.evaluate(preds_label_df)
```

```
Wall time: 423 ms
```

```
837.5357983096798
```

> `aggregate()` is very similar to the `reduce()` function from Python and Spark. The main difference is that we have to specify which is the initial value for the aggregation and provide a function that will take two elements (the current

---

[14] https://spark.apache.org/docs/3.3.0/api/python/reference/api/pyspark.ml.feature.ElementwiseProduct.html#pyspark.ml.feature.ElementwiseProduct

[15] https://spark.apache.org/docs/3.3.0/api/python/reference/api/pyspark.ml.functions.vector_to_array.html#pyspark.ml.functions.vector_to_array

[16] https://spark.apache.org/docs/3.3.0/api/python/reference/pyspark.sql/api/pyspark.sql.functions.aggregate.html#pyspark.sql.functions.aggregate

aggregation and the new element) and return the aggregated value (the sum of both in our case).

Let's compare with our previous implementation.

```
%%time
preds_labels_df = df.select(pred('features').alias('pred'), 'label')
mse_evaluator.evaluate(preds_labels_df)
```

```
Wall time: 6.77 s
```

```
837.5357983096799
```

This is much faster than the UDF! You could insert this in the gradient descent for loop and would clearly notice the difference.

> **Challenge #8.4**
>
> We did well with the linear regression. Could you modify the global linear regression algorithm we developed to learn a logistic regression model for classification? You will only have to consider two changes:
>
> - the logistic regression model is the linear regression model passed through the sigmoid function ($g(z) = 1/(1 + e^{-z})$);
> - the cost function is the binary cross entropy:
>
> $$J(\theta) = -\frac{1}{m} \sum_{i=1}^{m} y^{(i)} \log(h_\theta(x^{(i)})) + (1 - y^{(i)}) \log(1 - h_\theta(x^{(i)})).$$
>
> Despite these changes, the gradient update rule is exactly the same (except for the change in the model).

We first transform our problem to a simple classification problem, so that we can work with the logistic regression: we convert our house prices to "cheap" (class 0, costing less than €300k) and "expensive" (class 1, costing more than €300k) houses.

```
df = df.withColumn('label_clasif', sql_f.when(df.label < 300, 0)\
                                       .otherwise(1)).cache()
df.show(4)
```

```
+-----+--------------------+------------+
|label|            features|label_clasif|
+-----+--------------------+------------+
|282.5|[1.0,0.2254798291...|           0|
|329.5|[1.0,-0.219912425...|           1|
|287.0|[1.0,-0.025053314...|           0|
|257.5|[1.0,-0.386934521...|           0|
+-----+--------------------+------------+
only showing top 4 rows
```

We now need to introduce the two changes in our training loop. For our model, we will need to introduce the sigmoid function.

```
def sigmoid(z):
    return float(1 / (1 + np.exp(-z)))
sigmoid(-1), sigmoid(0), sigmoid(+1)
```

```
(0.2689414213699951, 0.5, 0.7310585786300049)
```

For the new cost function, we either program it from scratch in Spark or use `MulticlassClassificationEvaluator`, which provides us with the `'logLoss'` metric, which is the cross-entropy. In this case, we prefer to do it from scratch, since the evaluator requires a `Vector` of probabilities and we will avoid this for simplicity.

We make use of our faster implementation from Challenge #8.2 to compute the outputs. So let's first make a prediction for θs initialized to zeros, and then use those outputs to develop the cost function.

```
thetas = np.zeros(2)
# Error in current iteration
elementwise_product = ElementwiseProduct(inputCol='features',
        outputCol='pred_vec', scalingVec=Vectors.dense(thetas))
preds_label_df = elementwise_product.transform(df)
preds_label_df = preds_label_df.withColumn('logits',
        sql_f.aggregate(vector_to_array('pred_vec'), sql_f.lit(0.0),
        lambda acc, x: acc + x)).select('label_clasif', 'logits')
preds_label_df.show(4)
```

```
+------------+------+
|label_clasif|logits|
+------------+------+
|           0|   0.0|
|           1|   0.0|
|           0|   0.0|
|           0|   0.0|
+------------+------+
only showing top 4 rows
```

With this, the `'pred'` column will have what is usually known as the logits, the output values before passing through the sigmoid. We can implement the sigmoid function with Spark SQL functions:

```
preds_label_df.withColumn("prob",
        1 / (1 + sql_f.exp(-1 * sql_f.col("logits")))).show(4)
```

```
+------------+------+----+
|label_clasif|logits|prob|
+------------+------+----+
|           0|   0.0| 0.5|
|           1|   0.0| 0.5|
|           0|   0.0| 0.5|
|           0|   0.0| 0.5|
+------------+------+----+
only showing top 4 rows
```

In this case, using SQL expressions would make the code more concise and probably clearer:

```
preds_label_df = preds_label_df.selectExpr('*',
    '1 / (1 + exp(-1 * logits)) as prob')
```

```
+------------+------+----+
|label_clasif|logits|prob|
+------------+------+----+
|           0|   0.0| 0.5|
|           1|   0.0| 0.5|
|           0|   0.0| 0.5|
|           0|   0.0| 0.5|
+------------+------+----+
only showing top 4 rows
```

Now, the new column (`'prob'`) stores the probability of each example belonging to class 1 (in this case, the house being "expensive"). We could get the final prediction by imposing a threshold at 0.5.

```
preds_label_df.withColumn("prediction",
    sql_f.when(sql_f.col("prob") < 0.5, 0).otherwise(1)).show(4)
```

```
+------------+------+----+----------+
|label_clasif|logits|prob|prediction|
+------------+------+----+----------+
|           0|   0.0| 0.5|         1|
|           1|   0.0| 0.5|         1|
|           0|   0.0| 0.5|         1|
|           0|   0.0| 0.5|         1|
+------------+------+----+----------+
only showing top 4 rows
```

Anyway, we are interested in computing the binary cross-entropy, for which we only need the probability. To compute this, we can again use Spark SQL, since we will just be doing some logarithms and multiplications. Let's see it.

```
cross_entropy = (
    preds_label_df.selectExpr(
        "label_clasif * log(prob) + (1 - label_clasif) * log(1 - prob) AS
↪loss"
    ).agg(sql_f.mean("loss")).first()[0] * -1
)
cross_entropy
```

```
0.6931471805599452
```

We first computed the loss of each example, and then we computed the average loss that we refer to as the cost (note that we finally multiplied by −1 to make it positive, following the original equation). For brevity, we have written it again as an SQL expression.

We now put everything into our training loop and run it!

```
# Hyper-parameters
iterations = 10
alpha = 10
```

```
# Initialization
thetas = np.zeros(2)
errors = np.zeros(iterations)
# df is cached!! Don't forget to do so
thetas_bc = sc.broadcast(thetas)
for i in range(iterations):
    # Gradients computation
    gradient = sql_f.udf(
        lambda x, y: (sigmoid((x * thetas_bc.value).sum()) - y) * x,
        VectorUDT(),
    )
    grads_df = df.select(gradient("features", "label_clasif").alias("grad"))
    avg_grads_df = grads_df.agg(Summarizer.mean(grads_df["grad"]))
    avg_grads = avg_grads_df.first()[0]
    # Update rule
    thetas = thetas - alpha * avg_grads
    thetas_bc = sc.broadcast(thetas)   # broadcast the new thetas
    # Error in current iteration
    elementwise_product = ElementwiseProduct(inputCol="features",
        outputCol="pred_vec", scalingVec=Vectors.dense(thetas))
    preds_label_df = elementwise_product.transform(df)
    preds_label_df = preds_label_df.withColumn("logits",\
        sql_f.aggregate(vector_to_array("pred_vec"), sql_f.lit(0.0),
            lambda acc, x: acc + x,),)
    preds_label_df = preds_label_df.selectExpr("*",
        "1 / (1 + exp(-1 * logits)) as prob")
    cross_entropy = (
        preds_label_df.selectExpr(
            "label_clasif * log(prob) + (1 - label_clasif) * log(1 - prob) AS␣
↪loss"
        ).agg(sql_f.mean("loss")).first()[0]* -1
    )
    cost_history[i] = cross_entropy
    print(
        f"Gradients: {avg_grads.round(2)}\t"
        f"Thetas: {thetas.round(2)}\t"
        f"Cost: {cost_history[i]:.2f}"
    )
```

```
Gradients: [ 0.1  -0.34]        Thetas: [-1.    3.44]   Cost: 0.34
Gradients: [-0.04 -0.  ]        Thetas: [-0.55 3.48]   Cost: 0.33
Gradients: [0. 0.]      Thetas: [-0.57 3.47]   Cost: 0.33
Gradients: [-0.   0.]      Thetas: [-0.57 3.46]   Cost: 0.33
Gradients: [-0.   0.]      Thetas: [-0.57 3.45]   Cost: 0.33
Gradients: [-0.   0.]      Thetas: [-0.56 3.44]   Cost: 0.33
Gradients: [-0.   0.]      Thetas: [-0.56 3.43]   Cost: 0.33
Gradients: [-0.   0.]      Thetas: [-0.56 3.43]   Cost: 0.33
Gradients: [-0.   0.]      Thetas: [-0.56 3.43]   Cost: 0.33
Gradients: [-0.   0.]      Thetas: [-0.56 3.42]   Cost: 0.33
```

Note that we set an unusually high learning rate to make it converge in a few iterations, as we have already tested it in this problem.

Do you wonder if the implementation is right? Check the result with `LogisticRe-gression` from MLlib.

```
from pyspark.ml.classification import LogisticRegression
lr = LogisticRegression(featuresCol="features", labelCol="label_clasif")
lr_model = lr.fit(df)
lr_model.intercept, lr_model.coefficients
```

```
(-0.5621411174773147, DenseVector([0.0, 3.4097]))
```

Almost the same parameters and just a bit slower as we are implementing it in pyspark from scratch. Note that we should disregard the first coefficient as we did in Challenge #8.2.

8.6   Exercises

8.1 Enumerate three principles that we should bear in mind when designing a global-based solution for big data.

8.2 Briefly explain the main difficulties in parallelizing k-means for big data.

8.3 Does it make sense to implement a local approach for k-means? If yes, how would you go about it and what differences would you expect with respect to the global version?

8.4 We have discussed the implementation of the standard k-means algorithm. An alternative to k-means is called k-medoids (or partition around medoids, PAM), which, rather than computing centroids, uses existing data points in the training set as representative examples of a cluster. You are asked to investigate how this method works and discuss whether implementing a global solution for this would be as simple as for k-means, paying attention to the scalability.

8.5 What are the main challenges in designing a global-based implementation of the closed form for linear regression?

8.6 Indicate whether the following statements about designing a big data solution for linear regression are true or false:
   (a) The closed-form solution does not scale up well when the dimensionality (d) is large, but it may cope well with a high number of instances (m is large).
   (b) The implementation of gradient descent is not a great alternative when d is large, but much better than the closed-form solution when m is big.
   (c) The results obtained with gradient descent may differ slightly from those obtained with the closed-form solution, but it has nothing to do with the parallelization.
   (d) In both k-means and linear regression, we have some data that needs to be in both driver and workers (θs and centroids). This becomes the main weakness of these designs.

8.7 Let's assume that we want to compute the product of two matrices, as we did before with (X^TX). However, on this occasion, we have two different matrices X and Y which are stored in two different DataFrames. Could we do this with the sum of outer products? If yes, how would you do it? You can assume that the size of X is $n \times d$, and Y is $d \times n$, where n is big and d is small.

8.8 In this chapter we have implemented the traditional "batch" version of gradient descent. Alternatively, we could have used mini-batches. This means that instead of using all the examples to compute the gradients, we would only use a subset of the training data. Would it be possible to implement this in Spark? What are the advantages and disadvantages?

8.9 If we were to have a dataset with millions of features, but a relatively low number of examples (e.g., 10 000), how would you implement the first step of the closed-form solution (i.e., $X^{\mathsf{T}}X$)?

8.10 This exercise revolves around the design of a global-based solution for the k-nearest neighbor algorithm (Cover and Hart, 1967). This algorithm classifies a new instance based on the Euclidean distance of that instance against the entire training set, that is, it doesn't perform any training. Then, the labels of the k nearest instances in the training set are used to determine the class of the input test instance. You are asked to design a big data solution to parallelize the processing of the k-nearest neighbors to classify a single test instance using a global approach. The input instance would look like . . .
```
[feature 1, feature 2, ..., feature N],  unknown class
```
. . . and the training data would have a large number of instances:
```
instance 1: [feature 1, feature 2, ..., feature N],  class X
...
instance M:  [feature 1, feature 2, ..., feature N], class X
```
Your design should take these two as input, together with k, the number of nearest neighbors considered, and provide the predicted class. Your implementation should allow for an arbitrary number of neighbors k.

(a) Draw a MapReduce-like diagram explaining how you would design a solution for this. Similar to what we did in Challenge #8.1, indicate any key–value pairs if needed.

(b) Write down some (Spark-like) pseudo-code that explains how the solution would work. You can assume you have functions to compute the k nearest neighbors and their distances sequentially (e.g., from the scikit-learn library). For simplicity, you can assume an RDD-based implementation.

(c) Briefly discuss the expected advantages and disadvantages of your design.

(d) If, instead of a single input test instance, we wanted to classify a relatively small set of test instances, briefly explain what changes you would make to your solution (if any).

9 Advanced Examples: Semi-supervised, Ensembles, Deep Learning Model Deployment

Learning Outcomes

[KU]   Understanding different approaches to designing machine learning solutions that might go beyond local or global approaches

[IS, PPS]   Learning how to implement solutions for different stages of the machine learning life cycle in the presence of big data

In the previous two chapters we focused on the design and implementation of our own big data solutions to parallelize classical machine learning methods, including decision tree classifiers, linear regression, and k-means clustering. However, as we mentioned in Chapter 6, all the stages of the machine learning life cycle might be affected by big data, but that does not mean that we need to parallelize all of them, as that depends very much on the problem at hand.

This chapter aims to present some more examples from different stages of the machine learning life cycle. So far, we have only been designing solutions to distribute the learning phase, and we talked about local and global approaches for those. We now want to explore three distinct topics: semi-supervised learning, ensemble learning, and how to deploy deep learning models at scale. These will require different solutions, which may differ (to an extent) from the local and global ones we explained before. Each one of them is going to be introduced in detail, motivating why parallelization to deal with big data is needed, determining the main bottlenecks, designing and coding Spark-based solutions for them, and discussing the further work required to improve the performance.

For semi-supervised learning, we talk about the classical self-training algorithm, which could be seen as a preprocessing stage that consists of enlarging the labeled training set in the presence of large amounts of unlabeled data. Then, we cover ensemble learning as an advanced method for supervised classification and regression, which involves the learning of many classifiers. Finally, we show an example with deep learning, but rather than parallelizing the training of a model, which is typically easier on GPUs, we deploy the inference step for a case study in semantic image segmentation.

9.1   Semi-supervised Classification: Self-Labeling Approaches

In many real-world applications, it is common to automatically gather lots of data, but labeling that data could be a manual and laborious process, which requires lots of time and expertise in a specific area. For example, creating a dataset of spam emails would require a person to read emails and tag them as suspicious or not. The issue in supervised machine learning is that with very low amounts of labeled data, it is usually difficult to appropriately train a classifier or a regressor. Semi-supervised learning (SSL) is a paradigm that aims to exploit small amounts of labeled data and very large sets of unlabeled data. Aiming to perform classification or regression, the intuition behind SSL is that we could use the regularities and patterns in unlabeled data to improve what we could learn from using only labeled data.

> SSL sits in between supervised and unsupervised learning. Its goal is to improve the performance in one of these two tasks by making use of information typically associated with the other. Thus, we may not only find techniques for semi-supervised classification and regression, but also for clustering, which may benefit from knowing that certain examples belong to the same class.

This chapter is focused on classification, where we have to further distinguish between *transductive* and *inductive* learning. The former is devoted to predicting the correct labels for the set of unlabeled examples that are also used during the training phase. The latter refers to the problem of predicting unseen data by learning from labeled and unlabeled data as training examples.

In the literature, we may find a multitude of approaches to tackling semi-supervised classification, including graph-based models, generative models, semi-supervised support vector machines, and self-labeling methods. For simplicity, here we focus on *self-labeling* learning (Triguero et al., 2015) as one of the most intuitive ways to perform SSL; it aims to augment the amount of labeled data using supervised techniques. Self-labeling techniques can be seen as preprocessing techniques that, given a set of data with both labeled and unlabeled data, return a new dataset with more labeled instances to be used by a new classifier/regressor. In its simplest form, the self-training algorithm (Yarowsky, 1995) iteratively enlarges the labeled training set by adding the most confident predictions of the supervised classifier used, accepting their own (more confident) predictions as real labeled data. Although there are more advanced methods, in this section we will focus on how to enable self-training to tackle big data using Spark.

9.1.1   Self-Training for Classification

The self-training approach is characterized by the fact that the learning process uses its own predictions to teach itself. It is said to be a wrapper methodology because it iteratively uses a base classifier, which learns from the existing labeled data, and adds its most confident predictions to the pool of labeled instances. This process is repeated for a number of iterations.

More formally, let's assume we have a training dataset with both labeled and unlabeled examples, and a test set which will be used to validate the results. We will use the following notation:

Training data (TR), composed of two subsets:
- *labeled set (L)*: relatively small at first (e.g., 2% of the data);
- *unlabeled set (U)*: very large set of instances with unknown class.

Test data (TS), which is not used during the training phase (for validation only – inductive learning).

We need to use a base learner I, for example, a decision tree, from which we can not only make a prediction but can also infer a confidence or probability in the prediction. The goal of self-training is to extend the labeled set L with those examples from U that we are more confident on. To do this, self-training follows an iterative procedure in which, (i) a classifier is trained using L to predict the labels of U, then (ii) the most confident predicted examples from U are added to L, and (iii) this process is repeated for a certain number of iterations or until we have labeled the whole of U (or there is some other stopping criteria). In pseudo-code:

```
Input: L: Labeled Set, U: Unlabeled Set, TS: Test Set
       Learner: Base Learner, MaxIter
L' = {} ; z=0
For i in {1, ..., MaxIter}:
   Learner = Learner.fit(L)
   Confidences = Learner.predict_proba(U)
   L'= most confident instances for each class with predicted labels
   L = L.union(L')
   U = U.substract(L')
   if U is 0: Break
End For
Learner = Learner.fit(L)  # Could be a different learner
Learner.predict(U) # Transductive phase
Learner.predict(TS) # Inductive phase
```

Here are a few things to bear in mind about the above pseudo-code:

- Confidence in predictions: Determining the confidence in the predictions depends on the base classifier. Probabilistic classifiers provide a probability associated with the prediction, which can be used as confidence. Otherwise, we need to find ways to obtain that confidence. For example, if we used the nearest neighbor algorithm, this could simply be the inverse of the distance: the closer the example is, the more confident the nearest neighbor algorithm is about the prediction. In a decision tree, confidence predictions can be obtained from the leaf that makes the prediction, as the percentage of correctly classified training examples from the total number of covered training instances.
- Hyperparameters: The algorithm has two parameters, the maximum number of iterations `MaxIter` and how to select the most confident instances at each iteration

(for example, using a threshold for the confidence). It is typically suggested that the number of instances added to L should be proportional to the number of instances of each class in L, so that we avoid adding examples from a particular class, making our classifiers biased. It is important to note that the number of iterations does not have to be large to try to label all instances of the unlabeled set. It is common that only a subset of the unlabeled set is selected to train a final model.

> Caveats/known issues: If predictions are wrong and added to the pool of labeled instances, that might end up creating a wholly misled model. The aim of this section is not to control those issues but to parallelize the original self-training with its own merits and drawbacks.

9.1.2   A Global Solution for Self-Training

Apart from those details about confidence and hyperparameters, the algorithm itself seems simple enough to aim for a global-based solution. If we start thinking of the main bottleneck of self-training, we may believe that it lies in repeatedly training a supervised classifier. However, initially, the labeled set is so small that the training would be fast and could be done locally (in a single node), but we would have to predict a large unlabeled set and decide which of the instances should be added, and that should be done in parallel. As we progress, the workload is shifted, the labeled set is incremented, and therefore the training phase would become slower and may require parallelization, but there would be fewer unlabeled instances to predict.

Before we start with the distributed design and implementation, let's choose a dataset as case study and define some baselines.

Case Study: Spam Email Recognition

As a case study, we are going to use the example we mentioned to create a classifier for spam email recognition. For the purpose of illustrating the design, we have chosen the Spambase[1] dataset from the UCI Machine Learning repository. This contains 4601 instances and 57 attributes, including measures of word repetition, length of words, and so on, all of which are numeric. The last column of the data denotes whether the email was considered spam (1) or not (0).

> Spambase is certainly not a large-scale problem, but it is enough for the purpose of showing how to implement self-training with big data. We leave it to the reader to test the implementations that follow with a bigger dataset and study the scalability of the different solutions, following the guidelines from Chapter 7.

We have downloaded the data and put it in a CSV format without a header. Let's start Spark and read the data:

```
import pyspark.sql.functions as sql_f
from pyspark.sql import SparkSession
spark = SparkSession.builder\
```

---

[1] https://archive.ics.uci.edu/ml/datasets/Spambase

```
                        .master("local[*]")\
                        .appName("MLexamples - advanced")\
                        .getOrCreate()\
sc = spark.sparkContext

df = spark.read.format('csv').option("header", 'false')\
                .load("data/spambase.csv")
```

For the purpose of this section, we are not worried about the column names of most attributes, but we need to clearly identify the output column, so we rename it. Also, as all the columns are numeric, we coerce these columns to float.

```
df = df.withColumnRenamed("_c57", "output")
df = df.select([sql_f.col(c).cast("float").alias(c) for c in df.columns])
```

As usual, we split the data into train and test:

```
seed = 12345
train, test = df.randomSplit([0.7, 0.3], seed)
```

Let's check the class distribution, as we will have to use that ratio to determine the number of instances per class that we will add at every iteration of the self-training algorithm.

```
stats = train.groupBy("output").count()
stats = stats.select("*",
    sql_f.round((stats["count"] / train.count() * 100), 2).alias("ratio(%)"),
)
stats.show()
```

```
+------+-----+--------+
|output|count|ratio(%)|
+------+-----+--------+
|   1.0| 1280|   39.63|
|   0.0| 1950|   60.37|
+------+-----+--------+
```

To recreate an SSL problem, we should normally split the training set into two sets to artificially simulate a small labeled set and a large unlabeled set. For example, we could take 2% of the training data as the labeled set, and use the remaining 98% as unlabeled data. However, as we are going to base our implementation on DataFrames, we don't really need to "physically" split this into two sets. We could add an extra column called label; 2% of those instances would have the same output column, and the rest would be unlabeled, which we could represent as class 2.

How do we do this? We could use Spark SQL functions to add an extra column that would take 2% of the original labels from the train.output column. To do this, we use the when and rand functions; rand provides a random number between 0 and 1, so 2% of the time we keep the original class, and otherwise we set the class label to 2.

```
pct = 0.02
train = train.withColumn("label",
    sql_f.when(sql_f.rand(seed=12345) < pct, train.output).otherwise(2),
)
```

Let's check the class distribution again:

```
stats = train.groupBy("label").count()
stats = stats.select("*",
    sql_f.round((stats["count"] / train.count() * 100), 2).alias("ratio(%)"),
)
stats.sort("label").show()
```

```
+-----+-----+--------+
|label|count|ratio(%)|
+-----+-----+--------+
|  0.0|   44|    1.36|
|  1.0|   32|    0.99|
|  2.0| 3154|   97.65|
+-----+-----+--------+
```

> As we randomly sampled the labeled set, you may have noticed that we don't have
> exactly 2% of the data, but slightly more. Getting the exact number would be more
> complicated and not easily scalable, and certainly not very relevant/necessary for
> the experiments.

Defining Baseline/Comparison Models

Let's establish some baselines to understand how well we can do in the SSL context.
We are going to use the decision tree algorithm from MLlib as the base classifier of
the self-training. Thus, we should investigate how well we can classify the unlabeled
and test sets when training only on the small labeled set. This would serve as a lower
bound for us, the minimum we should expect from an SSL algorithm. That would mean
that by using unlabeled data we increase the performance, and not reduce it. However,
spoiler alert, that might not always be the case.

As we are going to repeatedly use the MLlib decision tree implementation, rather
than applying a pipeline (`VectorAssembler` + decision tree), we will work directly
with an assembled DataFrame.

```
from pyspark.ml.feature import VectorAssembler
# feature cols cannot include output or label
feature_cols = train.columns
feature_cols.remove('output')
feature_cols.remove('label')
assembler = VectorAssembler(inputCols=feature_cols, outputCol="features")
```

Let's transform both train and test:

```
train_features = assembler.transform(train)
test_features = assembler.transform(test)
```

Looking at the dataset, we can see that it is sparse (i.e., most features are 0), and MLlib
coded this with sparse vectors for efficiency.

```
train_features.select("features", "label").show(1, truncate = False)
```

```
+-----------------------------+-----+
|features                     |label|
```

```
+-----------------------------+-----+
|(57,[54,55,56],[1.0,1.0,1.0])|2.0  |
+-----------------------------+-----+
only showing top 1 row
```

We get rid of any column we no longer need, and cache it. Note that we keep the ground truth label 'output' to later compute the classification accuracy.

```
train_features = train_features.select("features", "output", "label").cache()
```

We can now filter instances by 'label' to obtain labeled and unlabeled sets, so that we can train a decision tree with the labeled set. For this experiment, we fix maxDepth to 5.

```
labeled = train_features.filter(train_features.label != 2.0)
unlabeled = train_features.filter(train_features.label == 2.0)

from pyspark.ml.classification import DecisionTreeClassifier
# Note that we use the 'label' column
dt = DecisionTreeClassifier(maxDepth=5, labelCol="label")
model = dt.fit(labeled)
```

After training the model, we can make predictions on the unlabeled set and the test set.

```
pred_unlabeled = model.transform(unlabeled)
pred_test = model.transform(test_features)
```

Finally, we can evaluate the model using the evaluation package of Spark. For simplicity, we want to measure the accuracy of the classification, and for that, we may again use the MulticlassClassificationEvaluator (note that the Spark BinaryClassificationEvaluator does not provide accuracy). Remember, the actual class label is available in the 'output' column.

```
from pyspark.ml.evaluation import MulticlassClassificationEvaluator
evaluator = MulticlassClassificationEvaluator(
    predictionCol="prediction",
    labelCol="output",
    metricName="accuracy",
)
```

We can now measure the *transductive* (performance on the unlabeled set) and *inductive* (performance on the test) accuracy of this model trained with 2% of labeled data:

```
evaluator.evaluate(pred_unlabeled)
```

```
0.8722257450856056
```

```
evaluator.evaluate(pred_test)
```

```
0.8672501823486506
```

Okay, so our first "baseline" that we will try to beat using self-training gives us around 86%–87% accuracy (the actual value may vary in different executions if we use a different seed). We consider this the lower bound for the performance, but how well could we do if we were to have the entire training set fully labeled? Let's figure it out, using the actual training labels (which are in the 'output' column).

```
dt.setLabelCol('output')
upperbound_model = dt.fit(train_features)
```

We only need to evaluate this model on the test set, as this is a standard supervised learning experiment, with all the training data labeled.

```
upperbound_pred = upperbound_model.transform(test_features)

evaluator.evaluate(upperbound_pred)
```

```
0.9080962800875274
```

This would be our upper bound; it would be difficult (but not impossible) to get over that, as here we are training with the correct training labels. Let's think how to design the self-training approach to see if we can increase the size of the labeled set.

Distributed Design

What are the main challenges of an SSL algorithm in large-scale data analytics? In SSL in general, the main challenge lies in the size of the unlabeled set, which could be really large. As discussed before, for the specific self-training algorithm, the workload shifts as the algorithm adds more instances to the labeled set. At first, the inference phase (predicting the unlabeled set and deciding which of them to add) would be the main bottleneck. But the labeled set will grow dynamically, and it could potentially become huge, so we will need to distribute the learning phase too.

Keeping this in mind, let's think carefully about the implementation of self-training in parallel. We have already anticipated that we would use the MLlib decision tree as the base classifier, which would already be distributing both building and inference phases. As we do not know in advance the size of the labeled set, we decided to train the base classifier in a distributed manner from the first iteration. You may be thinking that while the labeled set is very small we may not be exploiting all the capabilities of Spark well, and you would probably be right. That's one of the downsides of the design we follow here. You may think of more elaborate strategies to alleviate this, which is somewhat problem dependent (i.e., depends on the amount of initial labeled data, and how quickly it grows).

As we have already suggested, we are using a single DataFrame, adding columns with the labels. If we keep this idea, as opposed to really splitting the data into two DataFrames, we don't have to worry much about the size of the labeled set, as it is distributed together with the unlabeled instances. At each iteration of the algorithm, the labels should change as new instances are added to the labeled set, that is, they have a label of 0 and 1 in our example, but that would only affect one column of the DataFrame. Apache Spark is obviously a good framework for iterating multiple times through the same data. As we only change the labels, the features/attributes

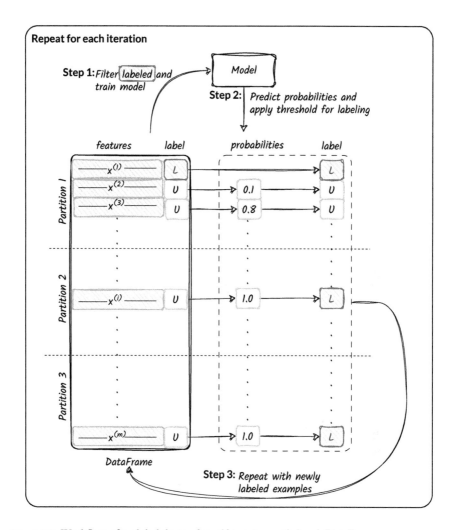

Figure 9.1 Workflow of a global design for self-training with Spark DataFrames.

of all the training instances can remain cached throughout the execution as they are not modified. This will probably be more efficient than working with a DataFrame of unlabeled examples and a Python structure or another DataFrame of labeled examples, constantly "moving" data from one to the other.

Figure 9.1 presents an overview of this distributed solution. This would consist of a loop that: (1) trains a distributed global model on the labeled instances (label != 2, in our example); (2) predicts the labels of the instances of the training DataFrame that are marked as unlabeled (label == 2) with a certain probability; (3) determines which of the most confident predictions should be marked as labeled, creating a new column. As we are using a single DataFrame, the last step is super efficient, and occurs fully in parallel (i.e., it is a narrow transformation).

Implementation

Let's focus on the implementation. As we are basing the implementation on a base classifier from MLlib, we have to check how to obtain probabilities. You may have seen before that when we do `model.transform(unlabeled)`, we not only get a `'prediction'` column, but also a `'probability'` column, which is what we want to use to determine which of the unlabeled instances will be "added" to the labeled set. Our previous model was trained with labeled data only (and the class column set to `'label'`), so we can use it to predict the entire `train_features` DataFrame directly and have a look at the probabilities.

```
preds = model.transform(train_features)

preds.select('probability').show(3, False)
```

```
+------------------------------------------+
|probability                               |
+------------------------------------------+
|[0.9767441860465116,0.023255813953488372]|
|[0.9767441860465116,0.023255813953488372]|
|[0.9767441860465116,0.023255813953488372]|
+------------------------------------------+
only showing top 3 rows
```

The first problem we encounter in our implementation is that the `'probability'` column is a `Vector` containing the probability of belonging to each of the classes (class 0 and class 1 in our example), and we do need to access each element. To do this, we have to transform that `Vector` into columns. We can do so using the function `vector_to_array`. If we put it together with the `array_max` function from Spark SQL, we can directly obtain the confidence for each prediction (as we are not interested in the probabilities over the rest of the classes).

```
from pyspark.ml.functions import vector_to_array
preds = preds.withColumn(
    "prob", sql_f.array_max(vector_to_array("probability"))
)
preds.show(3)
```

```
+-------------------+------+-----+-------------+--------------------+-------
---+------------------+
|           features|output|label|rawPrediction|
probability|prediction|        prob|
+-------------------+------+-----+-------------+--------------------+-------
---+------------------+
|(57,[54,55,56],[1...|   0.0|  2.0|   [42.0,1.0]|[0.97674418604651...|
0.0|0.9767441860465116|
|(57,[54,55,56],[1...|   0.0|  0.0|   [42.0,1.0]|[0.97674418604651...|
0.0|0.9767441860465116|
|(57,[54,55,56],[1...|   0.0|  2.0|   [42.0,1.0]|[0.97674418604651...|
0.0|0.9767441860465116|
+-------------------+------+-----+-------------+--------------------+-------
---+------------------+
only showing top 3 rows
```

We should typically set a threshold to decide whether or not an instance is considered to be added to the pool of labeled instances, and that is a hyperparameter of the self-training algorithm. For this example, we keep this hyperparameter fixed to 1. This means that we only consider those instances for which our base classifier is completely sure (prob == 1).

> This hyperparameter needs to be set depending on the base classifier. For decision trees, 1.0 makes sense, but other classifiers may never provide a probability of 1.0.

But, should we just simply add all of those with probability 1? We mentioned before that we have to control this to avoid adding too many instances of one class, neglecting others. As an example, let's investigate the probabilities of the previous prediction (remember, we used only the labeled instances to train a decision tree and predict unlabeled ones).

```
preds.filter("prob == 1").groupBy("prediction").count().show()
```

```
+----------+-----+
|prediction|count|
+----------+-----+
|       0.0|  109|
|       1.0| 1318|
+----------+-----+
```

Interestingly, we can see how the classifier is more confident to predict class 1 (spam emails) than class 0 examples (non-spam ones). Which instances should be added to L? The recommendation is to add the most confident predictions, but to add to L elements proportionally for each class. In our example, the ratio of non-spam to spam is around 1.5, meaning that if we add 15 examples of class 0 (non-spam), we should add at least 10 of class 1 (spam).

To prevent the classifier in the next iteration being biased, we need to consider the probabilities. From the above count, we should probably make sure we take the 107 from class 0, and two-thirds of those from class 1, roughly 70. Thus, we are "disregarding" quite a few of the most confident instances of class 1. We would need to choose those 70 randomly out of the 1287. As this operation will depend on the probabilities we get at each iteration, we define a function that, given a list of the labeled set class distribution and a list with the counts of the most confident instances per class (those greater than or equal to a threshold, 1.0 in our case), will return the number of instances of each class to be added.

```
import numpy as np
def instances_per_class(class_distrib, counts):
    # Works with respect to the class with the lowest proportion
    index_min = np.argmin(counts / class_distrib)
    new_counts = counts[index_min] * (
        class_distrib / class_distrib[index_min]
    )
    return np.round(new_counts).astype("int")
```

Let's test it quickly with the above numbers, first computing the class distribution in our labeled set. We create a function for this as we will be reusing it.

```
def df_count(df, group_col):
    return np.array(
        df.groupBy(group_col).count().sort(group_col).toPandas()["count"],
        dtype="int",
    )
```

> Using toPandas()['col_name'] is just the shortest way to get the column values into the Python list we need for our function. We can bring this to the driver as we already know that we will have as many elements as classes.

```
class_distrib = df_count(labeled, 'output')
class_distrib
```

```
array([44, 32])
```

We need an array with the counts of the most confident instances:

```
counts = df_count(preds.filter("prob == 1"), "prediction")
counts
```

```
array([ 109, 1318])
```

We are ready to test the function:

```
to_add = instances_per_class(class_distrib, counts)
to_add
```

```
array([109,  79])
```

Now the objective is to update the 'label' column in the train_features DataFrame to change the label of the most confident instances to the predicted one, taking the counts we computed into account. In this way, doing the next iteration will be straightforward.

So, to create the new column, we need to bear in mind that it should have a class probability of 1 and its previous label should be 2.0 (indicating it was unlabeled previously). Unfortunately, this limitation of adding an exact number of instances per class may complicate this implementation. To do this efficiently, we are going to have to sacrifice a bit of precision in doing it. Aiming to get the exact number would probably be more costly and complex. The simplest way of doing this is following the same idea as we did to split our training set into the labeled and unlabeled sets, that is, using random numbers to take approximately the estimated counts from each class. Therefore, for an instance to be labeled in the current iteration, it must fulfill three conditions:

- be unlabeled (label == 2);
- have a confidence/probability of 1 (we could set any other threshold);
- be randomly selected following the count distribution.

Let's compute the percentage of examples from each class we need to get from those having a probability of 1.

```
pcts = to_add / counts # elementwise operation
pcts
```

```
array([1.        , 0.0599393])
```

```
pcts[0]
```

```
1.0
```

For simplicity, we are going to do this in two steps. First, we create an additional column pcts, which will store the percentages needed depending on the class label of an example.

```
preds = preds.withColumn("pcts",
    sql_f.when(preds.label == 0, pcts[0]).otherwise(pcts[1])
)
```

Then, we can update the 'label' column using the rand function and the 'pcts' column:

```
preds = preds.withColumn("label",
    sql_f.when(
        (preds.label == 2) & (preds.prob == 1)
        & (sql_f.rand(seed=12345) <= preds.pcts),
        preds.prediction).otherwise(preds.label),
)
```

> The withColumn transformation will overwrite the column if it already exists in the DataFrame, so we can use it for updating the 'label' column with the newly labeled examples.

Let's see if that worked. Let's compute the number of labeled examples that are currently labeled and compare with those that we had before:

```
preds.groupBy('label').count().sort('label').show()
```

```
+-----+-----+
|label|count|
+-----+-----+
|  0.0|   51|
|  1.0|  102|
|  2.0| 3077|
+-----+-----+
```

Challenge #9.1

The above solution to add the most confident instances would only work for binary classification problems and would need changing depending on the number of classes. You are asked to investigate ways to improve this code. As a suggestion, you could use the create_map[2] function from SparkSQL, which will allow you to map each class label to the percentage of examples we have to take from that class within a single (when) condition. You could also take a look at the sampleBy[3] transformation and see if you could use it for this task.

We initially had 44 examples from class 0 and 32 from class 1, and we expected to add 109 to class 0 (all of them with probability 1) and 79 from class 1. The added figures are again not exact, but it is a good approximation with little or no real effect on the self-training methodology.

Okay, so we now have all the ingredients to define the final self-training loop. Let's define a function for it.

```python
def self_training(train_features, max_iter=10, seed=12345,
                  num_classes=2, max_depth=5):
    # define Decision Tree with column label set to 'label'
    dt = DecisionTreeClassifier(maxDepth=max_depth, labelCol="label")
    # obtain class distributions from the labeled set
    class_distrib = df_count(train_features.filter("label != 2"), "label")
    for i in range(max_iter):
        labeled = train_features.filter("label != 2")
        print(f"Iteration: {i} - labeled size: {labeled.count()}")
        # Train a model
        model = dt.fit(labeled)
        # Predict and obtain probabilities:
        preds = model.transform(train_features)
        preds = preds.withColumn("prob",
            sql_f.array_max(vector_to_array("probability"))
        )
        counts = df_count(
            preds.filter("label == 2 AND prob == 1"), "prediction"
        )
        # stop the loop if there aren't any instances to add from one of the
        # classes or if there are only instances from one class to add
        if 0 in counts or len(counts) < num_classes:
            break
        to_add = instances_per_class(class_distrib, counts)
        print(f"Adding {to_add[0]} instances from class 0, "
              f"and {to_add[1]} from class 1")
        # Calculate all instances that could be added
        pcts = to_add / counts  # elementwise operation
        preds = preds.withColumn("pcts",
            sql_f.when(preds.label == 0, pcts[0]).otherwise(pcts[1]),
        )
        preds = preds.withColumn("label",
            sql_f.when(
                (preds.label == 2) & (preds.prob == 1)
                & (sql_f.rand(seed=12345) <= preds.pcts),
                preds.prediction).otherwise(preds.label),
        )
        train_features = preds.select("features", "output", "label").cache()
    return train_features.filter("label != 2")


# reset train_features
train_features = assembler.transform(train)
%time enlarged_labeled = self_training(train_features)
```

---

2 https://spark.apache.org/docs/3.3.0/api/python/reference/pyspark.sql/api/pyspark.sql.functions.create
   _map.html#pyspark.sql.functions.create_map
3 https://spark.apache.org/docs/3.3.0/api/python/reference/api/pyspark.sql.DataFrame.sampleBy.html#py
   spark.sql.DataFrame.sampleBy

```
Iteration: 0 - labeled size: 76
Adding 107 instances from class 0, and 78 from class 1
Iteration: 1 - labeled size: 154
Adding 306 instances from class 0, and 223 from class 1
Iteration: 2 - labeled size: 427
Adding 168 instances from class 0, and 122 from class 1
Iteration: 3 - labeled size: 648
Adding 236 instances from class 0, and 172 from class 1
Iteration: 4 - labeled size: 902
Adding 242 instances from class 0, and 176 from class 1
Iteration: 5 - labeled size: 1162
Adding 22 instances from class 0, and 16 from class 1
Iteration: 6 - labeled size: 1182
Adding 28 instances from class 0, and 20 from class 1
Iteration: 7 - labeled size: 1199
Adding 9 instances from class 0, and 7 from class 1
Iteration: 8 - labeled size: 1210
Adding 9 instances from class 0, and 7 from class 1
Iteration: 9 - labeled size: 1221
Adding 9 instances from class 0, and 7 from class 1
Wall time: 10.9 s
```

```
print(f'Final size of the labeled set: {enlarged_labeled.count()}')
```

```
Final size of the labeled set: 1232
```

Now that we have the dataset "preprocessed" and enlarged. We can again use MLlib to predict the labels of the entire unlabeled and test sets:

```
model = dt.fit(enlarged_labeled)
preds_trans = model.transform(unlabeled)
preds_inductive = model.transform(test_features)
print(f"Transductive accuracy = {evaluator.evaluate(preds_trans)}")
print(f"Inductive accuracy = {evaluator.evaluate(preds_inductive)}")
```

```
Transductive accuracy = 0.9102726696258719
Inductive accuracy = 0.9088256746900073
```

In this particular example, the self-training is working great. The inductive accuracy is slightly higher than the upper bound, which is fantastic, although that's not due to our parallel implementation but the self-training. If we tested other hyperparameters for the base classifier, we may quickly see that the outcome can easily change.

Challenge #9.2

You are asked to design and implement a local-based approach for self-training. We would advise thinking a little bit differently from the local approach we described in Chapter 7, and not aim to build a model per partition. Alternatively, the complete self-training is run for each partition independently. Nevertheless, the aim is to enlarge the labeled set only as if it was a pure preprocessing stage.

In summary, we have provided a global design (and a local one in the challenge) to do self-training in large datasets. If you asked us what else could be done to improve this analysis, we would say:

- The implementation seems quite efficient, but we haven't analyzed in depth its scalability. We hope that keen readers use the knowledge gained in Chapter 7 to do so.
- We initially hard-coded the solution for binary classification problems, but some tweaks are needed to make it work with multi-class problems (see the solution to Challenge #9.1).
- We tested the self-training method with decision trees as a base classifier, but we haven't done much investigation of its behavior. It would be great to play with other classifiers and much bigger datasets.
- Last, but not least, the global design could be applicable to other self-labeling strategies that have proven to be more robust. They do, however, involve training more classifiers at each iteration, or manipulating the data a little. For example, in co-training (Blum and Mitchell, 1998), we would normally have to train two separate classifiers, splitting the training data by features into two different subsets.

9.2   Ensemble Learning: Bagging and Boosting

Ensemble learning (Kuncheva, 2014) is a very popular strategy in supervised machine learning. It is designed to increase the accuracy of a single classifier (or a regressor) by training a diverse set of classifiers and aggregating their decisions. Actually, you may remember that we have already seen an ensemble method when we did our local solutions for decision trees in Chapter 7. We simply put together decision tree classifiers trained in parallel with different subsets of the data, and we used those to make predictions, aggregating their decisions with a simple majority-vote rule. You may already have guessed that, of course, having more than one classifier/regressor implies more training, and therefore increases the computation costs. Hence, that's why we are interested in doing this efficiently in the context of big data. While we can do both regression and classification, we focus on an example with classifiers.

When we talk about ensembles, we must not forget to mention one key aspect: diversity. This refers to the fact that the models in an ensemble must provide different outputs for the same dataset. Otherwise, how can we improve a single model? If we have several models giving the same outputs, we won't get much from using them together, so we would rather choose one of them. Obviously, too much diversity can lead us to predict wrongly in many examples. We look for something in between. This is the accuracy–diversity dilemma: we want models that are individually accurate but that complement each other. In a nutshell, ensemble learning algorithms apply different strategies to achieve such diversity while maintaining the good accuracy of the individual models. This can be achieved, for example, by using different variations of the same classifier or by combining or hybridizing models from different learning paradigms.

Some may refer to ensemble learning as those collections of classifiers that are slightly different variations of the same classifier, as opposed to the more general multi-classifier systems term, which is typically used for the combination and hybridization of different models. On the one hand, having multiple classifiers may help alleviate the individual weaknesses of a single model. In fact, this type of multi-classifier has also become a powerful tool in state-of-the-art AutoML techniques, such as AutoGluon, ensembling/stacking a diverse suite of high-quality models. On the other hand, training slightly different variations of the same classifier by using the available data in different ways may provide different "views" of the data and mitigate various issues in machine learning. For example, this strategy has been demonstrated to reduce the variance of the individual models, leading to improved robustness to many machine learning issues such as imbalanced or multi-class problems. In this section we focus on the latter, ensembling "minor" variations of the same classifier.

Within the field of ensemble learning, we can find several approaches in the literature, of which we highlight *bagging* and *boosting* as the precursors of state-of-the-art ensembles such as random forest or gradient boosted trees (e.g., XGBoost). In brief, bagging trains multiple models on different random subsets of the training data independently, and then applies a voting strategy or averages the predictions of these models, whereas boosting sequentially trains a series of models so that each model focuses on correcting (reducing) the mistakes of the previous model. Bagging and boosting are two well-known classical ensemble approaches, and their ideas are still applied in more complex ensemble methods. There are other ensemble strategies such as stacking (more related to multi-classifier systems), where a new (meta-)model is trained to combine the predictions of multiple models. However, our focus here is to apply bagging and boosting to large-scale problems in Spark with what we have learned so far.

For both algorithms, we will be aiming to get a global-based solution. While a local model could also make sense, the solution would be very much the same as we provided in Chapter 7, but changing the scikit-learn classifier used. We encourage readers to look at ensembles in scikit-learn[4] and run those approaches sequentially and as a local-based model for big data. Both options would serve as relevant baselines to compare with our global-based solution.

9.2.1   A Global Solution for Bagging

The concept of bagging, or bootstrap aggregating, was first introduced by Breiman (1996) as a method for creating ensembles. It involves training multiple classifiers on random subsets of instances (taken with replacement) from the original training data. Therefore, each classifier is trained on a different subset of the data, generating the required diversity. When presented with a test instance, the ensemble's final prediction is determined by a majority or weighted vote of the classifiers' predictions.

Bagging requires a base learning algorithm, which should typically be a "weak learner," which means that minor changes in data produce big changes in the learned

---

[4] https://scikit-learn.org/stable/modules/ensemble.html

model. In a way, we are interested in overfitting the data with each base classifier, so that we generate diversity with just small changes in the data. The idea is that then, by aggregating all the models, the overfitting (variance) of each individual classifier will be reduced while improving the performance of each of the individual classifiers.

The algorithm has two main hyperparameters: the number of iterations/classifiers, and the bootstrap size. At each iteration the weak learner is trained on a different set, and the bootstrap size indicates the number (or percentage) of instances that will be randomly chosen with replacement from the original data. Typically, the boostrap size is set to the size of the training dataset, so that each classifier is trained with the same amount of data as that available.

Here is some brief pseudo-code of the learning phase of bagging:

```
Input: TR: Training set, n: Boostrap size, Learner: Weak learner, MaxIter
for t = 1 to MaxIter:
    TR_t = RandomSampleReplacement(n, TR)
    models[t] = Learner.fit(TR_t)
return models
```

Once the models are trained, we can predict new examples with simple or weighted voting, as we did in Chapter 7 with our local model. Note also that, when working with regression problems, we could just average the predictions to get the final output.

With this brief introduction, we are now ready to design a distributed solution for bagging.

Distributed Design

With the information presented so far about ensembles, we can quickly see that the main bottleneck for ensembles is the need to train multiple classifiers. Looking at the above description of bagging specifically, we also have to create that bootstrapped version of the dataset prior to training. We need to factor in these two aspects in designing a successful distributed solution. On the one hand, the base learners will have to be distributed versions to be able to tackle large datasets. As we did before for the self-training algorithm, we can simply rely on MLlib to help distribute the learning at each step. Once again, we will be using decision trees.

And what do we do about boostrapping? Well, luckily for us, there are some predefined functions in Spark that allow us to do the sampling very efficiently. Otherwise, we would have to implement it ourselves. Having said that, is boostrapping a time-consuming operation? We can do that for each partition of a DataFrame independently, without sending any data across the network, so we are talking about a narrow transformation. Thus, the design of bagging is extremely simple. Figure 9.2 shows the workflow of this distributed solution.

> Spark uses random numbers following two different distributions to implement an efficient distributed sampling (Poisson and Bernoulli for with and without replacement, respectively). Bernoulli is what we have been applying in the previous self-training implementation for sampling, whereas in Poisson we would get a number for each row indicating how many times it is sampled.

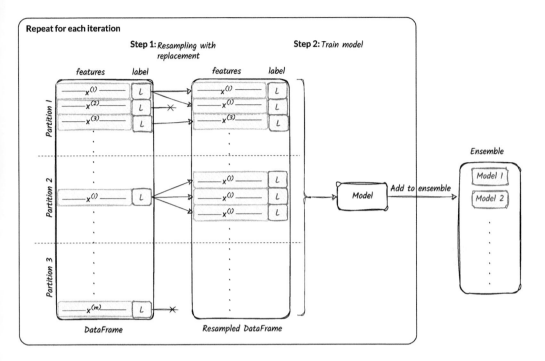

Figure 9.2 Workflow of a global design for bagging with Spark DataFrames.

Implementation

We use the Spambase dataset as before. Let's reset train and test:

```
train, test = df.randomSplit([0.7, 0.3], seed)
```

As we did before for self-training, it is probably best to not use a pipeline of Vec-torAssembler followed by classifier, as we are going to be reusing the very same assembled data with various classifiers. Let's transform both train and test:

```
train_features = \
    assembler.transform(train).select("features", "output").cache()
test_features = assembler.transform(test).select("features", "output").cache()
```

You may have noticed that we got rid of unused columns and cached the train_features, as we will have to bootstrap it at each iteration of the main loop, and we want to make sure this transformation only happens once.

To create one bootstrapped version of train_features, we could simply use the sample function of Spark:

```
bag = train_features.sample(withReplacement=True, fraction=1.0)
```

For this example, we have fixed the bootstrap size hyperparameter to 1.0, meaning that the size of the training data would be (almost) the same; the main difference is that there may be some instances that are repeated more than once, and others that have disappeared. That's what introduces the diversity. Let's compare this bag DataFrame against train:

```
bag.groupby('output').count().show()
```

```
+------+-----+
|output|count|
+------+-----+
|   1.0| 1309|
|   0.0| 1865|
+------+-----+
```

```
train.groupby('output').count().show()
```

```
+------+-----+
|output|count|
+------+-----+
|   1.0| 1280|
|   0.0| 1950|
+------+-----+
```

The total number of examples in bag is similar to what we have in train, but we are getting fewer examples from both classes due to the randomness of the sample function.

> You may want to explore this hyperparameter further. Lower values would normally speed up the processing, as it would make the training set smaller, but that might turn into lower performance.

Once we have created that bag, we should train a base learner with it. As before, we opt for a decision tree with maxDepth set to 5.

```
dt = DecisionTreeClassifier(maxDepth=5, labelCol="output")
```

We could now fit the model with model = dt.fit(bag). However, here is the only tricky bit in this implementation. As we are going to train multiple decision trees, when testing, we need to get the predictions from all of them for our data. To do so, we transform our test_features DataFrame with each decision tree, which will try to add its output columns. However, as they are named the same by default, we will get an error. Therefore, we should tell each decision tree to name the output columns differently; they are set by default to 'prediction', 'probability', and 'rawPrediction'. What we can do is add the number of the iteration to the column name very easily using the dt object:

```
dt.setPredictionCol(f'prediction_1')
dt.setProbabilityCol(f'probability_1')
dt.setRawPredictionCol(f'rawPrediction_1')
model = dt.fit(bag)
```

If we now make predictions on the test set . . .

```
prediction = model.transform(test_features)
```

. . . the resulting DataFrame would have those columns. Let's see:

```
prediction.show(1)
```

```
+-------------------+------+---------------+---------------------+-----------
-+
|            features|output|rawPrediction_1|
probability_1|prediction_1|
+-------------------+------+---------------+---------------------+-----------
-+
|(57,[54,55,56],[1...|   0.0| [1453.0,124.0]|[0.92136968928344...|
0.0|
+-------------------+------+---------------+---------------------+-----------
-+
only showing top 1 row
```

Alright, we are in a good position to put everything together in a function `bagging` that will return all the fitted models as a list:

```python
def bagging(train_df, weak_learner, bootstrap_size, max_iter=10):
    models = []
    for i in range(max_iter):
        bag = train_df.sample(withReplacement=True, fraction=1.0)
        dt.setPredictionCol(f"prediction_{i}")
        dt.setProbabilityCol(f"probability_{i}")
        dt.setRawPredictionCol(f"rawPrediction_{i}")
        models.append(dt.fit(bag))
    return models
```

```python
max_iter = 10
%time models = bagging(train_features, dt, 1, max_iter)
```

```
CPU times: total: 156 ms
Wall time: 5.11 s
```

The training phase of bagging is now implemented. Before we move to the test phase, we could investigate the individual performance of each one of the classifiers on the test. Let's define a simple function to do this, but first let's reset the `evaluator` for this section of the chapter:

```python
evaluator = MulticlassClassificationEvaluator(
    labelCol="output",
    metricName="accuracy",
)
```

```python
def test_individual_models(test_feat, models):
    for i in range(len(models)):
        prediction = models[i].transform(test_feat)
        evaluator.setPredictionCol(f'prediction_{i}') # Change column
        acc = evaluator.evaluate(prediction)
        print(f"Accuracy model {i}: {acc}")
```

```python
test_individual_models(test_features, models)
```

```
Accuracy model 0: 0.900072939460248
Accuracy model 1: 0.9059080962800875
Accuracy model 2: 0.9073668854850474
```

```
Accuracy model 3: 0.9066374908825675
Accuracy model 4: 0.8971553610503282
Accuracy model 5: 0.9029905178701677
Accuracy model 6: 0.9022611232676878
Accuracy model 7: 0.8971553610503282
Accuracy model 8: 0.8789204959883297
Accuracy model 9: 0.9029905178701677
```

Looking at that output, we can see how the performance varies quite a bit among classifiers. We expect the ensemble to improve upon those individual performances.

> Note that in the bagging function we didn't set a seed to sample the training set; this allows us to obtain different subsets for each classifier and therefore different results. To date, there is no option to set a global random seed in Spark.

Let's implement the test phase. We could reuse part of the previous function to append the predictions of each classifier. But let us show you a more elegant way of doing this. In models, we already have the fitted models, which have to be used to transform the test set. Therefore, we can put the list of models as the stages of a pipeline, just like this:

```python
from pyspark.ml import PipelineModel
pipeline_models = PipelineModel(stages=models)
```

> We directly created a PipelineModel instead of a Pipeline as all the components are Transformers and there is no need to fit the pipeline.

We can apply that pipeline of models to transform the test DataFrame, adding columns with the predictions of the number of classifiers we have used.

```python
prediction = pipeline_models.transform(test_features)
```

The last step of bagging is to aggregate those predictions to come up with a final prediction. We do this in two steps. First, we create a single column that will contain an array with all the predictions.

```python
ensemble = prediction.select(
    sql_f.array([f"prediction_{i}" for i in range(max_iter)]).alias("preds"),
    "output",
)
ensemble.show(1, truncate=False)
```

```
+----------------------------------------------------+------+
|preds                                               |output|
+----------------------------------------------------+------+
|[0.0, 0.0, 0.0, 0.0, 0.0, 0.0, 0.0, 0.0, 0.0, 0.0]|0.0   |
+----------------------------------------------------+------+
only showing top 1 row
```

Why are we doing this? This will now help us perform a Column operation to compute a majority vote in that array. You may remember that we did something similar with RDDs to implement the aggreggation of our local decision tree models. To do this, we use the mode class from the statistics package, which will allow us to compute the consensus between all the classifiers as the mode of the array of predictions. We will have to define a UDF to use it. We could probably try to do this with Spark aggregations, which would be more efficient, but more complex; given that this is not a really time-consuming operation, we have opted for simplicity.

```
from statistics import mode
from pyspark.sql.types import DoubleType
mode_udf = sql_f.udf(mode, DoubleType())
prediction = ensemble.withColumn("prediction", mode_udf("preds"))
prediction.show(1)
```

```
+--------------------+------+----------+
|               preds|output|prediction|
+--------------------+------+----------+
|[0.0, 0.0, 0.0, 0...|   0.0|       0.0|
+--------------------+------+----------+
only showing top 1 row
```

Let's evaluate the performance of the ensemble.

```
evaluator.setPredictionCol('prediction') # reset predictionCol
evaluator.evaluate(prediction)
```

```
0.9161196207148067
```

In this example, bagging with majority vote has resulted in an accuracy higher than any of the individual decision trees.

> ## Challenge #9.3
>
> We have simply used a majority vote to compute the final prediction of the ensemble. You are asked to implement the necessary code to calculate the prediction as a weighted vote.

9.2.2 A Global Solution for Boosting: AdaBoost

The idea of boosting was introduced by Schapire (1990). It is another ensemble method like bagging that, in each iteration, somehow alters the training set, so that diversity is produced in the final ensemble. However, the idea of boosting is a bit more complex than just resampling the training set. While bagging focuses on reducing the overfitting (variance) of a model by averaging prediction, in boosting the idea goes further, trying to build a strong classifier out of a weak base classifier, which is slightly better than a random one. Hence, it is also able to improve the bias or underfitting of a model.

AdaBoost (Freund and Schapire, 1997) was the first approach to boosting. In AdaBoost each example has an associated weight that represents its importance, and the models are learned sequentially using these weights, which are modified through iterations. Initially, it trains a model with all the examples having the same importance (weights). Then, the weights of the examples are modified. The weights of misclassified instances are increased. Conversely, the weights of correctly classified instances are decreased. The objective is to give more importance to the examples that are hard to classify.

> The base learner needs to have a way to weigh the importance of the different examples. For those models not capable of dealing with weights, this can be replaced by an approximation based on a weighted resampling of the training set.

In addition to the weights of the examples, in AdaBoost, a weight is assigned to each individual classifier, which is used when predicting new examples. This weight depends on the error each model makes on the training set (taking the weight distribution into account). The idea is to give more weight to those classifiers that perform better at that stage. As such, the method only has one key hyperparameter, the number of classifiers/iterations. Brief pseudo-code is shown below. The error rate is computed as the sum of the weights of those training instances that are misclassified. If the error is higher than 0.5 (a random classifier), the loop is ended. The pseudo-code also provides details about how the increase/decrease of weights works based on a formula, which is only for binary classification (it assumes predictions and labels are either 1 or -1).

```
Input: TR: Training set, n: Boostrap size, Learner: Weak learner, MaxIter
weights[i] = 1/size(TR) for i = 1,..., size(TR)
for t = 1 to MaxIter:
    models[t] = Learner.fit(TR, weights)
    predictions = models[t].predict(TR)
    error = Sum of weights of misclassified TR instances

    if error > 0.5:
        Disregard model and break

    alpha[t] = 1/2 * ln((1-error)/error)
    for i = 1 to size(TR):
        weights[i] *= exp(-alpha * prediction[i] * TR[i].output)
    Normalize weights to be a distribution (sum up to 1)
return models
```

We will use the same data as before and decision trees as the base learner. Fortunately, a decision tree can use weights to consider the importance of the different training instances when calculating dispersion metrics like Gini or entropy to decide at what feature and value to split a node, and this is already implemented in Spark.

Distributed Design and Implementation

As before, the main bottleneck will again be training the various classifiers, which we will also handle using distributed base learners. Actually, the design itself is also extremely simple and similar to the one for bagging. The main difficulty may lie in how to update the instance weights with DataFrames, but let's figure that out as we implement it. Figure 9.3 shows the workflow of this global design.

We are using the same data as before, and again, we use the assembled features version train_features. The first step of AdaBoost will be to add a column with weights for all instances. According to the pseudo-code, this should be 1 divided by the size of the training data, to give all instances the exact same importance. So, we count

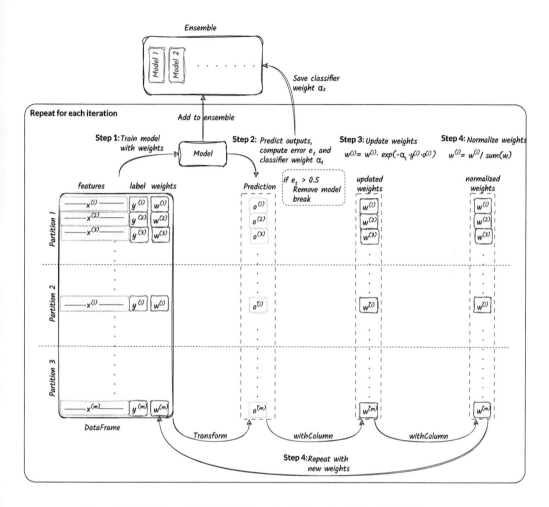

Figure 9.3 Workflow of a global design for AdaBoost with Spark DataFrames.

the number of elements of the DataFrame and add a column using the `lit` function to add the same literal number for all the elements of the column.

```
# re-setting train_features
train_features = assembler.transform(train)
train_features = train_features.select("features", "output").cache()
count = train_features.count()
train_features = train_features.withColumn("weights", sql_f.lit(1.0 / count))
```

We can train a decision tree that takes into account the column `weights` either when defining the object ...

```
dt = DecisionTreeClassifier(
    maxDepth=5, labelCol="output", weightCol="weights")
```

... or by setting the name of the column later on:

```
dt.setWeightCol('weights')
```

```
DecisionTreeClassifier_3a2d9e2c28db
```

We should now fit the model with those weights and predict the error rate.

```
model = dt.fit(train_features)
train_features = model.transform(train_features)
```

The error rate is the sum of the weights of misclassified instances (i.e., `prediction != output`):

```
err = train_features.filter("prediction != output")\
                    .agg(sql_f.sum("weights"))\
                    .first()[0]
err
```

```
0.07120743034055732
```

The algorithm would stop the loop if the error is higher than 0.5, and would disregard the last model trained.

The last step we need to implement before putting everything together is the update of the weights. First, we have to compute the weight for the current classifier `alpha[t]`.

```
alpha = 0.5 * np.log((1 - err) / err)
```

We will have to store that `alpha` for each model at the prediction phase, but it is also used to modify the weights of the examples.

To update the weights of each instance, we need to create an extra column following the formula specified before, which is the multiplication of the current weight and the exponential of minus the weight of the classifier times the prediction and the label. Something interesting here is that for the formula to work well, the prediction should either be +1 or −1, but the class labels in our dataset were 0 and 1. We could have changed this from the start, but the implementation problem here is that Spark ML expects classes starting from 0, so we need to think of something else. Let's recap the formula we need to implement:

```
weights[i] = weights[i] * exp(-alpha * prediction[i] * TR[i].output)
```

If you think about the formula a bit, you will notice that the multiplication of the prediction and the label will always be either +1 (if both agree) or −1 (if they disagree). Accordingly, the weight update formula is just multiplying each weight by `exp(alpha[t])` if it has been misclassified or by `1/exp(alpha[t])` if it has been correctly classified. Therefore, it may be easier to use an auxiliary column indicating whether the example is correctly classified (+1) or not (−1) corresponding to `prediction[i] * TR[i].output`. We then use this to update the weights.

```
train_features = train_features.withColumn("correct",
    sql_f.when(sql_f.col("prediction") == sql_f.col("output"), 1)
        .otherwise(-1),
)
train_features.show(1)
```

```
+-------------------+------+-------------------+-------------------+------
-------------+---------+-------+
|           features|output|            weights|       rawPrediction|
probability|prediction|correct|
+-------------------+------+-------------------+-------------------+------
-------------+---------+-------+
|(57,[54,55,56],[1...|
0.0|3.095975232198142...|[0.46191950464395...|[0.94550063371356...|
0.0|         1|
+-------------------+------+-------------------+-------------------+------
-------------+---------+-------+
only showing top 1 row
```

We can now create a new column with weights for iteration 1 of the algorithm. This uses the current weights, `alpha`, and our auxiliary column. We use the function `expr` from Spark to easily compute that exponential.

```python
train_features = train_features.withColumn(f"weights_1",
    sql_f.expr(f"exp(-1 * correct * {alpha}) * weights")
)
```

Finally, we need to normalize that new column, dividing all the weights by the total sum of weights.

```python
sum_weights = train_features.agg(sql_f.sum(f'weights_1')).first()[0]
train_features = train_features.withColumn(f'weights_1',
    sql_f.expr(f'weights_1/{sum_weights}')
)
```

To put everything into a loop, we again have to make sure we give a different column name for each output as we did for bagging. Other than that, we have all the pieces of this puzzle.

```python
def adaboost(train_features, weak_learner, max_iter=10):
    models = []
    clf_weights = []
    count = train_features.count()
    train_features = train_features.withColumn(
        "weights_0", sql_f.lit(1.0 / count)
    )
    for i in range(max_iter):
        dt.setPredictionCol(f"prediction_{i}")
        dt.setProbabilityCol(f"probability_{i}")
        dt.setRawPredictionCol(f"rawPrediction_{i}")
        dt.setWeightCol(f"weights_{i}")
        models.append(dt.fit(train_features))
        train_features = models[i].transform(train_features)
        # compute error
        err = train_features.filter(f"prediction_{i} != output")\
                            .agg(sql_f.sum(f"weights_{i}"))\
                            .first()[0]
        if err > 0.5:
            models.pop()
            n_estimator = i
```

```
        break
    alpha = 0.5 * np.log((1 - err) / err)
    clf_weights.append(alpha)
    # Create our auxiliary column
    train_features = train_features.withColumn(f"correct_{i}",
        sql_f.when(
            sql_f.col(f"prediction_{i}") == sql_f.col("output"), 1
        ).otherwise(-1),
    )
    # update and normalize
    train_features = train_features.withColumn(f"weights_{i+1}",
        sql_f.expr(f"exp(-1 *  correct_{i} * {alpha}) * weights_{i}"),
    )
    sum_weights = train_features.agg(sql_f.sum(f"weights_{i+1}"))\
                            .first()[0]
    train_features = train_features.withColumn(f"weights_{i+1}",
        sql_f.expr(f"weights_{i+1}/{sum_weights}")
    )
return models, clf_weights
```

Let's run our distributed version of AdaBoost.

```
# re-setting train_features
train_features = assembler.transform(train)
train_features = train_features.select("features", "output").cache()
%time models, clf_weights = adaboost(train_features, dt)
```

```
CPU times: total: 297 ms
Wall time: 14.1 s
```

As we did before, let's test the individual performance of the models:

```
test_individual_models(test_features, models)
```

```
Accuracy model 0: 0.9080962800875274
Accuracy model 1: 0.849744711889132
Accuracy model 2: 0.7848285922684172
Accuracy model 3: 0.5711159737417943
Accuracy model 4: 0.7067833698030634
Accuracy model 5: 0.7964989059080962
Accuracy model 6: 0.5412107950401167
Accuracy model 7: 0.6652078774617067
Accuracy model 8: 0.7177242888402626
Accuracy model 9: 0.7483588621444202
```

This is nothing like what we observed in bagging: the classifiers are mainly getting worse as iterations progress. Does it make any sense? It does! AdaBoost is focusing on the most difficult instances, giving less importance to the rest and losing overall accuracy. However, we also have an associated weight for each classifier that will balance this when using all of them together.

We still need to work a bit to get the ensemble prediction, as we now have to take the classifier weights into account. Let's first have a look at the classifier weights:

```
clf_weights
```

```
[1.2841441293635254,
 0.6783332771872561,
 0.641746188181348,
 0.39236410163552365,
 0.5732733374809456,
 0.5709714273382864,
 0.3391329388501538,
 0.28814688142847106,
 0.3033938710031082,
 0.42657214895332257]
```

To predict the class for a new instance, in AdaBoost we multiply the output of each classifier (either +1 or −1) by its weight and sum them. Then, we take the sign of that value as the class. Let's write it as pseudo-code:

```
class(x) = sign(sum([alpha[t] * model[t].predict(x) for t=1,...,maxIter]))
```

This is simply checking the predictions of which class adds up the most according to the classifiers' weights, and that class is predicted using the `sign` function, which returns +1 for positive values and −1 for negative ones. However, our Spark ML decision tree works with output values 0 and 1, so we can adapt this formula to make it easier. In this case, it would be equivalent to summing the values for class 1, and checking if the resulting value is above the threshold given by half of the sum of the classifier weights. In other words, the formula can be expressed as follows:

```
class(x) = sum([alpha[t] * model[t].predict(x) for t=1,...,maxIter]) >␣
↪sum(alpha) / 2
```

Let's implement this. First, we need to get the outputs of the classifiers for all the test examples. As before, we can now put the list of models in a pipeline and classify the test:

```
pipeline_models = PipelineModel(stages=models)
prediction = pipeline_models.transform(test_features)
```

We also put together all the predictions in a Column as an array:

```
ensemble = prediction.select(
    sql_f.array([f"prediction_{i}" for i in range(max_iter)]).alias("preds"),
    "output",
)
ensemble.show(1, truncate=False)
```

```
+-------------------------------------------------+------+
|preds                                            |output|
+-------------------------------------------------+------+
|[0.0, 0.0, 1.0, 1.0, 0.0, 0.0, 1.0, 0.0, 1.0, 0.0]|0.0   |
+-------------------------------------------------+------+
only showing top 1 row
```

You may think of many different ways of multiplying our `clf_weights` array by each row of the `'preds'` column. In this case, we have opted for something we challenged you with in the previous chapter: using the `ElementwiseProduct` function from Spark ML. With this, we can multiply a column of Spark ML `Vectors` by a scaling vector (in our case, `clf_weights`). To do so, we first need to convert our `Array` column to a `Vector` column from Spark ML. We have done this previously in the book using the `array_to_vector` function. Let's do this conversion first.

```
from pyspark.ml.functions import array_to_vector
ensemble = ensemble.withColumn("preds", array_to_vector(sql_f.col("preds")))
ensemble.show(1, truncate=False)
```

```
+---------------------------------------------+------+
|preds                                        |output|
+---------------------------------------------+------+
|[0.0,0.0,1.0,1.0,0.0,0.0,1.0,0.0,1.0,0.0]|0.0   |
+---------------------------------------------+------+
only showing top 1 row
```

The `ElementWiseProduct` has two main parameters: the input column (`'preds'`) and the scaling vector (`clf_weights`) that will be used to scale the input column. Note that the scaling vector should be of `Vector` type.

```
from pyspark.ml.feature import ElementwiseProduct
from pyspark.ml.linalg import Vectors
elementwise_product = ElementwiseProduct(
    inputCol="preds", outputCol="weighted_preds",
    scalingVec=Vectors.dense(clf_weights),
)
weighted_ensemble = elementwise_product.transform(ensemble)
weighted_ensemble.show(1)
```

```
+--------------------+------+--------------------+
|               preds|output|      weighted_preds|
+--------------------+------+--------------------+
|[0.0,0.0,1.0,1.0,...|   0.0|[0.0,0.0,0.641746...|
+--------------------+------+--------------------+
only showing top 1 row
```

We can observe how the ones in `preds` have been substituted by the weights of the corresponding classifier. The last step is to sum the values in each array in the `weighted_preds` column and compare this with half the sum of the classifiers' weights. If you are curious about this threshold:

```
sum(clf_weights) / 2
```

```
2.7490391507109706
```

If you have already completed Challenge #9.3 from this chapter, you will already know the solution for this last step, as it is the same as doing the weighted voting we proposed for bagging. To sum the values of a Spark SQL array, we use the `aggregate`[5] function, which is similar to a `reduce` except that we have to give an initial value for the aggregation. Note that we have to convert back our `Vector`-type column to `Array`.

---

[5] https://spark.apache.org/docs/3.3.0/api/python/reference/pyspark.sql/api/pyspark.sql.functions.aggrega te.html#pyspark.sql.functions.aggregate

```
weighted_ensemble = weighted_ensemble.withColumn("pred", (
        sql_f.aggregate(
            vector_to_array("weighted_preds"),
            sql_f.lit(0.0),
            lambda acc, x: acc + x)
        )
)
weighted_ensemble.show(1)
```

```
+--------------------+------+--------------------+------------------+
|               preds|output|      weighted_preds|              pred|
+--------------------+------+--------------------+------------------+
|[0.0,0.0,1.0,1.0,...|   0.0|[0.0,0.0,0.641746...|1.6766370996701339|
+--------------------+------+--------------------+------------------+
only showing top 1 row
```

Finally, we can compare the `pred` column with our threshold:

```
weighted_ensemble = weighted_ensemble.withColumn(
    "pred", (sql_f.col("pred") > sum(clf_weights) / 2).cast("double")
)
weighted_ensemble.show(1)
```

```
+--------------------+------+--------------------+----+
|               preds|output|      weighted_preds|pred|
+--------------------+------+--------------------+----+
|[0.0,0.0,1.0,1.0,...|   0.0|[0.0,0.0,0.641746...| 0.0|
+--------------------+------+--------------------+----+
only showing top 1 row
```

We added the cast to double so that we can make use of the Spark ML evaluator. Let's check our test accuracy.

```
evaluator.setPredictionCol(f'pred')
acc = evaluator.evaluate(weighted_ensemble)
acc
```

```
0.9321663019693655
```

It's not bad! It is the best performance we have achieved in this chapter. In this specific case, AdaBoost is performing better than bagging. But remember, this won't always be the case. You could also check different hyperparameters to make a fairer comparison. In terms of implementation and comparing with bagging, it has not been overly complicated, we mainly needed to take care of the examples' weights, and we have had to employ various tricks with Spark to make it more efficient and have a working distributed global version. In this case, the prediction part has also been somewhat more tricky.

To conclude this section on ensemble learning, we would like to flag some improvements that could be made to do ensemble learning in large datasets:

- Once again, both implementations seem quite efficient, but a detailed analysis of their scalability could shed light on their real capabilities, and find any other bottlenecks that would need to be addressed.

- We have implemented the classic version of AdaBoost, which would only work for binary classification problems. You could try and implement its multi-class extensions,[6] AdaBoost.M1 or AdaBoost.M2. While AdaBoost.M1 works directly with class labels, AdaBoost.M2 uses the confidence or probabilities of the predictions for each class. Implementing them wouldn't make much of a difference, since the main change is the way in which the weights are updated.
- As we mentioned with self-labeling, here we have used decision trees as base classifiers. We would recommend investigating other classifiers and bigger datasets as part of a larger analysis of the scalability of the solution.

9.3   Model Deployment: Case Study in Image Segmentation with Deep Learning

So far, we have mainly focused on how to train machine learning algorithms in the presence of large datasets. As we explained in Chapter 6, the machine learning life cycle has several phases, and not all of them may be equally affected by big data issues. For example, there are problems where capturing raw data may be challenging due to the velocity at which data is produced and the variety of sources from which it is gathered. However, after doing the data preprocessing and cleansing with Spark, we may end with a much smaller dataset that could be used to do machine learning locally without requiring Spark. Despite this, once we have our model learned, it may still be possible that we require large-scale inference as we have lots of testing data, for which we would resort to Spark again.

In this section we focus on an example of distributed inference. The initial data ingestion and preprocessing are generally very specific to the problem we are dealing with and can vary quite a bit from one use case to another, whereas distributed inference is perhaps a more recurrent and standard use case.

More specifically, our goal is to show an example of how we can distribute with Spark the inference of a convolutional neural network programmed in PyTorch, one of the most widely used frameworks for deep learning. Therefore, in this case we are not going to focus so much on the model learning, which will be done in a single machine (and hopefully with a GPU), but on the inference. Although we have not been especially focused on deep learning, Spark can also be a very helpful tool for working with very large problems in deep learning, either for training or inference. We won't dive deeply into this, but we recommend you take a look at Section 9.5 if you are interested in this.

9.3.1   Case Study on Remote Sensing: Building Semantic Segmentation

We are going to deal with a typical remote sensing problem, which consists of identifying buildings in aerial or satellite images. This is useful for multiple tasks, such as the

---

[6] www.sciencedirect.com/science/article/pii/S002200009791504X

generation of maps, analyzing the growth of human settlements, or other studies related to climate change such as pollution. This problem can be addressed as a semantic segmentation problem, which involves assigning a class (e.g., building or non-building) to each pixel of an image. Semantic segmentation is commonly addressed by fully convolutional neural networks, which can take an image as input and produce a mask (i.e., another image) with the class label for each pixel as output. We usually train these networks in a supervised manner, where we use training images paired with ground truth masks with the corresponding class label for each pixel.

In our case, we will consider images from the Sentinel-2 satellite as input data on which to identify buildings. The Sentinel-2 satellite was put into orbit by the European Space Agency (ESA) with the aim of providing high-resolution images for land monitoring free of charge. However, using this satellite has its drawbacks, mainly regarding the resolution of the images, which makes the problem really challenging. Sentinel-2 offers images with a maximum resolution of 10 m (for RGB and near-infrared bands), which means that each pixel of the image covers a space of 10 m×10 m, making it very difficult to identify small buildings.

Geospatial data management is quite complex and specialized, so we will try to perform a simple exercise that allows us to focus on what is important for this book, which is the distribution of the inference. Let's give a thought to why we would need distributed inference in this case. Assume that you already have a model for classifying Sentinel-2 images, how many Sentinel-2 images would you need to perform a classification on a global (worldwide) scale? If a Sentinel-2 image covers 100 000 m × 100 000 m (i.e., 10 000 km^2) and occupies approximately 600 MB, to process the whole world (i.e., to cover an area of approximately 149 000 000 km^2, we would need about 15 000 images (9 TB of data). Obviously, we could avoid classifying the seas and do other optimizations, but it is also true that the model will probably not be able to process the images as a whole and will have to slice them up. Anyway, it does not seem feasible for a single machine if we want to finish in a reasonable amount of time.

Fortunately, the advances in deep learning and the use of pretrained networks do allow us to train models with quite a good generalization capacity on single machines for the task we are going to face. Let's start with this part so that we have a model we can then use for distributed inference. To avoid getting lost in the training of the model and to make it as simple as possible, we are going to make use of the fast.ai library.[7]

> If you want to be introduced to applied deep learning and understand a little better the steps that we will carry out here, we recommend the fast.ai book (Howard et al., 2020), a good guide to deep learning. By the way, this book is also written in Notebooks and all its code is available at GitHub.[8]

Both the dataset and some of the ideas presented here are based on one of our research papers (Ayala et al., 2021). To simplify the problem, we use only a couple of cities: Pamplona, Mikel's hometown, to train the building prediction model, and Granada, Isaac's hometown, to check the performance of the model (test).

---

[7] https://docs.fast.ai/
[8] https://github.com/fastai/fastbook

> Even if you don't know deep learning, don't worry, we will simply train a model
> with labeled data and use it in other areas with unlabeled data to predict buildings
> with Spark.

Let's start looking at the data we have to better understand the problem. Our data is
located at data/dataset/, which is split into two additional folders, train and test,
with Pamplona and Granada images, respectively. In each folder, there is also a pair of
folders named images and labels. In the former we have the RGB images that are the
inputs to our model (we disregard the near-infrared band and other lower-resolution
bands), whereas in the latter we have the ground truth masks associated with each
image indicating, for each pixel, whether it belongs to a building or not. These will
be our targets for the input images. Before showing an example, we need to set up the
environment and load some libraries.

> You will be able to run the inference without a GPU. However, for the training part,
> we recommend you run it on a computer with a GPU with CUDA enabled. If you
> don't own one, don't worry, you could make use of Google Colab.[9] To facilitate
> working with Colab, you will find several specific code cells.

```
# Working with Colab? Install required libraries
colab = 'google.colab' in str(get_ipython())
if colab:
    # Install required libraries
    !pip install pyproj
    !pip install geopandas
    !pip install contextily
    !pip install owslib
    !pip install semtorch
    !pip install pyspark

    # Mount Google Drive
    from google.colab import drive
    drive.mount('/content/drive')

    # Copy data to working directory
    !cp "/content/drive/MyDrive/Colab Notebooks/data_chapter9.zip" .
```

```
# Decompress data
import shutil
shutil.unpack_archive('data_chapter9.zip', 'data/')
```

To simplify some operations we have created a Python file with several helper
functions in the helper_code folder (geo_helpers.py). Most of them have to do
with geospatial operations needed to work with geospatial data, so don't bother trying
to understand them unless you are very interested. We will also be using numpy,
matplotlib, and the fast.ai library, so we will import them.

---

[9] https://colab.research.google.com/

```
import helper_code.geo_helpers as geo
import matplotlib.pyplot as plt
import numpy as np
from fastai.vision.all import (
    torch, PILBase, PILImageBW, Path, L, SegmentationDataLoaders, Resize,
    get_image_files, foreground_acc, JaccardCoeff, Dice,
    LabelSmoothingCrossEntropyFlat, CrossEntropyLossFlat
)
if torch.cuda.is_available():
    torch.cuda.set_device(0)
```

Let's now look at one of our training samples .

```
# Image to show
image_name = "512_320"
# Read tile and mask
im = PILBase.create(f"data/dataset/train/images/{image_name}.png")
mask = PILImageBW.create(f"data/dataset/train/labels/{image_name}.png")
# Show tile and mask
# Create figure
fig, ax = plt.subplots(1, 3, figsize=(10, 10))
# Draw image
im.show(ctx=ax[0])
ax[0].set_title("Input image")
# Draw masks
mask.show(ctx=ax[1], cmap="binary_r")
ax[1].set_title("Target mask")
# Draw mask superimposed to the image
geo.show(im, mask, ax[2])
ax[2].set_title("Input and target");
```

| Input image | Target mask | Input and target |

> The masks have been automatically extracted from existing information in Open-StreetMap (OSM)[10] and are therefore in many cases not perfect or are incomplete. Despite this, deep learning models are usually able to generalize quite well.

As already mentioned, this is a semantic segmentation problem where, for each input image, we must classify every single pixel, in this case into building or non-building.

---

[10] www.openstreetmap.org/about

Fast.ai helps us perform this task with a few lines of code. We first only need to create some `DataLoaders` for the dataset:

```
# Use data from train folder (Pamplona)
dls = SegmentationDataLoaders.from_label_func(
    "data/dataset",
    bs=16,
    fnames=get_image_files(f"data/dataset/train/images"),
    label_func=lambda f: Path(str(f).replace("images", "labels")),
    codes=["background", "building"],
    item_tfms=[Resize(512)],
    valid_pct=0.2,
)
```

In this case we have created the training and validation `DataLoaders` with the images of Pamplona. In the `label_func` parameter, we indicate that to get the target mask of an image, it must simply replace `"images"` by `"labels"` in the input image file path. Note also that we are going to use a trick so that the output mask has more resolution than the original input image. According to the paper mentioned above, it is possible to segment Sentinel-2 images at sub-pixel resolution, which allows us to obtain segmentation masks at higher detail. In this case, we can obtain building masks at 2.5 m instead of 10 m. This means that the output mask is actually four times larger in pixel resolution than the input (512 pixels vs. 128 pixels). That's why we specify the `Resize(512)` in the `item_tfms` parameter. Thus, we make the input and output have the same dimension, which is what a semantic segmentation neural network usually expects. Finally, we use 20% of the images for validation (within the Pamplona images). We could use other strategies, like using another city, but let's keep it simple.

Now we can see what a batch (a set) of images from the dataset looks like with their masks overlaid.

```
dls.show_batch(max_n=2, figsize=(10, 10), cmap=geo.cm_build, alpha=None)
```

We are going to use a more powerful network than the ones included in the original fast.ai library, using the SemTorch library.[11] We create a DeepLabV3+ (Chen et al., 2018):

```
from semtorch import get_segmentation_learner
learn = get_segmentation_learner(
    dls,
    number_classes=2,
    segmentation_type="Semantic Segmentation",
    architecture_name="deeplabv3+",
    backbone_name="resnet50",
    metrics=[foreground_acc, JaccardCoeff(), Dice()],
    wd=1e-2,
    loss_func=LabelSmoothingCrossEntropyFlat(axis=1),
).to_fp16()
```

Don't worry if you don't understand every line of code. We will be using a pretrained ResNet50 backbone and some classical image segmentation metrics (Intersection over Union (IoU) and Dice).

Fast.ai allows us to find the best learning rate for a data problem with the learning rate finder. Note that the following two code cells are the only ones that require a GPU to finish in a reasonable time.

```
learn.lr_find()
```

```
SuggestedLRs(valley=0.00363078061491251)
```

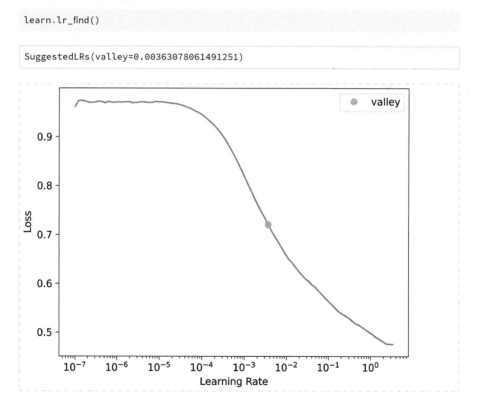

With this information, we can now train the model:

```
learn.fit_one_cycle(10, 1e-3)
learn.save('chkp-last')
```

```
epoch train_loss valid_loss foreg_acc  jaccard     dice  time
    0   0.539594   0.493933 0.054769 0.043582 0.083523 00:19
    1   0.387526   0.279760 0.146946 0.164553 0.282603 00:19
    2   0.324542   0.265769 0.358044 0.336097 0.503103 00:19
    3   0.292788   0.254464 0.587654 0.504649 0.670786 00:19
    4   0.273030   0.242437 0.657886 0.584619 0.737867 00:19
    5   0.260123   0.239863 0.669083 0.605212 0.754059 00:19
    6   0.251306   0.240204 0.630965 0.588000 0.740554 00:19
    7   0.244491   0.232856 0.758347 0.673183 0.804673 00:19
    8   0.239550   0.232060 0.738475 0.672972 0.804523 00:19
    9   0.236406   0.231507 0.772753 0.687287 0.814665 00:19
```

```
Path('data/dataset/models/chkp-last.pth')
```

Our trained model is performing reasonably well in the validation set (see the metrics from the last row of the table). We achieved a building detection accuracy (recall) of 0.77, an IoU (Jaccard coefficient) of 0.68, and a Dice (F-score) of 0.81. Of course, these are metrics computed from a subset of images of Pamplona. But, what about its generalization to other locations, like Granada? Maybe you don't know much about Spanish geography, but the differences from north to south are important, and so are the types of buildings. Let's see if the model is able to generalize.

We load our last model and change the loss function so that it works properly for inference.

```
learn.load('chkp-last', strict=False)
learn.loss_func = CrossEntropyLossFlat(axis=1)
```

To check this, we first need to create a test `DataLoader` for Granada.

```
test_dl = dls.test_dl(get_image_files('data/dataset/test/images'),
                      with_labels=True,
                      bs=16,
                      shuffle=True,
                      items_tfms=[Resize(512)])
```

We can now check some results. Using the `show_results()` method from the fast.ai `Learner`, we can easily show both the target (ground truth) and the prediction.

> Unfortunately, the ground-truth labels for the buildings in Granada are missing almost everywhere. This means that computing any accuracy wouldn't be very meaningful, but we can visualize the results to get an idea.

```
learn.show_results(dl=test_dl, max_n=2,
                   figsize=(10, 10), cmap=geo.cm_build, alpha=None)
```

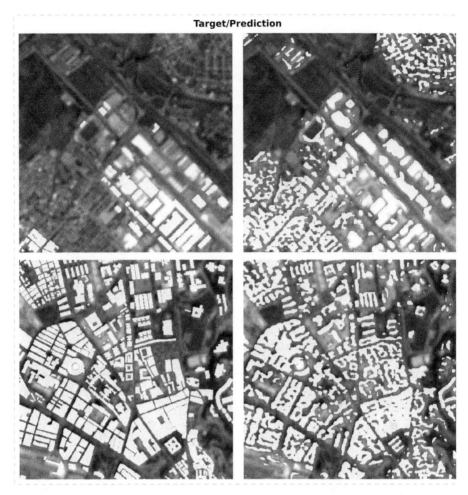

Target/Prediction

This is interesting, we have a model that works relatively well in other cities in Spain; in fact, the predictions (on the right) are much better than the targets generated with OSM (on the left). Getting these predictions has taken less than a second. However, as mentioned in the introduction to this section, what if we now wanted to predict larger areas? All of Spain? The USA? The world? In such cases the number of images would become large, and we would need to download and preprocess them before feeding them into the model, which would not be feasible on a single machine. So we should move to Spark! We were thinking of trying with Nottingham to see whether we could detect Isaac's office there; however, we could move to an even more different and bigger city. Why not New York? Well, if you have other interests, you will be able to do it in any area of the world just by following a few steps. Go to https://geojson.io/ and select an area with a bounding box. Then download the information as a GeoJSON. We have done it with part of Manhattan and saved it to manhattan.json. This JSON simply stores the coordinates of the area we will pretend to classify. Let's check it (we will be using the geopandas and contextily libraries for this):

```
import contextily
import geopandas
aoi = "manhattan"
gdf = geopandas.read_file(f"data/{aoi}.geojson")
ax = gdf.to_crs(epsg=3857).plot(
    figsize=(8, 8), edgecolor="k", facecolor="None")
contextily.add_basemap(ax, source=contextily.providers.Stamen.TonerLite)
ax.set_axis_off()
```

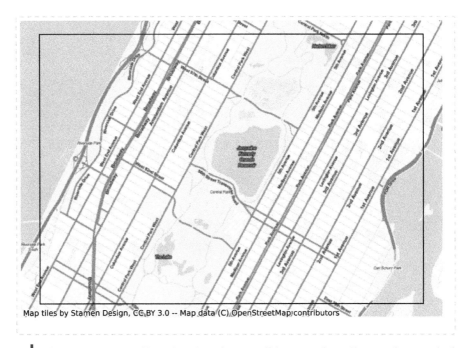

Map tiles by Stamen Design, CC BY 3.0 -- Map data (C) OpenStreetMap contributors

> Of course, this is still not big data, but it will be enough to illustrate how to deal with much larger areas with Spark.

When classifying a larger area like this, we may start facing limitations on how to deal with such a high-resolution image. That's why, in the geospatial domain, as in big data, the information is usually sliced up to ease processing. We usually define a grid that is used to divide the area into a set of tiles. For our example, the Manhattan area could be split following a 3×3 grid, generating nine tiles. This procedure is very common for representing maps and storing aerial/satellite imagery. Fortunately, tiling simplifies our distributed inference task, since, assuming disjoint tiles, we can easily work with them in parallel (e.g., classify each tile independently). Figure 9.4 illustrates this idea of tiling an area of interest.

> We mentioned before that Sentinel-2 images cover an area of $100 \, \text{km} \times 100 \, \text{km}$, so you may not understand why we need more than one single image for the Manhattan area. Sentinel-2 generates raw images of that dimension, but it is more

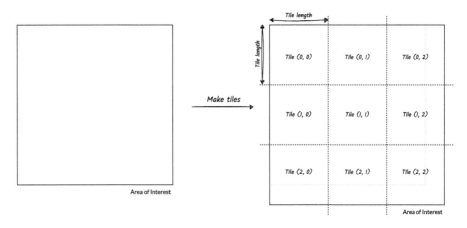

Figure 9.4 Tiling of an area of interest. If needed, the area of interest is increased to make its shape a multiple of the tile length.

> usual to then work with smaller tiles that are more manageable. For example, in our case using neural networks we couldn't process the whole image due to a lack of GPU memory.

Once we have clarified that we will be working with tiles, we need a source to get them. In a typical remote sensing pipeline, we would download complete Sentinel-2 images from a service like SciHub[12] (where all the data gathered by Sentinel-2 is available), combine the RGB bands we need (discarding the other bands), and then slice them up. For our purpose this could be a bit tedious, as we would need to perform some specialized tasks. Therefore, we will ease this task using the Web Map Tile Service (WMTS) provided by Terrascope[13]. This is like the Google Maps service, but provides Sentinel-2 images. It is a great resource for our illustrative purposes, although it may not be the best option for other multi-temporal analyses requiring multiple time steps through a year. Terrascope's WMTS offers Sentinel-2 images at different zoom levels (i.e., resolutions). At the maximum zoom level offered by Terrascope, we can get Sentinel-2 images in RGB at 10 m, exactly what we need. Note that by changing the zoom level we could obtain images with a coarser resolution, but, as we trained our model with a 10 m resolution, we should stick to that.

So, let's now summarize what we need to do to get our area of interest classified:

1. Define the area of interest as a GeoJSON (https://geojson.io/). In our case, Manhattan.
2. Tile the area of interest according to the tile length. In our case, this will be 256×256 as this is the tile size provided by Terrascope WMTS, that is, 2560 m × 2560 m (according to the Sentinel-2 10 m resolution).
3. For each tile:
   (i) Download it from the WMTS.

---

[12] https://scihub.copernicus.eu/
[13] https://viewer.terrascope.be/

(ii) Feed it to the network to get the prediction.

(iii) Store both the tile and the building mask.

You may have noticed that parallelizing the third step is quite straightforward, as we will be working with each tile independently. But you may be thinking, is this a global or local solution? Well, we are not building a model, so it is neither. We will follow a divide-and-conquer strategy, where each tile will be processed independently, so it will be more similar to a local learning approach. Nonetheless, we have already been doing this in the previous chapters each time we predicted the outputs for the examples in an RDD or a DataFrame. However, in this case it will involve some additional steps, as we are dealing with images that we need to download instead of tabular data.

Although we are interested in distributing this computation, let's start simple with a non-distributed implementation that we can parallelize later with Spark.

9.3.2   Non-distributed Implementation

We now start working on non-distributed inference using the WMTS service. To do so, we need to download all the tiles covering our area of interest in Manhattan and classify them one by one. We end by showing the results for this area.

We need to define some parameters for connecting to the WMTS:

```
zoom = 14
epsg = 3857
url   = 'https://services.terrascope.be/wmts/v2?'
layer = 'WORLDCOVER_2020_S2_TCC'
tilematrixset = f'EPSG:{epsg}'
tilematrix    = tilematrixset+f':{zoom}'
```

> Working with this will be a little harder, so we will need to use some of the helper functions we put in geo_helpers.py.

Using the helper functions, we download all tiles corresponding to the Manhattan area (the fetch_tiles function) and then we use the merge_tiles function just to show the complete area obtained from WMTS.

```
import os
# Remove existing data
tiles_dir = f"./temp/{aoi}"
merge_fn = f"{tiles_dir}.tif"
if os.path.isdir(tiles_dir): shutil.rmtree(tiles_dir)
# Fetch all tiles from the aoi (in gdf.total_bounds)
geo.fetch_tiles(url, layer, tilematrixset, zoom, gdf.total_bounds, tiles_dir)
# Merge all tiles into a single tif
geo.merge_tiles(tiles_dir + "/*.tif", merge_fn)
# Show the complete image
PILBase.create(merge_fn).show(figsize=(10, 10));
```

```
Fetching 9 tiles
```

We will take a deeper look at the `fetch_tiles` function, as we will be parallelizing it later (`merge_tiles` just combines the tiles, so we can show them in a single image). The `fetch_tiles` function takes the coordinates of our bounding box and downloads the corresponding tiles from the WMTS service. `bbox_to_xyz` is a helper function that converts our bounding box coordinates to tile indices so that we tell the WMTS exactly which tiles we want. We do this with a double loop to move along the vertical and horizontal axes.

```
def fetch_tiles(url, layer, tilematrixset, zoom, bounds, download_dir):
    wmts = WebMapTileService(url)
    x_min, x_max, y_min, y_max = bbox_to_xyz(*bounds, zoom)
    print(f"Fetching {(x_max - x_min + 1) * (y_max - y_min + 1)} tiles")

    os.makedirs(download_dir, exist_ok=True)
    for x in range(x_min, x_max + 1):
        for y in range(y_min, y_max + 1):
            tif_fn = os.path.join(download_dir, f"{x}_{y}.tif")
            im = download_tile(wmts, url, layer, tilematrixset, zoom, y, x)
            if im is not None:
                tif_fn = save_as_tif(im, x, y, zoom, tif_fn)
```

We have now downloaded the files and stored them in TIF files. The next step is to load and classify them with our model. We will do it as if we were in a new environment where we need to load our model from scratch. To do so, we need to create the `DataLoaders` again, and the `Learner`, and then load its weights (these steps are specific to fast.ai, and they will vary depending on the framework you use):

```
path = Path("data/dataset")
dls = SegmentationDataLoaders.from_label_func(
    path,
    bs=16,
    fnames=get_image_files(path / f"train/images"),
    label_func=None,
    codes=['background', 'building'],
    item_tfms=[Resize(1024)],
)
learn = get_segmentation_learner(
    dls,
    number_classes=2,
    segmentation_type="Semantic Segmentation",
    architecture_name="deeplabv3+",
    backbone_name="resnet50",
).to_fp16()
learn.cbs = L([])
learn.model = learn.model.eval()
learn.load("chkp-last");
```

Did you notice something different? We didn't provide a label_func; why? We will be broadcasting the Learner later, and the label_func doesn't pickle well (when broadcasting the learner, everything inside it needs to be serialized using the pickle library from Python). This is not a problem since in the inference phase we won't have labels. There is another difference in the item_tfms, whose resize is twice the one we used in training (from 512 to 1024). Although we haven't shown you, the tile we download from the WMTS is of size 256×256, exactly twice the resolution we used in training, so we also expect twice the resolution at the output (this won't be a problem for our network as it is a fully convolutional one). Finally, we also empty the Callbacks list (learn.cbs) to avoid problems with serialization.

In our non-distributed implementation, we just have to loop over each tile, get its predictions, and save them to disk. It will be a bit more complex because we will be showing the predictions and saving them georeferenced (so that they can still be used in software like QGIS[14]).

```
# Set prediction directory and clean existing files
predictions_dir = f'./temp/{aoi}_predictions'
os.makedirs(predictions_dir, exist_ok=True)

import glob
fns = glob.glob(f"./temp/{aoi}/*tif")  # Get tile list
fig, axs = plt.subplots(len(fns) // 3, 3,
                        figsize=(10, 3.25 * (len(fns) // 3)))
# Classify each tile one by one
for i, ax in enumerate(axs.flatten()):
    # Read tile
    im = PILBase.create(fns[i])
    # Predict buildings
    preds, _, _ = learn.predict(im)
    # Show predictions
```

---

[14] https://www.qgis.org/

```
    geo.show(im, preds, ax)
    # Save georefenced predictions/masks
    pred_fn = os.path.join(predictions_dir, os.path.basename(fns[i]))
    geo.save_mask(preds, fns[i], pred_fn)
plt.tight_layout()
```

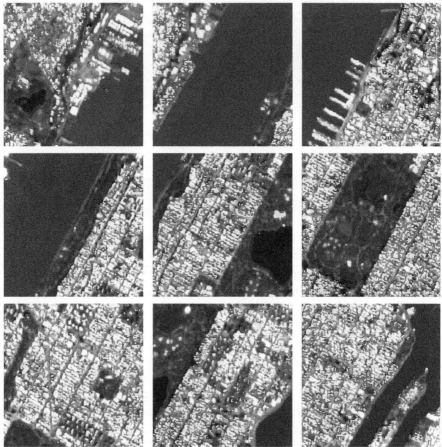

As before, we can use the merge_tiles function to combine the predictions and show all of them together with the complete image:

```
# Merge predictions
merge_prediction_fn = predictions_dir + ".tif"
geo.merge_tiles(predictions_dir + "/*.tif", merge_prediction_fn)
# Load complete image and predictions
preds = np.array(PILImageBW.create(merge_prediction_fn))
im = PILBase.create(merge_fn)
# Show image and predictions
geo.show(im, preds)
```

```
Merge tiles
Merge complete
```

Not bad at all! Our model trained with Pamplona is also able to do good work in Manhattan. Going back to our interest, we have been able to do this because they were just a few tiles. We should now think bigger: what if we had a million tiles? We should move to Spark and do distributed inference. Let's move on!

9.3.3   Distributed Implementation

We have already given some hints about how the distributed implementation should work. The idea is that each worker will be in charge of downloading a set of tiles, classifying, and writing them to a shared drive (e.g., HDFS). Since we can treat each tile independently, this shouldn't be hard to do with Spark.

Let's first present our design before focusing on the actual implementation. Figure 9.5 summarizes the steps we need to perform. On the left, we have an RDD of tiles, which stores the coordinates defining the tiles. The idea is then, working by partitions (e.g., using mapPartitions), to establish the connection to the WMTS and, for each tile in the partition, download, classify, and store both the tile and its predicted mask. As we have a single model that should be shared across workers, we will broadcast it beforehand. Of course, we could do this without working by partitions, but it wouldn't be as efficient, as you will see next.

We are now ready to start with the implementation. First, we need to ensure that our model is available to all workers. Neural network models can be quite big, so we'd better broadcast the model to the workers:

```
learn_bc = sc.broadcast(learn)
```

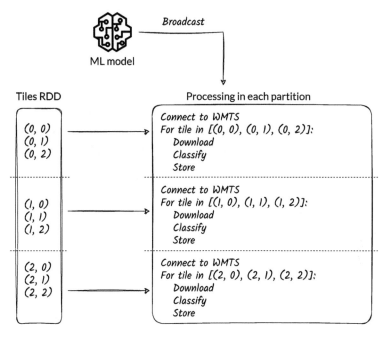

Figure 9.5 Diagram of the distributed inference implementation. The model is broadcast to all workers. In each partition, the connection to the WMTS is established before downloading the tiles, classifying, and storing them.

> We must be sure that learn is serializable. Recall that we made a few changes for this earlier (no label_func, and we also empty the Callbacks). This doesn't affect the inference but avoids problems serializing. There could also be other, more complex, solutions, and this will depend on the library we are using.

To parallelize the processing we need to do with each tile, we first need to identify which tiles we need to process. You may remember that we did this previously using the fetch_tiles function, where we directly downloaded each tile. In this case, we only need to get the (x, y) pairs indicating the tile indices we need to process. We can modify the function to return the (x, y) pairs instead of processing them. We have codified this in the fetch_tiles_xy function in our helper module:

```
def fetch_tiles_xy(zoom, bounds):
    x_min, x_max, y_min, y_max = bbox_to_xyz(*bounds, zoom)
    tiles_xy = [
        (x, y) for x in range(x_min, x_max + 1)
                   for y in range(y_min, y_max + 1)
    ]
    return tiles_xy
```

Let's now get the list of tiles we need to process:

```
tiles_xy = geo.fetch_tiles_xy(zoom, gdf.total_bounds)
tiles_xy[:4] # show first four tiles
```

```
[(4824, 6154), (4824, 6155), (4824, 6156), (4825, 6154)]
```

This is the kind of information we can parallelize in an RDD. We could also use DataFrames, but we won't get any advantage as we will be using `mapPartitions()` for simplicity.

```
rdd = sc.parallelize(tiles_xy)
```

Well, now we should take each tile index pair, download the tile, classify, and save both to disk. We could obviously make use of `map()`, but there is a good reason to opt for `mapPartitions()`. We will be opening a connection to the WMTS each time, which is costly (more than 1 s):

```
from owslib.wmts import WebMapTileService
%time wmts = WebMapTileService(url)
```

```
CPU times: total: 203 ms
Wall time: 2.06 s
```

If we do this with each tile, we will have to pay for a high overhead. Therefore, using `mapPartitions()` will be much more efficient: we will open the connection and iterate over all tiles in the partition, downloading, classifying, and storing them:

```
def classify_tile(coords):
    # Open connection to the WMTS
    wmts = WebMapTileService(url)
    for x, y in coords:
        # Download tile
        im = geo.download_tile(wmts, url, layer, tilematrixset, zoom, y, x)
        if im is not None:
            # Classify. Learn is already broadcasted
            preds, targs, probs = learn_bc.value.predict(im)
            # Save to disk
            geo.save(im, preds, x, y, zoom, tiles_dir)
```

The `download_tile` function is the same as we used previously. However, `save` is a bit different, since it stores both the tile and the predicted masks simultaneously in georeferenced TIFs. If you take a look at this function, you will notice that maintaining the georeferencing is the most complex part, but again, it is important to be make the resulting information usable for further geospatial processing and analysis.

We can easily check that the function is working with a single tile (don't forget to take look at the output directory).

```
classify_tile([[(4824, 6154)]])
```

If we apply this to our RDD, we will be carrying out the inference in a distributed manner. We mentioned `mapPartitions()` for this. But is it the best option available?

Given that we are downloading tiles, classifying, and storing them, does the `classify_tile` function return something to generate a new RDD? Not at all! So we have better methods for this; wouldn't it be better to use `foreachPartition()`? Recall that this is an action that runs the given function in each partition of the RDD and returns nothing (as it expects the function to perform some kind of work in that respect). Let's try it:

```
# Set the output dir and clean
tiles_dir = f'./temp/{aoi}'
if os.path.isdir(tiles_dir): shutil.rmtree(tiles_dir)
os.makedirs(f'./temp/{aoi}', exist_ok=True)
# Run the distributed inference
rdd.foreachPartition(classify_tile)
```

Work done! We should take a look at the output folder to see the generated TIFs:

```
glob.glob(tiles_dir+'/*')[:3]
```

```
['./temp/manhattan\\pred_4824_6154.tif',
 './temp/manhattan\\pred_4824_6155.tif',
 './temp/manhattan\\pred_4824_6156.tif']
```

We can take a look at each tile independently or merge all tiles into a single output as we did before with the non-distributed implementation. In both cases, we would observe exactly the same as we did with our non-distributed implementation. Of course, we wouldn't be able to merge the tiles if we were classifying a bigger area, which would require an appropriate viewer to load the tiles and their predictions.

In summary, we have seen a way to parallelize an inference phase, where the training did not require a complex (distributed) implementation. But keep in mind that creating a larger dataset for the same task would probably require Spark again: it would be necessary to download Sentinel-2 images, merge RGB bands and discard the rest, create the tiles, and so on. All this takes significant CPU time, and parallelizing it allows scaling much faster.

To close this section on model deployment, we would like to mention some points you could work on:

- As before, the implementation seems efficient, but we haven't really gone large-scale, so it would be great to try it with a larger area in a real cluster.
- There are several issues very specific to the case study we have worked on; we recommend you think of other case studies where you can further develop the ideas we have seen in this section. It could be an image classification problem, a natural language processing case study, dealing with time series, or any other problem requiring distributed inference.

> **Challenge #9.4**
>
> To perform a finer classification in semantic segmentation, it is common to work with overlapping tiles. This complicates the distributed processing a bit, as we should aggregate the predictions for the same pixel using the average of the probabilities or by simple majority voting. Assuming that you have a list of tiles already classified and a function `overlapping_tiles()` that gives you all the indices of all tiles overlapping a given tile, provide an overview of how you would use MapReduce to make that work in parallel.

9.4   Take-Home Message

In this final chapter, we have designed and implemented solutions for different advanced machine learning scenarios. Specifically, we have spoken about semi-supervised learning, ensemble learning, and model deployment for big data. While the topics were perhaps more advanced and complex, and we have had to provide more background information, the solutions were not necessarily more difficult than the ones presented in previous chapters. We have seen how many of the operations we have conducted have come down to utilizing DataFrame operations effectively, and MLlib underneath as well.

In semi-supervised learning, we have centered our attention on a family of methods called self-labeling, and particularly on the classic self-training method. The key take-away messages of this section are:

- We have seen that the underlying idea of self-training is to enlarge the number of labeled examples by iteratively using a supervised classifier to predict the labels of a large unlabeled set. As such, it can be seen as a preprocessing method.
- The complexity of self-training depends very much on the underlying base classifier. We have relied on MLlib, and used its decision tree as a base classifier, but others could be used. We have learned that it is not all about the cost of training a model, as this would initially be quick when the labeled set is small. There is a cost associated with making predictions and determining which of the unlabeled instances should be labeled. The computational cost is at the inference stage at first, but it moves to the building of a model as the self-training loop progresses.
- We have devised a simple global-based solution, which keeps a single DataFrame with labeled and unlabeled data. This has allowed us to perform most operations on the workers only. Of course, the base classifier is parallelized as well, and it may need to move data from workers to the driver, and vice versa.
- The proposed solution consists of training a model with the available labeled data and adding new columns with the labels predicted at each iteration. To do so, we have had to make some calculations to compute the most confident predictions, and then select some of them to avoid biasing the model towards a particular class.
- Through the challenge of the semi-supervised section, we have also learned that a local model does not always have to create an ensemble of models. We devised a local approach that acts as a preprocessing technique, so it does not return any model, but those instances that are labeled at each partition.

For ensemble learning, we have focused on the classical bagging algorithm, and AdaBoost as the most representative boosting algorithm. This chapter has focused on global-based solutions, as the local counterpart would be too similar to the one presented in Chapter 7. The main bottleneck for ensemble learning is typically the need to train multiple classifiers, but there are some other details that need to be considered:

- Bagging is a method of creating ensembles by training multiple classifiers on random subsets of the original training data. The final prediction is made by a majority or weighted vote of the classifiers' predictions. To implement this for big data, we first have to bootstrap the training data efficiently. Spark offers an operation for this, which is very efficient as it is a narrow transformation. Nevertheless, we could easily implement this ourselves, as we could do bootstrapping locally at each partition of the dataset and that would result in a very similar randomly chosen training set. Furthermore, the base learners will have to be distributed versions to be able to tackle large datasets. Once again, we use MLlib to train global classifiers.
- AdaBoost trains each classifier iteratively using the whole dataset and gives more importance to difficult instances in each iteration to improve the accuracy of classification. The weighting mechanism modulates the attention to the instances based on their classification results on the training data, with misclassified instances receiving more weight and correctly classified instances receiving less weight. Thus, the base learner must have a way to weigh the importance of instances. In addition, The overall error of the learned models to classify the training set is used to give more confidence/weight to those classifiers that perform better at that stage. Apart from computing the weights of each instance and each classifier, the design is purely based on using a distributed version of a learner.
- Some implementation tricks that are worth mentioning in this section include the creation of a pipeline of already fitted models, which is provided as a list of models to a Spark Pipeline, or using (and caching) a version of the dataset with assembled features.
- In both bagging and AdaBoost we needed to distribute the test phase. We developed the voting strategy with a simple UDF due to the simplicity of the operation. As we did with the weighted voting in the Challenge, we could have used more efficient Spark operations, although this becomes too specific to the framework we are using. We also took advantage of Spark ML functions such as ElementWiseProduct to develop the specific approach for boosting, where weights are given to each classifier. Remember that if we want to get the most out of distributed computing, we must know the details of the framework we are working with.

As a case study of model deployment, we have talked about image segmentation with deep learning. We have used fast.ai as a high-level library to train a building segmentation model on satellite images and then distributed the model's inference. With the appropriate hardware, we could go large-scale with this implementation, classifying anywhere in the world. There are several take-aways from this section:

- The need to use Spark or distributed computing in machine learning is not always in the training phase. It may be that the training is not a bottleneck, but other parts of the machine learning life cycle may require distributed computing, such as data preparation or inference, as in this chapter.
- Spark can be combined with deep learning frameworks such as PyTorch or TensorFlow. In this chapter we used fast.ai as a high-level library on top of PyTorch to train and classify our remote sensing images in a building segmentation problem.

- The way we approached it was to broadcast the model and distribute the inference of the images in each partition with `foreachPartition`. In this particular case, we had to download and preprocess each image before classification. The tasks we need to do will heavily depend on the specific problem we are solving.
- When broadcasting a model, we will be dependent on the library we use underneath. We must ensure that the model we broadcast can be pickled; otherwise, we should look for other solutions.
- Depending on the specific problem, we must decide whether to work by partitions or not. In our implementation, we did so as we had an expensive task that could be shared by a set of examples, such as the connection to the WMTS.

9.5   To Learn More

This chapter has covered a few advanced topics in machine learning you might not have heard about before. Here we provide some resources to learn more about semi-supervised learning, ensemble learning, and image segmentation.

> If you want to learn more about semi-supervised learning in general we recommend Chapelle et al. (2010), and a survey by van Engelen and Hoos (2020).

> Triguero et al. (2015) gives you an overview of the advantages and disadvantages of various self-labeling techniques. Apart from self-training, there are many other methods such as co-training, tri-training, or democratic co-learning, which you could explore and integrate with the above design.

> We highly recommend Kuncheva (2014) to get up to speed with ensemble learning, and the book chapter by Dr Galar on ensemble learning in imbalanced classification (Fernández et al., 2018).

> Minaee et al. (2022) and Zhu et al. (2017) are two great review papers on using deep learning for remote sensing related to the case study presented for model deployment.

The last section of this chapter has touched upon the idea of distributing deep learning, but it has focused on the inference step, as the training of deep learning models is usually accelerated with GPUs. However, there are some new big data platforms emerging to combine GPU processing with Spark. Some of our favorites are:

> Horovod Runner: Distributed deep learning with Horovod.[15] This API allows running distributed deep learning training on top of a Spark cluster. That's part of a bigger platform called Horovod,[16] which is a distributed deep learning training framework. You may read about Spark deep learning pipelines,[17] but note that they are already deprecated.

> TensorFlow on Spark by Yahoo[18] allows distributed deep learning with TensorFlow in a Spark cluster with either CPU or GPU servers.
>
> BigDL (distributed deep learning library for Apache Spark) by the Intel Corporation[19] is a collection of libraries that provides building blocks required to build and run distributed deep learning workloads.
>
> Elephas[20] (distributed DL with Keras and PySpark) is an extension of the Keras high-level library that works on top of Tensorflow to allow for distributing the training of deep learning models using Spark.

9.6 Solutions to Challenges

Challenge #9.1

The above solution to add the most confident instances would only work for binary classification problems and would need changing depending on the number of classes. You are asked to investigate ways to improve this code. As a suggestion, you could use the `create_map`[21] function from SparkSQL, which will allow you to map each class label to the percentage of examples we have to take from that class within a single (`when`) condition. You could also take a look at the `sampleBy`[22] transformation and see if you could use it for this task.

To write a solution for multi-class problems, we are going to learn a new function from Spark SQL, `create_map`.[23] To put it simply, it will allow us to map each class label to the percentage of examples that we should take from that class. Using this jointly with `rand`, we will be able to select approximately the expected number of instances from each class.

```
from itertools import chain
map_pct = sql_f.create_map([sql_f.lit(x) for x in chain(*enumerate(pcts))])
map_pct
```

```
Column<'map(0, 1.0, 1, 0.05993930197268589)'>
```

[15] https://docs.databricks.com/machine-learning/train-model/distributed-training/horovod-runner.html
[16] https://horovod.ai/
[17] https://www.databricks.com/blog/2017/06/06/databricks-vision-simplify-large-scale-deep-learning.html
[18] https://github.com/yahoo/TensorFlowOnSpark
[19] https://github.com/intel-analytics/BigDL
[20] https://github.com/danielenricocahall/elephas
[21] https://spark.apache.org/docs/3.3.0/api/python/reference/pyspark.sql/api/pyspark.sql.functions.create_map.html#pyspark.sql.functions.create_map
[22] https://spark.apache.org/docs/3.3.0/api/python/reference/api/pyspark.sql.DataFrame.sampleBy.html#pyspark.sql.DataFrame.sampleBy
[23] https://spark.apache.org/docs/3.3.0/api/python/reference/pyspark.sql/api/pyspark.sql.functions.create_map.html#pyspark.sql.functions.create_map

This column expression works like a dictionary but with Spark SQL columns. Therefore, we can use it to map our predicted label to the probability of labeling that example (our percentage). Let's see first an example with a toy DataFrame (forget about class 2 for now as it will be filtered).

```
toy_df = spark.createDataFrame([[0, 1.0], [0, 0.05],
                                [1, 1.0], [1, 0.05]], ['prediction', 'prob'])
toy_df.show()
```

```
+----------+----+
|prediction|prob|
+----------+----+
|         0| 1.0|
|         0|0.05|
|         1| 1.0|
|         1|0.05|
+----------+----+
```

If we apply the `map_pct` column expression to our `'prediction'` column, we will be mapping each prediction to the percentage of that class (i.e., the probability of labeling that example). In this case, examples from class 0 will get a percentage (probability) of 1.0, as we will be taking all of them, whereas those from class 1 will get 0.0599, since we have predicted many more examples from that class than the ones we need to maintain the class distribution.

```
toy_df.withColumn('pcts', map_pct[toy_df.prediction]).show()
```

```
+----------+----+-------------------+
|prediction|prob|               pcts|
+----------+----+-------------------+
|         0| 1.0|                1.0|
|         0|0.05|                1.0|
|         1| 1.0|0.05993930197268589|
|         1|0.05|0.05993930197268589|
+----------+----+-------------------+
```

The next step would be to take a random number for each example that will be compared with our new column to get only those examples obtaining a random number less than or equal to the percentage (probability).

```
toy_df.withColumn('rand', sql_f.rand(seed=12345)).show()
```

```
+----------+----+------------------+
|prediction|prob|              rand|
+----------+----+------------------+
|         0| 1.0|0.4181468371948335|
|         0|0.05|0.6027671297035345|
|         1| 1.0| 0.738817497584181|
|         1|0.05|0.8734885555942988|
+----------+----+------------------+
```

In our toy example, we would just label two examples as class 0, since there are only two examples from class 1 and both are getting random numbers above the percentage for class 1.

Let's now put it all together to update the `'label'` column with the examples fulfilling all three conditions we established.

```
preds = preds.withColumn("label",
    sql_f.when(
        (preds.label == 2) & (preds.prob == 1)
        & (sql_f.rand(seed=12345) <= map_pct[preds.prediction]),
        preds.prediction).otherwise(preds.label),
)
preds.show(3)
```

```
+--------------------+------+-----+------------+--------------------+-------
---+------------------+--------------------+
|            features|output|label|rawPrediction|
probability|prediction|                prob|                pcts|
+--------------------+------+-----+------------+--------------------+-------
---+------------------+--------------------+
|(57,[54,55,56],[1...|   0.0|  2.0|   [42.0,1.0]|[0.97674418604651...|
0.0|0.9767441860465116|0.05993930197268589|
|(57,[54,55,56],[1...|   0.0|  0.0|   [42.0,1.0]|[0.97674418604651...|
0.0|0.9767441860465116|                 1.0|
|(57,[54,55,56],[1...|   0.0|  2.0|   [42.0,1.0]|[0.97674418604651...|
0.0|0.9767441860465116|0.05993930197268589|
+--------------------+------+-----+------------+--------------------+-------
---+------------------+--------------------+
only showing top 3 rows
```

We also asked you to check the `sampleBy`[24] transformation, which does very much what we were looking for. However, in our case, this would return a new reduced DataFrame, which doesn't fit well with our implementation of self-training that uses a single DataFrame for both labeled and unlabeled data. However, it would be a good exercise to work with two DataFrames and take advantage of this to check its efficiency.

Challenge #9.2

You are asked to design and implement a local-based approach for self-training. We would advise thinking a little bit differently from the local approach we described in Chapter 7, and not aim to build a model per partition. Alternatively, the complete self-training is run for each partition independently. Nevertheless, the aim is to enlarge the labeled set only as if it was a pure preprocessing stage.

In Chapter 7, we implemented a local-based model for decision trees that consisted of learning a model per partition and concatenating those models as an ensemble. Here, we can opt for a slightly different divide-and-conquer strategy. As the initial labeled dataset will usually be small to start with, we could simply broadcast that to all executors.

> In some cases, this may be a strong assumption, but one could argue that SSL would make more sense when the amount of labeled data is actually very low.

---

[24] https://spark.apache.org/docs/3.3.0/api/python/reference/api/pyspark.sql.DataFrame.sampleBy.html#py spark.sql.DataFrame.sampleBy

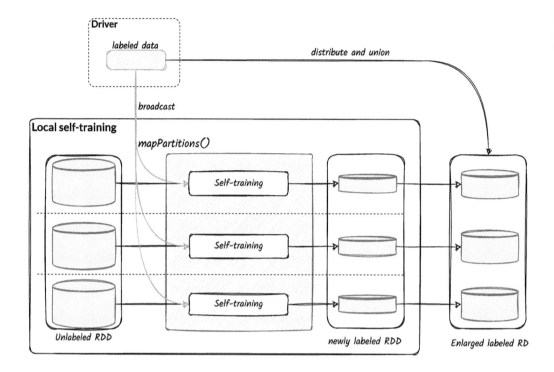

Figure 9.6 A local model for a self-training algorithm.

Then, at each partition, we can use a self-training algorithm (or basically any self-labeling method) to iteratively label the most confident unlabeled instances in that subset of the data. The map would only return the most confident unlabeled instances with their predicted labels, so it is "filtering" out those unlabeled instances in which the base classifier is not that confident. As the resulting set of newly labeled instances may be large, we don't have to collect the result back to the driver, but we can keep it distributed across executor.

Once done, we could just simply join those newly labeled examples with the original ones. We should do this in parallel, not in the driver, to avoid issues with memory. Thus, assuming that the labeled set was initially in the driver (as it was small), it would have to be distributed (i.e., a Spark DataFrame created with its content). The union of two DataFrames is a narrow transformation, and therefore it is efficient to join those two dataset. After obtaining the enlarged labeled set, we can just simply apply any MLlib classifier as we did with the global solution. Figure 9.6 shows a MapReduce-like workflow for a local-based approach for self-training.

How does this compare to the previous implementation? On the one hand, it is probably the most efficient way of enlarging the labeled set using unlabeled data. In contradistinction to the global counterpart that requires distributing the learning of the base classifier, it only launches a single Spark job, but we have to distribute the labeled set to merge it with the newly labeled instances. On the other hand, we could more easily replace the self-training algorithm with any other SSL method. Having said that, as with most local solutions, the result will vary depending on the number of partitions. If the unlabeled chunk available in one worker is not very representative or noisy, it could lead to misclassifications. Also, as stated above, its main limitation is that the labeled set does have to be very small for this approach to work.

Let's implement this. Now we do want to split the training data into two sets: labeled and unlabeled. For that, we could simply use the randomSplit() function.

```
# reset train and test DataFrames
train, test = df.randomSplit([0.7, 0.3], seed)
labeled, unlabeled = train.randomSplit([0.02, 0.98], seed)
```

To simulate the idea that the labeled set would live in the driver, we will collect it as a pandas DataFrame. Then, we broadcast it to make it available to all executors.

```
labeled_driver = labeled.toPandas()
labeled_bc = sc.broadcast(labeled_driver)
```

```
len(labeled_bc.value)
```

```
76
```

As a local model, we use mapPartitions() on the underlying RDD. But first, let us get the RDD and split it into four partitions.

```
unlabeled_rdd = unlabeled.rdd.repartition(4)
```

We need to create a function that will apply the self-training process, which will *only* return those instances that have been classified from unlabeled_rdd. But before that, we are going to need a function that gets some labeled data and trains a decision tree model with the scikit-learn library:

```
from sklearn.tree import DecisionTreeClassifier as DecisionTree_Sklearn
def wrapper_decision_tree(data_pd):
    clf = DecisionTree_Sklearn(random_state=0, max_depth=5)
    # Shape the Pandas DataFrame for scikit-learn (output in last column)
    X_train = data_pd.iloc[:, :-1]
    y_train = data_pd.iloc[:, -1]
    # Fit the model
    model = clf.fit(X_train.values, y_train.values)
    return model
```

If we were to use that function within mapPartitions(), we would get a decision tree for each partition (with a few changes to convert the partition iterator to a pandas DataFrame), but what we want to do is to use that within another function, local_self_training(), that will invoke it. Let's do that:

```
import numpy as np
import pandas as pd
from pyspark.sql import Row
# For simplicity, define column names as a global variable
```

```python
column_names = train.columns
def local_self_training(unlabeled_partition, max_iter=10,
                        seed=12345, num_classes=2):
    # For the sample from Pandas
    np.random.seed(seed)
    # We coerce the partition to a list to filter it when returning
    # Otherwise, the iterator can be traversed only once
    unlabeled_partition = list(unlabeled_partition)
    # Create the unlabeled DataFrame from partition data
    unlab_pd = pd.DataFrame(unlabeled_partition, columns=column_names)
    # Get labeled DataFrame from broadcast variable
    labeled_pd = labeled_bc.value
    # To store the indices of labeled instances
    labeled_indices = []
    # Obtain class distributions from the labeled set
    class_distrib = unlab_pd.groupby(["output"])["output"].count()
    for i in range(max_iter):
        print(f"Iteration: {i} - labeled size: {labeled_pd.shape[0]}")
        # Learn the model and predict unlabeled samples
        model = wrapper_decision_tree(labeled_pd)
        probs = model.predict_proba(unlab_pd.iloc[:, :-1].values)
        # Count examples that can be added (prob == 1)
        counts = np.count_nonzero(probs == 1, axis=0)
        if 0 in counts: break
        # Compute instances to add from each class
        to_add = instances_per_class(class_distrib, counts)
        print(f"Adding {to_add.tolist()} instances")
        pcts = to_add / counts  # elementwise division
        # Creating Pandas DataFrames with instances to add from each class
        instances_to_add = []
        for c in range(num_classes):
            instances_to_add.append(
                unlab_pd[probs[:, c] == 1].sample(frac=pcts[c]))
            instances_to_add[c]["output"] = c  # assign the predicted class
        # Put them all into a single DataFrame
        instances_to_add = pd.concat(instances_to_add)
        # Update Pandas DataFrames
        #    1. Remove labeled instances
        unlab_pd = unlab_pd.drop(instances_to_add.index)
        #    2. Add new instances
        labeled_pd = pd.concat([labeled_pd, instances_to_add])
        #    3. Save indices for the final output
        labeled_indices += instances_to_add.index.tolist()
    # Return the newly labeled instances from the partition data
    return [row
            for i, row in enumerate(unlabeled_partition) if i in labeled_indices]
```

We could first check this function on the driver. To do so, we can bring a manageable subset of unlabeled_rdd to the driver.

```python
newly_labeled = local_self_training(unlabeled_rdd.take(2000))
```

```
Iteration: 0 - labeled size: 76
Adding [1025, 582] instances
Iteration: 1 - labeled size: 1683
Adding [2, 1] instances
```

```
Iteration: 2 - labeled size: 1686
Adding [3, 2] instances
Iteration: 3 - labeled size: 1691
```

This is good practice because, otherwise, we could get lost on the tracebacks from Spark when our function does not even work locally. So, we can now apply the self-training as a filter in each partition of the unlabeled data:

```
newly_labeled = unlabeled_rdd.mapPartitions(local_self_training).cache()
```

```
%time newly_labeled.count()
```

```
Wall time: 8.88 s
```

```
2570
```

We can transform our resulting RDD into a DataFrame (as it is composed of Rows) and join it with our DataFrame of labeled examples (if we only had it locally, this would be the moment to distribute it).

```
new_training = labeled.union(newly_labeled.toDF())
```

We are ready to use MLlib with this new dataset! Let's test this, resetting the DecisionTree model with the right `labelCol`.

```
new_training_features = assembler.transform(new_training).cache()
unlabeled_features = assembler.transform(unlabeled)
dt = DecisionTreeClassifier(maxDepth=5, labelCol="output")
```

```
model = dt.fit(new_training_features)
```

```
local_preds_trans = model.transform(unlabeled_features)
```

```
local_preds_inductive = model.transform(test_features)
```

```
# Evaluate Local model accuracy
print(f"Transductive accuracy = {evaluator.evaluate(local_preds_trans)}")
print(f"Inductive accuracy = {evaluator.evaluate(local_preds_inductive)}")
```

```
Transductive accuracy = 0.920418516169943
Inductive accuracy = 0.9051787016776076
```

Comparing the global and the local solutions in terms of accuracy is a bit tricky. Our local solution uses the scikit-learn library during the self-labeling process, but the global one is using the MLlib implementation. Although both are implementing, in principle, the same decision tree algorithm, the actual implementation is different, and it is likely that the results are not fully comparable. In this dataset and with these hyperparameters, the local model seems to be performing better in the unlabeled set, but slightly worse in the test set. Further investigation, with additional datasets, and exploring the scalability of both solutions would be needed to establish a fair comparison.

> ## Challenge #9.3
>
> We have simply used a majority vote to compute the final prediction of the ensemble. You are asked to implement the necessary code to calculate the prediction as a weighted vote.

For simplicity, we have used a UDF to implement the majority vote. However, we will solve this challenge more elegantly using functions from Spark SQL.

First, we need to get the probabilities from the ensemble instead of the prediction of each tree. Let's get the outputs for our test examples again and extract the probability as we did before for the prediction.

```
prediction = pipeline_models.transform(test_features)
ensemble = prediction.select(
    sql_f.array([f"probability_{i}" for i in range(max_iter)]).alias("preds"),
    "output",
)
ensemble.show(1, truncate=70)
```

```
+------------------------------------------------------------------------+-----+
-+
|
preds|output|
+------------------------------------------------------------------------+-----+
-+
|[[0.9452411994784876,0.054758800521512385], [0.95,0.05], [0.9283935...|
0.0|
+------------------------------------------------------------------------+-----+
-+
only showing top 1 row
```

If you analyze what we get, it is an array of vectors (coming from Spark ML). To simplify this a little, we restrict our solution to binary classification problems. Hence, we can just work with one of the probabilities of each tree (typically, the probability of class 1).

To get those probabilities, we need to use a function we have used before, vec-tor_to_array, to convert the Vectors from Spark ML to Spark SQL arrays. Then, we could use the element_at[25] function to get the probability of class 1. Of course, as this is all already inside a Spark SQL Array, we can use the transform[26] function to apply the previous to each element of our array (works as a Python map function). Let's see it.

---

[25] https://spark.apache.org/docs/3.3.0/api/python/reference/pyspark.sql/api/pyspark.sql.functions.eleme nt_at.html#pyspark.sql.functions.element_at

[26] https://spark.apache.org/docs/3.3.0/api/python/reference/pyspark.sql/api/pyspark.sql.functions.transfor m.html#pyspark.sql.functions.transform

```
ensemble = ensemble.withColumn("preds",
    sql_f.transform(
        "preds", lambda x: sql_f.element_at(vector_to_array(x), 2)
    ),
)
ensemble.show(1, truncate=70)
```

```
+-----------------------------------------------------------------------+-----
-+
|
preds|output|
+-----------------------------------------------------------------------+-----
-+
|[0.054758800521512385, 0.05, 0.07160647571606475, 0.062150403977625...|
0.0|
+-----------------------------------------------------------------------+-----
-+
only showing top 1 row
```

We have the data ready to be aggregated. To do the majority vote, we need to compute the average probability of class 1, that is, the average of the probabilities in 'preds', and then check whether it is greater than 0.5. If the average is greater than 0.5, the class will be class 1, and class 0 otherwise.

To implement this, we need to take a look at another Spark SQL function: aggregate.[27] This function allows us to aggregate values in a Spark SQL Array. In this case, we sum all the values and then divide by the number of elements in the array. Finally, we check whether this value is above the 0.5 threshold.

```
prediction = ensemble.withColumn("prediction", (
        sql_f.aggregate("preds", sql_f.lit(0.0), lambda acc, x: acc + x)
        / sql_f.size("preds") > 0.5
    ).cast("double"),
)
```

The aggregate function has three parameters: the column where it is applied, the initial value for the accumulator where the aggregation is performed (0.0 in this case, given as a Column expression), and the function to be used to aggregate each element (x) to the accumulator (acc). You may also have noticed the casting to double. Remember that Spark ML codifies the classes in this way.

```
evaluator.setPredictionCol(f'prediction')
acc = evaluator.evaluate(prediction)
acc
```

```
0.9175784099197666
```

Perhaps surprisingly, we get exactly the same result! Anyway, this may not be always the case.

[27] https://spark.apache.org/docs/3.3.0/api/python/reference/pyspark.sql/api/pyspark.sql.functions.aggrega
te.html#pyspark.sql.functions.aggregate

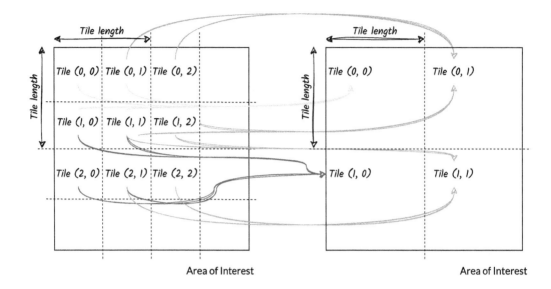

Figure 9.7 Segmentation with overlapping tiles. On the left, the outputs of each overlapped tile are available. On the right is how these tiles are combined to obtain the final output tiles with aggregated predictions. The arrows illustrate which tile on the left should contribute to each predicted tile on the right.

> ## Challenge #9.4
>
> To perform a finer classification in semantic segmentation, it is common to work with overlapping tiles. This complicates the distributed processing a bit, as we should aggregate the predictions for the same pixel using the average of the probabilities or by simple majority voting. Assuming that you have a list of tiles already classified and a function `overlapping_tiles()` that gives you all the indices of all tiles overlapping a given tile, provide an overview of how you would use MapReduce to make that work in parallel.

Now, we have our area divided into more tiles than before (see the left part of Figure 9.7), as there is now an overlap. Let's assume a 50% overlap in this case. We need to get a final set of tiles where there is no intersection among them, that is, no overlap. To do so, we need to send each current tile to those that depend on it to get its final result. That is, each tile will contribute to one or more tiles of the final output.

From a MapReduce perspective, for each tile, we will output several keys. The keys are the indexes of each tile to which it must contribute, whereas the value will be the tile itself (the predicted mask or probabilities). In the reduce, we will have, for each final tile, the list of masks that we must aggregate and obtain the final tile. Here we can apply a weighted vote or an average of the probabilities taking into account the part of the final tile that is covered by each tile. The specific implementation is a bit more complex than it sounds, but the MapReduce part is the one that we have just described.

Figure 9.7 depicts this process. Note that the tile indices are shown in the top-left part of each tile. We have an area divided into 3×3 tiles with 50% of overlap, so the final output (on the right) will just have 2×2 tiles. So we need to map the first nine tiles to the latter four, so that we can aggregate them in the reduce. We would apply a flatMap operation to compute and output, for each tile, which tiles in the right part it must contribute to (look at the arrows). We could write a function to know to which indices or coordinates each tile must contribute. For example, in this case, it would be enough to compute, for both (x, y) indices, round(x/2) and round(y/2), and for those tiles not in the edges (with either x or y 1 and 2 in this case), also output that same index plus one. In this way, we can observe that tiles in the edges contribute to one (if they are in a corner) or two tiles, whereas the others contribute to three or four tiles. In this specific example, all the final four tiles are obtained as the aggregation of four tiles.

9.7   Exercises

9.1 Briefly explain the main bottleneck of semi-supervised learning in large-scale data analytics.

9.2 Why is it important in self-training not to add all the most confident predictions at every iteration?

9.3 Indicate whether the following statements about designing a big data solution for self-training are true or false:
   (a) While possible, a local-based solution does not make much sense.
   (b) Initially, the main bottleneck of a global design is on retraining a classifier at each iteration.
   (c) The scalability of self-training is bound by the underlying base classifier.
   (d) If we can't get over the lower-bound baseline performance, it definitely means there is an error in the distributed implementation.

9.4 In ensemble learning we use multiple base learners, which are called weak learners. What do you think are the most desirable features of those base learners in the context of big data?

9.5 Bagging achieves diversity by boostrapping the training data. Briefly discuss the efficiency of carrying out such an operation/transformation in large datasets.

9.6 What are the main differences in the big data solutions presented for bagging and boosting?

9.7 Why did we deploy the inference phase of a deep learning model using Spark rather than a GPU?

9.8 Could you devise any different approach to deal with distributed inference rather than divide and conquer? For example, in our remote sensing case study we divided our area into tiles and processed them independently. Could we deal with this without this division?

9.9 Feature selection is a preprocessing technique to reduce the dimensionality of a problem. It allows us to identify relevant features. There are many approaches in the literature, including filter, wrapper, and embedded feature selection. Without considering what a given feature selection method does specifically, you are asked to design a local-based solution that takes some training data and will rank the importance of the features. Thus, the expected output is a list with the ranking of features sorted from the most important to the least. The list should simply have the indexes of those features. For example, the output [3, 1, 0, 2] in a dataset with four features would mean that the most important one is column 3. You can assume that the output of the feature selection algorithm chosen will also output the same kind of list.

(a) How would you solve this using Spark? Briefly describe a solution for this.

(b) Discuss the expected advantages and disadvantages of this local design.

9.10 In multi-label classification, an instance has to be classified along multiple categories at the same time. For example, in one image we could find a tree, a river, and a dog. The simplest strategy to do this is to train a separate machine learning model for each target variable independently. You are asked to design a global big data solution to tackle this problem. For simplicity, you could assume that we have three output variables, and the data will be split into three partitions. Assume that the test dataset will also be big.

(a) How would you solve this using Spark? Briefly describe a solution for this.

(b) Discuss the expected advantages and disadvantages of this global design.

Bibliography

Abuzaid, F., Bradley, J., Liang, F., Feng, A., Yang, L., Zaharia, M., and Talwalkar, A. 2016. Yggdrasil: An Optimized System for Training Deep Decision Trees at Scale. Pages 3817–3825 of: *Proceedings of the 30th International Conference on Neural Information Processing Systems*. NIPS'16. Red Hook, NY, USA: Curran Associates Inc.

Agrawal, R., and Prabakaran, S. 2020. Big Data in Digital Healthcare: Lessons Learnt and Recommendations for General Practice. *Heredity*, **124**(4), 525–534.

Akram, A. W., and Alamgir, Z. 2022. Distributed fuzzy clustering algorithm for mixed-mode data in Apache SPARK. *Journal of Big Data*, **9**(1), 121.

Ayala, C., Sesma, R., Aranda, C., and Galar, M. 2021. A Deep Learning Approach to an Enhanced Building Footprint and Road Detection in High-Resolution Satellite Imagery. *Remote Sensing*, **13**(16), 3135.

Bishop, C. M. 2006. *Pattern Recognition and Machine Learning*. Berlin, Heidelberg: Springer.

Blum, A., and Mitchell, T. 1998. Combining Labeled and Unlabeled Data with Co-Training. Pages 92–100 of: *Proceedings of the Eleventh Annual Conference on Computational Learning Theory*. COLT' 98. New York, NY: Association for Computing Machinery.

Breiman, L. 1996. Bagging Predictors. *Machine Learning*, **24**(2), 123–140.

Chapelle, O., Scholkopf, B., and Zien, A. 2010. *Semi-Supervised Learning*. Adaptive Computation and Machine Learning series. Cambridge, MA: MIT Press.

Chen, J., Li, K., Tang, Z., Bilal, K., Yu, S., Weng, C., and Li, K. 2017. A Parallel Random Forest Algorithm for Big Data in a Spark Cloud Computing Environment. *IEEE Transactions on Parallel and Distributed Systems*, **28**(4), 919–933.

Chen, L.-C., Zhu, Y., Papandreou, G., Schroff, F., and Adam, H. 2018. Encoder–Decoder with Atrous Separable Convolution for Semantic Image Segmentation. Pages 833–851 of: Ferrari, V., Hebert, M., Sminchisescu, C., and Weiss, Y. (eds), *Computer Vision – ECCV 2018*. Cham: Springer.

Chiusano, P., and Bjarnason, R. 2014. *Functional Programming in Scala*. Shelter Island, NY: Manning Publications.

Cover, T., and Hart, P. 1967. Nearest neighbor pattern classification. *IEEE Transactions on Information Theory*, **13**(1), 21–27.

Damji, J., Wenig, B., Lee, D., Das, T., and Lee, D. 2020. *Learning Spark*. 2nd edn. Sebastopol, CA: O'Reilly Media Inc.

Daniel, J. 2019. *Data Science with Python and Dask*. Shelter Island, NY: Manning Publications.

Dean, J., and Ghemawat, S. 2004. MapReduce: Simplified Data Processing on Large Clusters. Pages 137–150 of: *OSDI'04: Proceedings of the Sixth Symposium on Operating System Design and Implementation*, vol. 6. Berkeley, CA: USENIX Association.

Dean, J., and Ghemawat, S. 2010. MapReduce: A Flexible Data Processing Tool. *Communications of the ACM*, **53**(1), 72–77.

DeWitt, D., and Gray, J. 1992. Parallel Database Systems: The Future of High Performance Database Systems. *Communications of the ACM*, **35**(6), 85–98.

Ekanayake, J., Li, H., Zhang, B., Gunarathne, T., Bae, S.-H., Qiu, J., and Fox, G. 2010. Twister: A Runtime for Iterative MapReduce. Pages 810–818 of: *Proceedings of the 19th ACM International Symposium on High Performance Distributed Computing*. New York, NY: Association for Computing Machinery.

Esteves, R., Pais, R., and Rong, C. 2011. K-means Clustering in the Cloud – A Mahout Test. Pages 514–519 of: *2013 27th International Conference on Advanced Information Networking and Applications Workshops*. Los Alamitos, CA: IEEE Computer Society.

Fernández, A., García, S., Galar, M., Prati, R. C., Krawczyk, B., and Herrera, F. 2018. Ensemble Learning. Pages 147–196 of: *Learning from Imbalanced Data Sets*. Cham: Springer.

Freund, Y., and Schapire, R. E. 1997. A Decision-Theoretic Generalization of On-Line Learning and an Application to Boosting. *Journal of Computer and System Sciences*, **55**(1), 119–139.

García, S., Luengo, J., and Herrera, F. 2015. *Data Preprocessing in Data Mining*. Springer Series in Statistics. Cham: Springer.

Garreta, R., Moncecchi, G., and Hauck, T. 2017. *scikit-llearn: Machine Learning Simplified*. Birmingham: Packt Publishing.

Géron, A. 2022. *Hands-On Machine Learning with scikit-learn, Keras, and TensorFlow*. Sebastopol, CA: O'Reilly Media Inc.

Ghemawat, S., Gobioff, H., and Leung, S.-T. 2003. The Google File System. Pages 29–43 of: *Proceedings of the 19th ACM Symposium on Operating Systems Principles*. New York, NY: ACM.

Ginsberg, J., Mohebbi, M. H., Patel, R. S., Brammer, L., Smolinski, M. S., and Brilliant, L. 2009. Detecting Influenza Epidemics Using Search Engine Query Data. *Nature*, **457**(7232), 1012–1014.

Gropp, W., Lusk, E., and Skjellum, A. 2014. *Using MPI: Portable Parallel Programming with the Message-Passing Interface*. 3rd edn. Cambridge, MA: MIT Press.

Hai, M., Zhang, Y., and Zhang, Y. 2017. A Performance Evaluation of Classification Algorithms for Big Data. *Procedia Computer Science*, **122**, 1100–1107.

Hastie, T., Tibshirani, R., and Friedman, J. 2001. *The Elements of Statistical Learning*. New York, NY: Springer.

Howard, J., Gugger, S., and Chintala, S. 2020. *Deep Learning for Coders with Fastai and PyTorch: AI Applications Without a PhD*. Sebastopol, CA: O'Reilly Media Inc.

Hutton, G. 2016. *Programming in Haskell*. 2nd edn. Cambridge: Cambridge University Press.

Jain, S. M. 2020. *Linux Containers and Virtualization: A Kernel Perspective*. New York, NY: Apress.

Jogalekar, P., and Woodside, M. 2000. Evaluating the scalability of distributed systems. *IEEE Transactions on Parallel and Distributed Systems*, **11**(6), 589–603.

Juez-Gil, M., Arnaiz-González, Á., Rodríguez, J. J., López-Nozal, C., and García-Osorio, C. 2021. Rotation Forest for Big Data. *Information Fusion*, **74**, 39–49.

Kuncheva, L. I. 2014. *Combining Pattern Classifiers: Methods and Algorithms*. Chichester: Wiley.

Laney, D. 2001 (February). *3D Data Management: Controlling Data Volume, Velocity, and Variety*. Tech. rept. META Group. Available at: http://blogs.gartner.com/doug-laney/files/20 12/01/ad949-3D-Data-Management-Controlling-Data-Volume-Velocity-and-Variety.pdf.

Lazer, D., Kennedy, R., King, G., and Vespignani, A. 2014. The Parable of Google Flu: Traps in Big Data Analysis. *Science*, **343**, 1203–1205.

Luengo, J., García-Gil, D., Ramírez-Gallego, S., García, S., and Herrera, F. 2020. *Big Data Preprocessing: Enabling Smart Data*. New York, NY: Springer.

Lulli, A., Oneto, L., and Anguita, D. 2017. ReForeSt: Random Forests in Apache Spark. Pages 331–339 of: Lintas, A., Rovetta, S., Verschure, P. F. M. J., and Villa, A. E. P. (eds), *Artificial Neural Networks and Machine Learning – ICANN 2017*. Cham: Springer.

Maillo, J., Ramírez, S., Triguero, I., and Herrera, F. 2017. kNN-IS: An Iterative Spark-Based Design of the k-Nearest Neighbors classifier for Big Data. *Knowledge-Based Systems*, **117**, 3–15.

Marx, V. 2013. The Big Challenges of Big Data. *Nature*, **498**(7453), 255–260.

Mayer-Schönberger, V., and Cukier, K. 2013. *Big Data: A Revolution that Will Transform How We Live, Work, and Think*. Boston, MA: Houghton Mifflin Harcourt.

Meng, X., Bradley, J., Yavuz, B., Sparks, E., Venkataraman, S., Liu, D., Freeman, J., Tsai, D., Amde, M., Owen, S., Xin, D., Xin, R., Franklin, M. J., Zadeh, R., Zaharia, M., and Talwalkar, A. 2016. MLlib: Machine Learning in Apache Spark. *Journal of Machine Learning Research*, **17**(34), 1–7.

Minaee, S., Boykov, Y., Porikli, F., Plaza, A., Kehtarnavaz, N., and Terzopoulos, D. 2022. Image Segmentation Using Deep Learning: A Survey. *IEEE Transactions on Pattern Analysis and Machine Intelligence*, **44**(07), 3523–3542.

Ng, A. 2012. *CS229 Lecture Notes – Supervised Learning*. Available at: http://cs229.stanford .edu/lectures-spring2022/main_notes.pdf.

Ng, A. 2017. *Machine Learning Yearning*. DeepLearning.AI. Available at: https://info .deeplearning.ai/machine-learning-yearning-book.

Panda, B., Herbach, J. S., Basu, S., and Bayardo, R. J. 2009. PLANET: Massively Parallel Learning of Tree Ensembles with MapReduce. *Proceedings of the VLDB Endowment*, **2**(2), 1426–1437.

Pietsch, W. 2021. *Big Data*. Cambridge: Cambridge University Press.

Ramírez-Gallego, S., Fernández, A., García, S., Chen, M., and Herrera, F. 2018. Big Data: Tutorial and Guidelines on Information and Process Fusion for Analytics Algorithms with MapReduce. *Information Fusion*, **42**, 51–61.

Schapire, R. E. 1990. The Strength of Weak Learnability. *Machine Learning*, **5**(2), 197–227.

Segatori, A., Marcelloni, F., and Pedrycz, W. 2018. On Distributed Fuzzy Decision Trees for Big Data. *IEEE Transactions on Fuzzy Systems*, **26**(1), 174–192.

Severance, C., and Dowd, K. 2010. *High Performance Computing*. Available at: https://open .umich.edu/sites/default/files/downloads/col11136-1.5.pdf.

Triguero, I., García, S., and Herrera, F. 2015. Self-Labeled Techniques for Semi-supervised Learning: Taxonomy, Software and Empirical Study. *Knowledge and Information Systems*, **42**(2), 245–284.

van Engelen, J. E., and Hoos, H. H. 2020. A Survey on Semi-supervised Learning. *Machine Learning*, **109**(2), 373–440.

White, T. 2015. *Hadoop: The Definitive Guide*. 4th edn. Sebastopol, CA: O'Reilly Media Inc.

Xia, M., Saxena, M., Blaum, M., and Pease, D. A. 2015. A Tale of Two Erasure Codes in HDFS. Pages 213–226 of: *Proceedings of the 13th USENIX Conference on File and Storage Technologies*. Berkeley, CA: USENIX Association.

Yarowsky, D. 1995. Unsupervised Word Sense Disambiguation Rivaling Supervised Methods. Pages 189–196 of: *Proceedings of the 33rd Annual Meeting on Association for Computational Linguistics*. Stroudsburg, PA: Association for Computational Linguistics.

Zaharia, M., Chowdhury, M., Franklin, M. J., Shenker, S., and Stoica, I. 2010. Spark: Cluster Computing with Working Sets. In: *Proceedings of the 2nd USENIX Workshop on Hot Topics in Cloud Computing.* Berkeley, CA: USENIX Association.

Zaharia, M., Chowdhury, M., Das, T., Dave, A., Ma, J., McCauley, M., Franklin, M. J., Shenker, S., and Stoica, I. 2012. Resilient Distributed Datasets: A Fault-Tolerant Abstraction for In-Memory Cluster Computing. Page 2 of: *Proceedings of the 9th USENIX Conference on Networked Systems Design and Implementation.* Berkeley, CA: USENIX Association.

Zhu, X. X., Tuia, D., Mou, L., Xia, G.-S., Zhang, L., Xu, F., and Fraundorfer, F. 2017. Deep Learning in Remote Sensing: A Comprehensive Review and List of Resources. *IEEE Geoscience and Remote Sensing Magazine*, **5**(4), 8–36.

Index